COMMUNICATION CONCEPTS AND SKILLS

COMMUNICATION CONCEPTS AND SKILLS

ROBERT HOPPER
and
JACK L. WHITEHEAD, JR.
University of Texas

HARPER & ROW, PUBLISHERS
New York, Hagerstown, Philadelphia, San Francisco, London

PHOTO CREDITS

Page 4, Leo De Wys; 9, TWA *Ambassador Magazine*; 16, UPI; 34, Kimberli Hymas; 39, Jack L. Whitehead; 51, Geoffrey Watson; 57, Sarita Brown; 65, Sarita Brown; 76, Robert Hopper; 88, Southwick, Stock, Boston; 101, Robert Hopper; 106 (#3), Kimberli Hymas; 119, Kimberli Hymas; 124, Corry, DPI; 173, Valerie Newman; 177, Chester, DeWys; 197, David Anderson; 200, Forsyth, Monkmeyer; 226, Geoffrey Watson; 239, Jack L. Whitehead; 248, Jack L. Whitehead; 258, Geoffrey Watson; 273, 282, Jack L. Whitehead; 306, Southwick, Stock, Boston; 312, Berndt, Stock, Boston; 332, Tom Taylor; 354, Geoffrey Watson; 365, Jack L. Whitehead; 378, Forsyth, Monkmeyer.

Sponsoring Editor: Alan Spiegel
Project Editor: Karla Billups Philip
Designer: Gayle Jaeger
Production Manager: Marion A. Palen
Photo Researcher: Myra Schachne
Compositor: Progressive Typographers, Inc.
Printer and Binder: Halliday Lithograph Corporation
Art Studio: J & R Technical Services Inc.

COMMUNICATION CONCEPTS AND SKILLS
Copyright © 1979 by Robert Hopper and Jack L. Whitehead, Jr.

All rights reserved. Printed in the United States of America. No part of this book may be used or reproduced in any manner whatsoever without written permission except in the case of brief quotations embodied in critical articles and reviews. For information address Harper & Row, Publishers, Inc., 10 East 53rd Street, New York, N.Y. 10022.

Library of Congress Cataloging in Publication Data

Hopper, Robert.
    Communication concepts and skills.

    Bibliography: p.
    Includes index.
    1. Communication. I. Whitehead, Jack L., joint
author. II. Title.
P90.H66   001.5   78-27482
ISBN 0-06-042903-8

We dedicate this book to our fathers, Jack H. Hopper and Jack L. Whitehead, Sr. In our lives, they wrote the book on self-improvement of communication skills.

CONTENTS

CONTENTS IN DETAIL

ix

TO THE INSTRUCTOR

There are few books that stress both communication concepts and communication skills. The traditional text format has provided practice in a set of skills such as public speaking, discussion, and reading aloud in the belief that such skills transfer automatically into improved communication in everyday situations. More recently, authors have stressed communication concepts such as information processing, transactional perspective, and source credibility in the belief that such theories matter more than skills practice. There have been books that attempted to combine theories and practice but, for the most part, these books offer a surface treatment of theory and a watered-down discussion of skills.

The heart of *Communication Concepts and Skills* is a series of 117 experiences for students to use in order to refine their communication skills. These experiences offer improvements over those of other texts in four ways: First, the experiences appear in the flow of the text, not at the back of the book or at the ends of chapters. Students complete the experiences as they read related conceptual materials. Second, these experiences have been tested by hundreds of our own students. Third, most of the experiences can be completed by the individual student outside class, providing bases for class discussions. (An accompanying *Instructor's Manual* provides numerous other experiences for in-class use.) Fourth, the experiences provide opportunities to work on a much broader set of skills than most books present, including conflict resolution, interviewing, and relationship development, in addition to time-honored presentation and discussion skills.

Skills practice does not water down this book's presentation of concepts. The book's 14 chapters offer coherent presentations of theory and research in human communication. Perception, self-concept, language, nonverbal communication, intercultural communication, persuasion, organizational communication, and a number of other topics are explored. These topics are discussed without the extensive use of jargon or footnotes. However, both authors are practicing communication researchers weaned on the value of recent experimental findings. We advance only those communication concepts that are based on solid evidence.

We believe that improved human communication requires both concepts and skills. To teach one but not the other is as futile as applauding with one hand. That is why *Communication Concepts and Skills* combines both.

Dozens of people have been helpful to this project, including Ronald Bassett, Nancy Wrather, Richard Street, D. F. Gundersen, Robert Jeffrey, and Genine Oestrick.

Robert Hopper
Jack L. Whitehead

Are you completely satisfied about the ways in which you communicate? Are you satisfied with your social life? Are you content about transactions with your family? Are you satisfied with your daily work? Are you confident of your ability to speak in public?

If the answer to any of these questions is no, this is the book for you. It challenges you to change, to take some chances. Readers who are not entirely satisfied will have the most to learn from this book.

At times you may think this book is unusual. We will ask you to do some things that you do not normally do while reading a book. Sometimes, we will ask you to write something in the book before continuing. Sometimes we will ask you not to continue reading until you go through an exercise by yourself, with someone else, or with a group. Sometimes you may say, "This doesn't make sense." "This doesn't apply to me." That is a good sign. You may be on the brink of a significant breakthrough in communication skills. The discomfort you feel is a fear of the unknown; it is healthy and natural. At such times, it is imperative that you proceed with redoubled enthusiasm. If you do not, fear of the unknown may well conquer you.

We have tried to keep the language in this book "untechnical." We want you to learn the materials in this book in two ways: First, we want you to master the *concepts* we describe. In this, our goal is similar to the goal of most textbooks. Second, we want you to practice communication *skills*. To learn about communication concepts is desirable, but our essential goals will be reached only when you communicate effectively in your everyday life. We challenge you to break out and break through, to become more knowledgeable, more skilled communicators. That more effective communicator you may become is someone you have known for a long time.

R. H.
J. L. W.

CHAPTER 1
STUDYING COMMUNICATION

βefore you begin to read this chapter, please respond to Experience 1.1. It will help you to check your present understanding of some of the ideas we will be discussing.

EXPERIENCE 1.1 SOME STATEMENTS ABOUT COMMUNICATION

DIRECTIONS   Several statements are listed below. To the right of each statement are the letters *A* and *D*. Circle *A* if you tend to agree with the statement or think it is essentially correct; circle *D* if you disagree with the statement or think it is essentially incorrect.

1 Communication occurs when one person sends a message to another person. A D

2 The actual sending of the message is the most important event in communication. A D

3 A conversation between two people takes place in discrete segments; that is, one persons sends a message, and the other person receives the message. Then the process is reversed as the other person sends, and the first person receives. A D

4 Communication occurs when a receiver of a message assigns meaning to it. A D

5 Communication between two people is a relatively simple matter. A D

6 Feedback is information a person gets by scanning the environment to see how well his or her actions are adapting to the context. A D

7 The more people have in common, the better they can communicate. A D

8 Most of the world's problems are communication problems that could be solved if people simply understood each other better. A D

9 Feedback is necessary to increase the accuracy of communication. A D

10 Whenever there is a breakdown in communication, it is usually the fault of the message sender. A D

11 Most communication transactions are quite simple once you understand what is going on. A D

   The statements in Experience 1.1 focus on the content of this chapter. We agree with statements 4, 6, 7, and 9; we disagree with statements 1, 2, 3, 5, 8, 10, and 11. Now you may question our thinking about these statements, but when you have finished this chapter, you will understand why we responded as we did.

It is easy to send a message; it is somewhat more difficult to communicate. Communication is a sort of sharing that takes place when messages get received and interpreted.

Imagine two people, one of whom is sending a message. The second person, who is facing in the other direction, never notices the first person. There has been no communication from A to B. There may have been some communication from B to A.

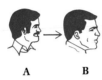

A   B

Imagine the same two people facing each other. The same person is speaking, and the other person is now listening. It seems that some form of communication is now taking place from A to B.

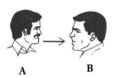

A   B

Next, imagine the same two people facing each other, but the first person is not talking. For the sake of argument, assume that the first person is trying to send no message at all to the second. Is

A   B

communication taking place? Yes. The second person is still receiving and interpreting messages from A because even silence can be a message. You cannot stop sending messages, but sending messages does not by itself constitute communication.

You are probably sending messages right now, but you are not sending messages right now that we will receive. We are not sending messages to you right now; we sent them when we wrote this book. You are now reading and interpreting those messages. Yet, it is correct to say that communication is happening between us now, although the messages were sent long ago. *Communication happens when messages*

Communication is message reception and interpretation. Describe some messages these communicators are receiving from each other? What kind of situation is this? How do you know?

are received and interpreted. It is not communication when we write a book. It *is* communication when you read and understand one.

If you give a speech and nobody comes to hear it, there is likely to be no communication. If you go outside and yell but get no response, chances are that you did not communicate. But if you are sitting alone in your room and you hear the scream of one of your classmates who went outside to yell, then you are participating in an act of communication.

At least two kinds of things happen when people communicate with each other. One is *message transportation.* If a sender of a message talks to a receiver of a message, the message travels from one person to the other in much the same way as you walk from your room to class. The transportation analogy is widely used in theories of communication. Television, for instance, involves a sort of mass transit for messages; it allows a message to be transported to millions of homes from one central location.

If you think about communication as transportation, you focus on the source of the message and on the message itself. This kind of thinking raises certain questions. For example: What can a speaker do to make a presentation more effective? What kind of television commercial is going to transport itself most effectively to a large number of listeners? Most books about communication discuss communication primarily as transportation. They place emphasis on how to construct messages and how to deliver them so that you will get your point across as often as possible.

A second activity happens during communication that is more subtle than transportation, but equally important. As the transported message reaches you (its destination), a change takes place inside your head. Nobody knows precisely what that change is. But somehow the message picks up a meaning. You *interpret* it. The meaning in one head was not simply transported to some other head through communication. Rather, you have taken the message that was transported to you and given it a meaning. This interpretation process is crucial to communication. Whenever it occurs, communication has taken place, and no communication can take place without it. Communication can thus be defined as *what happens when a receiver of a message assigns meaning to it.*

To emphasize the interpretation function of communication is to emphasize the role of the receiver in communication. If we are sending messages to you (in this book), then our effectiveness depends on your receiving behavior as much as our sending behavior. You must be paying attention, you must be interested, you must have some means of understanding what we are saying. If these things do not happen, our sending has been a waste of time.

In summary, people often emphasize message transportation when they think about communication. This emphasis focuses on the role of sources of messages and effective message construction. Such a perspective is useful, but there is also value in viewing communication as interpretation of messages and emphasizing effective processes of assigning meanings to messages. In this book, we explore with both perspectives, but our major commitment is to this definition: *Communication is message reception and interpretation.*

When you have completed Experience 1.2, you will have a clearer idea of the importance of interpreting messages. But first, let us explain why we want you to respond to this experience and the others in this book. We have designed them to demonstrate our view of how people acquire knowledge and make that knowledge meaningful. We believe that you will learn best when you are actively committed to learning and when you are involved in the process of learning. The experiences are designed to get you to respond actively to what we say. If the knowledge you gain from a textbook is going to mean anything to you, it must be discovered by you and grounded in your own experience. That is why we seek your involvement and commitment through completing the exercises as you read the text. Take time to respond to each experience as you come to it. Your effort will pay off in increased understanding and skill development.

To get the most out of this book, we ask you to:

1   Be a little dissatisfied with your present communication behavior and understanding of the process of communication. Only when you are dissatisfied can significant learning take place.

2   Seek out reasons why a particular skill or understanding might be important to you. Having a good reason for learning can facilitate the process.

3   Complete each of the experiences as they occur in the text.

4   Enjoy the experiences.

5   Try to draw a conclusion from each experience. Make some personal observation or generalization.

6   Discuss what you are learning with someone. Try out your insights about communication on your friends. Ask for their reactions.

7   Put what you have learned into practice in your daily communication with others.

8   Write in this book. Become its third author. Write your name in as the third author on the title page. Make notes in the margin. Write down your thoughts on the experiences and the text. Our experience in using these materials in our own classes show that the students who do a lot of writing master the material best and show the greatest improvement in their communication skills.

EXPERIENCE   1.2   HOW DO YOU SPEND YOUR COMMUNICATIVE DAY?

DIRECTIONS   **The left-hand column lists seven forms of communicative activity you might undertake during an average day. For each activity, describe some actual instances of such communication behavior that you engaged in on one day last week. Then, in the right-hand column, estimate how much time you spent on each activity.**

Activity   *Amount of time*

1   **Reading** _Minimal - Just paper work_

2   **Watching TV** _when arrived home from work_   _1½ hrs_

3   **Listening to radio** _all day - backround music at work_

4   **Talking to others (friends, teacher, and so on)** _____   _____
all day & night -

5   **Listening to others talk (friends, teachers, and so on)** _____   _____

6   **Delivering prepared messages to groups of people** _____   _____

7   **Writing** orders - paperwork   2 hrs
messages - notes

8   **Other** Selling   4 hrs

Most of our students express surprise at the results of Experience 1.2. They have found that they spend more time in receiving behavior (such as listening, reading, and watching TV) than in sending messages. You may say that is because you are a college student, you listen to hours of lectures every week. That is true, of course. But chances are that you also watch less television than nonstudents. The content of your activities may be different, but the basic behavior is the same as that of most people.

Studies of communication have routinely found that nearly everyone listens more than he or she talks, reads more than writes, and in general spends a lot more time receiving messages than sending them. Yet, although people really spend a great deal of time listening, they usually give very little thought to listening skills. Perhaps people think about listening so rarely because it seems easy and natural to interpret messages.

Actually, listening is not so easy as it seems. Most people are quite inefficient at it. No matter how carefully they think they are listening, they probably remember less than they hear. In other words, most people listen *ineffectively* most of the time. That is important because receiving is a key to communication. Remember, no communication happens without receiving behavior (listening). It follows logically that no *effective* communication happens without effective listening.

Misunderstandings occur to all of us each day. After a misunderstanding, your first thought usually is to ask how the sender of the message might have said it better. You rarely stop to think that you, the receiver of the message, might have listened more effectively. Yet effective listening could resolve more communication problems than effective talking could. In the first place, it does not matter how well you say something if nobody listens. Did you ever have the experience of saying something eloquent only to have your listener misunderstand? In contrast, have you ever said something perfectly horrible, but a caring response from someone else saved the day? Do you begin to see the importance of effective listening?

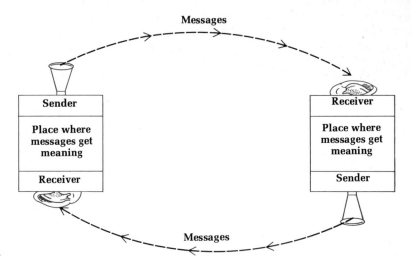

Figure 1.1

Figure 1.1 presents a detailed diagram (model) of what happens when people talk and listen. The two squares in the diagram represent two people sending messages to each other and receiving messages from each other. The messages form a continuous flow around the two people. One person does not simply talk and then listen to the other talk, the way you might think it works when you see dialogue written in a book. Rather, both people send messages constantly and just as constantly monitor messages coming in. For instance, suppose you are talking to a friend. While you are talking, your friend is responding to you by nods, by smiles, by occasional chuckles, by looking at you. You do not stop talking to process each of these messages. You keep talking. Sometimes, the other person interrupts you to finish a sentence. So, you see, it is not so simple as you talking and your friend listening. There is an all-at-onceness to interpersonal communication.

The speaking-listening diagram is a popular representation of the communication process. Wilbur Schramm, a pioneer in the study of communication, used a similar diagram as a model of the communication process more than twenty years ago. The model is elegant because it captures aspects of both the transportation and the interpretation views of communication.

We have introduced the diagram here because it helps to illustrate the importance of what happens at the end of the receiving part of any message transaction. At that point (just past the ear), the message is taken into the receiver and interpreted as a set of meanings. This is the moment of impact, the moment in which a message creates effects. Without suggesting that any part of the message cycle is unimportant, we argue that the moment a message is given meaning in the mind of the receiver is the most critical moment of any communication act.

What does that mean to you? Plenty. Most of us yearn to talk. We want center stage. If you listen to any casual conversation between friends, you will probably note that most of the participants spend much of the conversation paying maximum attention to what they are going to say next. We do it, too. We go to parties and act as if we have a little writer in the back of our heads spinning out new bits of message to impress our friends with. As we listen to others, we spend a

When you listen, are you really listening, or just waiting for a turn?

lot of time thinking about the next time we will be speaking. People want to speak because they think that the speaker is the most important part of any communication event. But did you ever stop to consider whether the message-receiving part of your communicative day might be more vital than the speaking part? Sometimes, that is so.

Here is another example: You are watching television. A station transmitter sends a program to your TV set; the content of that program is a film made by some famous Hollywood stars. As you watch the film, you may envy the movie stars because they get to be on center stage before millions of people. That is a common response. But perhaps the most important part of the transaction is taking place at your end, the viewing-listening end.

A lot of people complain about the poor quality of television programming, and a good case can be made for that point of view. But did you ever stop to think that the real moment at which TV programming has its effects is the moment at which your mind assigns meanings to it. You may not be able to change television programming, but there are some things you *can* change. You have lots of choices. You can change channels, turn the device off, or interpret the programming differently, just to name a few. All these choices involve the television programs only indirectly. The one thing they involve directly is the place where communication makes the greatest difference. It also happens to be the only place where you can make important changes. That place is inside you.

This chapter is about working on yourself. That is the most direct way to improve your communication skills. Working on yourself includes work on what you think and on ways you listen, as well as on how you speak. It is partly a matter of practice and partly a matter of awareness, of understanding the messages that are buzzing around you all the time.

We invite you on a journey into yourself by way of some training in communication skills. We will also show you some ways you can speak more effectively, but they will work only if your listeners receive and interpret effectively. That is because the receiver usually holds most of the keys to effective communication.

Like almost anything, this emphasis on the receiver can be used as a cop-out. You can excuse any failure to speak effectively by blaming it on the foibles of other people who just would not listen. Ineffective speakers often blame their failures on others by claiming that the others misunderstood them. But blaming others is almost always futile. There is only one person over whose sending and receiving behavior you have significant control. That is the person we suggest you work on, using the materials in this book. The point is really what *you* do, whether you are acting as sender or as receiver (and you are almost always both). *You are somebody whose behavior you can change. Are you listening?*

Now, you are ready to proceed to Experience 1.3.

EXPERIENCE 1.3 AREAS OF COMMUNICATION SKILL NEEDING IMPROVEMENT

DIRECTIONS (Part 1) Rate each of the following areas of communication skill according to how interested you are right now in improving your own skills in it. Indicate your rating by circling one of the numbers in the Ratings column. Use the following system:

1 = It is very important that I improve in this area.
2 = It is quite important that I improve in this area.
3 = It would be nice if I could improve.
4 = This is not a priority area for me to improve in.
5 = I am adequate enough in this area. I do not need to improve much.

Rating	*Task*
1 2 ③ 4 5	meeting people
1 2 ③ 4 5	getting along with friends and family
①② 3 4 5	being able to conduct successful interviews
⋆ 1 ② 3 4 5	working in group settings
1 ② 3 4 5	succeeding in a job setting
1 ② 3 4 5	preparing messages intended for others
⋆ ① 2 3 4 5	delivering a speech
1 2 ③ 4 5	getting my way with others (especially clerks, bureaucrats, and people asked for favors)
1 2 ③ 4 5	understanding and appreciating cultural differences
1 ② 3 4 5	resolving conflicts
⋆ ① 2 3 4 5	understanding my own communication behavior
1 2 3 4 5	others [please list]

_____

_____

_____

DIRECTIONS (Part 2) List four people with whom you would like to improve communication. Also list one institution you would like to communicate with   more effectively (such as a company, a government, a church).

Boss
Wife
Daughter
Brother

N&L Catevers

DIRECTIONS
(Part 3)

Review all the items in Parts 1 and 2, and put an asterisk (*) next to the three items you are most interested in improving. Write a sentence about each of these items (or people) explaining what you would like to accomplish.

1. _Understanding my own communication Behavior & being in Control_

2. _Being able To Solicit accounts effectively._

3. _____

We have been suggesting that you work on yourself as a communicator. Experience 1.3 allowed you to analyze your impressions of your own present strengths and weaknesses as a communicator and of the areas in which you are most interested in improving. It is important for you to know which areas of communication behavior you most wish to improve because those are areas in which you can expect to see improvement as you progress through this book. All the task areas in Experience 1.3 will receive detailed treatment in later chapters.

Your ratings of the skills listed in Experience 1.3 are likely to change over time. For instance, you may be most interested now in getting over stage fright when giving a public speech. But after you have given a few speeches or have had other strengthening experiences, you may be less worried about stage fright and more worried about composing your ideas so that you will present them as forcefully as possible. Similarly, you may be interested now in effective ways to meet people. Later, your interests might switch to how to deepen existing friendships.

We suggest that you return to Experience 1.3 at least once a month while you are working with this book. Analyzing your priorities for improvement is always helpful. Those things you care most about improving at any given time are those areas in which your behavior is most likely to make a dramatic change for the better.

As you work on yourself and make progress in awareness, in knowledge of communication codes, in concrete problem-solving skills, you may find that you get your way more often. If you do, that is fine, but do not let your success go to your head. If you totally lose the ability to look at yourself critically, if you become too self-satisfied, you may find yourself unable to change when you need to.

COMPLEXITY IN COMMUNICATION SYSTEMS

There is a lot going on each time people communicate. A supposedly simple act of communication, two people having an idle chat, is far from simple. Each person has a vocabulary of several thousand words, and many of these words have several meanings. Each person may speak an average of 120 words per minute, with gusts of up to 160 words. Each of these words is made up of several sounds. Each word is also part of a phrase or sentence, a group of words that hang together in some way to form meanings. Each group of sentences, in turn, may cluster around a topic of conversation. Each speaker is also sending a large number of nonverbal messages that are at least as complex as the phrases and sentences they are speaking. In addition, each speaker is a member of cultural, ethnic, and social groups. Each speaker is fond of certain expressions, and each is likely to interrupt the other at any time. Each person simultaneously sends and receives messages and is also planning what he or she wants to say next.

Did you ever stop to think that you process all this information in each simple communicative interaction? Communication is indeed complex. Perhaps it gets more complex than it needs to be. If an American engineering company were asked to design a communication system for a humanoid species, the result would probably be much simpler than the one human beings have to work with today. Each word would probably have only one meaning. All words would probably sound just the way they were spelled. Nonverbal signals might also be assigned definite meanings. Apparently, such a company was not consulted because none of those things are true of human communicative systems. Like most aspects of our world, communication systems turn out to be intricate, confusing, and mysterious.

Responsibility and choice

You may believe that you know about the complexity of communication, but chances are that on a day-to-day basis you act as if you did not. For instance, suppose you had an argument with a friend last week. You are still mad. When asked why, you respond, "The argument was all her fault!" That statement makes the matter sound deceptively simple: You and your friend were sailing along with an OK relationship. Then she did something that caused difficulties, and now things are worse. In fact, whatever your friend may have done, chances are that it is not so simple.

In the first place, your friend did not do one thing. Rather, she did a number of things, sent a large number of nearly simultaneous messages. You probably had a number of reactions to those messages. The meanings of the situation were things that you and your friend created together in the situation. You had little control over what your friend said and did, but you did have some control over the meanings that you assigned to the messages and the ways that you chose to react.

"Wait a minute," you protest. "I still had no control over the situation. My friend just picked a fight with me 'til I lost my temper. She made me do it."

Read the last paragraph again. It sounds like a lot of things people say. *But it is not true.* We often phrase our excuses in terms of things other people "caused" us to do. Such explanations might be valid if we lived in the simple world designed by that hypothetical engineering firm. There might be such simple causes and effects in that world. But there are none in this world.

Suppose, for a moment, that you are arguing with your friend. The argument is extremely important to you. Your friend has just said something that made you so angry that you want to hit her. You are so furious, you can hardly see. You reach for something to throw, and your hand settles firmly around the handle of a heavy cast-iron skillet.

At that moment, the telephone rings. What do you do? About 95 percent of our students admit that they would stop to answer the telephone, even in the middle of a fight. Furthermore, most say they would answer the phone in a polite voice, as if nothing special were going on.

So much for the notion that the other person *made* you do something. Apparently, you have a choice, even a number of choices.

Suppose, further, that the phone call is from an old friend you have not seen in two years. The friend wants to meet you in an hour at a local pub to discuss old times. How likely are you to say, "Look, Joan, could you call back some other time. Evelyn and I are having this big fight now, and she just was making me throw the skillet at her when you interrupted?" Perhaps you *would* say that. But there are a number of other things you might say, too. You have a choice. If you want to see Joan, you may even decide to conclude your crucial fight another night.

Multiplicity and change

There are always a number of communication events going on, even when you are alone. Set aside five minutes to spend by yourself in your room tonight, and listen to yourself. Do not say anything. Turn off the TV and the radio. Just sit. Remain quiet. You will probably be amazed at the gaggle of old tunes, parts of past and planned conversations, jingles from TV, and other drivel chattering through your brain even though you are alone and silent. It is rather like Muzak; you do not really notice it 'til everything is quiet, but it is always there. So are the songs of birds. So are thousands of messages from other people during each day.

Given the number of factors working on you all the time, no one factor acts as a simple cause of other factors. Rather, whole *complex systems* of variables are interacting all the time. The friend you talked to yesterday is not exactly the same person today. You may notice some similarities, but that person has changed since yesterday. Do you notice the changes?

Do you notice such changes in yourself? Do you ever stop to notice that you do not act the same all the time? Do you realize that you assume different roles depending on how you see particular situations? (We discuss the concept of roles in detail in Chapter 3.) For example, you may notice some things that are always the same about your friend Larry. You may say that Larry is a happy-go-lucky jokester. You believe that those traits are part of Larry's personality, things he carries around with him that do not change. Well, that may be. But did you ever stop to think that Larry may act in many different ways when you are not present? In fact, the reason why Larry acts happy-go-lucky around you may have as much to do with *you* as with Larry. Maybe Larry thinks that is the kind of person you like best, and Larry wants you to like him. Seen that way, Larry's behavior reflects as much about you as it does about Larry. That is one more way message receivers are important.

We suggest examining complex systems of factors so that you can learn to tell how large numbers of simultaneous events affect each other. All items in a situation that affect the messages sent in that situation can be referred to as the *context* for communication. You take communication contexts into account in deciding what you will say and in interpreting the messages you get from others. Context is like the background material in a play: the scenery, who is on stage, what has happened before, the value systems of the characters, and so on.

FEEDBACK

How do communicators manage to keep track of all the events that constitute communication contexts? Suppose that someone invented a machine that could respond appropriately to contexts as people routinely do. There is some sense in which communicators act as information machines: People scan their environment to see what factors are relevant to communication, they take in information and interpret it, they make predictions about what will happen next, and they formulate an appropriate set of reactions. Then they observe the way others react to their messages. They do all that routinely. In addition, they pay some attention to the words, sentences, and particular nonverbal cues that they use and interpret.

The analogy that people process information by using some of the techniques of machines has been expanded into an area of study called *cybernetics*. Cybernetics examines uses of feedback to keep systems running as effectively as possible. *Feedback* is information from the environment about how well your last actions adapt to a particular communication context.

The word *cybernetics* comes from the Greek word *kybernētēs*, meaning "pilot" or "steersman." The pilot of a ship stands on the deck and scans the sea, looking for information. If the pilot sees no information, then no changes are made in the ship's course. The wheel is held steady, and the whole system goes sliding along the ocean. But if the pilot sees that the ship has drifted off course or notices a rock, an iceberg, a coral reef, or another ship, that information serves as the feedback the system needs to change course, and correction is made using the steering wheel.

Like a ship's pilot, you steer a communication course through your day. Your communication course may seem less well defined than that of a ship bound for Madagascar, but you still steer your way through the day, avoiding danger spots and keeping an eye on your goals. Certain objectives are set for events. Also, you use sets of values, more general guides, that help you to make decisions. You move through time and space, getting feedback from others' reactions to your messages. That feedback is similar in principle to the information that the pilot of a ship gets from visual scanning of the horizon and from use of navigational instruments. You use feedback to adjust your next messages and keep yourself on course.

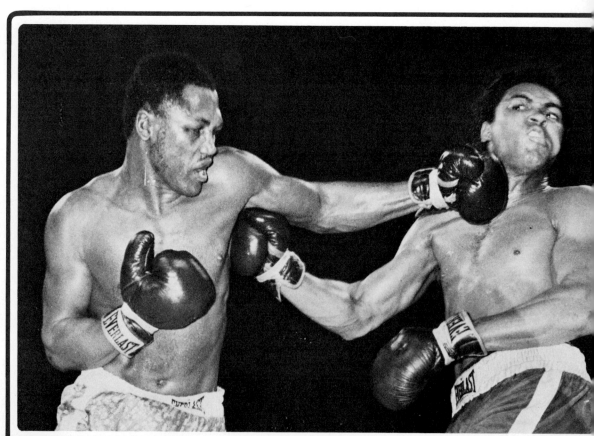

Feedback guides communicators' adjustments to one another.

To get a clear picture of the importance of feedback, try your hand at Experience 1.4.

EXPERIENCE 1.4 FEEDBACK AND ACCURACY

DIRECTIONS **To show you how much feedback adds to the accuracy of communication, we have provided ten geometric shapes. You need a partner for this experience. Position yourself so that you cannot see what your partner is drawing and so that he or she cannot see the shapes on this page. Try to describe one of the shapes, and have your partner try to draw it, but read the rules on page 18 first.**

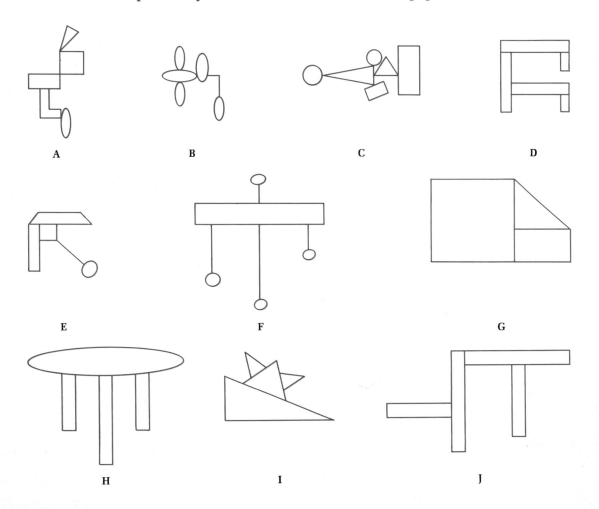

A

B

C

D

E

F

G

H

I

J

1. The first time you do this, your partner must remain silent. He or she may not ask you any questions, and you are not allowed to look at your partner's drawing until it is finished.
2. When the drawing is finished, have your partner draw another shape as you describe it. But this time, let your partner ask questions about the shape or ask you to look at the drawing to see if he or she is doing it correctly.
3. Compare the accuracy of the two drawings.
4. Change places, give your partner the book, and have him or her describe a figure for you to draw—first without feedback, and then allowing you to ask questions.

In most cases, the difference between the accuracy of the feedback drawings and the accuracy of the no-feedback drawings is dramatic. A speaker may actually try to mimimize feedback because a lot of audience response makes the event more unpredictable and increases the chance that the speaker may not get to put the message in exactly the words originally planned. But that tactic is generally shortsighted. When someone is trying to get a message across, his or her chances of success are increased if listeners are allowed and encouraged to ask questions, to evaluate what is happening, to venture opinions, to check their understanding.

However, hoping for and encouraging feedback are not always enough. A listener may fail to provide feedback even when it is encouraged. Remember, you can control only your own behavior. All you can do in such instances is remain aware of nonverbal cues and other signals of the ways in which the communication context changes.

If your listener cooperates by providing some feedback, this still does not ensure that messages will be accurate or useful. Each communicator comes from a different background and has had a different set of experiences. Therefore, a message will mean something just a little different to each individual. When you have completed Experience 1.5, you will have a better understanding of how these subtle differences work.

EXPERIENCE 1.5 PARAPHRASING SKILLS

DIRECTIONS   You need another person for this experience. The two of you must have a conversation lasting five to ten minutes. Talk about a recent political issue, your hobbies, or your attitude toward grades.

Your conversation should be like any normal, friendly conversation except for one rule: After the first speaker finishes talking, the second person must paraphrase what the first said, using some different words but saying as close to the same thing as possible. The original speaker will then agree or disagree about what was said and may offer some clarification if needed. If the first speaker is not satisfied with the paraphrase, the second must try new paraphrases until the first speaker is satisfied. It is not at all uncommon for four or five paraphrases to be necessary. When the second speaker has completed a successful paraphrase, he or she should *respond to* what the first person said. The first person must then try to paraphrase this response. Continue this way until the process feels familiar.

Here is a sample of such a conversation:

First: *I'm extremely interested in the election for governor next month.*

Second: *I think you're saying that the governor's election campaign has been extremely exciting to you.*

First: *Well, no. Actually, it's been dull, but I'm interested in the issues.*

Second: *Oh, I hear you saying that the personalities in the campaign are dull but that the issues are things that you think are important.*

First: *That's closer to it, but I don't think the issues are all that vital. They're just issues that are fascinating because there's so much name-calling and so many sides to every issue.*

Second: *I see. Do you mean that actually it's the exchange of arguments that you find most fascinating about this campaign?*

First: *Now you've got it.*

Second: [Responding to the first speaker's original statement] *I actually think that most of the issues in the campaign are quite trivial.*

First: *Do you mean to say that. . . .*

Most students express surprise at how difficult and involved this Experience 1.5 can become. A common reaction during the experience is, "If you meant that, why didn't you just say that?" Experience 1.5 highlights the difficulty of getting meanings across to other people even under conditions in which there is plenty of feedback. That difficulty seems to spring from the fact that each person has a unique set of experiences to draw on and therefore assigns a unique set of connotations to many words and expressions. The following imaginary conversation demonstrates the problems these differences can cause.

I just bought a car.

Great. Is it a new car?

No, it's an old car.

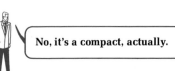

Oh, a classic, I suppose?

No, a five-year-old Ajax.

Oh, is it in good shape?

Yes, the salesperson said it was owned by a little old lady.

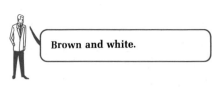

Does it have a big engine?

No, it's a compact, actually.

Oh. What color is it?

Brown and white.

Oh, why didn't you just say that you had a brown and white compact car that's five years old?

I thought it was important that we have this exercise in feedback and communication accuracy.

Well, we certainly did a good job, didn't we?

Each of us has a field of experience. If our fields of experience do not overlap much, it is difficult for us to communicate. Notice the word *communicate*. The root word is *common*, which is also the root word for *community, commune, Communist,* and *communion*. In England, there used to be meadows called the *commons* in every town on which everyone's animals could graze. The word *communication* refers to the sharing of messages. To communicate, humans must establish a common field of experience, a set of notions with shared meanings, so that they will both be referring to approximately the same thing when talking to each other.

Thinking about communication as such a sharing enterprise helps us to understand why people who have a great deal in common find it easy to understand each other's problems, joys, pet peeves, and other kinds of message content. People in this fortunate circumstance discover large overlaps in their common field of experience. In other words, two such people share a lot of assumptions. When you talk on any subject, you say some things, and you leave some things unsaid. If you are telling off-color jokes to your friends, you are assuming that they find such stories humorous. If they do not react the way you expected them to (i.e., if they do not laugh or indicate that they are amused), it may be that your friends' assumptions about what is funny are different from yours.

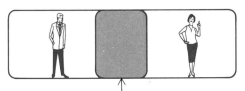

Common field of experience

Given each person's unique set of experiences, it is remarkable that messages get shared at all. Take a teacher and a group of students, for example. At the start of a class, the teacher and students often have little in common. The teacher is usually older, almost always more educated in a specialized field, and often from a different cultural background. Teacher and students are likely to have different values and to care about different things. How are these two sets of communicators going to establish some common assumptions so that messages can be shared by them? Teachers usually offer a set of definitions of key terms so that everyone will assign similar meanings to important words that will be used a number of times throughout the course. Some key terms for an introductory course in human communication are included in the Mini-Glossary.

Communication The assigning of meanings to messages by receivers.
Receiver A person who senses and interprets messages.
Encoder A person (or some other entity such as a machine or an animal) who sends a message. Persons cannot stop sending messages.
Channel The medium through which a message travels to receivers. In interpersonal communication, it is often simply the space between persons, which allows visual and auditory signals to pass back and forth.
Mass medium A mechanized vehicle for transmitting messages uniformly to large numbers of receivers who may be removed from the senders in time and space.
Messages Pieces of information that seem to travel to and (usually) from humans. They are the raw materials of communication. The sharing of messages is the object of communication. (Chapters 4 and 5 focus on elements of messages.)
System A set of interacting variables. Most communication phenomena seem to be complex systemic events.
Context The system background against which a message occurs. The context is made up of those other things that are happening that give the message its meaning.
Common field of experience Meanings that are quite similar in minds of parties to communication. For example, the words in this Mini-Glossary are now part of the common field of experience we share with you.

Do you understand each of the terms in the glossary? If any of the terms are unfamiliar to you, stop and reread the Chapter. You will find a discussion of each term. If you still have questions, ask your teacher or a classmate for clarification. It is critical that we have a common field of experience so that we can proceed.

Study the terms in the Mini-Glossary. Memorize the definitions. Now, look at the following list of terms and recite each definition without looking back at the Mini-Glossary.

Communication	Channel	System
Receiver	Mass medium	Context
Encoder	Messages	Common field of experience

When you are satisfied that you know each definition, proceed to Experience 1.6. Be certain that you have mastered the definitions before you continue. Do not try to respond to the Experience if you are not fully prepared for it.

EXPERIENCE   1.6   GLOSSARY QUIZ I

DIRECTIONS   Without looking back to previous pages, fill in all the blanks in this quiz just as if you were taking an in-class test.

1   Communication: The assigning of _meanings_ to _messages_ by _recievers_.

2   Receiver: A person who _senses_ and _interprets_ messages.

3   Encoder: A person who _sends_ a _message_.

4   Channel: The _medium_ through which a message _travels_ to receivers.

5   Mass medium: A man-made vehicle for _transmitting_ messages _uniformly_ to large numbers of receivers who may be removed from _senders_ in _time_ and _space_.

6   Messages: Pieces of _information_ that seem to travel to and (usually) from humans. Raw materials for communication. The _sharing_ of messages is the object of communication.

7   System: A set of _interacting_ variables.

8   Context: The system _background_ against which a _message_ occurs.

9   Common field of experience: _Meanings_ that are quite _similar_ in the minds of parties to communication.

10 Martha wants to make sure that Edgar remembers to pick up his laundry. Martha asks Emily to remind Edgar when she sees him and tells Emily to emphasize the point that Edgar will have nothing to wear unless he picks up his clothes. Martha also asks Bill to tell Edgar to pick up his laundry if Bill should happen to see him. Edgar picks up his laundry but complains to Martha that she did not have to tell everyone to remind him. Emily's reminder to Edgar can be described as a _____. Bill functions as a _____.

HOW TO READ THE REST OF THIS BOOK

How did you do on the test in Experience 1.6? If you got 90 percent correct, then you are ready to go on. If you did not, go back and review the pivotal terms until they are clear to you. There is a review quiz in Experience 1.7 for you to take when you are sure that you are ready.

A tip about how to read this book is worth repeating: Be sure to follow directions. The book is written so that each part leads to the next. If you skip an experience because you do not feel like doing it or because it does not make sense to you, you will not learn what the book is designed to teach you.

We have arranged the chapters in the order that we believe makes the most sense. Remember to read each chapter from start to finish and to complete each Experience as you come to it.

The order of chapters calls for some explanation. As we noted earlier in this Chapter, we begin the study of communication concepts and skills with you as an individual. If you do not begin by sorting out your own self, no amount of training can make you an effective communicator. For this reason, Chapters 1 to 3 are devoted to you as a communicator, quite aside from messages you send to others. Topics discussed include the role of perception in interpreting messages and the relationships between self-concept and communication. Chapters 4 and 5 focus on messages, describing how language affects the ways that people communicate and the role of nonverbal codes in communication.

Whereas Chapters 1 to 5 focus on the various components of the communication process, Chapters 6 to 11 explore the situations in which you are most likely to find knowledge of these components useful: conflicts, intercultural communication, building relationships, interviews, task-oriented small groups, and larger work organizations.

Chapters 12 to 14 apply these concepts and skills to the development of messages to inform or persuade large numbers of listeners and to the public delivery of such messages.

EXPERIENCE 1.7 GLOSSARY QUIZ II

DIRECTIONS   Match each of the following terms with its correct definition by writing the appropriate letter in the blank next to each term.

	1	Communication	a. A person who sends a message.
B	2	Receiver	b. A person who senses a message.
A	3	Encoder	c. A set of interacting variables.
	4	Channel	d. The assigning of meanings to messages.
	5	Mass medium	e. The system background against which a message
	6	Messages	occurs.
C	7	System	f. Meanings that are quite similar in the minds of
e	8	Context	the parties to communication.

_____ 9   Common field of experience   g. Pieces of information that seem to travel to and (usually) from humans.
                                                 h. A man-made vehicle for transmitting messages uniformly to large numbers of receivers who may be removed from the senders in time and space.
                                                 i. The medium through which a message travels to receivers.

Now, read each of the following statements carefully. Write *T* next to the statement if it is true or *F* if it is false.

_____ 10   In interpersonal communication, a person can start and stop sending messages whenever he or she wants to.

_____ 11   The sharing of messages is the object of communication.

_____ 12   Most communication phenomena seem to be simple systemic events.

CAUTION   We conclude this Chapter with a vital point: Many people believe that most of the world's problems are problems of communication. Do not believe that for a moment. There are many problems that have little to do with faulty or ineffective communication. Better communication will do little to feed the hungry or clothe the poor. More effective communicating will do only a little to make you happier or richer than you are. There is no program for improving communication skills that will allow you always to get your way by persuading other people that you are right. Even if you communicate effectively, other people may be working against the very issues you support. Many times, people communicate effectively and still fail.

      Do not expect to be able to be the master of complex systems that nobody understands thoroughly. There are no mysterious, foolproof formulas for success. You usually get what you pay for in life. Sometimes, of course, you get lucky, and sometimes you get gypped.

      Effective communication is not everything. But it can be very helpful. If you are persistent in your studies, you will develop understandings and skills that will enable you to ride the wave more often than you get knocked over by it.

      Welcome, good luck, and have a fun trip through this book.

CHAPTER 2
PERCEIVING MESSAGES

A great deal of light falls on everything.
—VINCENT VAN GOGH

hapter 1 emphasized the importance of reception and interpretation in the communication process. This chapter examines some principles of perception that underlie receiving and interpreting messages. Paying attention does not, by itself, ensure effective listening. An effective listener must also be able to understand some ways that our perceptual system works on a message.

Perception is not a simple process of understanding a factual world out there. People do a lot of selecting and interpreting when they think they are only sensing. This chapter begins with a discussion of how we perceive objects *selectively*, that is, how we notice some things while ignoring others. However, perception of persons is quite different from perception of objects. The chapter concludes with an exploration of the application of person perception skills to interpersonal communication.

How do you perceive something? That is, how do you receive messages from others and from the world and arrange those messages so that they mean something to you? Experience 2.1 will help you to sort out your current understanding of these questions.

EXPERIENCE 2.1 AGREE-DISAGREE STATEMENTS ABOUT PERCEPTION

DIRECTIONS **Read each of the following statements carefully. Circle A if you tend to agree with the statement; circle D if you disagree with it.**

1 **What people perceive generally depends on what their environment and culture have taught them to see.**   (A) D

2 **People perceive what they wish to perceive, regardless of reality.**   (A) D

3 **Our perceptions are real, but when we try to talk about them, the words distort reality.**   (A D)

4 **We can never see reality.**   A (D)

5 **Generally, a careful, sensitive person can tell what others are thinking.**   A D

6 **Stereotypes distort perception and are responsible for many tragedies.**   (A) D

7 **A person who observes things carefully can see "what is" clearly.**   (A) D

8 **Only scientists see reality.**   A (D)

9 **The perception of an object depends more on the object than the perceiver.**   A (D)

28

10 **The way we perceive a person affects how he or she acts
    toward us.**   (A) D
11 **Perception is direct and clear.**   A (D)

People's attitudes toward perception vary as much as individual
perceptions do. Experience 2.1 serves as a rough indicator of your
confidence in your own perceptions and of how you feel about
perception. It will be interesting for you to review and revise these
opinions after you have experienced this chapter.

**HOW ACCURATE IS
PERCEPTION?**

Perception processes are at the heart of most communication
theories. If perception does not work accurately, no message can be
effective on its own terms. For many reasons, perception may be the
weakest link in the communication chains that connect us. Most people
go through most days with the feeling that what they perceive is real.
They behave as though receiving messages and figuring out what they
mean are the most natural and simple of processes. To a certain extent,
these assumptions are true. But sometimes our senses and perception
play tricks on us that make us wonder how close to reality our
perception can actually come. In the next few pages, we will show you
how the perception process allows you to see some strange things.

What shape is represented by the series of dots below? Connect
the dots with lines to form the shape you see.

•

•   •

Most people see a triangle with three equal sides.

But why do they not see any of these shapes?

It is difficult to say *why*. Perception is a very rapid process. The dots
are simply *seen* as forming a triangle. This set of lines is also ordinarily
seen as a triangle.

∧

∠   ⅃

But that perception changes if the size of the angles change. Draw lines to complete the figure described by these angles.

Most of our students have tried to draw the connecting lines as concave sides.

Why? Because that is the way the human eye (and nervous system) fills out the figure. But why do people not complete the figure with lines that bulge outside the angles?

Furthermore, why are the figures perceived as completely closed rather than open, like this:

The eye (and other senses, too) takes incomplete information and manufactures a hypothetical complete picture. That is a prediction process because the whole picture often cannot be sensed. Ordinarily, this information processing procedure produces accurate predictions that aid communication. Nevertheless, it is important to be aware of the nature of the process because sometimes perceptual predictions go awry. For example, look quickly at the following figure, and guess whether the sloping line at the left and the one at the right could be joined to form one *straight* line.

The two lines look as though they are not on the same path. To most people, they *look* as though they cannot be connected. But, in fact, they can. Take a ruler or the edge of a piece of paper, and place it along the line; then you will see.

This figure, like a mirage of water on the desert, is an *optical illusion*; it is a trick of the eye. Optical illusions are interesting because the objects that cause them can often be examined from other angles and seen differently. Optical illusions are good lessons in the nature of the predictive information processing mechanisms that underlie perception.

Another visual trick our perceptions can play involves *impossible objects*. These are objects that can be drawn in three-dimensional form but that could never really exist in three dimensions. This figure is an example of an impossible object.

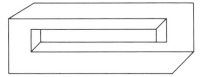

Perception is a process of predicting, of guessing, of jumping to conclusions. For this reason, perception produces error. You may think that you will make fewer mistakes if you make sure that you have all the facts before reaching any conclusions. In a sense, that is correct. But you will *never* be able to get *complete* information because perception processes always eliminate some information and simplify the situation. For instance, many stimuli pass into the eyes and ears but are not of sufficient size or loudness to excite the nervous system's receptors. Such stimuli are said to be below *threshold*. Even after messages get into the nervous system, they are further simplified by a process called *inhibition*, which eliminates messages that do not agree with the dominant messages being received. Thus, because of threshold and inhibition, you never receive complete information from the nervous system. Perception is always a process of simplifying, of prediction, of jumping to conclusions.

Breakdowns in perception often lead to communication problems. Experience 2.2 presents you with a perception problem.

CONTEXTS AND EXPECTATIONS IN PERCEPTION

(handwritten margin note) * Inhibition eliminates messages that do not agree with the Dominant message!

EXPERIENCE   2.2   THE NINE-DOT PROBLEM

DIRECTIONS   Connect *all* nine dots using only four straight lines and without lifting your pencil from the paper or retracing a line. It *is* possible. Before you read on, work on this puzzle for at least ten minutes.

. . .

. . .

. . .

The solution to Experience 2.2 seems elementary once you see it. If you found the answer, congratulations! But very few people can solve the problem the first time they try it. Why is it difficult for most of us to see the solution? Because most people *impose one additional assumption* that is not part of the puzzle. Rather, this assumption is an information processing rule that applies to most such puzzles. That assumption is that the four straight lines cannot go past the square formed by the eight outside dots. It makes the puzzle impossible to solve. Did you make this erroneous assumption? We did when we first tried the puzzle.

The lesson of this experience is that it is useful to maintain an awareness of the assumptions that underlie your perception of any object, person, or problem. Those assumptions will color what we see. If we are unaware of them, successful communication will be more difficult.

In order to solve the puzzle of the dots, you must examine assumptions and then change the frame of reference implied by the assumption that the dots form a square which is the outer limit of the problem.

Like the puzzle of the dots, every communication event that you witness comes to your perceptions embedded in various contexts. The way you interpret those contexts is based on your assumptions about what they mean. These assumptions are your *expectations* about the communication event. The uncritical use of one set of expectations from one situation to another is a common communication difficulty.

Each of us holds expectations to which we sometimes cling tenaciously. To get a better idea of the strength of expectation systems, count the number of times the letter *F* occurs in the following passage:

> *Mr. Farlay followed the '63 Ford to the corner of Fifth and Vine, when from out of the car stepped a dapper fellow in a tall felt hat, with the sack full of frozen waffles across his back and a pocketful of money.*

Write the number of *F*'s here: _____. Now count again to be sure that your total is correct.

Most students miss several of the *F*'s because it is difficult to count the *F* in the word *of* because the letter is pronounced like a *v*. Perhaps you, too, expected all the *F*'s to sound like *F*. Can you see now how an expectation can interfere with accurate information processing?

Read the following passage aloud.

A bird in the
hand is worth
two in the
the bush.

Read it again. Do you note anything strange? Most readers do not. But in fact, a word (*the*) is repeated. Most people do not normally notice this until it is pointed out to them. It is not expected; hence it went unseen.

Remember what you have already learned about expectations as you respond to Experience 2.3.

EXPERIENCE   2.3   EXPECTATIONS AND STEREOTYPES

DIRECTIONS   **Complete the blanks in the following set of statements as *quickly* as possible.**

1   **Women with big _____ are very _____.**
2   **A person must work hard in order to _____.**
3   **Frenchmen and Italians are excellent _____.**
4   **Politicians are usually _____.**
5   **Football players usually _____.**
6   **If it is made in _____, it may be cheap and worthless.**

A major difficulty can develop when you generalize from too little information and form expectations about people based simply on the racial or membership group to which they belong. That process is known as *stereotyping*. (We will have more to say about stereotyping in Chapter 7, "Crossing Cultural Differences.")

You may have thought that only stupid people hold strong expectations that interfere with communication. But the way you filled in the blanks in Experience 2.3 probably helped to convince you that almost everyone holds strong expectations. Even if you did not actually write sexist or racist responses, such possibilities probably flashed through your mind. People tend to forget about such expectations when things are going well, just as a fish forgets that its environment is wet. But just as soon as you forget about expectations and begin to use them uncritically, a situation is likely to occur in which new contexts call for new assumptions.

Experience 2.3 differed from the preceding visual puzzles in at least two important ways: First, it dealt with issues that are more likely to affect everyday communication than are puzzles involving sets of dots or counting occurrences of the letter *F*. Second, the optical illusions and the puzzles had correct answers that you could eventually see, and those answers showed that what you had thought before were, in fact, illusions. There is a *reality* that solves the puzzle: You really can connect all the dots; there really are 17 *F*s. But in everyday communication, there is rarely such an easy reality to appeal to. Rather, communicators are likely to hold competing views of reality, and neither can show the other his or her error. Therefore, perceptions are always guesses, and perception is inevitably strongly molded by expectation.

SELECTIVE PERCEPTION

So much there is to see, but our morning eyes describe a different world than do our afternoon eyes, and surely our wearied evening eyes can only report a weary evening world.
—John Steinbeck

Every eye sees a different world—a communicator's point of view influences what is perceived.

In many of the examples used in this chapter, there is a right answer that you can eventually see if you are clever enough. But human communication is rarely like that. If your friend tells you he lied before, did he really lie before or is he lying now? If you pledge eternal love, what is really happening? Different people often see the same event in different ways, and those differences are largely results of individual systems of expectations. Experience 2.4 demonstrates one example: your perception of smells.

EXPERIENCE 2.4 EVERY NOSE SMELLS A DIFFERENT WORLD

DIRECTIONS   Here is a list of eight smells. Rank them in order from the one you would *most* like to smell right now (number 1) to the one you would *least* like to smell now (number 8).

Ranking	Smell	Ranking	Smell
_____	peppermint	_____	cooking hamburger
_____	oranges	_____	lilacs
_____	garlic	_____	onions
_____	paint	_____	your own body

Wait a day or two, and then rank the list again. But be sure to do so at a different time of day and without looking at your first set of rankings.

Ranking	Smell	Ranking	Smell
_____	peppermint	_____	cooking hamburger
_____	oranges	_____	lilacs
_____	garlic	_____	onions
_____	paint	_____	your own body

Now, compare your rankings with those of others in your class.

We think you will be surprised at how much your rankings differ from those of others and even how much your own ratings differ from one time to another. Which rankings are right? Do onions smell better than oranges? The question is absurd. It is all in the nose of the smeller. It is virtually meaningless to call one set of preferences superior to another. You may love the smell of hamburger *before* lunch and detest the same smell half an hour after lunch. A similar illustration could be made using preferences in music, art, or interior decoration.

Perceptions of communication events may be as subjective as preferences for certain smells, but sometimes communicators treat such perceptions as facts. Others see different facts, and subsequent arguments are often problematic:

"George, I can't understand why you want to go to the Harrison's tonight. Just last night you said you'd never spend another evening with them."
"Agnes, that's not what I said at all. You asked me if I wanted to play bridge with them, and I said not really."
"George, that is *not* what you said at all."
"All I said was. . . ."

Like George and Agnes, most communicators see only part of the picture, their own point of view. And a person's point of view grows from his or her expectations. People see what they expect or wish to see—in football games, in their love lives, in political campaigns. What they really see is their own selves. (Think about this when you read Chapter 3.)

And like George and Agnes, most people spend their communicative energies defending, justifying, and rationalizing their own point of view instead of trying to understand what anyone else is saying.

Expectations lead to *selective perceptions* about people and things around us. Different perceivers sense different facts in many communication situations. Years ago, psychologists Gordon Allport and Leo Postman showed subjects a drawing of a crowd of people on a streetcar. One of the people was a well-dressed black man; another was a white man holding a knife. Later, when asked to recall which person in the picture held the knife, many subjects chose the black man. The subjects' prejudices and stereotypes actually led them to *see* inaccurately. Of course, such flagrant stereotyping may seem foreign to you, but it is a fact that most of us see what we expect to see much of the time. If you believe that most women lack intelligence, chances are you will find evidence to confirm this view in the behavior of the women you meet. Similarly, if you plan to vote for the Democratic candidate in an upcoming election, you will probably note only the smart things that your candidate says and only the bloopers made by the Republican, that is, if you pay any attention to the opposition at all.

The preceding examples represent concrete instances of selective perception, of actually perceiving the world's operations in terms of previous opinions and biases. Each of us perceives (and thus understands) the world in a unique set of ways. That fact is illustrated both by different interpretations of simple experiments (what you would like to smell; whether you see a young or old woman) and by different perceptions of everyday events.

In what ways is your perception selective? What you perceive can be heavily influenced by what you expect. When you expect others to act in a certain way, you may communicate your expectation to them in subtle ways, thereby increasing the probability that they will act as you expect them to. This phenomenon is known as a *self-fulfilling prophecy*. When it occurs, it makes you more confident of your predictions and therefore of the accuracy of your expectations. Consequently, your expectations will be even more definite the next time you have a similar encounter.

Examples of self-fulfilling prophecies are legion. The salesperson with "positive mental attitude" knows that he or she will sell the product, and that expectation is communicated to the customer. Studies in persuasion have shown that if a speaker is introduced to an audience as "an expert" in an area, he will be more persuasive than if there is no such introduction because listeners *expect* to be moved by the opinions of an expert. Self-fulfilling prophecies work in school, too. Before the start of a school year, teachers often inspect the records of their students or hear gossip about students from other teachers. On the basis of this information, teachers form expectations about which students will do the best work, which students will be troublemakers, and so forth, and treat those students accordingly. These expectations make it difficult for students to act in ways other than those the teachers expect. For example, the habitual troublemaker who suddenly does good work may be suspected of cheating.

Self-fulfilling prophecies are not necessarily bad. Often, expectations are fulfilled simply because they are accurate. At other times, self-fulfilling prophecies are helpful. The salesperson uses the self-fulfilling prophecy to maintain stable relationships with customers. Nevertheless, it is important to be aware that expectations influence perception. After all, perceptions are predictions. People often make such predictions on the basis of little information but with great confidence. Think, for example, of the confidence with which you put your weight on your feet when walking without ever testing whether the ground will hold you. People often put a lot of stock in their opinions without double-checking to see whether they are on solid ground.

PERCEIVING OTHER PEOPLE ACCURATELY

Up to this point, we have discussed examples of both object perception and person perception. Of course, there are differences between what happens when you perceive an object and what happens when you perceive a person. In studying human communication, we are primarily interested in how impressions of people are formed. People are more active than most objects and harder to predict. Also, people have more emotional significance than objects, and that makes judgments about them riskier. Finally, most objects do not perceive you as you are perceiving them. But people *do* perceive you at the same moment that you form impressions of them, and how you perceive them affects how they perceive you. In other words, person perception is interactive. Perception of another person can change from moment to moment much more rapidly than perception of an object. In summary, person perception is more complex than object perception, although it seems to involve similar perception processes.

Person perception is the process of making judgments about others' feelings, attitudes, and purposes. It is the process of forming and changing personal impressions of others. The rest of this chapter discusses communication concepts and skills that help to make person perception accurate. A good way to introduce you to this issue is to have you record your impressions of several people. That's the task set for you in Experience 2.5.

EXPERIENCE 2.5 PERSONAL EVALUATIONS

DIRECTIONS For each of the following sets of blanks, fill in the name of one *real* person you are interested in. You may choose a friend, a teacher, a relative, or a public figure (a politician, an artist, and so on). Then place a check mark on one of the spaces between each pair of adjectives indicating your feelings about this person. The middle blank indicates a neutral feeling or no opinion; the blanks on the end represent extreme evaluations; and the other blanks correspond to more moderate evaluations.

1. Name _____

active	___	___	___	___	___	___	___	passive
trustworthy	___	___	___	___	___	___	___	untrustworthy
knowledgeable	___	___	___	___	___	___	___	uninformed
good	___	___	___	___	___	___	___	bad
warm	___	___	___	___	___	___	___	cold
strong	___	___	___	___	___	___	___	weak

2. Name _____

active	___	___	___	___	___	___	___	passive
trustworthy	___	___	___	___	___	___	___	untrustworthy
knowledgeable	___	___	___	___	___	___	___	uninformed
good	___	___	___	___	___	___	___	bad
warm	___	___	___	___	___	___	___	cold
strong	___	___	___	___	___	___	___	weak

Person perception is a process of making judgments about others' feelings, attitudes, and purposes. How do these communicators use feedback to aid impression formation?

3. Name _____

active	___	___	___	___	___	___	___	passive
trustworthy	___	___	___	___	___	___	___	untrustworthy
knowledgeable	___	___	___	___	___	___	___	uninformed
good	___	___	___	___	___	___	___	bad
warm	___	___	___	___	___	___	___	cold
strong	___	___	___	___	___	___	___	weak

4. Name _____

active	___	___	___	___	___	___	___	passive
trustworthy	___	___	___	___	___	___	___	untrustworthy
knowledgeable	___	___	___	___	___	___	___	uninformed
good	___	___	___	___	___	___	___	bad
warm	___	___	___	___	___	___	___	cold
strong	___	___	___	___	___	___	___	weak

5. Name _____

active	____	____	____	____	____	____	____	passive
trustworthy	____	____	____	____	____	____	____	untrustworthy
knowledgeable	____	____	____	____	____	____	____	uninformed
good	____	____	____	____	____	____	____	bad
warm	____	____	____	____	____	____	____	cold
strong	____	____	____	____	____	____	____	weak

Most students do not find it difficult to make judgments such as these about people they know or even about politicians, artists, or movie stars. In fact, going through this evaluative process usually helps people to see that they intuitively make such judgments about those they interact with every day. You may not stop to think about it, but these evaluations of others help to shape the ways you form meanings from their messages.

The scales you filled out in Experience 2.5 are related to some of the most important sets of decisions you make in interpersonal communication. The good-bad judgment seems to lie at the base of most evaluation. Communicators tend to feel and express approval and disapproval toward others at all stages of communication processes. Warm-cold judgments are closely related to good-bad judgments. Warmth, which is usually associated with friendliness, is an important characteristic of people's perceptions of others.

Judgments about a person's activity level (active-passive) and strength (strong-weak) are also important in person perception. Our culture, for example, generally admires people who demonstrate strength and activity in most settings. Finally, judgments about trustworthiness and knowledgeability seem highly related to how well people believe what others tell them.

Look back over the five sets of judgments you made in Experience 2.5. In your style of judgment, did certain characteristics seem to cluster with others? For instance, if you rated a person trustworthy, did you also rate that person good? This raises an important question: Is that relationship a characteristic of the persons you evaluated, or is it a characteristic of your perceptual style?

Each of us makes hundreds of evaluative person perception judgments during an average day. Such judgments are far-reaching and resistant to change. They form a kind of self-fulfilling prophecy in themselves. For instance, people usually perceive others in terms of personality characteristics that the others possess or demonstrate. People are seen as kind or charitable or harsh or bitter or cheerful. Experience 2.6 demonstrates how such judgments work.

EXPERIENCE 2.6 PERCEPTION OF COMMUNICATORS' TRAIT CLUSTERS

DIRECTIONS Check either the Agree or the Disagree blank next to each adjective to indicate the best completion of the following statements:

1 People who are *inconsiderate* are also

	Agree	Disagree
aggressive	_____	_____
hostile	_____	_____
honest	_____	_____
irritable	_____	_____
warm	_____	_____
sincere	_____	_____

2 People who are *optimistic* are also

	Agree	Disagree
friendly	_____	_____
cold	_____	_____
unsympathetic	_____	_____
reserved	_____	_____
cheerful	_____	_____
good	_____	_____

Chances are that you feel that people who are inconsiderate are also aggressive, hostile, and irritable and that people who are optimistic are friendly, cheerful, and good. The point is that traits usually seem to occur in clusters. That is, the presence of one characteristic seems to predict the presence of certain other characteristics. This kind of perceptual prediction should not be too surprising to you by this time. Your impressions of another person usually start with small things: a smile, a handshake, a descriptive phrase, an indication of an attitude. These bits of information generate in your perceptual apparatus a swarm of inferences about the characteristics or motives of the other person. That is, when one trait or characteristic is inferred to describe a person, it suggests other traits.

The point of this discussion is not to make you doubt your perceptions. Your perceptual information processing system ordinarily works quite effectively. Rather, we want you to realize that some perceptions which might seem to be facts are actually rather abstract inferences. For example, you know that Eloise, your best friend, is optimistic, honest, and sincere but also rather aggressive. The first three characteristics cluster together rather well and could perhaps be predicted from each other. The fourth, however, often is believed to indicate lack of sincerity, lack of consideration, and the like. If someone met Eloise for the first time and noticed mainly her aggressiveness, that person might conclude that Eloise is dishonest and insincere. Such misperceptions can be minimized if we remember that perceptions are inferences which can easily be overgeneralized. The best rule of thumb is to avoid rigid categories in evaluating others.

Communicators sometimes show rigidity in discussing personality characteristics as if they were possessions. They say, "He has a warped outlook," or "he is unselfish." Actually, people are much less static than such statements indicate. People can change or choose to act in ways that differ from their usual behavior. Even a very unselfish person does things that might seem selfish. Treating perceptions as predictions that may be fallible can help you to avoid errors of stereotyping.

To understand another person, to perceive another person accurately, you must practice empathy; that is, you must try to understand what the other person is feeling. You might say that, in effect, you need to walk in the other person's shoes. We will discuss empathy in detail in Chapter 8. For now, try to practice empathy by the deceptively unsimple act of listening to the details of what is said. So, listen, look for clues, empathize, and ask questions to get feedback.

Experiences 2.7 and 2.8 provide some practice in the skills we have discussed in this chapter.

EXPERIENCE 2.7 PERCEPTUAL PREDICTIONS

DIRECTIONS   **Read each statement in the left-hand column. Try to predict the feelings that prompted the person to make the statement. Note your predictions in the right-hand column.**

EXAMPLE   *The person says:*
"I really enjoyed this evening."

The person probably feels:
Pleased, anxious, asking you for your reaction, wishes to see you again.

The person says:
1   "I can't see why she doesn't want to go steady this summer just because we won't see each other every day."

The person probably feels:
_____

_____

2 "My boss never seems to tell me whether he thinks I'm doing a good job." _____

3 "What did you get on the test?" _____

4 "I'm awful thirsty, Sally. Want to go over and have a soda with me?" _____

5 "I think Professor Widget is really arrogant. He's so insulting, I wouldn't give him the time of day." _____

6 "Doing a group project is really a a bad idea. Last time, I did all the work, and the loafers got just as much credit." _____

7 "I'm sorry about what I said on the phone last night. I'll always care for you." _____

8 "I can't believe you still think there's a God. What do you think about Santa Claus?" _____

EXPERIENCE 2.8 USING THE SENSES

DIRECTIONS Increasing your awareness of what is coming at you through your senses is bound to improve the accuracy and usefulness of your interpersonal communication skills. Eat an orange, paying close attention to everything you touch, smell, and taste, as well as see. You may be surprised to realize how many times you have eaten an orange with some of your senses turned off. Some doctors claim that obese

Hear no evil.   See no evil.   Speak no evil.

people eat so much because they do not really taste their food. The point we want to emphasize is that much of the time people keep their senses closed to much of the reality around them.

Read the following selection from Annie Dillard's book *Pilgrim at Tinker Creek,* in which she discusses two kinds of seeing and, by implication, two kinds of perception.

I chanced on a wonderful book by Marius von Senden called **Space and Sight.** *When Western surgeons discovered how to perform safe cataract operations, they ranged across Europe and America operating on dozens of men and women of all ages who had been blinded since birth. Von Senden collected accounts of such cases. . . .*

For the newly sighted, vision is pure sensation unencumbered by meaning: "The girl went through the experience that we all go through and forget, the moment we are born. She saw, but it did not mean anything but a lot of different kinds of brightness." Again, "I asked the patient what he could see; he answered that he saw an extensive field of light, in which everything appeared dull, confused, and in motion. He could not distinguish objects." Another patient saw "nothing but a confusion of forms and colours." . . .

Many newly sighted people speak well of the world, and teach us how dull is our own vision. . . . A little girl visits a garden. "She is greatly astonished, and can scarcely be persuaded to answer, stands speechless in front of the tree, which she only names on taking hold of it, and then as 'the tree with the lights in it.'" . . .

Seeing is of course very much a matter of verbalization. Unless I call my attention to what passes before my eyes, I simply won't see it. . . . When I see this way I analyze and pry. I hurl over logs and roll away stones; I study a bank a square foot at a time probing and tilting my head. . . .

But there is another kind of seeing that involves a letting go. When I see this way I sway transfixed and emptied. The difference between the two ways of seeing is the difference between walking with and without a camera. When I walk with a camera, I walk from shot to shot, reading the light on a calibrated meter. When I walk without a camera, my own shutter opens, and the moment's light prints on my own silver gut. . . .

When the doctor took her bandages off and led her into the garden, the girl who was no longer blind saw "the tree with the lights in it." It was for this tree I searched through the peach orchards of summer, and in the forests of fall and down winter and spring for years. Then one day I was walking along Tinker Creek thinking of nothing at all and I saw the tree with the lights in it. I saw the backyard cedar where the mourning doves roost charged and transfigured, each cell buzzing with flame. I stood on the grass with the lights in it, grass that was wholly fire, utterly focused and utterly dreamed. It was less like seeing than being for the first time seen, knocked breathless by a powerful glance. The flood of fire abated, but I'm still spending the power.

The following questions will help you to record your impressions of Dillard's ideas on perception.

1   Describe in your own words two kinds of seeing.

_____

_____

_____

_____

2   Have you ever experienced anything like "the tree with the lights in it"? If you have, describe it briefly. If you have not, describe how you *think* you would react to such an experience.

_____

_____

_____

_____

3   How do you think Annie Dillard would respond to the agree-disagree statements in Experience 2.1? Choose one or two particular statements with which you agreed but with which you think Dillard would have disagreed.

_____

_____

4   Describe how Dillard's two ways of seeing might apply to persons as well as objects.

_____

_____

SUMMARY

Perception can best be thought of as a prediction process. Your senses pick up incomplete information from the environment that is transmitted by the nervous system to the brain and interpreted. Because perception always simplifies the environment, your brain must fill in the missing pieces; that is, your brain must make predictions and jump to conclusions.

Perception often involves habit patterns. People perceive what they are used to perceiving. To some degree, they manage to perceive what they expect to perceive. People also make assumptions about situations that affect what they perceive. It is important to be aware of the assumptions you are making about a communication situation. When you uncritically transfer a set of assumptions from one situation to another, these expectations are likely to get you into communication difficulties. For instance, you may often communicate very subtly that you expect others to act in a certain way. Sure enough, they often behave in the way you expected them to. That is a self-fulfilling prophecy.

People tend to perceive others by making judgments about them according to a series of dimensions, including such characteristics as good-bad, warm-cold, active-passive, and strong-weak. Many other judgments may then be inferred on the basis of these judgments. A serious problem occurs when you rigidify a person's traits and begin to talk about the person's personality characteristics as if they were possessions. People are much too dynamic for such characterizations to be accurate. For this reason, it is important to regard perceptions of people as possibly fallible predictions.

People seldom utilize their full potential for perceiving the world. Open up your senses. As your awareness of your perceptual abilities increases, you will be able to improve your interpersonal communication ability and accuracy.

CHAPTER 3
COMMUNICATING THE SELF-CONCEPT

If you're not able to communicate successfully between yourself
and yourself, how are you supposed to make it with the
strangers outside?
—JULES FEIFFER

In Chapter 2, we asked you to examine how you perceived objects and other communicators. In this chapter, we ask you to examine how you perceive yourself. Your self is where your messages come from. Therefore, your concept of yourself, the way you regard yourself, the goals you set for yourself—all these factors are important to effective communication.

The connection between communication and self-concept may not seem obvious to you at the moment. Yet, every communication act you undertake is a presentation of your self and of the image of yourself that you want others to see. And do you not find that you see others as ambitious, self-righteous, or selfish on the basis of messages you receive from them? In fact, most messages in everyday interpersonal communication can be seen as reflections of the selves of those who compose them.

Once you understand that every message you send carries some of yourself in it, you must face some important questions. Would you prefer to know about this aspect of your messages? Or are you willing to leave the kinds of messages about yourself that you send out to chance? Socrates said that an "unexamined life is not worth living." We believe that an unexamined self is not worth giving. In other words, a communicator who is not in touch with the self-elements in his or her messages may end up being ineffective and never understand why.

Increased self-understanding leads to messages that are more creative, more self-fulfilling, and more effective. In *Wampeters, Foma, and Granfalloons*, novelist Kurt Vonnegut suggests that creative writing should be taught as a process for getting out what already exists in your self-concept. He says that each person has a self-concept and a set of ideas that are like a spool of ticker tape sitting in the back of the throat. The student who is unaware of self cannot get the words out; they are stuck in the back of the throat. The role of the teacher, in Vonnegut's view, is to reach into the student's throat, grab hold of that tape, and "pull it out inch by inch, so the student and I could read it." In essence, this is the goal of this chapter. We provide some means for you to pull out that ticker tape of self-concept in the back of your throat so that you can examine it. Our goal is to help you speak and write about what is on that tape. Once you have done so, we think you will find that your communication will improve and that you will be more aware of your own interests and the goals you wish to achieve as you continue to study communication.

Another reason for studying your self-concept in relation to communication goes back to the main message of Chapter 1, working on yourself. Your self-concept is something that you can work on by yourself and that you can change in ways that will make you a more effective communicator.

In summary, effective communication depends to a great extent on understanding the self who is communicating. In this chapter, we ask you to complete a number of experiences that are designed to increase your awareness of the concept of self in general and of your concept of self in particular. We hope that these experiences may well prove interesting and engrossing in their own right; we know that they will improve your interpersonal communications.

Experience 3.1 is aimed at getting you to answer various forms of a key question: Who am I? You must be able to answer this question before you can go on to answer the major questions of this chapter: Do you have one self or many selves? How consistent with each other are the various parts of your self-concept? There are no correct or incorrect answers to these questions, but your answers obviously have a number of effects on the kind of communicator you are and can become. Some communicators base their effectiveness on having one self; others, on having several. The important thing is to know which is which.

The remainder of the chapter deals with more detailed questions: How fully do you accept yourself? How is that acceptance related to your attitudes toward others? How is self-concept formed? Do you wish to explore yourself in depth? Can you change yourself? What impact would such changes have on your communication behavior?

Experience 3.1 will help you to answer the question: Who am I? Be sure to complete this experience before reading any further.

EXPERIENCE   3.1   WHO AM I?

DIRECTIONS   **Please write answers to the question "Who am I?" in each of the following blanks. Remember that the answers are for yourself only. Students who have completed this experience have responded with "woman," "Jewish," "good-humored," "ambitious," and hundreds of other words. Write your answers as quickly as possible and in the order that they occur to you. Some of the answers may seem inconsistent and illogical. That is perfectly natural; write them down anyway. For now, ignore the numbers below the lines.**

Who Am I?

1 _____
   1   2   3   4   5   6   7

2 _____
   1   2   3   4   5   6   7

3 _____
   1   2   3   4   5   6   7

4 _____
   1   2   3   4   5   6   7

5 _____
   1   2   3   4   5   6   7

6 _____
   1   2   3   4   5   6   7

7 _____
   1   2   3   4   5   6   7

8 _____
   1   2   3   4   5   6   7

9 _____
   1   2   3   4   5   6   7

     Most students have responded with two groups of descriptive terms about themselves: personal attributes and separators.

     Personal attributes include most of the items that did not surprise you at all by their presence on your list. They are your own individual characteristics: your looks, bodily attributes, personal abilities, sense of moral worth, intelligence, persistence, fussiness, strong temper, independence, and so on. Many students' responses in this category can be called *evaluative* responses. That is, they contain a component of goodness or desirability (or the opposites). It is interesting to note that basic responses to oneself are so emotionally charged.

     Separators include terms that differentiate you from others. Separators are usually phrased in terms of larger units of society to which you belong: your sex, your age, your job category, political affiliation, your ethnic group, your family position (i.e., son, mother, sister). Sometimes these terms also identify your position in these larger groups. Separators are usually somewhat more stable than personal attributes; that is, they change slowly or not at all. One day you may feel elated about your personal worth or intelligence or independence; the next day you may be quite depressed about the same thing. If fact, the elation seems to imply the depression. But whether elated or depressed, you do not routinely change your sex, ethnic group, or family position.

     Now turn back to Experience 3.1, and identify each statement about yourself as either a personal attribute or a separator by placing a *P* or an *S* next to it in the left margin. If you are unsure of any item, review the definitions of the two categories. Count the *P*s and *S*s. Did you have a greater number of one or the other, or were the descriptors about equally split? Does the number of each tell you anything? Which did you tend to list first, personal attributes or separators? (The majority of our students listed separators first.)

Finally, reread the list of items that describe you, and rate each statement in terms of importance to you. Circle the number 7 below the blank for items extremely important to you, and 1 for items of little importance.

Did you surprise yourself at all? Which turned out to be most important, your personal attributes or your separators? Most of our students report being surprised at several of the descriptions they used.

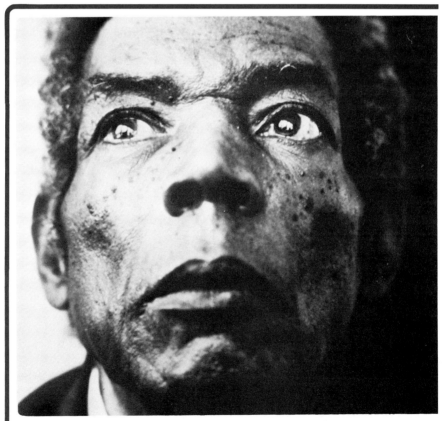

Separators include terms that differentiate you—which divide you from others.

One of the most consistent surprises has been the degree to which we depend on others for what we think of ourselves. Most people think of themselves as sturdy organisms who react to the world whatever it brings. If others do not like them, that is unfortunate, but it does not change what they are. This assumption is false. In reality, people find out what they are like largely through the actions of others. That is, the way you see yourself is essentially a summary of ways others have reacted to you. This may be an overstatement, but it is surprisingly true.

When you were small, did your parents and others talk about your characteristic ways of acting? Did they say and do things that helped you to feel competent, or clumsy, or athletic, or a good reader? Did parental messages contain characterizations like "she's pretty brash" or "he's shy," which may have actually changed your way of seeing yourself.

The main point is that your self-image is shaped by the ways that others act toward you. Your self-image, in turn, shapes the way you behave toward others, which further shapes the way they react to you. The process looks something like this:

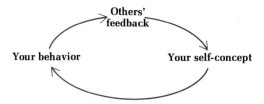

When you were a child, what was dinnertime like? Were you called a "picky eater"? Were you told you had a "hollow leg"? Did people say such things to you because of what you did, because of your self-concept, or because others said these things about you? In fact, all these forces were probably acting and interacting. The use of such expressions affected your self-concept, which affected the way you ate next on other occasions, which affected what others said about your eating habits.

Communication is the process through which all this takes place. Now do you understand why it is important to study your notion of yourself in order to become a more effective communicator? People ordinarily act in concert with the way they think they are. That is, you continue to be the kind of person you seem to yourself to be. If you do not understand yourself, you surely cannot understand, let alone control, the messages you send to others.

People also develop concepts of *themselves as communicators*. Just as a child's eating habits may be labeled, his or her way of speaking and communicating with others may be labeled by others as outgoing, shy, daring, conservative, and so on. Suppose, for instance, that you give a short talk at a meeting of your favorite social youth group. Afterward, a number of people tell you that they liked what you said as well as how you said it. Such information from others may change your concept of yourself as a communicator by making you feel more effective as a public speaker. Or suppose that the people you date tell you that you are shy and considerate. You may come to believe you actually do communicate these qualities. Consequently, your future communication with such persons is more likely to appear shy and considerate.

So far, we have talked about the notion of self-concept in general. At this point, a definition may be useful: *Self-concept is a set of perceptions and attitudes about oneself that affect communication.* Your self-concept is your composite view of your characteristics and abilities as sharpened and differentiated by your awareness of others and by comparisons with relevant others (those who are important to you and who influence your life).

CONSISTENCY AND SELF-CONCEPT

As we have already noted, you may have a large number of perceptions of yourself that may not all be consistent with each other. For instance, in Experience 3.1, you listed a number of items about yourself. Perhaps they formed a coherent picture. However, a number of our students wrote down apparently contradictory qualities. For example, some indicated that they were both happy-go-lucky and shy and sensitive. Ordinarily, it is difficult to exhibit both characteristics at the same time. Yet many people report having inconsistent parts of their self-concept. That is not good, nor is it harmful. It is simply true. To get an idea of how consistent *your* self-perceptions are, complete Experience 3.2.

EXPERIENCE   3.2   SELF-CONSISTENCY

DIRECTIONS   **Select five items from each of the following lists, and write them in the appropriate places on both sides of the matrix.**

Positive	*Negative*
optimistic	**impatient**
studious	**worrier**
honest	**self-conscious**
considerate	**moody**
reliable	**rebellious**

kind	immature
sincere	quick-tempered
friendly	easily influenced
cautious	lazy
independent	gullible
practical	envious
happy	often feel misunderstood
sensitive	disorganized
tolerant	guilt-ridden
idealistic	stubborn
adventurous	self-centered
intelligent	noisy

In each box where two terms from the two sides of the matrix intersect, write the number that indicates *how compatible* the terms are with each other. Use the following key:

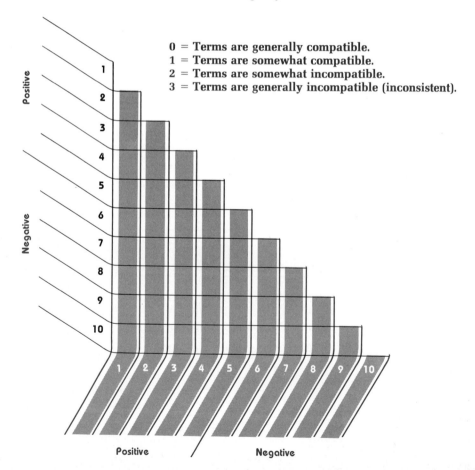

0 = Terms are generally compatible.
1 = Terms are somewhat compatible.
2 = Terms are somewhat incompatible.
3 = Terms are generally incompatible (inconsistent).

**Finally, add up the numbers that you have placed in the boxes.
Sum of all numbers = _____. This total represents a measure of
your self-consistency.**

Experience 3.2 was adapted from a test formulated by Gergen and
Morse. These researchers felt that the total of the numbers entered in
all the boxes of the matrix would constitute a measure of how
consistent a person perceived his or her personality to be. The average
undergraduate, they report, scored about 36. Therefore, if you scored
between 30 and 42, your response was quite typical. If your score was
over 55, you probably perceive your personal characteristics to be more
inconsistent with each other than the average college student does. If
your total was less than 15, your perception seems to be that your traits
are more consistent than most of your peers believe is true of
themselves.

At this point, we feel that it is important to emphasize, once
again, that there is no best way to be. If your score is extremely high
(over 60) or extremely low (under 10), it does *not* mean that you should
be in psychotherapy or that you are a leader of the human race. The
number simply indicates how consistent you see your various selves as
being.

Is it desirable to be consistent? That is an old argument. The most
famous statement on this subject was made by Polonius in
Shakespeare's *Hamlet*. Polonius, you may recall, was sending his son
off to college and was giving fatherly advice to the young man. The last
and most important piece of advice was this:

> This above all: to thine own self be true,
> and it shall follow, as the night the day,
> thou cans't not then be false to any man.

In other words, if you figure out what your self is, you can act
consistently with that single entity at all times, and that would be an
excellent way to live. You should act in the way you are. At those
times that you do not act as you are, you are being a hypocrite.
Polonius would prefer that you score a low total (10 to 20) on the
Gergen and Morse consistency scale.

Many people today still feel as Polonius did. Some therapists and
counselors emphasize getting to know yourself. Many college students
state that they are "trying to find themselves"; that is, they are trying to
discover what their selves are like so that they can act accordingly.
Many people seem to feel that the only road to being satisfied with
your actions is to act in a way that is consistent with a single,
consistent self.

However, to say that you have one consistent self is not to say that
you always should act the same way, regardless of the situation. What
you do in various everyday situations is play roles; that is,

communicate in familiar situations according to familiar patterns. But beyond these roles, you have a self; or to put it more precisely, you *are* a self. The roles you play should reflect that self.

If the roles you play are inconsistent with your self, or if you do not know what your self is like, then you have a problem. To discover your self is personal growth, progress. Self-discovery leads you to act in ways that are consistent with the self. That is the essence of the Polonius position.

The most vocal critic of the Polonius position has been psychologist Kenneth Gergen. In his book *The Concept of Self,* Gergen argues that there really is no single consistent self and that to figure out what the single self is is to deceive yourself. Rather, says Gergen, the self is a collection of roles or masks that you use at various times when they best suit your purposes. What you are changes constantly. Gergen devised a set of experiments to test whether people possess a coherent sense of who they are (the Polonius position) or whether the sense of who they are changes with circumstances. In one experiment, an interviewer talked with 18 undergraduate women. Earlier the women had filled out self-evaluation questionnaires in which they stated how much they approved of themselves and various things they did. During the interviews, the researcher responded to everything the undergraduates said in a friendly, accepting way, nodding, smiling, complimenting. After the interviews, the undergraduates filled out another questionnaire. A comparison of the two sets of questionnaires revealed that the women felt better about themselves after the interview experience. Their notions of self actually seemed changed by the positive reactions of another person.

In another experiment, applicants were waiting to be interviewed for a job. While they waited, they took several pencil-and-paper tests, including an appraisal of themselves. During the test, another person who was actually working for the experimenter, arrived late. In one set of experiments, this newcomer was well dressed, neatly groomed, smooth in demeanor, and he carried a briefcase. Gergen called him "Mr. Clean." A second experiment introduced "Mr. Dirty," who was sloppily dressed and carried a trashy paperback. Comparisons of the self-evaluations showed that Mr. Clean made the others feel relatively inferior and that Mr. Dirty made them feel more secure and confident.

Gergen's experiments demonstrate that the way people see themselves is largely a matter of comparing themselves with others they associate with. He states flatly that the way others act and have acted toward a person most of the time *becomes* the person's self-concept and that changes in how others act bring changes in the individual's self-concept. According to Gergen, there probably *is* no one self. Rather, there are many selves, each created out of the old selves (roles and reactions) in the crucible of a new communication situation.

If Gergen is correct, then it may not make a great deal of sense to worry about your real self. Polonius would like you to have a low score on the Gergen and Morse test (Experience 3.2), but Gergen might prefer a high score because it would show versatility. To get a clearer idea of the difference between the two positions, suppose that you do something selfish: like eating a whole box of candy that was to be shared. Polonius might ask you how you can act in such a selfish way when your real self is generous. The inconsistency in your behavior does not make sense from his point of view. Gergen would ask a different question. He would ask why you acted selfishly under this set of circumstances when last week and on several other occasions you have acted more generously. Gergen would expect to find the explanation, not in you, but in the situation and in how others have treated you.

A second suggestion that Gergen makes is even more startling. He questions the value of long-term relationships such as lifetime friendships and marriages. Such relationships, he argues, may actually create rigid expectations of how it is best for you to act and prevent you from becoming and changing in ways you otherwise might have. Polonius, we suppose, would argue in favor of long-term relationships because by getting to know another person thoroughly you would get to know your real self better.

Both Polonius and Gergen seem to make some good points. Which view sounds most like you? Which view would lead to more effective communication for you? Use Experience 3.3 to sort out some of your attitudes.

Do you consist of many selves?

EXPERIENCE 3.3 POLONIUS VERSUS GERGEN

DIRECTIONS
(PART 1)

The large square represents your self or selves. Each of the smaller shapes within it represents some aspects of you: roles, traits, characteristics. Fill in as many of the shapes as you can with statements or descriptions about yourself. Any of the descriptions of yourself that you used in Experiences 3.1 and 3.2 will be OK or you can use anything else you think of.

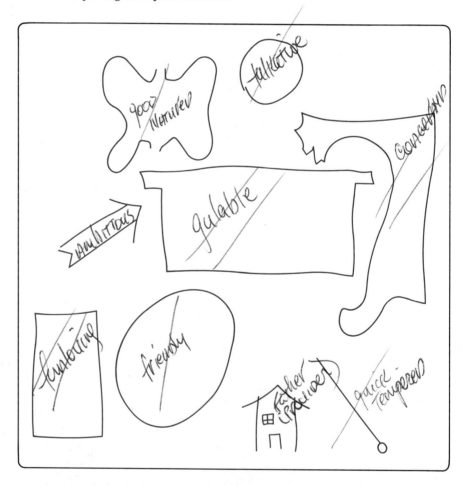

DIRECTIONS
(PART 2)

After you have filled in all the shapes, cross out the trait that seems least necessary to you, the one that you could get along without if you had to. Now cross out another. Keep track of the order in which you cross out the shapes. Cross out a third, and continue until there are only two left. Now think about what you are that encompasses these two items as the major aspects of your self, and answer the following questions.

1   What am I that is made up mostly of these two things?
_____
_____

2   What important people, such as friends and relatives, can I think of who would most approve of the two important things I chose as representative of me?
a _____
b _____
c _____

3   What important people would disapprove of my choices?
a _____
b _____
c _____

    Now, cross out one of your two remaining characteristics.
4   What do you think of what is left?
_____
_____

    Finally, cross out the last characteristic. Now there is nothing left except the background of the square. Presumably, that background is your real self; it is what is left after all personal characteristics or roles have been taken away.

5   Can you describe what is left? Try.
_____
_____

6   How do you feel about what is left?
_____
_____

SELF-ACCEPTANCE   Our students have shown a wide variety of responses to Experience 3.3. Some have found it meaningless and unhelpful; others have found interesting descriptions for the background part left over (the soul, pure things, skin and bones, a consciousness, and so forth). Some have simply found the experience frightening. "It's like going to my own funeral," one student told us after crossing out the last item.

    We interpret the results of Experience 3.3 in terms of the Polonius-Gergen argument. If you had a difficult time imagining what would be left after all your roles and self-descriptions were taken away, your response supports Gergen's position. If you found that you approached your true self only when the roles and descriptions were removed that certain roles *were* your true self, your response supports Polonius' notion.

Experience 3.3 can also be interpreted in terms of self-acceptance. By *self-acceptance* we mean the degree to which you perceive yourself as OK, as not so bad in spite of weaknesses. Self-acceptance is *not* the same as conceit. Most people who act in an overbearing or self-centered way put on that role as a defensive response because they actually have strong feelings that they are not all right.

Ordinarily, the person who feels OK does not show overbearing conceit. That person likes himself or herself and does not have anything in particular to prove. The person who is high in self-acceptance may work to improve, to become better at something, but will not be driven to achievement by inner feelings of worthlessness because he or she is able to include both positive and negative attributes into his or her self-concept.

In *On Becoming a Person*, Carl Rogers, an influential psychologist, says that people come to feel positive about themselves as a result of positive regard from others. These people consequently are less threatened by their own feelings and others' feelings about them and are less defensive about accepting other people. Explore this idea further in Experience 3.4

EXPERIENCE 3.4 SELF-ACCEPTANCE

DIRECTIONS   Indicate your preferred response to the following statements by circling that response. There are no right or wrong answers. The best answer is the one that applies to you.

_____ 1   I do not question my worth as a person, even if I think others do.

1	2	3	4	5
Not at all true of me	Slightly true of me	About half true of me	Mostly true of me	True of me

_____ 2   When people say nice things about me, I find it difficult to believe that they really mean it. I think that maybe they are kidding me or just are not being sincere.

1	2	3	4	5
True of me	Mostly true of me	About half true of me	Slightly true of me	Not at all true of me

_____ 3*   The person you marry may not be perfect, but I believe in trying to get him or her to change along desirable lines.

1	2	3	4	5
True of me	Mostly true of me	About half true of me	Slightly true of me	Not at all true of me

_____ 4   I look on most of the feelings and impulses I have toward people as being quite natural and acceptable.

1	2	3	4	5
Not at all true of me	Slightly true of me	About half true of me	Mostly true of me	True of me

_____ 5*   I usually ignore the feelings of others when I am trying to accomplish some important end.

1	2	3	4	5
True of me	Mostly true of me	About half true of me	Slightly true of me	Not at all true of me

_____ 6   I do not say much at social affairs because I am afraid that people will criticize me or laugh if I say the wrong thing.

1	2	3	4	5
True of me	Mostly true of me	About half true of me	Slightly true of me	Not at all true of me

_____ 7*   There are very few times when I compliment people for their talents or jobs they have done.

1	2	3	4	5
True of me	Mostly true of me	About half true of me	Slightly true of me	Not at all true of me

_____ 8*   I can be friendly with people who do things that I consider wrong.

1	2	3	4	5
Not at all true of me	Slightly true of me	About half true of me	Mostly true of me	True of me

Now write the number you circled for each statement in the blank to the left of it. Add up the numbers for the statements that have an asterisk (*) and write that number here_____. Add up the numbers for the statements without asterisks and write that number here _____.

We asked you to separate the items in Experience 3.4 that had an asterisk next to them. These items measured *acceptance of others*, a variable closely related to self-acceptance. Note that there were four statements with asterisks and four without and that you could score from 1 to 5 on each. So for each category, self-acceptance and acceptance of others, you could have a score of from 4 to 20.

There are two pieces of information you can get from Experience 3.4: First, the higher your score on either item, the more acceptance you demonstrated. Therefore, a score of 12 or 13 is about average in the self-acceptance category, and a score of 10 or 11 is average in acceptance of others. Second, and more important, about 90 percent of our students found that their self-acceptance score was within 3 points of their acceptance-of-others score. In other words, people who accept themselves also accept others, and people who feel that they are inadequate also fail to be accepting of others.

Research using longer forms of Experience 3.4* has indicated that self-acceptance and acceptance of others vary together. That is, if you have a high degree of self-acceptance, you will also tend to accept others. For example, if you perceive yourself as outgoing and likeable, you do not need to be constantly concerned about whether others are going to reject you. Thus, you are able to be more open and less defensive in your relationships with others. When others behave positively toward you, your regard for them increases. In turn, you come to see yourself in a more favorable light, and that carries over into other relationships. A positive response cycle is established. Falling in love is the most obvious example of this: The strong caring response of another is likely to increase your self-acceptance, which in turn affects your communication behavior toward others.

These speculations deal with a general tendency. There is no right or wrong way to be. You do not get extra points in Experience 3.4 for being accepting of yourself and others. You do not rate as "more together" if your scores for the two kinds of acceptance are similar. All you get, if you are honest with yourself, is a glimpse of what you are like. The only way you can win this game is to see what is true about you. The only way you can lose it is to deceive yourself.

Experience 3.5 will help you to explore self-acceptance more fully.

* E. M. Berger, "The Relation Between Expressed Acceptance of Self and Expressed Acceptance of Others," *Journal of Abnormal and Social Psychology* 47 (1952): 778–782.

EXPERIENCE 3.5. THE THREE SELVES**

DIRECTIONS   **Communicators seldom take an opportunity to look at themselves as others see them and as they would like to be. This experience involves a list of terms that can be used in various degrees to describe people. Begin by taking each term in column 1 and applying it to yourself by completing the following sentence: "I am a (an) _____ person." The first word in the list is** *academic.* **Substitute this term in the sentence, so that it becomes: "I am an academic person." Then use**

** Adapted from R. E. Bills, E. L. Vance, and O. S. McLean, "An Index of Adjustment and Values," *Journal of Consulting Psychology* 15 (1951): 257–261.

the following key to decide how much of the time this statement describes you, and write the appropriate number in column 2.

1 = *Seldom* is this like me.
2 = *Occasionally* this is like me.
3 = *About half the time* this is like me.
4 = *A good deal of the time* this is like me.
5 = *Most of the time* this is like me.

EXAMPLE   If you feel that this statement applies to you occasionally, write the number 2 beside the term *academic.* That is, *"Occasionally,* I am an <u>academic</u> person."

Now, using the same term, complete the following sentence: "Other people see me as a (an) _____ person." Decide how much of the time this term describes the way others see you. If you feel that other people see you as academic about half the time, write the number 3 in column 3. That is, *"About half the time,* others see me as an <u>academic</u> person."

Finally, using the same term again, complete the following sentence: "I would like to be a (an) _____ person." Then decide how much of the time you would like this trait to be a characteristic of you. If you would like to be an academic person most of the time, write the number 5 in column 4 beside the term *academic.* That is, *"Most of the time,* I would like to be an <u>academic</u> kind of person."

EXAMPLE

(1) *Description*	(2) *How I describe myself*	(3) *How others see me*	(4) *How I would like to be*
Academic	2	3	5

(1) *Description*	(2) *How I describe myself*	(3) *How others see me*	(4) *How I would like to be*
1 affectionate	_____	_____	_____
2 aggressive	_____	_____	_____
3 ambitious	_____	_____	_____
4 assertive	_____	_____	_____
5 bold	_____	_____	_____
6 charming	_____	_____	_____
7 clever	_____	_____	_____
8 competent	_____	_____	_____
9 confident	_____	_____	_____
10 considerate	_____	_____	_____
11 dependable	_____	_____	_____

12	cruel	_____	_____	_____
13	economical	_____	_____	_____
14	efficient	_____	_____	_____
15	fair	_____	_____	_____
16	friendly	_____	_____	_____
17	good follower	_____	_____	_____
18	helpful	_____	_____	_____
19	honest	_____	_____	_____
20	intellectual	_____	_____	_____
21	kind	_____	_____	_____
22	leader	_____	_____	_____
23	logical	_____	_____	_____
24	mature	_____	_____	_____
25	moral	_____	_____	_____
26	nervous	_____	_____	_____
27	normal	_____	_____	_____
28	optimistic	_____	_____	_____
29	poised	_____	_____	_____
30	relaxed	_____	_____	_____
31	responsible	_____	_____	_____
32	sincere	_____	_____	_____
33	successful	_____	_____	_____
34	tolerant	_____	_____	_____
35	competitive	_____	_____	_____

Experience 3.5 probably required quite a bit of thought on your part. As you were completing the scales, you may have been impressed with the differences between your actual self-ratings and your ideal ratings or with the difference between the way you see yourself and the way you perceive others to be responding to you.

There was probably some correspondence between the way you perceive yourself and the way you perceive that others regard you. After all, communicators define themselves primarily through interactions with other people. The process becomes circular, and a type of self-fulfilling prophecy develops. For example, if others respond to you as though you are a confident person, you will probably behave in ways that exhibit confidence; that behavior is reinforced by others because it meets with their expectations of you. At some point, you come full circle and actually *are* more confident because of the way others perceive and respond to your behavior.

The discrepancies between the way you perceive that you actually are and the way you would like to be were probably not great. One reason for that is the natural tendency to emphasize those aspects of the actual self that provide positive confirmation of the ideal self. This

To see ourselves as others see us: A promoter of communication accuracy or a pain in the neck?

tendency is called *biased scanning*. In essence, people remember those events and interactions that fulfill their expectations of their ideal selves. Similarly, people may suppress those events and interactions that do not confirm images of their ideal selves and that thus are punishing. Biased scanning was reflected in this experience by your liking those aspects of yourself for which you found both consistency between your actual and ideal selves and confirmation from others.

It seems worthwhile to maintain as accurate an image of yourself as is possible. In that way, you ensure yourself against receiving unexpected reactions from others that you are not able to deal with in a positive way. Such reactions could lead to anxiety and defensive reactions on your part, which would be likely to elicit other nonreinforcing behaviors on the part of others.

Sometimes these cycles become self-perpetuating, and that makes it hard for a person to change how he or she behaves from one occasion to the next. We recently had a discussion with a student who was graduating from college. He had been a member of the school's golf team and had ambitions to become a professional golfer on the PGA tour. However, he needed about $20,000 to sustain him on the first year of the tour, and he was not from a wealthy family. Most people in this situation find backers who are willing to invest in them for a return of a certain share of the winnings. But although this student was an excellent golfer and was likely to succeed on the tour, he was having trouble getting a backer. His major problem as he described it was that he was reinforced during his college years for exhibiting carefree, uninhibited, happy-go-lucky behavior and had come to see himself and behave in this manner. Backers willing to put up $20,000 were looking for people who would take the game seriously and make good on their investment. Such conflicts can make the transition from one portion of a person's career to another difficult.

Are there ways to change selves or to become more knowledgeable through such conflicts?

EXPLORING THE UNCHARTED SELF

It would have been thrilling to have been Magellan or Columbus and set sail for unknown worlds. Those explorers must have felt both a sense of seeing things nobody had seen before and a sense of adventure because they could not be sure of returning. Lewis and Clark may have had very similar feelings. Today, most geographic frontiers are well explored. Only those who journey to outer space are likely to experience precisely the feelings of adventure known by early explorers.

But there are also frontiers of inner space. Parts of everyone's self are as unknown as the farthest star in the galaxy. Few maps show how to get there, and some people feel that if they journey to these parts of themselves, they may end up on an uncharted reef somewhere or be unable to find their way back. Psychiatrist R. D. Laing argues that many psychotics are inner space explorers who cannot get back easily and that we should treat their explorations with as much respect as we have granted to Columbus and to present-day astronauts.

We believe that if you look deeply into yourself, you are likely to change through the experience, usually for the better, because you will gain increased self-knowledge and self-acceptance. Experiences 3.6 and

3.7 are exercises in self-exploration. If these experiences seem odd to you at times that is because your habit in the past has probably been to avoid such lines of thought. But it also means that you are making progress. Plunge on. Do not talk yourself out of the experience and the exploration.

EXPERIENCE 3.6 OUTLINE FOR AN AUTOBIOGRAPHICAL NOVEL

DIRECTIONS   You have been offered a lucrative contract to write a novel loosely based on your own life. By autobiographical novel, the publisher means that it should be based on your life but that if some detail comes into your mind that is more interesting than the corresponding part of your life, you should feel free to use it. In other words, your job is to present a true picture of your life without having to stick to the actual facts.

The publisher wants you to begin by making an outline to guide your writing. The following topics are those the publisher would like you to cover. Write a few notes about each question in order to give the publisher an idea of what the finished autobiographical novel will be like. You will notice that the outline covers an entire life, including things that may not have happened to you yet. Pretend that these things have happened. Remember that you can use fictional details.

1   Describe your looks and behavior patterns at age one.

_____
_____
_____

2   What was your major way of saying no as a small child? How well did this method work?

_____
_____
_____
_____

3   Who were the two most important people around when you were very small? Tell a story about your relationship with one of these people.

_____
_____
_____
_____

4   **Tell an early story about school.**

_____
_____
_____

5   **What could you do as a child to make a parent laugh?**

_____

6   **What is the worst punishment you recall?**

_____

7   **What was your life like at college? What was your favorite activity at that time?**

_____
_____
_____

8   **What was your first permanent job? What was the biggest frustration you experienced in this job?**

_____
_____
_____

9   **Of all the possessions you have had in your life, which was the most prized?**

_____

10   **In your whole life, what was your biggest lucky break?**

_____

11   **What should the title of your autobiography be?**

_____

Obviously, writing about yourself and including those parts of you that have not yet revealed themselves to you can help you to learn about yourself. Some theorists contend that people work out a detailed script for many parts of their lives and then try to act out as much of the play as they can. In fact, they may get upset with others who refuse to follow their parts in the script. It can be helpful to realize that others are acting out their own scripts and that maybe we are not satisfying their expectations either.

Did you find it disturbing to write about portions of your life that have not happened yet? Many students report difficulty with those parts of the autobiography. Some say they are afraid to write anything down for fear that things will happen that way just because that is what they wrote. They do not want to create any self-fulfilling prophecies for themselves. One student found the experience frightening because it made her admit that she already had a script figured out for her life.

"What's all this creative writing about?" you may ask. "What can it do for me?"

We believe that it is wise to know the ways you describe yourself. If you have such knowledge, you are more likely to understand and appreciate more of your own actions. You are also less likely to think you are controlled by others. You will see more clearly what your own behavior means.

Furthermore, when you plan things you want to accomplish, you improve your chances of success. For instance, one person is able to sit at a typewriter and compose sentences until a book is finished. Another cannot do that but can persuade voters to support a favorite candidate, a task that the first person would find impossible. A third person may be able to do neither of these but is still an effective appliance salesperson, someone who eases tension in work groups, or a humane, caring parent.

You do not have time to do everything. Therefore, why not choose for yourself those communication tasks at which you are likely to be effective? The experiences in this chapter have not given you enough self-knowledge to choose a college major or a career, but they can help you to choose the kind of communication settings in your everyday life that will accent your strength as a person and as a communicator.

Experience 3.7 demonstrates our point.

EXPERIENCE 3.7 TASK-TRAIT MATCH

DIRECTIONS **Think of six traits (or descriptors) that have emerged in the preceding experiences as being most typical of you. List these across the top of the matrix. Then look at the list of communication tasks, and decide whether each trait is an asset (+), a liability (−) or neither (0) for performing that task. Enter the appropriate symbol in each trait column.**

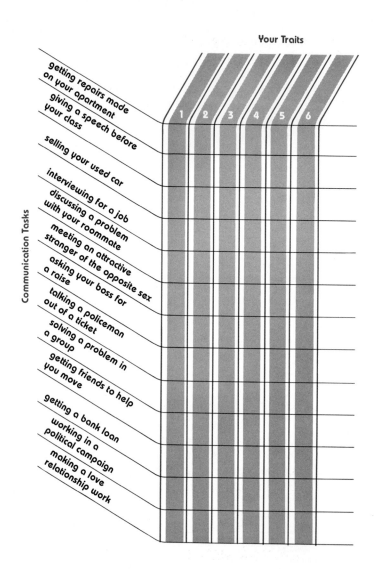

Your Traits

Communication Tasks

getting repairs made on your apartment

giving a speech before your class

selling your used car

interviewing for a job

discussing a problem with your roommate

meeting an attractive stranger of the opposite sex

asking your boss for a raise

talking a policeman out of a ticket

solving a problem in a group

getting friends to help you move

getting a bank loan

working in a political campaign

making a love relationship work

In the following matrix, list some tasks that we have not mentioned but that you need or want to accomplish through communication.

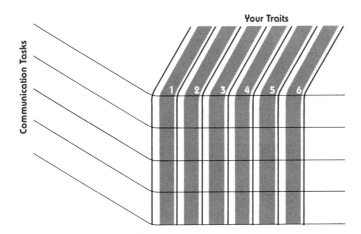

Experience 3.6 illustrated a point about your multiple selves. You may be disturbed at some of the traits you have chosen to describe yourself in this chapter's experiences. You may not like to think of yourself as moody, bashful, or self-centered. After completing the experience in which we asked you to cross out each of the parts of your personality, one student remarked that she was actually relieved to do that because all her traits were negative; she was glad to be rid of them. But almost any trait has some value. If it did not give you some payoff, you probably would not behave that way.

Experience 3.7 may lead you to ask what you get out of your traits. Choose your most negative trait; then look down its column to see how you rated it for every task that was suggested. You will probably find that even your most negative characteristics help you to do some communication jobs. For example, you may see yourself as stubborn and dislike that trait in yourself. But if you are trying to get repairs made on your apartment or to resist a high-pressure salesperson, your stubbornness might come in handy. Examine each of the traits you listed in Experience 3.7; look for the minus ratings for your positive traits and the plus ratings for your negative ones. These ratings will help to show you what you get out of acting the way you usually do. You will see that flexibility, the ability to exhibit different traits at different times, increases your chances of communicating effectively.

Developing communicative flexibility is something we have been leading up to throughout this chapter. We favor Gergen's notion of many selves over Polonius's notion of one self. One implication of Gergen's position is that you have the freedom to respond differently in different communication settings. By the time you have completed the course of study in this book, you may find that you have developed skills in areas in which you felt weak when you responded to Experience 3.7. One reason that communicators shy away from certain kinds of situations is lack of experience. With a little experience and a few new concepts, you will be surprised at how effectively your selves can communicate.

SUMMARY

Although getting to know themselves is a very desirable thing to do, most people find it really difficult. Usually, people respond to the question "Who am I?" by describing themselves in terms of both personality attributes or characteristics and separators that differentiate them from others. Others are important in forming a self-concept because it is through patterns of interaction with others that people define themselves. Self-concept is a set of perceptions about the self that affect communication. Your self-concept is your composite view of your characteristics and abilities, sharpened and differentiated by your awareness of others and by comparisons with others.

There are essentially two positions with regard to the consistency of a person's self-concept. One advises you to determine the essence of your self and to act according to that single entity in all facets of your life. The other advocates that the self-concept is composed, not of a single consistent self, but of many selves that reveal themselves through roles that you play.

It is vitally important to recognize what your self consists of and to accept it. That self should be as accurate an image as is possible. People who accept themselves tend to accept others as well.

Most people find it a valuable experience to look inside themselves. They are able to see more clearly what their own behavior means. Also, the acceptance of an accurate self-image enables them to determine what they are best at and therefore to make the most of their abilities.

CHAPTER 4
UNDERSTANDING LANGUAGE

Life isn't simple; it's overwhelmingly complex. The love of
simplicity is an escapist drug, like alcohol. It's an antilife attitude.
—TOM ROBBINS, Even Cowgirls Get the Blues

Speech uses language in oral communication. Language provides the building blocks for messages. The quality of a message, like that of a building, depends on the quality of the material—language—used to construct it. In this chapter, we provide experiences that will help you to check and to improve your language skills. We begin by reviewing some basic principles of linguistics. Then we turn to a series of techniques for making language increasingly clear and dynamic. We focus on written examples because they are easiest for you to practice in a book, but all the techniques we discuss apply equally to speaking.

Human language is more than a miracle. It is nothing less than a strange and wonderful system of intricacies that can be used for art, seduction, command giving, and many other purposes. Imagine the task of trying to program a computer to speak the English language. How many sets of formal programming symbols would it take to make a computer talk? (In fact, there have been dozens of researchers trying to do this for some time now.) Suppose you finally succeeded in programming the computer so that it could speak grammatical English. You would still only have scratched the surface of things that every human knows about language. People know when to speak and when to be silent, when to ask for a favor, how to lie, how to recognize good poetry or a pun. Theoretically, it might be impossible to number all the things that would have to be programmed into such a computer. Yet, you already know most of the things that the computer could not be taught.

Most people rarely stop to think how smart they must be to know so much about language. In fact, most people are rather matter-of-fact about their language knowledge. What they know seems simple to them. Most of our students think that they do not know very much about language. How much do you know? Experience 4.1 will show you how much you know instinctively about language.

EXPERIENCE 4.1 LANGUAGE POP QUIZ

DIRECTIONS **Answer each of the following questions by checking the correct response or writing in the answer in your own words.**

1 **Which of these groups of letters is a word?**
_____ a. **language**
_____ b. **agguael**

2 **Which of these groups of letters could not possibly be an English word?**

_____ a. mgreo
_____ b. grome

3 How can you tell that *mgreo* can or cannot be an English word?

_____

4 Is the following group of words a sentence: "The automobiles behind roared hear stones"?

_____ a. yes
_____ b. no

5 What makes you think that the group of words in item 4 is or is not a sentence?

_____

We have never run across a student who had tremendous difficulty telling the difference between words and nonwords or between sentences and nonsentences. However, we have found that most students have trouble being very precise in answering items 3 and 5 in Experience 4.1. It is easy to tell the difference between things that are part of the language and things that are not, but it is more difficult to explain why. Most students tell us that the nonwords and sentences just do not look right. Some students note that the nonword *mgreo* has too many consonants in a row or that the nouns in the nonsentence seem in funny places. But most have simply noted that the nonwords and sentences did not look or sound right.

You know these things about language subconsciously, intuitively, even though you may not know the scholarly ways to explain them. This kind of linguistic knowledge is called *linguistic competence.* Linguistic competence allows you to speak intelligibly. All speakers who can make themselves understood possess this competence. An analogy may clarify this point: We know that a fish knows how to move efficiently in water because it swims well. Obviously, the average fish has not been to engineering school any more than you have studied linguistics in some formal way. Still, you know linguistics. As Molière put it in *Le Bourgois Gentilhomme,* "For more than forty years I have been talking prose without knowing it." Sometimes the things we know best are the very things we think about least—talking, breathing, walking, sitting. People happen to be animals that speak. The language they speak is so immensely complex that they cannot imagine anyone but people handling it.

In fact, language may be more complex than it needs to be. If we were to make up a language, for instance, every word would be paired with just one meaning in order to avoid confusion. But language does not act that way. The 100 most common words in the English language have between 50 and 100 meanings each. How can someone tell which

This child cannot tie a shoe, yet he speaks coherent prose.

meaning you mean when you use a common word. For example, what does the word *out* mean in each of the following sentences?

Get *out* of here.
Something is *out* of order in my car.
Something is *out* of order in your alphabetical file.
That dress is too long; it is *out* of style.
I'm going to fight this one *out*.
The truth about Watergate got *out* at last.
I'm really feeling down and *out*.
Let's go *out* to eat for dinner.
Mr. Samuel is *out* to lunch. He will be back at one.
Mr. Samuel is *out* to lunch. He has been for 20 years.
She has really been *out* of it lately.
We are *out* of luck.
Out, out damned spot!
She really looks *out* of sight.
Out of sight, *out* of mind.
He tricked John *out* of his money.

He really stands *out* in his class.
Cattle are fed *out* and then sent to market.
She could *out* shout any other cheerleader.
We need to check *out* the new computer system.
I checked the book *out* of the library.
That item you want is *out* of stock.
Cut that *out!*
Sally is cutting *out* the material for the new dress.
I'm not getting anything *out* of my history course.
She moved *out* of town.
Lately, my in box has been really full, and my *out* box has been empty.
Sam and the boss had a falling *out,* so he is *out* looking for another job.
He got that information *out* of the encyclopedia.
She got kicked *out* of school for cheating.
He found *out* about her.
She took *out* her pen and signed the paper.
Far *out!*
He dropped *out* of high school.
You are *out* of your mind.
That well is *out* of oil.
The man at the record store said that item was sold *out.*
The miners are going *out* on strike.
I'm really put *out* over all these meaning of the word *out.*
We are cheating the buyers of this book *out* of some money.
Well, they picked *out* the book themselves.
For crying *out* loud!
I'm tired *out.*
We have a recession because too many people are *out* of work.
Over and *out,* Captain.
Nagusky went all *out* to win the game, but when he went *out* for a critical pass in the fourth quarter, he was knocked *out* of bounds, and his shoulder was thrown *out* of joint. His team had to call a time *out* to get him off the field. He will be *out* for six weeks.
I'm tired of reading these sentences. I want to get *out* of doing more.
Fill *out* the following form:

1   Define the word *out.*

    _____

2   Are all the meanings of *out* related in some way? How?

    _____

3   Why does our language have many words with many meanings?

    _____

    _____

What does a child think when he or she hears someone say, "We're coming to a fork in the road." "Feel a bit hoarse today, Fred?" "Be a dear, and stop acting like a pig." A delightful children's book by Fred Gwinne, *The King Who Rained*, gives a child's-eye view of sentences such as "The king reigned [rained] forty years" and "We should always live in the present [gift]." To an adult, those expressions are puns. Linguists would call them *homophones*—meaning words that sound the same but have multiple meanings. But a child just calls them confusing. Would it not be easier if each word had just one meaning? Maybe. But the only languages that work that way are the languages people have invented for talking to computers. Linguists point out that homophones rarely cause serious communication difficulty for adults. But when you hear a homophone that you are not familiar with, it can be startling. Most Northerners notice that Texans commonly pronounce the words *pin* and *pen* identically. But the words *cot* and *caught* are pronounced identically in Vermont, as are the words *God* and *guard* in several places. In fact, homophones are common in every known dialect of every language in the world.

Why, then, does a visitor from Chicago find it disturbing to hear *pin* or *pen* pronounced differently? The reason seems to have something to do with habits. The things you are used to hearing seem natural to you; things that sound different seem strange. Actually, you are, in effect, assuming that most words have only one meaning—your meaning.

Homophones are just one example of the misunderstandings that can result simply from not knowing a few facts about language or from not having sufficient reverence for what a complex business talking a language is. In Chapter 7, we will discuss how dialects work and how language can trick you into making wrong judgments about people and cultures that are different from your own.

MAKING LANGUAGE DYNAMIC AND PRECISE

We have been pointing out what a complex business any language is. There are a lot of things rattling around a language that most people rarely stop to think about but that often clog up communication. The intricacies of language often trick people into assumptions that cause problems. In Experience 4.2, you will explore some of these problems.

EXPERIENCE 4.2 AGREE-DISAGREE STATEMENTS

DIRECTIONS   Read each of the following statements. Circle *A* if you tend to agree with the statement; circle *D* if you tend to disagree with it. When you have finished, compare your reactions to the statements with those of two other people in your class.

1 All politicians are opportunists.   A   D
2 Most people do not really know what is good for them.   A   D
3 Interpersonal communication systems are highly integrated
   optimal decision processes.   A   D
4 Monitoring of interpersonal communication theoretical
   paradigms can be accomplished through an amalgam of
   techniques.   A   D
5 Implementation strategies for optimal organizational change
   should involve processes whereby personnel cognizant of
   human resource utilization establish programmatic
   goal-directed procedures.   A   D
6 Republicans do not really care about people.   A   D
7 The United States is the only country on earth where personal
   liberty, freedom, and dignity are cherished.   A   D
8 When our liberties are threatened by outside totalitarian
   nations our only choice is to use force.   A   D
9 Familiarity breeds contempt.   A   D
10 There is nothing new under the sun.   A   D

Our students often had arguments about the sentences in Experience 4.2. These arguments normally sprung from lack of agreement about their meanings. The sentences in Experience 4.2 are intentionally negative examples. That is, we wanted to show you examples of language that fails in clarity and precision. When you discussed the experience with your classmates, you probably found that some statements that seemed clear enough to you and clear enough to someone else led to disagreements. Those disagreements probably resulted because what was clear to you was equally clear but also different to them. Who is to say one of you is correct and the other wrong? A word or sentence functions in the way that speakers and listeners *think* it functions.

A word can mean many different things. Yet none of the meanings of *out*, for example, has much logical connection with the series of letters and sounds that form the word. Any other word used in the same way would do just as well as the present word. That is true for most words in the English language. There is no necessary connection between a word and its meanings. Words like *buzz*, *ding-dong*, or *swish* sound like what they mean; but most words do not. Most words are *arbitrarily paired* with meanings. Did you ever wonder why we call a horse by that name? The word for horse could be anything. Whatever you chose, it would not change the horse. The word *horse* is not the same thing as the thing horse. The word *horse* is a lot like the word *house*, but the things they refer to are completely different.

Semanticist Alfred Korzybski noted the difficulties we have described and compared the relationship between language and the life events it talks about to the relationship between a map and the territory it represents. The map is obviously not the territory. If you tried to vacation on a map of California, it would not take you long to see that you had made a mighty mistake. Rather, the map is a description of the territory, related to it by a set of rules. For example, the red lines that represent highways bear little resemblance to the highways themselves. The lines and colors that represent elevation make sense only if you know what they stand for. If you do not know the rules of mapmaking, you will get little information from a map.

When you talk to a person, you and the person are assuming agreement on a fantastically intricate set of rules more sophisticated than the most advanced and detailed mapmaking conventions. But that assumed common knowledge is rarely thought about because you know it intuitively and subconsciously. You and the other person may experience communication problems because of differences in politics or lack of skill with words, but some of these problems actually stem from unexamined assumptions about language. The main assumption is that talking is simple. Because everyone talks with little apparent effort, most people fail to realize the number of places in which language habits can lead to communication breakdowns.

Some words and expressions are particularly likely to be culprits. One of the most persistent sets of nagging language problems concerns the verb *to be*, which appears more frequently than almost any other item in English. To show you how pervasive *is* is, we have written this rather typical paragraph:

> Dr. Blank *is* a psychologist and *is* a senior staff member of a university counseling center. In this capacity, he *is* engaged in a number of activities, including one-to-one psychotherapy, group therapy, and supervision of trainees. He *is* short and fat. Sometimes he *is* quite rude to his co-workers. He would like *to be* chairman of his local professional group, but it *is* likely that his reputation for *being* rude may *be* working against him.

The paragraph contains nine instances of the verb *to be*. Many English paragraphs of this length contain twice as many. Routine use of *is* implies a permanence about the universe that probably does not reflect reality. The Greek philosopher Heraclitus claimed that a person never sets foot in the same river twice because both the person and the river exist in constant states of change. The statements "George Smith is a farmer," "your buddy Elizabeth is a fool," "the new child in class is a slow learner," and "I don't think Annie will succeed in fifth grade" all imply stability.

The statement "George Smith farms a small plot of land outside town" does not imply that George Smith never did anything else. In fact, George Smith serves as friend, father, farmer, pipe smoker, and gin rummy player. He may quit farming the next time prices go down. The statement "I got offended by Elizabeth's joke last night" does not put Elizabeth in the class of persons whose behavior is stupid. The statement "The new child's records show that last year's teacher reported difficulties in reading" does not consign the student forever to low achievement levels.

Each of those preferred statements recognizes two facts:

1   The subject of the sentence might change.
2   The sentence represents only somebody's opinion, not a fact about the person being discussed. For example, Elizabeth *is* not a fool, but I observed her acting like a fool on two occasions.

Both facts can be obscured by the use of the verb *to be*.

Here is how we rewrote our paragraph about Dr. Blank:

Dr. Blank, a psychologist, works at a university counseling center. His activities include one-to-one psychotherapy, therapy groups, and supervising trainees. Short and fat in appearance, Dr. Blank cuts an unusual figure. He sometimes seems rude to co-workers. His reputation for rudeness may undermine his ambition to chair his local professional group.

Can you see the principle? There are many ways that a sentence can be rewritten, not one right answer. Experience 4.3 will give you practice in writing more precise sentences.

EXPERIENCE   4.3   SCRATCH THAT "IS"

**DIRECTIONS
(PART 1)**

Rewrite each of the following statements, omitting all uses of *to be*, including *is, was, will, shall, be, being, been*. Often, you will have to supply new details to make the meaning more precise.

EXAMPLE

Tom is a student.
Tom studies at City College.

1   Is your roommate home tonight?

_____

_____

2   The test should be easy.

_____

3   My mom is a pushover.

_____

4   George is a thief.

_____

5   Tom said that his car is a lemon.

_____

6   Sam was sick yesterday.

_____

7   Sally is a poor communicator.

_____

8   You are a liar.

_____

9   Are you going to finish your paper before the end of the semester?

_____
_____

DIRECTIONS (PART 2)   Rewrite the following paragraph, eliminating all *to be* words.

Mr. Lawrence's work is in both casualty and life insurance sales. The receiver in the casualty sales interview is already educated concerning his needs. Most of the time it is the receiver who has initiated the interview, and he is seeking the best plan to fill his needs. Mr. Lawrence need only persuade this receiver that his plan is best. In life insurance sales, the receiver is usually not fully aware of his needs, so there are two points of persuasion: The first is persuading the receiver to be a further receiver (setting up an interview), and the second is persuading him of his need and the product's ability to fill that need.

_____
_____
_____
_____
_____
_____

_____
_____
_____

Most students tell us that Experience 4.3 provides a push to write more concisely. Some students have resolved to omit all *to be* words from their speech and writing. To the extent that this can be accomplished, it probably adds to the immediacy and impact of messages. Sometimes you have to do a lot of rearranging of entire sentences to avoid *is*. And do not expect immediate change. Even we still use a lot of *is* words.

The problem that all language appears to share with *is* is permanence. Just as few things "are" in a world of change, few facts are immutable. The truth, as it seems to us, may be a belly laugh to you. The truth to a Communist may seem propaganda to you, and vice versa. These examples suggest that communications can gain precision if messages include not only a description but also the *point of view*. Consider this statement:

Julie is intelligent.

It specifies no point of view from which Julie appears intelligent. If you add a point of view, the utterance grows more precise:

To me, Julie appears to act intelligently.

Note that this example also eliminated *is*. The statement can be even more precise if you also specify some rationale for the point of view by citing some evidence to substantiate it:

Julie's performance in yesterday's class discussion seemed intelligent to me.

Note that this example specifies whose opinion is being stated, omits *is* words, and states the occasion on which Julie behaved as specified.

It is possible to go still further. You could describe just what Julie did to be considered intelligent:

Julie followed directions to the letter during yesterday's discussion, which seemed the intelligent thing to do.

Now you can begin to see how disagreements are born. Suppose we said

Julie is a Fascist.

and you said

Julie is intelligent.

We might get into an argument about who has warped perceptions. But if we both stated that Julie followed directions well, which we detest and you admire, then we understand each other much more clearly.

In summary, language becomes more precise through

1 Specifying a point of view.
2 Specifying observable evidence to support that point of view.

These two principles underlie many of the communication skills that are discussed in this book. If you specify a viewpoint and offer good evidence, your chances of having your message understood increase dramatically. Experience 4.4 gives you some samples to practice on.

EXPERIENCE 4.4 MAKING PRECISE STATEMENTS

DIRECTIONS Rewrite each of the following statements in order to make it more precise. Be sure to eliminate all *to be* words, specify a point of view ("I think that. . . ."), and specify what acts or time periods are involved so that it is clear that your judgment is not meant to hold for all time.

EXAMPLE Mr. Jones is a wonderful man.
I think that Mr. Jones displayed problem-solving skills when he tried to help the group solve its problem last night.

1 Ed is a computer programmer.

2 I was in a bad mood yesterday.

3 I am angry at you.

4 Dr. Olds is a terrible teacher.

5 The students in my geography class just are not very bright.

6 You were not paying attention to my argument.

7 The university administration is not responsive to the needs of students.

Do you see how techniques we asked you to use in Experience 4.4 aim at greater clarity and precision in the use of language? Each technique cites as many observable facts as possible to clarify the statements and reduce the abstractness of language.

Separating facts and inferences

In his book *Science and Sanity*, Alfred Korzybski introduced a distinction between facts and inferences in language use. *Facts* include items of sense data; they refer to objects or events that can be seen, touched, heard, and so on. *Inferences* include conclusions reached on the basis of probability, guesses, and assumptions. Obviously, to conclude that Julie is intelligent or a Facist on the basis of her performance in yesterday's class constitutes an inference. It is less obvious that many everyday things which you think you are sure of are also inferences. For example, if it is raining in a given place, people commonly assume that it is raining several blocks away. It usually is, but that can rarely be observed. If a house is painted pink on one side, the side you can see, chances are that the other sides are painted the same color. But unless you have seen those other sides, you are only guessing.

Many items that are considered facts are actually probability-based inferences. You can use language more precisely by making a clear distinction between inferences and facts. For example:

It is raining here; I would guess that it is raining at my house.

By specifying which of your statements are inferences, you will add another dimension to precision. Such a distinction is more important in communication than examples about weather or the colors of unseen walls suggest. How often do you say something like "Jan is upset today" or "Allen seems conceited"? Even if you eliminate all *is* words from such statements, you must be admit that they represent inferences. You did not see Jan's anger or Allan's conceit. You saw their bodies and faces; you heard their talk. You received some concrete messages from what you saw and heard. You noted some of these messages and made inferences about the person's moods or attitudes.

Most speakers treat a statement such as "Jan is upset today" as a statement of fact. Ask the speaker "How do you know?" He or she will probably reply, "Well, I saw her!" A more precise reply would be: "Her face flushed bright red when I told her Allen got a better grade than she did." That response makes the description more factual because it describes what message behaviors led to your inference about Jan's anger.

We do not advocate that you give up the process of making inferences. After all, you make inferences every time you proceed through a green light or decide how you are going to spend Friday night. Life would be impossible without inferences. But language use becomes more precise when speakers consistently separate statements of fact from inferences. And the more precise you are in your use of language, the more effective you will be as a communicator.

Unfortunately, the line between facts and inferences is not always clear. Maybe Jan's face did not flush red at all. Maybe the sunset was reflected on her face; maybe she was trying out new makeup; maybe you just expected her to blush and saw what you expected. If you want a good example of how the line between fact and inference can become blurred, attend any sporting event. When a close call is made or when a penalty is ruled, the partisans of each team see the facts very differently, depending upon which team they are rooting for.

One area in which the tension between fact and inference becomes particularly important is news reporting. Reporters receive training in objectivity and in separating facts (news events) from inferences (editorial opinion), but that theoretical division does not always work. Ordinary events do not come with *fact* labels; rather, facts and inferences mix freely. A journalist can approach fairness, objectivity, precision, and clarity in reporting, but each of these qualities also represents the impossible.

All communicators experience this problem to some degree. The recommendations we make in this book can help you to make your verbal messages more precise and clear. But every new sentence or utterance provides opportunities to show that the structure of language makes what you are trying to do impossible. For example, in this chapter we have attempted to write in accordance with the principles we have been advocating. We believe that we have succeeded to a certain extent. We have used fewer *is* words, given more precise behavioral description, and made separation of fact from inference. But we have also failed on each of these counts plenty of times. To get a clearer idea of just how impossible the task is, try Experience 4.5.

EXPERIENCE 4.5 REPORTING FACTS AND MAKING INFERENCES

DIRECTIONS **There has been an accident in which the victim has been knocked unconscious and suffers amnesia. Assume that the victim is from out of town and is unknown to you. You work for the hospital; your supervisor hands you the victim's wallet and asks you to write a short description of the victim for use by the hospital staff. Base your description upon the items in the wallet. For purposes of this experience, take out your own wallet, and assume that it is the one given to you by your supervisor. Do not add any other details; stick to what a careful examination of your wallet and its contents reveals. Write in the space below.**

_____

_____

_____

_____

_____

_____

_____

After you have written the description, read it over carefully, and label both facts and inferences.

SPOTTING GOBBLEDYGOOK

Senator Fogbound, who is running for reelection, was asked by a reporter on an interview show what U.S. policy should be toward a certain Latin American country. Here is his reply:

> I'm glad you asked that question. Our relations with that country have been under careful scrutiny by the committee I chair for some time. Let me say that I consider that question to be of utmost importance not only for the nation but for the whole of Latin America. We have taken under advisement several staff recommendations and will issue a formal report in the near future. Let me assure you, however, that whatever is decided will support and respond to vital American interests in that part of the world.

You probably noted that the senator did not have much to say. Of course, there are many pressures on a U.S. senator, and the double talk he used serves some positive functions. Furthermore, he suspects that it will help him gain reelection. But he did not answer the question. As George Orwell noted, "Political language . . . is designed to make lies sound truthful and murder respectable, and to give an appearance of solidarity to pure wind."

You cannot change the way public figures talk, as you can prevent your own abuses of language. But you can learn to spot such gobbledygook when it appears. To do this you must root around in a message until you thoroughly understand what it says. Because there are plenty of messages of pure wind circulating in society, we recommend that you remain suspicious of any message until you are able to certify that it means something definite.

Many people feel that they lack background to understand what some expert says about welfare or race relations or whatever. Do not fall into that trap. Except for those rare cases of technical reports intended for an audience of specialists, most public communications should be understandable to a mature fifteen-year-old. Certainly you are capable of making informed judgments about most of what you see on television. If you start by practicing spotting gobbledygook on TV, you will soon be able to detect it in many other places, too.

Language—the primary tool of public life. It can be used to avoid clarity as well as to achieve it.

Gobbledygook often uses many of the hallmarks of imprecise verbal expression that we have discussed in this chapter. For example, when you see a lot of *is* words or a failure to separate facts and inferences, you can be suspicious. When your suspicions are aroused, use the following checklist as a guide. As you get experienced at this, you may want to make up your own terms, add to our list, or replace it entirely. These are the categories of absolute nonsense or worse that we believe are most abundant in popular media and politics:

1   euphemism
2   pseudoscience
3   bifurcation
4   cheap shot

Euphemisms

A *euphemism* is a word or phrase that is coined or stretched to take the place of a word that might prove offensive. We learned many euphemisms during childhood. Words such as *toilet, penis, died, nursing home,* and *urination* were rarely acceptable in polite conversation. Families become adroit at spotting potentially uncomfortable situations and inventing words that can be used in place of such difficult-to-say words. *Restroom, john, passed away, retirement communities,* and *discussion* are some of the most common and durable examples. Terms relating to sex and disposal of human wastes (note the euphemism) are more difficult to come by.

Euphemisms often appear harmless, and it is usually fairly clear what the speaker is talking about. But most euphemisms indicate people's attitudes. The phrase *passed away* indicates our culture's strong fear of dying and reluctance to accept death as one of the things that is going to happen to us. Sex inspires the most avoidance. Specialists who counsel couples experiencing sexual problems report that many couples seem unable to talk about sex with any precision. The parts of the body used for sexual intercourse seem embarrassing to name, even in intimate company. The frank seeking of sexual pleasure is frowned on by a little demon that occupies part of many minds.

In politics, euphemisms are used to justify a candidate's position. The candidate is not a *racist;* rather, the candidate stands for *states' rights, freedom of choice,* and *neighborhood schools.* The candidate wishes to help the *disadvantaged,* somehow, that seems much better than calling people *poor.* Nations that once were *backward* became *underdeveloped* and now are *developing.*

War has been an especially fertile producer of euphemisms in the past generation. An aggressive bombing raid becomes *protective retaliation.* A retreat becomes a *phased withdrawal.* Villages are destroyed in order to *save* them from the enemy.

Some people do not like the titles of their jobs. Job satisfaction may be enhanced by changing the job name through euphemism. *Janitors* became *custodians. Speech therapists* became *clinicians. Undertakers* became *morticians* several generations ago; now the same occupational category is called funeral director.

Then there are the advertising euphemisms: *regularity, dentures, personal hygiene, homemaker, problem perspiration, monthly blues, blemishes, halitosis.* Euphemisms are also prevalent in everyday life. Next time someone asks you if they can *borrow* a pencil, you might consider asking when they will give it back. We know students who use the word *studying* to describe sitting listening to the radio.

Interpersonal euphemisms are more slippery. It depends on whose ox is being gored. The coat you just bought on sale for a *good price* may seem *cheap* to me. Jane says her new boyfriend is *mellow* and *mature.* You may call him *wishy-washy* and *drab.* You dress *casually,* but others who dress similarly may be *careless* or *sloppy.* The point is that meanings reside, not in words, but in *people's minds.* That is, a given act is interpreted differently according to who does it. Your good friend is *conservative;* his good friend, whom you hate, is *reactionary.*

You are an *extrovert,* your roommate *talks a lot,* but Joyce is a *bigmouth.*

Try your hand at euphemisms by completing Experience 4.6.

EXPERIENCE 4.6 THE EUPHEMISM-MANUFACTURING GAME

DIRECTIONS

1 Some verbs conjugate irregularly. For example,
I give information; you argue; he propagandizes.
I am traditional; you are slow to change; she is oldfashioned.
Conjugate the following verbs:
a. I look for tax loopholes; you _____; he

_____.

b. I enjoy a wild party; you _____; she

_____.

c. I am quiet; you are shy; George is _____.
d. I _____; you are sullen; Audrey is

_____.

2 Truckers using citizen's band radios refer to a truckload of pigs as a load of *go-go girls.* Make up euphemisms for the following words:
a. headache _____
b. acne _____
c. alcoholic _____
d. crazy _____
e. loafing _____

3 Negative euphemisms (dysphemisms) are also popular. A *wife* becomes the *old battleax;* a *salesperson* becomes a *con artist.* Invent dysphemisms for the following words:
a. college _____
b. professor _____
c. mechanic _____
d. mother-in-law _____
e. presidential candidate _____
f. priest _____

4. List your favorite six euphemisms (or dysphemisms).
a. _____   d. _____
b. _____   e. _____
c. _____   f. _____

Compare your list with those of others, and come up with a master list of the 30 best.

Pseudoscience

Pseudoscience sounds a lot like euphemism, but there is often no precise meaning that is being euphemized. Jargon is invented by scientists and specialists to add precision when talking about fairly technical matters. The general public is used to not understanding jargon, so those who are good at jargon (professors and others) simply string out some jargon words together whenever they get into a tight spot. For example, "This is an example of the excessive dependency syndrome" has no clear meaning, but sounds scholarly and impressive.

If you can sound scientific or objective, your argument may succeed. Science is highly respected in the United States. For that reason, pseudoscientific talk has become depressingly common. It sometimes is easy to spot. Think of words that come in threes ("excessive dependency syndrome"). However, pseudoscience can also be less obvious. How often have you heard someone refer to "statistical tests," and "research proof," and "studies have shown."

What does "Blather Toothpaste has been shown in tests to be unsurpassed in reducing new cavities" mean? It says that Blather is not surpassed. That means that Blather and something else are about the same in reducing new cavities; it does not mean that Blather is better. And what is the something else to which Blather is being compared? "Tests at a major hospital show that Kumfurt's Pills were effective in reducing pain other than headache." Why were the tests done on pain other than headache? What kind of pain? Does it have any relevance to headaches, which is what you would take the pills for? What are these two commercials hiding?

"Our new ingredient, PX-50, reduces grease by 50 percent and kills millions of germs." Sounds impressive, but can you paraphrase what it means?

To get a good handle on how to sound important without saying much, try the game in Experience 4.7

EXPERIENCE 4.7 ROLL YOUR OWN BUREAUCRATIC JARGON

DIRECTIONS **Select any three-digit random number from the following list. Then refer to the list of words for each of the digits, and create a bureaucratic phrase. Use that phrase in a sentence. The phrase you create likely will sound impressive but will probably not be very meaningful. For example, the first number, 912, gives you "balanced organizational capability." Circle the numbers of the ten most interesting phrases that you create using this technique.**

```
912   618   995   085   950   495
683   096   179   088   135   696
290   960   192   402   903   065
288   235   984   771   757   627
770   023   307   388   308   906
405   337   840   858   938   939
775   564   590   566   159   966
010   444   450   316   629   589
828   738   752   935   631   576
014   526   328   557   855   439
045   944   375   544   305   240
067   281   065   797   869   972
516   690   101   367   041   546
499   115   789   979   527   137
675   447   930   399   499   324
646   152   045   278   025   284
983   940   998   898   762   961
665   200   426   838   302   608
539   055   082   805   673   444
600   447   492   422   070   323
543   442   594   980   974   424
622   645   830   792   926   649
700   450   166   739   685   358
666   780   248   142   419   631
031   699   504   488   038   521
```

First digit	*Second digit*	*Third digit*
0 compatible	0 monitored	0 dichotomy
1 integrated	1 organizational	1 contingency
2 synchronized	2 reciprocal	2 capability
3 responsive	3 policy	3 concept
4 total	4 management	4 projection
5 parallel	5 incremental	5 flexibility
6 optional	6 logistical	6 alternatives
7 functional	7 transitional	7 mobility
8 technical	8 systematized	8 programming
9 balanced	9 management	9 forecast

Compare the phrases you create with those in a government report or a speech. Do you notice any similarities?

_____

_____

_____

_____

Bifurcation

Bifurcation refers to pairs of words that are opposites. It can trap you into black-or-white thinking. Consider the following pairs of adjectives:

deep-shallow   happy-sad   good-bad   sacred-profane

But reality, the territory that the language map refers to, is not a matter of black-and-white categories. Reality is made up of millions of shades of gray and other colors.

It is easy to see how bifurcation comes about. There are words for extremes; whereas more precise description requires qualification and an admission that the description still cannot do justice to the actual event. Bifurcation is seductive because it implies that the world is simple. For example, it can trick you into thinking that people are good or bad. "If you're not for us, you're against us." "If you won't protest this war, you're a tool of the establishment."

Also, when you think of a word, its opposite is usually right on the tip of your tongue. In word association tests, a word's opposite is the most common response. Opposites are quite similar semantically. Imagine that all meaning is an enormous space. A word and its opposite would actually be quite close together in that space, rather than widely separated, as you might suppose.

One way of making an opposite is to add *no* to almost anything. That is how a small child makes opposites and negatives. That is also how the traditional American protestor, from striking laborer to war protestor, communicates his or her point of view.

Learning to say no is of course, very important. It is a critical step in a child's development because when a child says no, he or she takes a first step toward separate identity. Some people never really master the ability to say no.

A recent best seller titled *When I Say No, I Feel Guilty* attempted to teach adults how to say no without getting all worked up about it. One thing it demonstrated is the weakness of yes-no categories. Acceptance of yes-no alternatives leads to stereotyped action. A communicator who confines himself or herself to such alternatives gives away most of his or her powers of decision. Such a person cannot act; he or she can only react. During the most difficult phases of the Indochina War in the 1960s, American leaders claimed that because of the actions of the enemy, this country's only choices of action were escalation and retaliation. But such a statement did not reflect reality. To accept the assumption that there are only two alternatives is to let the categories of language play a cruel hoax. In the case of Indochina, succumbing to the trap of bifurcation led to a small country controlling the actions of the world's greatest power by a trick of language.

In Chaucer's *Canterbury Tales*, there is a story of a young knight who is saved from death by an old witch. The witch claims the right to marry the knight, and the marriage is accomplished. On the wedding night, the young man is horrified at the thought of sleeping with the hag. The witch allows him two choices: Either she can stay old but be a faithful wife, or she will turn young but play him false. Can you see the trick of bifurcation?

To sharpen your ability to spot bifurcation, complete Experience 4.8.

EXPERIENCE 4.8 BIFURCATION

DIRECTIONS   Read each of the following examples of bifurcation, and indicate what is wrong with the reasoning. Then write each sentence so that it makes more sense. If a statement does not exhibit false reasoning, indicate why it is correct.

1   Either an unborn fetus is a human being, or it is not.

_____

2   You are either for me or against me.

_____

3   We must strive to make our institutions more democratic, or we will become a totalitarian nation.

_____

4   High unemployment or high rates of inflation are our only choices.

_____

5   You cannot be a scientist and be religious at the same time.

_____

6   The light switch is either on or off.

_____

7   You can get either fuel economy or comfort in an automobile but not both.

_____

8   When I pull the trigger, either the gun will fire or it will not.

_____

9   The patient's illness is due to either a physical or a mental problem.

_____

As you have guessed, most of the sentences in Experience 4.9 are examples of faulty reasoning.   They fail to allow for other positions. However, there are a few truths included in the experience. An electric light switch is either on, or it is off; when the trigger is pulled, a gun will either fire or not. In short, there are some cases in which bifurcation is realistic. But usually there is room for suspicion when others offer you bifurcated choices.

Cheap shot

When a boxer punches below the belt, the whole fight is ruined. The same thing is true in politics and love. The cheap shot in communication can be defined as any speech act designed to hurt another person as seriously as possible. The cheap shot ordinarily changes the course of a conversation to abuse the other person.

> *Jane:* Harry, while I was doing the dishes, I was thinking about what name I should call your mother.
> *Harry:* I'm glad you finally did the dishes. It was starting to stink in the kitchen.

What actually happened in this exchange? Harry did not want to talk about his mother; such a conversation might have been uncomfortable. He avoided it by taking a cheap shot at Jane. A fight about housekeeping ensued, and they never did talk about Harry's mother.

A common use of the cheap shot in interpersonal communication involves a shift to the metacommunicative level. *Metacommunication* is a message about a message. You can resist talking about anything by calling attention to characteristics of the other person's message.

> *Child:* Daddy, can I get an ice-cream cone?
> *Father:* You mean, *may* I get one?

> *Wilbur:* Y'all wanna go the game tonight?
> *Chuck:* Why do you talk like a hillbilly?

A related variety of cheap shot is used by the teacher who grades a paper by putting red marks on all mechanical errors in order to avoid making a judgment about its content.

Cheap shots abound in politics. For example, there is the *guilt-by-association* trick used by Senator Joseph McCarthy in the 1950s: "If Mr. Jones was a good college friend of Mr. Smith, and Mr. Smith has admitted becoming a Communist while in college, then Mr. Jones was also a Communist in college." Closely related is the tactic of *affirming* by denying: "I'm not saying that my opponent is soft on Communism, but there would be rejoicing in Moscow if she got elected." Another cheap shot is the *scare issue:* "If we allow abortions to remain legal, our whole society will come to value life cheaply, and there will be widespread murders and lack of respect for humanity." This tactic is designed to scare people and to divert their attention from other issues.

Another diversionary tactic is the *straw person* argument. A straw person is created when a position is defined in such a way that it is easily destroyed in subsequent argument. "A conservative is a person who doesn't care about little people, and is only interested in protecting special interests." If this definition is allowed to stand, it is easy to attack the conservative position because the argument is constructed in a way that cannot withstand a challenge.

Another type of cheap shot is the *self-evident truth:* Everyone knows that nuclear energy is unsafe and that a massive accident is likely to occur." Here the speaker suggests that everyone already agrees with the argument and that therefore the question is not worth discussing.

Test your ability to detect fallacies of language by responding to Experience 4.9.

EXPERIENCE 4.9 LABELING FALLACIES

DIRECTIONS   Each of the following statements is an example of a fallacy of language. Read each statement, and identify the fallacy, using the following key, by placing the appropriate letter in the blank to the left of the statement.

a = bifurcation
b = cheap shot, interpersonal communication
c = cheap shot metacommunication
d = guilt by association
e = denying by affirming
f = scare issue
g = straw person
h = self-evident truth

_____ 1   Everyone knows that most welfare recipients are cheats.
_____ 2   Either we allow coal mining on federal lands, or we will be freezing in a couple of years.
_____ 3   She: *I'd like to talk about next month's budget.*
                        He: *I'm glad you washed the car. It was really filthy.*
_____ 4   I am not saying that Senator Schwamproot is a tool of the oil industry, but the oil executives in Houston treat him royally when he comes to town.
_____ 5   My opponent once was a good friend of Senator McClugg. Senator McClugg is a self-confessed Communist. Therefore, my opponent is a Communist sympathizer.
_____ 6   Daughter: *Can I stay out late tonight?*
                        Father: *You mean, may I stay out late tonight.*

_____ 7   National health insurance will destroy the doctor-patient relationship. It will take years to get an appointment with your doctor. You could die while waiting for one.

_____ 8   Modern liberals are not interested in the majority of hard-working Americans. They simply want to give vast powers to Washington bureaucrats to tell us how to run our lives.

SUMMARY

Human language is an incredibly complex phenomenon. It would be virtually impossible to program a computer to perform all the functions that a human language processor performs. People have a lot of intuitive and subconscious knowledge about language. This linguistic competence allows you to speak the English language intelligibly. Part of linguistic competence is tied to habit. Consequently when you hear a usage that sounds different from what you are used to, you may think that it is strange or incorrect.

A problem with language occurs when words are confused with the objects or events that they represent. People often forget that a map is not the same thing as the territory it describes. This problem is particularly apparent with the use of *is* words which tend to create an image of permanence that does not square with the process nature of reality. This can be avoided by avoiding the use of *is* words as much as possible and using more precise descriptions instead. Stating a point of view, talking about actual behavior rather than making evaluations, and differentiating between facts and inferences are all ways of being more precise.

Political language is particularly susceptible to a lack of precision. Such abstract-sounding, ambiguous language is known as gobbledygook. Whenever you hear it, your suspicions should be aroused. Types of gobbledygook include euphemism, pseudoscience, bifurcation, and the cheap shot. Spotting the use of these fallacies of language in personal and public messages can help to make you a more effective message receiver.

CHAPTER 5
EXPLORING NONVERBAL COMMUNICATION

βefore you read any further, complete Experience 5.1.

EXPERIENCE 5.1 MESSAGES FROM THE ENVIRONMENT

DIRECTIONS   Your task in this experience is to describe in writing the place you are in, any other people who are around, and what messages you are receiving from them and from your surroundings. Take at least ten minutes to make your observations before you begin to write, and do not talk with anyone during this experience.

1   Describe the setting (room, furniture, plants, arrangements of items, and the like).

_____
_____
_____
_____

2   Describe any people who are present (age, sex, dress, appearance, behaviors, and so on).

_____
_____
_____
_____

3   Describe the messages being received right now by each of your five senses.
a. sight

_____
_____

b. smell

_____
_____

c. hearing

_____
_____

d. touch

_____
_____

e. taste

_____
_____

4   What messages are you getting from your environment?

_____

_____

5   What inferences are you making on the basis of these messages?

_____

_____

Some students were not able to write much for Experience 5.1. Others wrote a good deal. But almost all expressed dissatisfaction with what they wrote because they said that not too many messages came through. In fact, most people are dissatisfied with their awareness of subtle messages that surround them.

The theme of this chapter is that if you maintain a state of awareness—that is, if you keep your senses open for messages from

Facial expressions may indicate emotional states. What can you infer about this person? What message cues key your impression?

other people, from yourself, from your environment—you will be able to observe hundreds of *nonverbal* communication messages every day of your life. The messages have been there all along, but communication takes place only when messages are received and interpreted. Hence, it is your active receiving process that makes nonverbal communication work.

Most people are aware that they send and receive many nonverbal messages in the course of an average day, and nonverbal communication is a very popular topic today. Several best-selling books have been written on the subject, and students often indicate that they find this area more intriguing than any other aspect of human communication. Most of those popular books promise that with some knowledge and practice, you can become an effective sender of nonverbal messages and an infallible reader of others' nonverbal messages. They suggest that you will then become a social success who knows what that new person thinks of you and a business success who knows just when to press for a commitment on the big transaction. Naturally, many people would like to be able to do these things. But to expect such powers is not realistic. Those who make such promises have an oversimplified notion of nonverbal communication.

There are two basic reasons why you cannot become an infallible and manipulative nonverbal communicator even if you want to do so.

First, nonverbal signs are usually sent involuntarily and received subconsciously. Ordinarily, you do not think about nonverbal communication. In fact, thinking about it changes the whole system. If you go around analyzing everyone's nonverbal behavior, you will change your own nonverbal messages and therefore the ways in which others will see you. There is no easy-to-learn, straightforward way for you to learn to be nonverbally effective in the sense that there are established ways to learn arithmetic, to play the piano, or to compose a five-minute speech.

Second, books translate nonverbal signs into words. That is what we asked you to do in Experience 5.1. But nonverbal communication cannot be adequately translated into words. Such messages are often ambiguous in terms of words. For example, lovers often send each other simultaneous unspoken messages of anger and continuing love that are meaningful in context of the relationship but meaningless if one of them tries to translate by saying, "Now exactly what did you mean by that look?" Furthermore, many nonverbal messages have no exact language equivalent. What is the verbal equivalent of a kiss or a pat on the head? You can make some approximation that will help you to understand the situation, but word approximations are not the same as the nonverbal messages themselves. When asked to explain the meaning of one of her performances, the famous dancer Isadora Duncan replied, "If I could tell you what it meant, there would be no point in dancing it."

We believe that it is more important to dance well than to understand the dance precisely. In other words, keep your senses open. You will be surprised.

EXPERIENCE 5.2 WHAT IS NONVERBAL COMMUNICATION?

DIRECTIONS Spend five minutes discussing some topic that interests you, such as sports, politics, God, or campus activities, with one other person. Hold the discussion while sitting *back to back* on the floor or on two straight chairs so that neither of you can see the other. Try to make the conversation as normal as possible, but avoid the temptation to look at each other. When you have finished your conversation, answer the following questions.

1   What kinds of information that you normally use in everyday interaction were missing in this conversation?

2   What information was still useful in this conversation? Did being unable to see the other person change how you used spoken words?

3   What kinds of things were most difficult to say in this conversation? Why?

4   Did you notice yourself using facial expression and gestures even though they could not be seen?

5   On the basis of this experience define nonverbal communication.

Visual cues constitute a large part of nonverbal communication. But in Experience 5.2, you were forced to communicate with another person without using such cues and to rely primarily on verbal cues instead. That experience has probably given you some idea of the value of nonverbal communication, but it has not cleared up all the puzzles.

The nature of the nonverbal code is by no means clear. Even the term *nonverbal communication* is a bit strange because it classifies its subject matter in terms of what it is not. That is, it is *not verbal*. Nonverbal communication is often considered to include literally any code items that are not strictly part of language, including the way you use gestures, the way you grow and comb your hair, the way you dress, the items that you carry with you, how close you stand to strangers, and how you make eye contact with others. All these things have some message value, but they are not primarily verbal. These diverse elements do not have much in common except their lack of verbalness, and that kind of classifying makes about as much sense as deciding to marry a person because both of you are not British.

Clearly, different authors and researchers disagree on what constitutes nonverbal communication. People use several communication systems besides language: expression and body movement, space, messages of smell, touch, and taste, and so on. People send and receive messages through all these modes most of the time. What do all these message forms have in common? Well, that is hard to pinpoint. They are *not* all visual. Nor is it as simple as saying that there is a system for each sense; more happens visually than with the other senses. In the end, therefore, we come back to saying that what all these systems have in common is the fact that they are not verbal. We must keep limping along with the term *nonverbal communication*. The most precise definition we can give you is that nonverbal communication is what was left out when you sat back to back with another person (in Experience 5.2) and tried to communicate. But even that definition is obviously not complete. You may have smelled each other; you had some spatial orientation toward each other; you made use of silences and other time-related matters in your conversation. All three kinds of messages are also nonverbal.

There is, however, one other clue to the nature of nonverbal codes: Nonverbal messages are generally more closely tied to feelings and emotions than verbal messages are. There may be many reasons for this relationship. First, there is the evolution explanation: Many animals use facial expressions and other nonverbal codes to express emotions such as fear or aggression. Courtship displays among apes and birds reveal almost unbelievable nonverbal skills. One conclusion that seems justified is that such signs are very ancient in origin, probably much older than language is. The carryover of emotional expression in nonverbal systems of communication can thus be seen as a simple matter of evolutionary history.

Second, communicators do not usually think of nonverbal messages as coded in the sense that language is. For instance, if you listen to someone speak or watch TV or read a book, your awareness is focused partly on the fact that you know that words are messages. If you have a strong reaction to the message, you realize that the message is only words and that there could be some explanation for your reaction. But if someone snubs you nonverbally or stands too close to you or smells "terrible" or calls you on the phone at 4:00 A.M. for a casual chat, your reactions are stronger, more emotive, more instinctive. You do not think of these items as coded messages, you just think of them as awful.

The reverse is equally true. Nonverbal expressions of love are far more emotive (and believed) than verbal expressions. This point is clearer in the case of nonverbal insults or behavior taboos. It might not be so hard for you to insult someone verbally. But could you go to his or her wedding wearing no shoes? Could you talk to a person while keeping your back turned to them?

In sum, nonverbal cues are messages that people respond to that are neither spoken nor written. Of course, all that this definition tells you is that nonverbal communication is not verbal. In fact, except for noting the fact that many nonverbal cues relate rather directly and strongly to emotions, it is rather difficult to define them precisely.

However, we *can* tell you some definite things about some specific aspects of specific nonverbal codes. The rest of this chapter will concentrate on an examination of four systems of nonverbal messages:
1   body movement and expression
2   communicative uses of space
3   communicative uses of smell, touch, and taste
4   communicative uses of objects and concepts

Keep in mind that our descriptions of these systems are valid only for most communicators in the United States. Different cultures speak different nonverbal codes just as they speak different languages.

KINESICS: COMMUNICATION THROUGH BODY MOVEMENT

Kinesics is the study of face and body movement. The term was coined by anthropologist Ray L. Birdwhistell, the pioneering theorist in this area. Kinesics researchers have tried to describe the rule-governed ways in which items of body movement are formed and combined into messages and how these messages are assigned meanings by receivers.

Experience 5.3 introduces you to one important area of kinesics: *facial expression.*

EXPERIENCE 5.3   MAKING INFERENCES ABOUT EMOTIONS

DIRECTIONS (PART 1)   **Look carefully at each of the following pictures. Then write your reaction to the picture, and indicate the emotions or messages that you think are being expressed.**

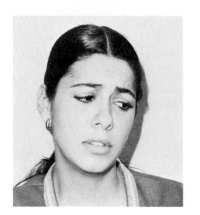

1

2

1. _____
_____
_____

2. _____
_____
_____

3

4

3. _____
_____
_____

4. _____
_____
_____

At your next class meeting, compare your reactions to these pictures
with those of other people in the class. Discuss the similarities and
differences in reactions, and speculate on what you feel causes them.

_____
_____
_____

DIRECTIONS   What is the most kinesically expressive part of the body? Most
(PART 2)   communicators consider the face the most expressive part of the body
            and the eyes the most expressive part of the face. Turn back to the
            pictures you studied in Part 1, and cover everything but the faces.

1   How much information do you lose?
_____

2   What kind of information do you lose?
_____
_____

Now cover everything in the pictures *except* the eyes.

3   Can you identify emotions just from expressions of the eyes?
_____

4   Write other reactions to this here. What appears to be the primary
    information sources in these photographs?
_____
_____
_____
_____

Experience 5.3 demonstrates that many emotions can be reliably
identified by looking at the eyes only but that there is loss of
information each time some part of the total picture is covered up. You
might have been able to guess a message, but you were probably less
confident of your guess because you had so little information.

What about the eyes? They certainly are powerful communicators.
Verbal expressions of the power of eye messages abound in the English
language: "If looks could kill." "He looks right through you." "Don't
slip on his icy stares." American teachers of public speaking have
ordinarily tried to teach speakers to maintain as much eye contact with
members of their audiences as possible. In our own experience in
teaching public speaking, those speeches that seemed ineffective could
be criticized more for lack of appropriate eye contact than for any other
reason. In face-to-face interaction, eye contact is often used to express
willingness to communicate, and avoiding another's stare is evasive.
Again, however, contexts are critical. In some subcultures within
American society, a child being chastised by an adult should look at
the adult earnestly. In others, the young person shows a similar
earnestness by looking away; if the youth returns the adult's eye
contact, it is an expression of defiance. A problem arises if two
communicators (e.g., a teacher and a child) come from different
cultural groups and therefore understand such messages differently.
The resulting breakdown in communication can have serious

consequences. For example, the teacher may feel that the child is either evading or defying the discipline.

Suppose that one communicator attempts to maintain more eye contact than the other. That person will feel that the other is avoiding his or her glance; the other person will think that the first is staring. In our culture, staring is impolite and taboo.

Eye contact is often used as a primary expression of affection. Watch the eyes of courters. And the closer together two people stand, the more eye contact becomes an effective "come-on." Is that why most people close their eyes during a kiss?

The rest of the face may not be so expressive as the eyes, but the mouth and the muscles that surround it can communicate emotionally charged messages. That popular contemporary social symbol the happy face demonstrates the importance of the mouth as a communicator. The entire message of the happy face is in the mouth, yet the whole face seems happy. Clearly, one detail in a nonverbal message can set the emotional tone of an entire context.

The *hands* and *arms* of communicators can be eloquent message carriers. A few decades ago, students of public speaking were taught detailed series of hand gestures that were supposed to evoke particular emotions in an audience. That practice is no longer favored, but a listener's interest can still best be held by a speaker who makes effective yet natural use of hand gestures to illustrate, amplify, and punctuate a speech.

The use of the hands is equally important in everyday interpersonal settings. When you tried to hold a conversation with another person while sitting back to back (Experience 5.1), you probably still tried to clarify what you were saying by use of hand gestures, even though you realized how futile that was. How often have you heard someone say something like, "Jane talks with her hands. If you tied her hands behind her, you wouldn't be able to understand a thing she said." When someone talks with their hands, just what are the hands saying? The question is meaningless out of context. Most gestures are more difficult to identify outside the situation in which they occur than facial expressions are.

The following passage from Robert Ardrey's book *The Territorial Imperative* describes some of the ways that hand and arm movements and facial messages can be communicative in men and animals. As you read this passage, compare it with your own experience.

> Watch a prizefight on television, or small boys in a schoolyard fight. Hesitant, uncertain as to whether to attack or back away, antagonists will dab at their noses. Care of the nose is an important human outlet; in moments of indecision, women will powder it. Hair, however, is just as important. Whether I am a Filipino or a New York executive or a tribesman in Ruanda, when I do not know what to do, say, or think next,

*I shall probably rub my chin or scratch my head. . . . But if I am a
woman I shall almost never rub my beardless chin; I shall feel around
instead in my back hair where it is longest. Yet there is something about
attention to hair which seems associated with sexual maturity. Children
rarely do it, tending instead to bite their fingernails. The adult is unlikely
to bite his fingernails, but in moments of inner stress or distraction or
embarrassment will carefully inspect them.*

The gestures described by Ardrey can be called *adaptors* because
people use them in responding emotionally to messages around them.
Scratching, doodling, fiddling with the hair, picking the nose, and
striking a casual pose by leaning against something are all examples of
adaptors. In contrast, many gestures function as *illustrators* because
they amplify and expand upon some oral messages. The gestures of
public speakers or of people who talk with their hands are illustrators.
Some gestures serve primarily as *regulators* of conversation because
they signal things about relationships between communicators. If you
raise your hand in class or pat a child on the head, you are using a
regulator. A final category of gestures, *emblems*, actually have
meanings in much the same sense as words do. In many cultures,
specific hand gestures have obscene meanings. Another example of an
emblem is the hitchhiker's outstretched thumb.

In summary, kinesic behaviors are heavily message-laden. In
Silent Messages, psychologist Albert Mehrabian estimates that how
much you like someone is determined 7 percent by the other's verbal
messages, 38 percent by paralanguage (vocal cues), and 55 percent by
visible messages. Those particular percentages are not important in
themselves. Rather, the significant finding is the predominance of
kinesics over speech. If a person says he will do something for you but
his face makes you think he is lying, which message will you believe?
Most people seem to trust their kinesic judgments. Use Experience 5.4
to sharpen yours.

EXPERIENCE 5.4   OBSERVING KINESIC BEHAVIOR

DIRECTIONS   **Station yourself in some setting where you can observe others without
necessarily being able to hear what they are saying and, most
importantly, without being observed by them. A park bench, a study
room in a library, a lounge in a large apartment building or
dormitory, a public beach or pool, a waiting room in an airport or bus
station are all excellent choices. Observe the kinesic behavior of two
groups of people. Concentrate on each group for several minutes, and**

spend about a half hour altogether in observing. Describe as many specific behaviors (things that you can state definitely happened) as possible. If time permits, jot down your conclusions about what was happening, but be sure to complete the description first. In your description, try to construct nonverbal contexts as completely as you can; include not only facial expressions but also body posture, position, and gestures. Note also how far from each other communicators keep their bodies during particular kinds of acts. Record your notes on the following checklists.

KINESICS CHECKLIST 1

1 Describe the setting or context.
   _____

2 Give an overall description of each person you are observing.
   _____
   _____
   _____

3 Describe the facial expressions noted.
   a. eyes
   _____
   b. mouth
   _____
   c. total facial expression
   _____

4 Identify the kinds of gestures observed.
   a. adaptors
   _____
   b. illustrators
   _____
   c. regulators
   _____
   d. emblems
   _____

5 What emotions or ideas were communicated?
   _____

6 What is your assessment of the situation?
   _____
   _____
   _____

KINESICS CHECKLIST 2

1   Describe the setting or context.
_____

2   Give an overall description of each person you are observing.
_____
_____
_____
_____

3   Describe the facial expressions noted.
a. eyes
_____

b. mouth
_____

c. total facial expression
_____

4   Identify the kinds of gestures observed.
a. adaptors
_____

b. illustrators
_____

c. regulators
_____

d. emblems
_____

5   What emotions or ideas were communicated?
_____
_____

6   What is your assessment of the situation?
_____
_____

PROXEMICS: USING SPACES TO COMMUNICATE

While observing nonverbal ways in which people relate to each other in public places (Experience 5.4), you probably noticed that people use the spaces between them as important carriers of messages. Such messages primarily concern the state of the relationships between the people.

In Chapter 8, "Developing Relationships," we will examine two major dimensions of relationship communication, dominance and friendliness. Spaces between people are used to communicate one or both of these dimensions. For example, lovers station themselves near each other on many occasions, and this proximity is both part of their closeness and a symbol of that closeness. Note that even the word *close,* which is often used to describe intimate relationships, is a word about spaces. Although there are exceptions (remember the importance of context), closeness in spatial orientation ordinarily indicates closeness of relationship.

Closeness can also indicate dominance, and distance can indicate submission. You avoid standing too close to someone you fear. In contrast, you may stand quite close to someone you feel superior to or even pat that person on the head or the back. Spaces, like gestures, thus serve as regulators.

This generalization—that closeness indicates affection and/or dominance—must be qualified on many occasions, but it provides the most logical introduction to *proxemics,* which is the study of how people use spaces for purposes of communication. The term *proxemics* (which has same root word as *proximity*) was coined by anthropologist Edward T. Hall. In *The Silent Language,* Hall presents many interesting and entertaining examples of how space can be used to communicate. He emphasizes the problems that result when communicators from different cultures that use space codes somewhat differently try to understand each other. For example, many people from Latin America habitually stand closer to each other during conversation than North Americans do. Two North Americans who are informal business acquaintances will usually stand about three feet apart while talking; two Latins will generally stand much closer. An amusing phenomenon can occur when a North American talks to a Latin. The Latin will edge closer in order to feel comfortable, and the North American will edge away for the same reason. The two may back across an entire room in this awkward dance. The American is likely to regard the Latin as pushy and aggressive; the Latin will feel that the American is aloof and standoffish.

Zones of personal space
As you can see, although the meaning of space may universally concern friendship or dominance, the meaning of two feet of space varies by culture. In our culture, we interpret spaces between people in terms of five zones of distance surrounding each person.

1. *Intimate zone* (0 to 2 feet). In America, a person who stands this close to another person would, in most instances, have to be a very close friend or a family member. At this distance, you can easily smell and touch the other person, signs of strong intimacy in our culture. Only under extenuating circumstances, such as a fight or in a crowded subway, would an American be this close to someone who is not an intimate. When two people talk at this distance, their tones are often hushed, and physical touching may be quite common.

2. *Personal zone* (2 to 4 feet). Even at this distance, Americans tend to be comfortable only if they are fairly well acquainted with the other person. This is a common distance for people to stand or sit from

each other at parties. But if a stranger walked up to you in a public place and got this close to you, you might feel uncomfortable or even frightened.

3. *Businesslike zone* (5 to 8 feet). This is the distance at which Americans usually stand when they meet for the first time. At this distance, speech is full-throated. This is a *safe* distance. It is the distance you might stand when talking to a policeman or when receiving an order from your boss. The inner edge of the businesslike zone is the distance you stand from another during a very formal handshake.

To find the outer limit of your businesslike zone, note how you move your eyes when you walk outdoors in a public place, such as a college campus or a zoo. One of the primary attractions of walking in such places is the interesting diversity of people you see. And it is ordinarily OK to watch people in this fashion until you get closer to them than about eight feet. Observe yourself as you approach people. When you are about eight feet from strangers, you will probably avert your gaze suddenly. If you think this habit is just a meaningless custom, try to keep looking at people as you pass within a foot or two of them on the sidewalk. If you continue to look at them the entire time, you will probably feel your heart beating rather rapidly, and perhaps the other person will show discomfort by hurrying past or looking at you as though there is something wrong with you.

4. *Public zone* (more than 10 feet). A distance of more than ten feet from another person is safe. At this distance, interaction is usually avoided. If you do say something, you almost have to shout to be heard (both because of the distance and because the other does not expect you to speak). The next time you go to a fairly crowded beach, take note of the distance that you must put between yourself and another sunbather in order to feel comfortable.

Each person carries a *bubble of personal space* around wherever he or she goes. Actually, there are several bubbles. They look like this:

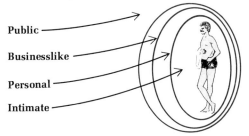

Public
Businesslike
Personal
Intimate

Notice that the bubble is biggest in front of the person and smaller on the sides and in the back. For some reason, it makes a person less uncomfortable to stand beside someone than to stand facing them at some close distance.

Personal space is a system that is quite consistent and simple when you are free to choose how and where you encounter others. Unfortunately, there are many circumstances that do not allow you that luxury. For example, riding a bus, sitting in a library, going to a ball game, attending a concert, sunbathing on a crowded beach, getting caught in a traffic jam, and being one of a million shoppers in a store on a sale day are all very common situations in twentieth-century America, and each constitutes a unique context. Most of the time, most people find ways to adjust to the fact that society seems to require infringements on their personal space. These adjustments can demonstrate a good deal of ingenuity. Consider the ways in which people compensate for lack of space in the following situations: in an elevator, at a crowded party, on a bus or subway, in a library—an invasion of personal space and other entries into an individual's territory require special handling.

The elevator

Everyone's personal space must be routinely violated in an elevator in order to get the maximum number of people to their floors with the minimum waiting time. The way people act on an elevator shows that they know this.

When you get on an elevator, you avert your gaze from the other riders, just as you avert your gaze when you pass strangers on the sidewalk. Avoiding eye contact is probably the most useful defense against necessary violations of personal space. Rather than looking at the other people, you customarily gaze at the indicator lights as if very interested in what floor you are on. Another thing people do on a very crowded elevator is to turn around while entering and back toward the others on board. They do this because their personal space is smaller in back and because such a move assures the others of their docility. Finally, people usually stop talking or avoid starting conversations because talk could increase personal closeness.

A crowded party

At a party, eye contact is again critical. You are often elbow to elbow with people you do not know. So long as you do not speak to them and face away from them, there is likely to be little problem—as long as you have *someone* to talk to. If you are alone in a crowd of partygoers you do not know, you will probably be very uncomfortable. A related problem occurs when you go to the bar or refreshment table to get a drink or a snack and then try to return across a crowded room to people you were with. There often seems no way to do this without going right through others' conversations. How do you do it? You murmur, "Excuse me," lower your gaze, and just stumble through.

The subway or bus

A crowded vehicle can be one of the most extreme cases of invasion of personal space. People sit and stand pressed against each other. Under normal conditions, such physical closeness is reserved for intimates. But *these* people are strangers. Matters become more intolerable if the bus careens around a corner or if the subway jerks to a stop, forcing the parties to lean or fall against each other and touch in ways they would not choose even with close friends. Nevertheless, regular commuters still manage under these circumstances. Again, the eyes are averted. You particularly do not look at the people you lean against. You probably turn your back to the person closest to you. Unless you are standing and need your hands for balance, you may fold your arms across your chest to give yourself some feeling of distance. A book or newspaper can provide additional distance. If you are involved in a book or newspaper, it not only helps you to forget the circumstances but shows the others that you are not emotionally involved with the crowded setting.

The library   College students are especially familiar with this situation. If the library study room is not crowded, studiers sit far away from each other. This preserves a sense of personal space. As the room gets more crowded, new arrivals have to sit between others. Usually, when you sit next to someone in a crowded library, you ask, "May I sit here?" or "Is this seat taken?" This question serves the same function as "excuse me" at a party. It shows that you have no aggressive intentions in entering the other's personal space. It is also customary to avoid looking at others as much as possible, to pretend, in essence, that they are not there. Finally, you arrange your books and papers so that there is a clear division between your things and theirs. If you begin to spread out your things and crowd the other person, your behavior could begin to constitute an invasion.

An invasion   *Invasion* is a dramatic or sudden entry into another's personal space. It is sure to cause discomfort. There are many sets of circumstances that constitute invasion. Consider, for example, a person who likes you better than you like him or her. The person tries to show this by standing closer to you than you wish. You probably respond by averting your eyes, by sounding unpleasant, by crossing your arms, by leaning away, or by turning your body sideways. All these maneuvers are substitutes for having more space.

Try staging an invasion and observing the other's behavior. But be careful how you go about it. We suggest you choose persons of your own sex; otherwise the other person may suspect criminal intent. Pick out your "victim" in some public place, perhaps the library when it is not crowded. Invade the person's space by sitting right next to him or her and then spreading your books and papers out so that you begin to infringe on his or her territory.

Territory   Territory is closely related to personal space. It is a safe zone, a place where you can rest from the rigors of defending your personal space from invasion. Examples include your favorite chair, your bedroom, your house (home as castle). Animals usually have their own turf that they will defend from attack. Nations behave in the same way; so do street gangs. The instinct to take and hold pieces of space permanently seems to be very old and widespread.

Watch students as they approach professors' offices. There may be hesitation, formality ("Are you busy?"). The lower-status person asks permission to enter the dominant one's territory both because the lower-status person is in some sense afraid of the dominant person and because the dominant person is on his or her own turf. Similarly, a subordinate asks permission to enter the boss's office; whereas the boss may just barge in on the subordinate. When the underling enters the boss's office, he or she stands until invited to sit and often maintains considerable distance from the superior. But when the superior enters the subordinate's office, he or she may stride right up to the desk. Clearly, uses of territory relate primarily to the dominance-submission dimension of relationships.

You now have some background information about kinesics and proxemics. The best way to learn more about these areas is through systematic observation. Experience 5.5 provides a format for your observation.

EXPERIENCE 5.5 OBSERVING KINESICS AND PROXEMICS IN ACTION

DIRECTIONS
Perform each of the following sets of behaviors, and record your reactions by answering the list of questions that follows each set of instructions.

1 **Go to a library and stay for about an hour. Select a table with people seated around, and observe them. Note where people sit, how they react to each other, and how they stake out personal space.**
a. Draw a diagram of the table, noting where people sit.

_____

_____

_____

_____

_____

_____

b. How do the people stake out their territories?

_____

_____

c. What happens when a new person sits at the table? What are the reactions of others sitting at the table?

2   Turn on the TV set but keep the sound off. Watch for 30 minutes
(including commercials).
a. How much of the message are you able to follow?

b. What ambiguities in the message emerge?

c. What added information could have resolved the ambiguities?

d. What aspects of these messages do you note with the sound off that
you have never noticed before?

3   Perform an act that calls attention to personal space. Invade
someone's territory, perhaps by sitting in someone's favorite chair or
talk without lowering your voice after getting on an elevator or by
keeping your back to the door of the elevator and facing the other
passengers.
a. How do the other people react to your invasion?

b. Why do you suppose that reactions to these behaviors are usually
so intense?

c. How did you feel while performing your invasion?

COMMUNICATION THROUGH OBJECTS AND CONCEPTS

A final category of nonverbal communication messages involves a
variety of objects and concepts. For example, in most mystery stories,
the messages sent by objects are critical. The detective is
superobservant about the way people use objects and leave subtle
indicators of their presence that become circumstantial evidence. The
master detective of them all is, of course, Sherlock Holmes. That
famous detective was able to solve fictional mysteries by paying
attention to tufts of grass on shirtsleeves, pieces of clothing left at the
scene of a crime, or unusual bulges in coat pockets. In Conan Doyle's

novel, *A Scandal in Bohemia,* Holmes demonstrates his mastery over physical cues by abruptly pronouncing that his associate, Dr. Watson, has taken a recent walk in the mud, and had hired an inept servant. The predictions were based upon several deep scrape marks on the soles of Watson's boots, which resulted from careless boot cleaning after a wet walk.

To most of us, the inferences of insightful detectives, real or ficticious, seem amazing or hard to believe. That is what makes Sherlock Holmes interesting. Still, the kinds of data used by legendary sleuths are available to us all. We use these items—clothes, contents of wallets, grooming, decoration of living rooms, or a make of automobile—to make inferences about the meanings of messages and the motives of communicators.

Of course, such inferences are fallible (see the discussion of fact and inference in Chapter 4). Great detectives are interesting precisely because they make inferences that we admire and that usually prove to be correct. Most of us are more in the category of Dr. Watson, of whom Holmes says, "You see, but you do not observe."

Still, you send messages every day with objects. Furthermore, an article of clothing may send one message to your friends and a very different message to your parents. The contents of your wallet can mean different things to different people, as you learned in Experience 4.5. Experience 5.6 will help you to examine some of those messages.

EXPERIENCE 5.6 COSTUME AS MESSAGE

DIRECTIONS **Think about the clothing you are wearing right now. List as many items as you can, and describe each briefly in the Items column. In the Messages column, note any messages about you that each piece of clothing might send to others.**

Items	*Messages*
_____	_____
_____	_____
_____	_____
_____	_____
_____	_____

How do you think you present yourself to yourself and to others?

_____

_____

How do you vary these self-presentation messages to suit different contexts?

_____

_____

All people carry around with them many messages about themselves: clothes, hairstyles, makeup, the contents of their pockets, their cars. Children already know how to do this. If you empty the pockets of any five-year-old, you find an amazing assortment of artifacts that tell you about the child's taste and temperament.

Even strangers can receive messages from your choice of clothing and other artifacts. What can you infer about this person? What message cues key your impressions?

Communicators learn to read such messages quite astutely, although the process may remain largely subconscious. In that sense, we are all reaching the same kinds of conclusions that Sherlock Holmes did.

Communicators also manipulate entire environments in ways that send messages. A teacher often arranges furniture in a classroom to facilitate a certain kind of interaction. The furniture in a professional person's office may point to aspects of his or her personality or attitudes.

Again, professors' offices provide an example. One professor might place the desk between his or her chair and chairs for students, thus putting greater personal space between communicators and emphasizing the professor's status. A more informal professor might turn the desk to allow closer contact with others. Such changes in environment can affect communication patterns. Having students sit in a circle, for example, appears to increase participant interaction. Nightclubs and restaurants are often dark so that patrons can leave some inhibitions at the door. Such places are often used for courtship, and it is easier to let others into intimate space zones when a room is dark.

Concepts also communicate, often nonverbally. The United States has a flag, an eagle, and money—all used as emblems. Emblems are powerful communicators. The mere sight of a swastika still fills many people with a sense of dread.

Time is a made-up concept that all people use for messages. Most Americans wear watches and subscribe to a concept that time is finite and constantly moving onward. For example, a wife may become unhappy with her husband because he spends insufficient time with her or the children. Asking someone for a date for five minutes from now and asking to see someone several days from now convey two very different messages. If when you show up for a date, the other person makes you wait an hour, you will probably be offended. If you only have to wait a few minutes, you will not mind. Why? Hall claims that people attach many social and cultural values to time: "Time talks. It can speak more plainly than words. The message it conveys comes through loud and clear. Because it is manipulated less consciously, it is subject to less distortion than the spoken language. It can speak the truth where words lie." Hall offers many examples of cross-cultural misunderstandings that result from lack of comprehension of how others perceive time. For instance, in America, a dinner guest is expected to arrive on time. A dinner guest who arrives on time in India would be insulting the host or hostess because the custom there is to arrive several hours late. The Latin American custom of resting in the afternoon (siesta) has become a stereotype of laxiness in the U.S. popular media. Hall reports an even more dramatic case from the South Seas. American supervisors of a factory had blundered by hiring too many workers from one native group and not enough from another. Because the Americans were too ignorant of the problem to solve it, leaders of the rival native groups met and arrived at a solution. They hurried to tell the plant manager. Unfortunately, the visit occurred at about 3:00 A.M. They did not realize that to wake an American in the middle of the night was a sign of great crisis. When the plant manager saw the natives coming, he called out the marines.

CONTEXT ANALYSIS

Any nonverbal event you observe may mean different things in different settings. A message that has a strong emotional message to you might not even be perceived as a message by someone with different expectations. Any given gesture or movement might take different meanings, depending upon how other communication systems interact with visual systems. We have made this point in discussing other aspects of communication, but it seems most strongly true with respect to visual messages. Meanings of communication events emerge from interaction of verbal, vocal, visual, and other code systems with past events, personal styles and preferences, and the goals of the communicators. Consequently, it is not unusual for messages to contain conflicting information.

Consider, for example, the wife who smiles at her husband, stares him in the eye, and remarks with heavy vocal irony, "I'm glad you could make it home so soon." It is 4:00 A.M. The husband has been late before. He is unlikely to believe the wife is delighted. But the situation is slightly ambiguous, and that is not all bad. The ambiguity in such situations allows expressive forms of communication that would be impossible if all messages were consistent. People's feelings are not always consistent. A wife might well wish to indicate both that she is displeased by her husband's actions and that her basic feelings for him remain unchanged. Thus, conflicts between verbal and nonverbal messages (and within nonverbal messages) can actually contribute to precision in expression of feelings. Expressing feelings is, after all, what visual messages do best. Who says feelings have to be one-dimensional?

Another example may help to show the importance of context. Nonverbal code elements can be extremely subtle; sometimes they are literally nothing, as in the case of silence. Silence is usually thought of as a space between messages, not as a message in itself. Yet everyone realizes that silence, whether in a phone conversation, on a date, at the dinner table, or in church, is a powerful communicator. Ray Birdwhistell writes, in *Kinesics and Context,* that his mother "could emit a silence so loud as to drown out the scuffle of feet."

But the meaning of silence in church is different from the meaning of silence at the dinner table or in a phone conversation. However, it would be inaccurate to say that most nonverbal signs have any particular meanings, as words are believed to have. It would be impossible to compile a dictionary of nonverbal signs. Silence, for example, can mean anything from fury to reverence. (And, of course, these words are inadequate to express what the silences really signify.)

Many popular writers who discuss nonverbal communication make a very important mistake on this issue. They imply that particular gestures, expressions, and postures have rather specific meanings. For example, women who cross their arms and legs tightly are not available, and people who lean away from you are expressing dislike. But in many cases, such interpretations prove to be wrong because they do not take into consideration the differences in the *context* in which the nonverbal messages occur.

A number of middle-class caucasian Americans, including both authors of this book, can feel quite uncomfortable about silence. If our students are too quiet, it may indicate extreme boredom or hostility. When we meet new people, we feel some compulsion to make conversation so that there are not long, unfilled pauses. But not every cultural group or every individual feels this way. Many use long silences as messages, and the typical talkative American reaction would be inappropriate in such settings. For instance, anthropologist K. H. Basso reports that Apache Indians use silence as a get-acquainted message at the beginning of relationships. Two Apaches would normally not introduce themselves to each other upon meeting, nor would they be likely to talk. Rather, both would remain silent for a period of time that we (Whitehead and Hopper) would find quite unnerving. Basso illustrates the function of silence by relating the story of a cattle drive on which four Apaches worked as cowboys. Two of the Apaches were strangers to each other, and neither spoke a word to the other for three days. On the fourth day one of the strangers said to someone else he knew, but within the other stranger's hearing, "Well, I know there is a stranger to me here, but I've been watching him and I know he is alright." After that, the two strangers talked to each other.*

If one of us had met one of those Apaches, we might have interpreted his behavior as unfriendly. Conversely, the Apache might have perceived us as pushy or glib. This kind of situation would represent a failure of context analysis. Such failures can sometimes be averted by learning about other cultures and their customs (see Chapter 7, "Crossing Cultural Differences"). Different cultures use different nonverbal codes, just as they speak different languages. People are *aware* that they speak different languages. For example, Americans do not expect to understand Russian speech. But somehow, this awareness of difference does not usually extend to nonverbal communication. Maybe that is because messages such as holding hands, smiling, shrugging, and eye contact look universal. If a European gestures at an American, the American feels less need to translate. Such an inference is dangerous, of course because nonverbal codes vary across cultures just as much as language varies.

* K. H. Basso, "To Give Up on Words: Silence in Western Apache Culture." In Pier, Giglioli, ed., *Language and Social Context*, London: Penguin Books, 1972, pp. 67–87.

However, not all failures of context analysis represent cross-cultural problems. Even good friends or members of the same family may feel differently about something like the meaning of silence. Start your practice of context analysis by completing Experience 5.7.

EXPERIENCE 5.7 THE IMPORTANCE OF CONTEXT

DIRECTIONS **Look at the photograph, and try to decide what the person is feeling. Do *not* read ahead. Base your judgment on nonverbal cues only.**

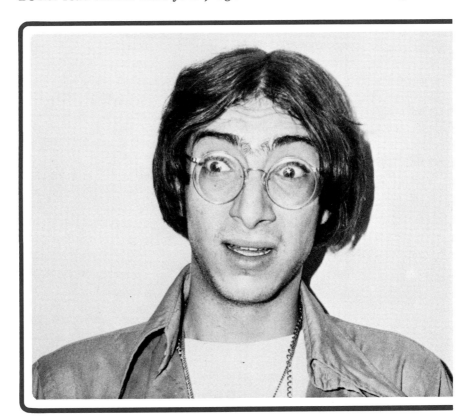

1 **Describe how this person is feeling.**

_____

_____

Now, suppose that the picture illustrates the following scene: This man has just returned to his house. It is three o'clock in the morning, and he has often stayed out late. The wife was waiting for him when he came in and greeted him by saying, "I see you're late again." The picture was taken just as she finished speaking.

2   Using this additional information, describe what you think the man in the picture is feeling.

_____

3   What is his face expressing?

_____

This picture was taken as the wife greeted her husband.

4   On the basis of this further information, reassess the situation.
    a. What is the man feeling?
    _____

    b. What does his face express?
    _____

    c. What is the wife feeling?
    _____

    d. What do her words express?
    _____

    e. What does her face express?
    _____

5   What is your total assessment of the situation, based on all the
    information available to you?
    _____
    _____

6   What do you predict will happen next?
    _____

The situation portrayed in Exercise 5.7 is not really tricky. It is
rather typical of many communication situations. That is, it
demonstrates that various contextual factors are important in deciding
what a given facial expression or arm gesture really means.
    For example, a smile is usually taken as an indication of
friendship or affection, but there are many contexts in which this is not
so. A salesperson often smiles when trying to overcome a hostile
customer's resistance. Hostile parents may smile at their children and
not show affection. It is a stereotype that Orientals smile to indicate
hostility as well as friendship. Are you certain you can always tell the
difference between a smile, a sneer, and a grimace? Is the difference
between the three a matter of the position of the lips? Usually, it is not.
Differences are often found in the position of and expression of the
eyes. Furthermore, all these inferences about smiles are also fallible.
    It would be next to impossible to put together a checklist of
nonverbal expressions and their meanings within certain contexts
because so many fine shades of meaning and intonation are involved.
Yet, communicators can usually make judgments of others' reactions to
them and simultaneously program nonverbal messages of their own.
People do all this intuitively.
    To understand the meanings of complex messages, you must
analyze entire contexts of communication events. Why does the
salesperson work so hard on the initial approach to a customer (see
"Proxemics")? Why are students of speech communication, who are
taught to speak clearly, not told to use clear facial expressions? Why do

lonely people so often appear aloof and unfriendly when, in fact, they desire to interact? One answer is that there is a low level of awareness in our culture of the importance of visual communication. Education concentrates on the verbal. Consequently, nonverbal messages do not receive official recognition as messages.

SUMMARY

Nonverbal communication is a very popular topic, having received widespread attention in the mass media and in popular books. Some of these books and articles suggest that people can become infallible, manipulative nonverbal communicators. However, that is unlikely because most nonverbal signs are sent involuntarily and received subconsciously. Furthermore, the words that writers use to describe nonverbal communication do not adequately represent the actual events of nonverbal communication. In addition, the meaning of nonverbal communication depends heavily on the context in which it occurs. Thus, it would be practically impossible to construct a dictionary of nonverbal cues.

It is easier to describe what nonverbal communication is not than to define what it is. Usually, the term *nonverbal communication* refers to any code items that are not strictly a part of language. These include body and facial movement, space, time, smell, touch, taste, objects, and concepts. Nonverbal cues are more directly and strongly related to the emotions than words are.

Kinesics is the study of face and body movement. Many emotions are communicated by facial expression, particularly by the eyes. Other types of kinesic communication include adaptors, illustrators, regulators, and emblems.

Proxemics is the study of how people use space for communication. In most cases, Americans interpret spaces between people in terms of a number of zones surrounding people: the intimate zone (0 to 2 feet), the personal zone (2 to 4 feet), the businesslike zone (5 to 8 feet), and the public zone (more than 10 feet). Often people are crowded by environmental conditions and must find ways to adapt to various invasions of the intimate zone.

Although nonverbal communication is dominated by sight, the senses of smell, touch, and taste are also important modes of communication. Concepts such as time and objects such as clothing or furniture can also be powerful nonverbal communicators.

Usually, the meaning of a whole message can be determined only through a detailed analysis of the total context. This task, so massive that it boggles the minds of most theorists, is handled as routine by most people every day. They examine nonverbal signs in context and intuitively interpret a large number of such cues simultaneously.

CHAPTER 6
RESOLVING CONFLICTS

At first, Harry felt scornful when Jane suggested that she keep her own last name after their marriage. Then he felt surprised and finally afraid. He thought, "Why doesn't she want us to share a name? What will my family think? How will children feel if their parents have separate last names?"

Harry remembered that his mother had once said that a woman who did not want to take her husband's name did not have a permanent stake in the relationship. Harry knew Jane better than that. Still, the request surprised him, and he found himself wondering if maybe his mother might be right. That thought was terribly unnerving to Harry. He was not used to thinking that his mother could be right. He wondered whether he really minded Jane keeping her name. Was he just blindly accepting his mother's opinion because he had never given the matter much thought. It was hard to be sure.

Harry looked at Jane closely, trying to guess what was on her mind. Neither had spoken for several minutes. Her chin was trembling slightly, but the line of her mouth was firm. She was not likely to back down without a battle. Harry was not even sure he opposed her idea. But if he gave in now, the issue would be settled, and he might decide later that he had made a big mistake.

He spoke slowly. "If our names were different, what last name would we give our children?"

In this example, Harry and Jane find themselves in conflict with each other over a concrete policy issue. In addition, Harry is in conflict with himself. Jane's intrapersonal conflicts are probably just as severe.

The potential for entering into conflicts is constant. You are faced with decisions. You must deal with numerous individuals who will have an impact on your future. You also have encounters with institutions. For example, you must deal with the telephone company when your bill contains a charge for a long-distance call that you did not make. Each encounter that you have with a person, institution, or even yourself allows and sometimes even invites conflict.

In America, conflict is usually considered undesirable. Whenever conflict can be avoided or toned down, most people are relieved. The belief seems to be that people are normally loving and care for each other and that events (conflicts) which get in the way of this cooperative spirit are unfortunate disruptions of the familyhood of humanity. That view is probably too simplistic. We are not suggesting that you should go around looking for a fight, but not all conflicts are tragic and not all evasions of conflict lead to harmony.

In reality, people are sometimes cooperative, sometimes competitive, and sometimes hostile and bellicose. None of these behaviors is the natural or best way to act in all circumstances. Conflict is a part of communication. Therefore, it is better to learn what it is about than to pretend you can and should always avoid it.

A second set of misconceptions about conflicts is that they result from poor communication and that good communication can resolve them. That is simply not true. Think about Harry and Jane's conflict. They are facing a problem, and they seem to be communicating about it accurately, caringly, and with a certain degree of efficiency. They do not seem to be violating any of the principles that we discuss in this book. They are probably on a productive road to a better relationship, but they are also heading into a storm. In their case, effective communication brings on conflict rather than avoids it.

What might have happened if Harry and Jane avoided a conflict? Jane might have decided not to bring up the issue in order to avoid conflict, but she might have gone on resenting the name she bore for the duration of the marriage. That would have avoided conflict but it would not be healthy. Harry might have avoided conflict by simply giving in, especially because he was not sure how he felt. But later, he might have regretted his decision.

A third misconception about conflicts is that all conflicts can or should be resolved. According to that point of view, conflicts (wars, arguments, and so on) are unfortunate and should be ended as soon as possible so that people can live in harmony. Some of the greatest tragedies in the news are the traditional disputes—between Indians and Pakistanis, Arabs and Jews, Hatfields and McCoys, civil rights activists and bigots. Such disputes seem so futile. Sides are entrenched and therefore unable to see each other's point of view. Many Americans believe that the only good conflict is an ended conflict. Our society loves the peace treaty, the labor pact that averts a strike, the marriage counselor who transforms a warring couple back into lovebirds.

But are conflicts always unfortunate? Do you know any conflicts that have essentially good outcomes? Sporting events are conflicts. Would you want to end all sporting events? When the conflict is over, the game has ended. Perhaps the world should not aim for perfect harmony.

It is, as we have said, unrealistic to expect to end many conflicts. For that reason, it is important to understand how conflict can be dealt with. There *are* better and worse ways to proceed. This chapter aims to help you find some of the better ways.

You should begin by finding out where your major conflicts live. Experience 6.1 will help you to do just that.

EXPERIENCE 6.1 CONFLICT CHECKLIST

DIRECTIONS **Look at the following list of areas of potential conflict, and rate each item as "very important to me now," "somewhat important to me** now," or "not important to me now." Indicate your rating by circling the appropriate number. Add any potential conflicts that are important to you but that we have omitted. Finally, circle the two items about which you feel that major conflicts are currently going on or may start soon.

	Importance		
Area of potential conflict	Very important to me now	Somewhat important	Not important now
My religious views	1	2	3
My likely career choice	1	2	3
How much I study	1	2	3
Relationships to parents	1	2	3
My political views	1	2	3
Will I marry?	1	2	3
Can I get credit at local stores and banks?	1	2	3
Do I vote in elections?	1	2	3
Can I convince my teachers that I deserve better grades?	1	2	3
Relationships with roommates	1	2	3
Relationships with landlord	1	2	3
Relationships with persons of the opposite sex	1	2	3
Relationships with people from whom I purchase goods and services	1	2	3
Relationships with teachers	1	2	3
_____	1	2	3
_____	1	2	3

INTRAPERSONAL CONFLICT

Some of our students have expressed surprise after completing Experience 6.1 because they found that many of their most vital conflicts were not with other people but with themselves. Harry was in conflict with his own feelings and expectations as much as he was in conflict with Jane's decision. Most conflicts have both intrapersonal and interpersonal aspects (which are usually more obvious). Interpersonal conflict is more obvious because it is observable. You could observe Harry and Jane arguing, but Harry's intrapersonal conflicts would be harder to follow. Even if you asked Harry about his inner conflicts, you might get less than a straight answer.

Intrapersonal conflict is experienced by every human early in his or her development. Maybe you can remember situations when you were growing up in which you had to make a decision between two alternatives that both seemed like fun. We can remember, for example, having to choose whether to study or play baseball, whether to go out for a pizza with one group or go bowling with another. We could either go to the movies or listen to records, but we could not do both. Because we could not do both, we experienced intrapersonal conflict.

Learning to deal with the sources of intrapersonal conflict may be one of the most important aspects of growing up as a communicator. You probably learned to make a decision and then enjoy your choice. You probably also learned to be expert in the art of rationalizing, that is, thinking and talking about how well you chose and how miserable you would have been if you had decided otherwise. The rationalization process is employed to make sense out of what would otherwise be an ambiguous situation. Rationalization is a form of intrapersonal conflict resolution.

The necessary decisions in life often lead to intrapersonal conflict. Describe this picture in terms of the nonverbal variables introduced in Chapter 5.

Decisions about what to do for fun do not require a great deal of data; you tend to reply on your mood or feelings at the time. But there are bigger decisions—for example, what school to attend, which camera or automobile to buy, whether to marry, whether to have children—that require a great deal more thought and that usually result in more internal conflict. Most people prefer to think that they make these decisions rationally, evaluating their needs, considering all alternatives, and then deciding the best course of action. Yet, people often make such decisions on impulse. Later, they may feel guilty, resentful, or victimized.

Over time, collections of such decisions play a big part in forming your opinion of what kind of person you are or at least what kinds of rules you are assuming at the present time. In Chapter 3, we discussed the notion of multiple selves. We noted that the different roles people play in different communication contexts may not be consistent with each other. Often, it is not so much inconsistencies among roles that lead to intrapersonal conflict as it is inconsistency between multiple roles and the idea that the roles should fit reasonably with each other. If that idea is not completely clear to you, wrestle with it for a minute.

You serve out time in various roles. You are a student, a family member, a close friend to a few people, a member of some organizations, perhaps an employee. Use Experience 6.2 to organize your thoughts about some of the roles you play and about the potential relationships or conflicts among them.

EXPERIENCE 6.2 ROLE EXPECTATIONS

DIRECTIONS **In the first column, list three major roles that you fulfill. In the second column, describe some of the expectations that others with whom you interact have of your behavior in that role. In the third column, describe the situation in which you perform the role, including the rewards or punishments associated with performing the role and the appropriateness of the expectations others have of you in the role.**

EXAMPLE

Roles	*Expectations of others*	*Role situation*
College teacher	**Have interesting lectures and classes. Spend time meeting and giving students individual help outside of class. Give students prompt and helpful feedback on their work.**	**Paid by state for role performance. Evaluated by students and peers for promotion. Expectations are appropriate.**

	Roles	Expectations of others	Role situation
1	_____	_____	_____
		_____	_____
		_____	_____
2	_____	_____	_____
		_____	_____
		_____	_____
3	_____	_____	_____
		_____	_____
		_____	_____

If you are like most of the students we know, you had little difficulty completing Experience 6.2. It is not difficult for most people to outline some major role performances that they feel they are expected to fulfill. But it probably occurred to you that the different expectations of the different roles you play sometimes come into conflict with each other. It is hard to fulfill one set of expectations without violating another set. For example, you may be both a student and a part-time employee. In your role as a student, you are expected to attend classes, take exams, and turn in assignments on time. In your role as a part-time employee, you must be at work on time, perform assigned tasks, and put in some extra time during rush periods of the year. Suppose that the Easter season is approaching. It is a busy time where you work and also a time at which there are several exams at school. You must decide which role, student or employee, will get *first priority* when you run out of time.

The role that gets priority is the role you act out while you let others slide. Suppose that you see yourself primarily as a student and that your work is simply something you do for needed money. You will probably tell your boss that you cannot work overtime because of upcoming exams. Now suppose that your job is in the field in which you hope to work fulltime after graduation and that the job experience is therefore as important to you as getting good grades is. Then your decision is more difficult because the conflict between roles is more intense.

Talk is an indicator of role conflict, but probably not the best one. People often talk about the role conflicts they are going through, but what they say is not really evidence of role priority. Talk is filled with excuses, rationalizations, and attempts to be acceptable that often mask role preferences. Actions are better indicators. In other words, you may declare loudly your interest in your studies, but if you let your boss browbeat you into working long hours and then do poorly on your exams, your actions speak louder than your words. That is an oversimplification, of course. One complicating factor might be that you see one of your roles as a person who gives in to the demands of others. Thus, when your boss asks you to work overtime, your work-interest role combines with your give-in-to-others role to overpower your interest-in-studies role.

Such role conflicts sometimes lead to procrastination. Difficulty in deciding which role to follow can be made more acute by a feeling that if one role is selected, the person will then be heavily responsible for work related to that role. For instance if you were to decide that you were superserious about your studies and you did not then receive acceptable grades, you might begin to doubt your abilities. But so long as you can put off making a serious commitment to your studies, there is less risk. You may get mediocre grades, but that is because your studies have not been really interesting or because you are more interested in your part-time job. As you avoid commitment to a role, there are plenty of excuses for lack of excellence. But if you make a priority decision, excuses (rationalizations) may be in shorter supply.

Closely related to role conflict is value conflict. *Value* is a rather loose term referring to the items or behaviors that are of worth to you. As you play roles, you try to gratify as many values as possible. Money, giving to others, avoiding sin, possessions, high-status jobs—these are some of the objects and actions that Americans commonly value. Values, like roles, are subject to priority conflicts. For example, some individuals primarily seek jobs with security; in doing so, they must make some trade-offs in such areas as money, personal freedom, and autonomy. In order to get a job he wants, a male student may have to cut his hair, dress in a suit, get up early in the morning, and give up frequent traveling. Many different values may be called into play by such decisions. Find out what some of these might be by completing Experience 6.3.

EXPERIENCE   6.3   VALUE CONFLICT AND EMPLOYMENT

DIRECTIONS   **In the first column, list three kinds of jobs that you might take immediately upon leaving school. Pick jobs that are as different as possible, that is, one job that would allow maximum opportunities for money or power and another job that would allow maximum personal freedom or that would make the most important contributions to society. In the second column, list some advantages for each job. In the third column, list some disadvantages for each job, stressing your personal values.**

EXAMPLE

Job	Advantages	Disadvantages
Teacher	Would have contact with people. Would have summers off. Could help children develop.	Low pay. Indoor work. Nonflexible hours. Rigid structures in school system.

	Job	Advantages	Disadvantages
1	_____	_____	_____
		_____	_____
		_____	_____
2	_____	_____	_____
		_____	_____
		_____	_____
3	_____	_____	_____
		_____	_____
		_____	_____

There are values involved in occupational decisions that many people rarely think about. In completing Experience 6.3, some of our students found that, for example, they valued personal autonomy more than they had realized. Some were surprised to find that they wanted the best kind of job at any personal cost. Others were worried about their long-term health if they assumed a stressful occupation. Making such value-related decisions is not easy, but examining your values may provide you with data that are already in your head but that you had not much thought about.

Another source of value conflict emerges when a person must make decisions about political and social problems. Such conflicts are usually easiest to note during important election campaigns.

Consider, for example, the frequent public debates about how best to make urban streets safe for transportation, taking walks, and other enjoyable activities, especially at night. One proposal for improving conditions is to punish street criminals severely and to have police officers hassle anyone who looks suspicious. That solution would serve values associated with safe streets, but it would sacrifice some values that many Americans hold about fairness and justice. If there is widespread police harassment on the streets, it is likely to focus unfairly on members of minority groups and others who dress less than formally or who maintain life-styles that differ from the majority's. Thus, the value of safe streets comes into conflict with values of justice and fairness. Everyone experiences such value conflicts, not just the voter who votes for a candidate who holds opposing values, because everyone holds values that are, to some degree, in opposition.

Value conflicts are not easy to resolve. Many cannot be resolved at all. In fact, you may not want to resolve them all. But many Americans seem to believe that it would be good to resolve all conflicts, a value that has been called the *utopia syndrome*. According to the utopia syndrome, ideal solutions should be worked toward, and such work is likely to improve the day-to-day quality of human life.

There are many illustrations of the value of perfection to Americans. Look at any magazine cover. If there is a human being pictured, chances are the picture looks perfect. Think of the models in advertisements and women's magazines. They have perfect figures and never a blemish. You might see one person like that a day, and that person is probably a model. But if you only looked at the covers of *Seventeen*, *Vogue*, or *Ladies' Home Journal*, you would begin to believe that all the people looked like that. Living with a utopian idea can make life difficult for people. We must admit that looking in the mirror is not always altogether pleasurable because the images that we see in the mirror are not comparable to those we see on TV or in the magazines. You have probably felt the same way, too.

The utopian syndrome affects many students in their daily work. Those who procrastinate about writing papers often tell us that they have an idea of what the paper should be like and that when they begin writing, they feel the actual product is not measuring up, and they stop writing. They fall further behind because they do not want to create a paper that is not perfect. We sometimes suggest that such students write three pages each evening, regardless of the quality, until they are finished. What they produce under such circumstances is often as good as the paper that they would have handed in three weeks late.

The utopian syndrome also troubles interpersonal relationships. Many Americans want to be in a perfect relationship. For example, they want to have a perfect lover or be a perfect friend to someone. But the actuality often seems to leave a bad aftertaste. Could the aftertaste be a result of the ideal they are comparing themselves with? Do you expect such perfection in your relationships?

Many students answer that question by saying something like, "Well, I feel that I've got to try my best." You read Chapter 8, "Developing Relationships," and you decide you can improve your life; you buy a book on transactional analysis, or the joys of sexuality; you take a workshop in assertiveness training. These teach strategies to lead you to fantastic peak experiences or to get your way with people. Can you see the problem in this picture? Those of you who see, read on. The rest of you should go back and study until you get it perfect. Can you see the trap there? Good. Read on.

In *Zen and the Art of Motorcycle Maintenance*, Robert Pirsig speaks of one possible outcome of value conflict: the "value trap." The value trap is what you end up in if you do not examine your values and ask what good they are doing you right now. Pirsig's example of a value trap is a device used in India to trap monkeys, a coconut chained to a stake. The coconut is filled with rice and has a hole in one end large enough for the monkey to get its paw inside but too small for the animal to pull its paw out after it has grabbed some rice. The monkey reaches in, takes some rice, pulls to get its hand out, and is caught. Escape is still possible, but only if the monkey lets go of the rice. The monkey seems unable to compare the value of having rice with the value of losing freedom and life, and so it is trapped. If the monkey could compare the importance of values, the trap would not work, and the whole situation would change. The same may be true for your values. Have you thought about the value of excitement, of freedom, of peak experience, of money, of belief in something bigger than yourself? Chances are that if you think of such issues, you will understand some of your own priorities about values.

Can you revalue your values? If you can, does the revaluing reframe your life? Is the job you thought you wanted (Experience 6.3) worth the price you will have to pay for it? Is the seeking of utopia worth the cost? We are not trying to tear down your value system. You may well give positive answers to the last two questions; about half our students do. If you do, you probably already knew what your values are. But some of our students say that they have never thought about it before.

Violence provides another example of value conflict. Primitive peoples survived by hunting successfully and keeping their neighbors from conquering them. Successful violent behavior seemed essential for survival. In the Old West a useful function was served by successful adaptation to violence. Today, however, it rarely pays to get violent. Yet, many people cannot reframe their violent world picture. And many people fear that if they reframe their violence values but others do not, they might get wiped out by violence. They might be right, but such a conflict is *interpersonal*. The conflict over violence values is intrapersonal. Do you see? If so, you are ready to examine what people usually think about when they use the word *conflict*: conflicts among persons.

INTERPERSONAL CONFLICT

When you think of conflict, you probably think of disagreements between persons. Harry and Jane, for example, were about to have an argument with each other. Each also had some intrapersonal conflict about the topic, but the main arena of their disagreement was to be interpersonal. That is the way things usually seem to happen, if only because interpersonal communication is so much easier to observe than intrapersonal communication.

The potential for interpersonal conflict is present in almost all relationships and within all groups and organizations. You can get involved in many sorts of conflicts, including conflicts about when and how to have conflicts. You can get into conflicts about how an organization or committee should operate. You can encounter conflicts about whether your best friend of the opposite sex should date other people.

Such conflicts are part of the human landscape and are not always harmful. In fact, conflict can be a positive force for improving relationships and improving the ability of groups and organizations to adapt to change. However, conflict is also potentially disruptive to communication. For instance, a game such as tennis provides a conflict setting that can provide entertainment for the parties as well as exercise. But if either party to the game begins to feel that his or her self-esteem is threatened by losing, however, the game conflict may degenerate into scenes that could carry competition or bad feelings beyond the tennis court.

The rest of the chapter aims to get you thinking about some of your own interpersonal conflicts, and how to deal with them. In Experience 6.1 you rated some of the most important sources of conflict you are now dealing with. Use the interpersonal conflicts you noted there, or use anything else that occurs to you, and respond to Experience 6.4.

EXPERIENCE 6.4 INTERPERSONAL CONFLICTS LIST

DIRECTIONS **Recall at least three interpersonal conflicts which have been important to you lately. It is vital that these conflicts be both *recent* and *important*. In the first column, describe the *problem* in the conflict (who was involved and what was at issue). In the second column, describe *what happened* during the conflict. If the conflict has ended, how did it end? In the third column, describe the *results* of the conflict. (How do you feel? How do the others feel? Are you pleased with your own actions and the outcome?)**

EXAMPLE

The problem (parties, issue)	*What happened* (events, end)	*Results* (feelings, outcomes)
My boyfriend became jealous because an old boyfriend arrived	I spent little time with my current boyfriend and refused to stop seeing my old	I feel great. I am not ready to be tied down, even though I still like my current boyfriend.

from New Zealand. I hadn't seen the latter for eight months, and I spent every moment with him.

boyfriend. I refused to give up my New Zealand boyfriend. My current boyfriend had no choice but to end the relationship or put up with my dating others. He puts up with the latter and keeps his protective attitudes to himself.

I am pleased with what happened, but I suspect my current boyfriend is still not particularly pleased.

1 _____   _____   _____
  _____   _____   _____
  _____   _____   _____

2 _____   _____   _____
  _____   _____   _____
  _____   _____   _____

3 _____   _____   _____
  _____   _____   _____
  _____   _____   _____

Scarce resources   One of the first things our students have noted about about the three conflicts they list in Experience 6.4 is that *all conflicts are not alike.* Your responses to all conflicts may have been one-dimensional (until now), but the conflicts themselves differ in many ways. Some are conflicts over *scarce resources,* things that not everyone can have. The outcome of a sporting event is the best example of a scarce resource. There may be two teams in a volleyball game or seventy golfers in a tournament, but there can be only one winner. Everyone competes for a position that can go to only one person or team. When one team or person wins, the resource is used up. There is no other way to arrange it without changing the whole game.

A conflict over scarce resources becomes a win-or-lose situation. You may not be all that interested in winning, but win and lose seem the only possibilities. People often program themselves for win-lose situations that are unnecessary. Consider, for example, this conflict over design of work space (see Chapter 5): A new faculty office building has only a very small number of offices with windows. The windows are wonderful, whole-wall picture windows; the offices without windows seem drab in contrast. Naturally, there are conflicts about which people should get the window offices. The conflict-producing value of the resource is created by the scarcity of the resource. If most of the offices had windows, there would be no conflict on this issue. The resource would have been abundant.

Some situations are even more ambiguous. Consider your best friend of the opposite sex. Do you date only each other? Why or why not? If you do date only each other, is it because your affections for each other are in some sense scarce resources? Time is certainly a scarce resource. If your friend spends Saturday with someone else, he or she cannot spend that same time with you (unless the three of you are together, which may not be the kind of situation you had in mind). But suppose that you are out of town next weekend and that you and your best friend have agreed to date only each other. Then time scarcity is not a problem. In many relationships there is another scarcity ethic: If certain affections can be shown more than one person, they lose their value. In other words, monogamous sexual relationships in our society have defined affection as a scarce resource. There is no necessary reason why it has to be that way, but that is how it is defined. (We do not suggest that it be defined differently; we simply want to point out how scarce resources can be created.)

Psychologists have spilled a lot of ink on the subject of sibling rivalry. Brothers and sisters fight each other, undercut each other, upstage each other all in the name of trying to get the most affection from the parents. There were seven Hopper children and three Whiteheads, and neither family was without that sort of conflict. We both had to grow pretty far into adulthood before we were able to see our brothers and sisters as something other than competitors. Competitors for what? For the scarce resource of parental affection and esteem. But where did the notion that parental affection and esteem have to be a scarce resource come from?

In summary, all conflicts are not alike. Some conflicts are over scarce resources; others are over abundant resources. It can be revealing to examine a conflict in terms of the relative scarcity of resources.

Goals

Conflicts can differ in terms of the *goals* of the participants. Sometimes participants seek the same goals; sometimes they seek different goals. In tennis games and in sibling rivalry, both parties seek the same goals. In a classical debate, parties argue opposite sides of a question; they may both have a common goal of winning the debate, but there the similarity of their goals ends.

It is vital to analyze the goals of parties to a conflict because parties often assume either that their goals are the same or that each other's goals are mutually destructive. For example, if a married couple begins considering a divorce, one party to the discussion may wish to keep the marriage together and therefore assume that the other party also wants to keep the marriage together. The other party, however, may wish to terminate the marriage. The parties must understand each others' goals if the conflict is to have fortunate outcomes. Discussion and educated guesswork about the goals of other parties to a dispute can be a key to conflict resolution.

Finding out the other party's goals can be difficult. Sometimes parties are reluctant to reveal their exact goals because certain strategies they plan to use in the conflict depend on secrecy or surprise. Sometimes people are not certain of their own goals and do not fully understand their own actions.

Power of the participants

The *relative power of the participants* can have a great impact on the outcome of a dispute. Power is a curious term. One way of assessing a person's power is to see how he or she has done in similar conflicts in the past. For instance, if your team is playing a basketball team that has won only two games in a long season, you would have different expectations about the outcome of the conflict than you would if your team were playing the defending champions.

Why analyze power? If you find out how powerful a person is, will it hinder rather than help you? That is a good point. But there is another approach: You can take a good look at the sources of the other person's seeming power. For example, you may see that the other basketball team plays a certain kind of basketball (i.e., a run-and-shoot or a ball-control game). You can then adjust your own tactics to do best against that team.

Suppose that you see a probable conflict shaping up between yourself and your boss over a project you are doing together. You are able to see that his sources of power are aggressiveness and the ability to bowl over his opponents with a verbal barrage, often without backup facts and data. Therefore, you go assemble a great deal of evidence for your position and begin asking detailed questions that your boss cannot answer without data. When he is unable to answer, you begin to reveal the data you have collected and support your position with facts. Thus, you are able to counter his verbal aggressiveness with facts and evidence.

In summary, interpersonal conflicts (such as those you listed in Experience 6.4) can be analyzed according to the following questions:

1   Is the resource scarce? (Can both parties win?)
2   Are the goals of the parties the same or different? (And are the goals clear?)
3   Are the participants equal or unequal in power?

To learn more about how these questions work and how they can help you toward increasingly rational conflict experiences, complete Experience 6.5.

EXPERIENCE 6.5   CONFLICT ANALYSIS WORKSHEET

DIRECTIONS   Write down a brief description of two conflicts you have been involved
in lately, one whose outcome you felt good about and one whose
outcome you were less satisfied about. Include a description of how
the conflict was resolved. Then describe each conflict in terms of the
three issues listed.

1   The conflict I feel good about was:
_____
_____

a. Was conflict over scarce resources? Describe.
_____
_____

b. What were the goals of the conflicting parties? Were they the same
or different?
_____
_____

c. Describe the relative power of the parties.
_____
_____

2   The conflict I feel bad about was:
_____
_____

a. Was conflict over scarce resources? Describe.
_____
_____

b. What were the goals of the conflicting parties? Were they the same
or different?
_____

c. Describe the relative power of the parties.
_____
_____

3   What will you do that is different the next time you are party to a
conflict?
_____
_____

Problem solving   In the past, students' responses to Experience 6.5 have shown
three basic styles of resolving conflicts. The method chosen often had a
lot to do with the satisfaction of the parties over the outcome.

For example, the majority of the decisions that students have expressed satisfaction about have employed an approach called *problem solving*. Several clues will tell you whether a conflict should be approached through problem solving. First, both parties to the conflict should believe that the dispute can be resolved in ways that will please everyone. In other words, both parties should believe that they win. In such a situation, both parties understand that the conflict is not over scarce resources. As we noted earlier, it is often difficult to know whether some resources, such as another's affection, are scarce. However, if both parties *believe* that there is enough of the needed resources to please everyone, they can expect to be satisfied with the outcome.

Second, each party must understand the goals of the other. Their goals do not need to be the same, but they must be clearly understood. Empathy for the other party goes a long way toward creating a problem-solving atmosphere.

In a problem-solving atmosphere, there are few power or status differences between the parties. That is, they are either actually equal in power or power and status differences are not much referred to in the discussion because they are not considered important. Neither party tries to overpower the other to get his or her way. Instead, a primarily rational atmosphere pervades, and attention is centered on the problem.

Problem-solving techniques have been used by professional bargainers to get out of the problems created by win-lose situations. For example, a strike is near, and management and union negotiators meet to try to work out a settlement. The union representative presents a series of twenty demands at the start of the negotiation. At that point, management representatives often reject the demands as ridiculous. In problem-solving, experts recommend moving toward a suitable climate by accepting the demands as good-faith proposals that could serve as bases for discussion. Next, each demand can be discussed separately by a two-person team consisting of one manager and one union representative. The fact-finding teams then report back to the main groups. By that stage, the members of the groups have been working together long enough to begin to understand each other's viewpoints. Next the group again divides into subgroups to evaluate all possible solutions according to how well they satisfy the expressed needs of *both* sides. Notice that a scarce resource is treated as abundant. The bread-and-butter issues may be economic, but an approach to conflict that stresses understanding the other's point of view makes money seem less scarce.

In summary, a problem-solving atmosphere is a rational climate that allows open discussion of issues on the assumption that both parties can be winners. Each side understands the goals of the other, and power differences between the parties are minimized. The atmosphere may seem rather artificial, and it takes work to maintain, but those who use the problem-solving approach are usually satisfied with the outcome, as our students discovered. (Students reported satisfaction with the outcomes of 90 percent of the conflicts that they described in problem-solving terms.) In problem-solving conflicts, the parties follow the three criteria:

1   They define the resources of the conflict as plentiful.
2   They describe their goals to each other as clearly as possible.
3   They de-emphasize any power differences between them.

Look back to the conflicts you described in Experience 6.5. Do these three criteria fit any of the conflicts you discussed? Were you satisfied with the outcomes of such conflicts? We suggest you ask your friends or survey your classmates to see if our 90 percent finding holds up.

Forcing

Students were not delighted with all the conflicts they reported. Many conflicts with unhappy outcomes were described by students in terms of one party forcing the other party to do things against his or her will. Such *forcing* strategies create and maintain a win-lose atmosphere, in contrast with the win-win atmosphere of problem solving. The assumption of the forcing tactician is that only one party to the conflict can win. Both victory and the issues of the conflict become scarce resources.

In forcing situations, goals are kept secret as much as possible. If one side knows the other's goals, it will try to keep them from achieving those goals, even if they have no real effect on their side's own goals, because victory is seen as a scarce resource. The recent history of warfare is full of tragic examples of forcing strategies. Since 1950, most wars have taken place in small countries. The big countries supply arms and sometimes soldiers primarily to gain influence on the government that survives the war. Usually, if one major power sends guns to one side of a war, its enemies send arms to the other side. The goal is to frustrate the goals of the enemy, whatever they might be. In order to prevent such blocking moves, forcing enemies keep their goals as secret as possible.

Finally, the relative power of the parties is emphasized in a forcing atmosphere. The most powerful party wins. The other party may be bitter but is powerless to do anything. The actual conflict may be quite short and quiet (if the most powerful party bluffs the other into submission) or long and messy (if both parties feel they have a chance to win). In either case, the loser is unlikely to emerge from the conflict satisfied. Even the winner may find that the victory has not been worth the cost. Most of the conflicts about which our students expressed unhappiness were settled by forcing strategies. (It must be admitted, on the other hand, that one-fourth of the conflicts about which students expressed satisfaction were settled by forcing. In all such cases, they were the winners of the disputes.)

Participants in forcing conflicts seem blinded by the need to defeat their opponents. They do not search for creative solutions that could satisfy both sides. In fact, groups involved in forcing strategies select leaders on the basis of ability to destroy the enemy, not on the basis of ability to search for alternative solutions. The conflicting parties direct their energies and efforts at defeating each other rather than at the common problems they face. Each party attempts to present a united front to the opposition, minimizing internal arguments. Any communication between the two parties tends to be evaluative, and reactions are generally defensive. The conflict goes on until one party gives up.

Many conflicts settled by forcing do not look like conflicts at all because one party, seeing the other's power, simply gives in. Although that may seem less costly than other forms of conflict, long-term problems are likely to result. The conflict is simply put off, not settled.

Compromise

The strategy of *compromise* has a good image. Marriage counselors, for example, urge compromise, and undoubtedly compromise is necessary. But how does a compromise atmosphere define a conflict? A compromise strategy treats the conflict as being over scarce resources. It is impossible for both sides to win and either impossible or undesirable for one party to overcome the other. Although the parties may be aware of each other's goals and may wish to satisfy them, those goals seem irretrievably in conflict. In contrast with problem solving, which creates a win-win situation, and forcing, which creates a win-lose situation, compromise creates a *lose-lose situation*. That is, neither side can win without crippling the other, but each can keep the other from winning.

The prototype compromise occurs in the Bible. Two women come to King Solomon, each claiming to be the mother of the same child. There seems to be no way to decide who is telling the truth. Solomon decides on a compromise: He will cut the child in half and give half to each mother. Can you see how compromise creates a lose-lose situation?

Consider an everyday situation. Two brothers are fighting over a newspaper. Each is grasping it, and both want to read it right now. They finally compromise and cut the newspaper in half. And both parties lose. This demonstrates one of the problems with the compromise strategy: The brothers never really explored the dynamics of the conflict. In compromise, as in forcing, there is a tendency not to discuss goals in order to prevent those goals from being blocked. Had the two brothers discussed their newspaper needs, they might have discovered that one wanted to look only at the sports page and that the

Table 6.1   **Three conflict strategies**

	Problem-solving	Forcing	Compromise
Is the resource seen as scarce?	*no*	*yes*	*yes*
Are the goals of both parties clear?	*yes*	*rarely*	*sometimes*
Are the participants equal in power?	*yes*	*no*	*yes*

other was interested primarily in the editorials. If the brothers had chosen the problem-solving approach instead, both could have been satisfied.

As you can see, the definition of resources as scarce or plentiful is the key to what kind of conflict you will have. If the resource is seen as scarce, you either force or compromise. If you see the resource as plentiful, you have options that the problem-solving strategy makes possible. It is the same newspaper either way. The difference is in how you see it. (If you think that point is frivolous, reread Chapter 2.) The three styles of conflict resolution are summarized in Table 6.1.

On some occasions, of course, compromises are necessary. If a husband and wife wish to vacation together but he prefers the woods and she prefers the beach, both sets of goals cannot be satisfied at once. Even in this case, however, a constructive, problem-solving atmosphere can lead to a better decision. That is, each party can assume that the other is bargaining in good faith and lay out all his or her goals clearly. Then there may be basis for negotiating a solution that allows both parties at least a partial win. The parties might discover, for example, that they do not really have to be together and take separate vacations or that there is a cabin in a secluded woody area near a beach or that they can afford two short vacations. Even in compromise, a large number of alternatives can be considered in a problem-solving climate, thus increasing the chance of hitting on a win-win solution.

To examine your own conflict strategies, complete Experience 6.6.

EXPERIENCE   6.6   PROVERBS ABOUT INTERPERSONAL CONFLICT

DIRECTIONS (PART 1)   Indicate your opinion of each of the following short proverbs as a conflict strategy. In each case, ask this question: How desirable is this strategy as a method for resolving conflicts? Use the following key, and write the appropriate number in the blank to the left of each proverb.

1 = completely undesirable		4 = desirable	
2 = undesirable		5 = very desirable	
3 = neither desirable nor undesirable			

_____ 1 You scratch my back; I'll scratch yours.

_____ 2 When two quarrel, he who keeps silent first is the most praiseworthy.

_____ 3 Soft words win hard hearts.

_____ 4 A man who will not flee will make his foe flee.

_____ 5 Come and let us reason together.

_____ 6 It is easier to refrain than to retreat from a quarrel.

_____ 7 Half a loaf is better than none.

_____ 8 A question must be decided by knowledge, not by numbers, if it is to have a right decision.

_____ 9 When someone hits you with a stone, hit him with a piece of cotton.

_____ 10 The arguments of the strongest always have the most weight.

_____ 11 By digging and digging, the truth is discovered.

_____ 12 Smooth words make smooth ways.

_____ 13 If you cannot make a man think as you do, make him do as you think.

_____ 14 He who fights and runs away lives to fight another day.

_____ 15 A fair exchange brings no quarrel.

_____ 16 Might overcomes right.

_____ 17 Tit for tat is fair play.

_____ 18 Kind words are worth much and cost little.

_____ 19 Seek till you find, and you'll not lose your labor.

_____ 20 Kill your enemies with kindness.

_____ 21 He loses least in a quarrel who keeps his tongue in check.

_____ 22 Try and trust will move mountains.

_____ 23 Put your foot down where you mean to stand.

_____ 24 One gift for another makes good friends.

_____ 25 Don't stir up a hornet's nest.

DIRECTIONS (PART 2) Now that you have indicated the desirability of each proverb, transfer your rating numbers to the following blanks. The numbers correspond to the proverb numbers. Then add up the numbers in each column.

5. ____	4. ____	1. ____	2. ____	3. ____
8. ____	10. ____	7. ____	6. ____	12. ____
11. ____	13. ____	15. ____	9. ____	18. ____
19. ____	16. ____	17. ____	14. ____	20. ____
22. ____	23. ____	24. ____	21. ____	25. ____

TOTALS

_____	_____	_____	_____	_____
Problem solving	Forcing	Compromise	Withdrawing	Smoothing

Your numerical totals, in Experience 6.6 do not mean much by themselves, but the differences among the totals *are* significant. Your highest total indicates that the word at the bottom of the column describes your predominant problem-solving style. Other high totals indicate tactics you are likely to use sometimes. Comparatively low totals indicate the methods you are least likely to use.

Withdrawing and smoothing

Two additional conflict styles, withdrawing and smoothing, are primarily used to avoid or put off conflicts, not to resolve them. We alluded briefly to the withdrawing strategy when we noted that some people seem to avoid conflicts by simply refusing to fight. Smoothing is similar in principle. It emphasizes what conflicting parties have in common and encourages pleasant and friendly messages. In essence, the smoothing strategy tries to get around the fact that conflict exists and to establish warm ties in spite of it. Both smoothing and withdrawing can lead to serious problems if they are used as primary or exclusive ways of dealing with conflicts because conflicts do not disappear if retreated from or ignored. Nevertheless, these strategies can be very useful in preventing serious forms of hostility.

As we have emphasized, conflict is normal and often useful. But some of the forms of violence and hostility to which conflict sometimes lead—wars, fistfights, strikes, lawsuits, lovers throwing frying pans at each other—produce more trouble than good. Each of these eventualities represents a conflict that could have been better managed but was allowed to get out of hand. When such a danger arises, smoothing and withdrawal can perform important functions.

The cooling-off period, which is used in labor-management negotiations, is a clear example of smoothing. A strike deadline approaches; the two sides begin to trade insults; tempers flare. Both parties are cornered. Neither can see alternatives to the outright battle of the strike. Waste and tragedy may result. At this point, a mediator (often a court) may impose a 90-day cooling-off period during which work will proceed as usual while tempers have a chance to cool.

Suppose that you have a serious argument with your parents and a resolution seems impossible. You could begin to trade insults or threats, but that would be unfortunate. Smoothing gives you valuable room. Both parties to the conflict can state that they want the best for each other and that they will sleep on the problem. By taking time out, it becomes possible to bring problem-solving strategies into play.

A withdrawing strategy performs the same general function. If you are having an argument with your father, and you know your father tends to use forcing strategies, you may be able to defuse the conflict temporarily by refusing to fight or by claiming that you do not have time to talk about it now. However, it is important to remember that the problem remains unresolved. Unless you can bring some problem-solving strategies to bear, you will eventually end up where you started.

Reframing

Conflict escalates because of the ways that the parties see the situation. Ordinary arguments are unlikely to change the way the parties see the situation. Somehow, the perception of the situation needs to be changed. What is needed when serious conflict (war, strikes, violence and so on) threatens is some kind of reevaluation of the situation.

We have already referred to this reevaluation process: *reframing*. The term was coined by Paul Watzlawick and his associates in their innovative book *Change*. In some ways, everyone performs reframing operations every day. The simplest example of reframing is a dream. If your dream turns into a nightmare, you may scream, you may fight, you may suffer, you may argue, but the situation remains the same. But if you wake up, the whole situation is changed. The nightmare is no longer real; it has lost its power. The situation has become reframed.

Another example is the American custom of the surprise party. The party is a kind of practical joke in which friends scheme to trick somebody into going to some routine occasion and the subject suddenly finds himself or herself at a place where friends jump out and yell "Surprise." At the moment that the subject realizes what has really been going on, the situation is reframed. Strange things that the friends have been doing are recognized as part of the plot. Reframing thus offers a new theory to explain events.

How does reframing apply to conflict? If a situation in which conflict may escalate out of control can be changed into a different kind of situation, violence may be averted, and the parties may even work toward a problem-solving atmosphere. For instance, a married couple argues every day. They do not get enough sleep, their sex life deteriorates, and they act nasty to each other. They seek marriage counseling. The counselor listens to their complaints and informs them that they argue so much because they really care deeply for each other. If they regard arguing as a sign of their special relationship, there is no need for them to be defensive or to worry about who wins the fight. The important thing is that the fight itself takes place and thus reaffirms their relationship. This is not so implausible as it may seem to you. A new definition of the situation has been offered that changes the meaning of some of the fight behaviors and makes it possible for the couple to engage in problem solving.

Watzlawick and his associates describe an incident that occurred in France in the nineteenth century. A series of disturbances led to chaos in a town. It was announced that there would be a public rally one afternoon. The mayor ordered the police chief to go to the rally and "disperse the rabble." Confrontation was imminent. The police surrounded the public square; the crowd grew threatening. At any moment, violence might flare. Then the chief of police stepped forward and raised his hands. "Ladies and gentlemen," he began, "I have orders to disperse all the rabble from this square. Since all I see before me are respectable ladies and gentlemen, I ask that you leave at once so that I can find the rabble." The square was clear in minutes, and violence was avoided.

What did the police chief do? He offered a redefinition of the situation that allowed the parties to put off the conflict for a while. He did not solve the conflict, but he did prevent serious hostilities that could have made the conflict unsolvable.

In many difficult conflicts, some degree of reframing is a necessary part of a solution. For example, labor-management negotiators often spend a great deal of time together and become close friends. The friendship provides a reframing of their adversary relationship that makes it possible for them to reach agreement on some difficult issues.

Reframing is not rare. When you fell in love, you reframed. When you decided that your parents' words were advice, rather than orders, you reframed. The challenge is in getting someone else to share your reframing. How do you get your parents to see you as a grown-up. Chances are their frame still looks the same to them. Experience 6.7 lets you practice the gentle art of reframing.

EXPERIENCE   6.7   REFRAMING

DIRECTIONS   **Read each of the following problems, and rank the solutions according to the instructions provided.**

1   **You have a part-time job that produces most of your income. It is nothing outstanding, but the people you work with are nice. Your supervisor is hard on everyone, but you have learned how to tolerate the tactics, which are used almost every day. One day, without any warning, your supervisor accuses you of loafing on the job. You have taken sometimes a few extra minutes for coffee breaks, but everyone else does that quite regularly. The supervisor adds that you will be watched and that any questionable behavior will be dealt with severely. After a week of cold looks, oppressive comments, and constant nonverbal harassment, you are really shaken.**

Here are four possible solutions to this problem. Assume that there are no other alternatives. Choose the solution you would be most likely to try first, and write 1 beside it. Rank the remaining solutions 2, 3, and 4 in the order in which you would use them.

_____ a. Work through all the pressures that the supervisor is using, and prove that the charges are untrue.

_____ b. Go to the supervisor, admit that he/she is probably right, and ask him/her to tell you some things you can do in the future to improve your behavior.

_____ c. Go to the supervisor, and tell him/her that you are innocent of the charges and that unless the pressure is stopped you will quit immediately.

_____ d. Get together with the rest of the workers, and attempt to plan and use a group technique for solving your common problem in dealing with the supervisor.

2   You have been living for a year with one other person, a roommate of the same sex. You are not the closest of friends, but your roommate certainly knows you well, and you appreciate his/her company. Then financial problems force you to get a second roommate. After a few weeks, your two roommates begin complaining about your enforced rules of neatness. You attempt to explain your feelings rationally, but a shouting match breaks out. For two days, you and your roommate have not talked to each other except for "phone for you," "you have a letter," and the like.

Here are four possible solutions to this problem. Assume that there are no other alternatives. Choose the solution you would be most likely to try first, and write 1 beside it. Rank the remaining solutions 2, 3, and 4 in the order in which you would use them.

_____ a. Initiate conversation with your roommates by apologizing for how hard you have been on them, and offer to be more tolerant of their messiness in the future.

_____ b. Search for a living situation with people who are neater and more cooperative, and move out at the first opportunity.

_____ c. Talk with your old roommate, and try to get him/her to agree to force out the person who brought the problem with him/her.

_____ d. For ten days, try being sloppier than your roommates are. Adopt their life-style completely, and be better at it than they are.

HOW DO YOU FIGHT CITY HALL?   We have already noted that power differences among individuals and groups can have a significant impact on the outcome of a conflict. One common kind of conflict pits the individual against the massive organization—the government, the telephone company, the company you work for. In such a situation, most of the power is on the side of the big organization. This is one of the most common and frustrating conflicts Americans have to deal with today.

What can you do when you have to fight city hall? The large organization has large resources. It is probably in no hurry to settle such disputes. It is probably used to having people gripe and may even employ professional flak catchers (euphemistically called *customer service representatives*) whose major job is to listen to complaints and attempt smoothing maneuvers while doing little or nothing to settle the conflict.

Here are a few examples of cases you might run up against.

1   A store does not wish to give you credit because you are a student.
2   An airline loses your luggage.
3   The phone company bills you for three long-distance calls that you did not make.
4   You return some tires that have worn out halfway through the warranty period, and the company claims you mistreated the tires.
5   An expensive pair of shoes splits at the sole after you have had them four months. You did not keep the sales slip.
6   Your landlord refuses to refund your security deposit when you move, but you know that the damages he wants to charge you for were done by former tenants.
7   The city changes the zoning of the vacant lot next door, allowing a builder to erect a catsup factory there.
8   You have reason to believe that the police are tapping your phone.

Because the parties to conflicts such as these do not have approximately equal powers, the transactions can prove very difficult for communicators who are inexperienced in handling them. Nevertheless, there are some things that you can do. Experience 6.8 will help you explore some of the options.

Procedural persuasion involves an appeal to the rules.

EXPERIENCE   6.8   THE SHOE STORE CAPER

DIRECTIONS   You bought a pair of shoes three months ago for $70, which is more than you have ever spent for shoes. Last night, you were caught in the rain, and the shoes got wet for the first time. The sole split; apparently it had been glued defectively. You are not a shoe expert, but that is your opinion. You did not keep a sales slip, but you feel that the store should give you at least 80 percent of your money back. What would you do?

1   Describe what you would do. For example, if you decide to go to the store or to write, what would you say?

_____

2   Assume that you got no satisfaction from your first tactic. You are not ready to give up yet. What would you try next? Whom would you address, and what would you say or write?

_____

3   Assume that you are still dissatisfied with the store's response. You are probably quite angry by now. What would you do? If this attempt also fails, will you give up, or do you have more tactics in mind? Describe what you would do, and guess the probable final result.

_____
_____
_____

In his article "Communication Strategies in Conflicts Between Institutions and Their Clients," John Bowers lists some strategies that individuals commonly use in conflicts against large organizations: petition, appeal, promulgation, organizing, and resistance. In all probability, the strategies you decided to try in Experience 6.8 appear on Bowers's list. An interesting feature of that list is that it follows a sequence from the least serious and disruptive strategies to the most seriously disruptive. If we were to evaluate what you wrote in Experience 6.8, we would give you most points if your strategies occurred in the same order as those on Bowers's list. In other words, his first or second strategy should be what you try first, and you should resort to the last items on the list only in desperation. Do not hunt fleas with elephant guns; you would probably miss the flea but do damage to other parts of the scene.

Petition   Petition is a simple request for better treatment. In Experience 6.8, petition probably involved going to the store and asking the first clerk you saw for a partial refund. Petition is a necessary and useful tactic, but in most difficult cases, it is highly unrewarding. It can be useful, however, to put petitions in writing, particularly when you are dealing with mail-order firms and government bureaucracies. A written petition has several advantages: You can carefully consider your words; you need not worry about being betrayed by nonverbal cues that you feel uneasy; the respondent is also under less pressure because a letter can easily be shown to several people and responded to coolly. If you are in no hurry, writing is often effective. But in a tough conflict with a powerful organization, petition is usually insufficient.

Appeal   When you go to the shoe store, the first clerk you see will probably give you little satisfaction. One way or another, you will get the brush-off. You may even get blamed for the damage: "I'm sorry but we don't even carry this shoe." "Our policy is not to accept returns without a sales slip." "This shoe has obviously been mistreated." It rarely proves productive to argue with such responses. The clerk, who probably lacks authority to make a controversial adjustment anyway, will just become defensive.

Ask for the supervisor. "May I speak to your supervisor, please?" will usually do it. Stick to your guns. The employee may tell you that the supervisor cannot help you or is not there. Then ask who is present that can help. There usually is someone. If nobody is available, ask for an appointment to see someone who can help. Ask for the phone number of the store owner. Be polite.

All these tactics are examples of an appeal. Frequently, just the show of determination to appeal ends the conflict. For example, one of the authors had a small conflict with city hall about maintenance of a drainage ditch behind his home. The person reached by petition was unhelpful, so the author asked for a supervisor with authority to make a decision. The employee said he would speak to the supervisor himself. The next morning, the work was performed. There was no further interaction with the city on this subject.

Appeals can themselves be appealed; it works like the court system. You can ultimately appeal to the chief executive of any company. In fact, higher-ups are frequently more sensitive to customer and citizen gripes than the front-liners. The higher-ups have more to lose if the dispute escalates to more serious tactics. In that sense, appeal is a kind of implied blackmail. If your car dealer will not give you warranty service, write to the company's district headquarters or to the top man in Detroit.

Promulgation   Suppose that you take your case to the owner of the shoe store and the owner tells you to go fly a kite. What then? Usually, the next step is *promulgation*, telling someone who is outside the company or organization involved but who may be able to assist you with your problem. For example, you might complain about the shoe store to the Better Business Bureau or to some other consumer protection organization. You might write to the attorney general of your state to complain. You might write to Ralph Nader or some other advocate who often proceeds publicly against large organizations.

Promulgation can also have a less specific target, the general public. You might get an interview on TV to complain against the shoe seller, or you might distribute leaflets urging other customers to avoid such a gyp. You might decide to write to a local newspaper. However, some caution is called for in this type of promulgation. The line between legitimate public complaint and semilegal slander or libel can be foggy. For example, a dissatisfied car customer who parked his lemon, with a big sign on it, next to the dealership got a lawsuit for his trouble.

Organizing

One way to fight an organization is to form a counterorganization. Labor unions are the best-known examples. When they could not get satisfaction for their gripes (petitions, appeals, promulgations), workers banded together in order to proceed against employers from some kind of power base. That power came from the fact that employers needed *somebody* to run the factories. When workers agreed that nobody would work until conflicts got settled, then management often listened for the first time.

Consumer boycotts use a similar principle. Buyers band together and agree that they will not purchase certain products or shop at certain stores; until a given conflict is settled. Sometimes the conflict is their own; sometimes consumer groups support workers' grievances (as in the case of the grape boycott).

Organizing is often combined with promulgation. A boycott needs publicity if it is to work effectively.

As you have probably realized by now, the cost of settling a conflict increases as it becomes necessary to use increasingly serious tactics. Petition is easy, although it is more trouble than ignoring the issue. Appeal is more trouble and hassle. Promulgation can be hectic. Organizing people often proves to be a full-time job. An important question is: How much do you care about this conflict? How far are you willing to go? You must realize that you cannot even every dispute. If you spend energy on every conflict that comes at you, you will never have peace or quiet. You must evaluate each situation.

Resistance

The most expensive and serious option is resistance. For example, you could sit in the shoe store with a big sign about the store's shoddy merchandise around your neck and refuse to leave. You could combine resistance with organization and get twenty friends to come to the store with you and sit in all the available chairs. Everyone could wear signs. You could ask to try on shoe after shoe. You could stay for hours and frighten other customers away. Such tactics take determination and planning. You could end up spending the night in jail if the owner of the store calls the police.

Resistance can be highly disruptive. The big-city riots in the 1960s have been characterized by conflict theorists as resistance when petition, appeal, promulgation and organization had failed.

Occasionally there are dramatic payoffs when resisters display innovative planning and a willingness to put themselves on the line. For example, Martin Luther King's nonviolent demonstrations and other forms of organization and resistance changed many attitudes and a lot of behavior. Saul Alinsky, a Chicago organizer, may have been the most innovative of all resisters. He once threatened to direct his workers to descend on O'Hare Airport by the hundreds during the rush hour. They were to occupy every toilet and stand in front of every urinal in the airport. The dispute was settled before this tactic was actually used.

Of course, organizations have some countermoves of their own. Bowers ranks them from cheapest and easiest to most difficult and expensive: avoidance, procedural persuasion, substantive persuasion, adjustment, and suppression.

Avoidance   Avoidance is least expensive and most effective when used against written petitions. The letter just does not get answered, or the official promises to decide your case soon but does nothing. In the case of an in-person appeal, the clerk or official may simply try to avoid dealing with you.

Procedural persuasion   The organization can appeal to the rules. "I'm sorry, our policy doesn't allow us to do that." "I don't make the rules." Or it can tell the petitioner that his or her message takes the wrong form. "You have to put that in writing using form 11-27-B." "I'm sorry, adjustments have to be accompanied by sales slips."

An interesting form of procedural persuasion was born in the computer age. A petition or appeal is not spotted by the computer, which processes your payments and statements, and the organization can claim that the petitioner was not following procedures. This is also a convenient form of avoidance. Procedural persuasion is often used against promulgation, organization, or resistance. The buzz phrase is that the complainer "isn't going through proper channels."

Substantive persuasion   Your appeal may be denied on the grounds that you do not deserve it. "You have clearly mistreated the shoes." "Shoes can't be expected to last longer than that." The representative of the organization may even try to make you feel guilty or cheap for making your request, hoping that you will stop bothering the organization.

Adjustment   The organization makes an offer or simply gives in. This may well end the conflict in a way suitable to one or both parties. Adjustment is usually costly for the organization.

Suppression   Suppression is fairly rare, but a big organization can take you to court, or assess you back taxes, or sabotage your credit. Organizations usually find the threat of such measures fairly effective. Actually performing these measures can be costly in terms of damaged public relations and also in actual financial outlay.

Here is an example that demonstrates the use of the categories listed by Bowers. Assume that you buy a used car. After you get it home, you find that the transmission leaks and slips when you drive. You take the car back to the dealer who sold it to you, and he sends you to a transmission repair shop, where the transmission is worked on at the dealer's expense. You have made an oral petition, and the institution has responded with an adjustment. The transaction involved some cost to you. You had to take the car to the transmission shop and do without the car while it was being repaired. It also involved some cost to the dealer. He had to pay the repair shop for working on the car.

When you get the car back, you find that the transmission still does not work properly and is still leaking in your driveway. Now you feel hopelessly caught between two institutions. Should you take the car back to the transmission shop that botched the job or to the dealer? You opt for taking the car to the dealer and trying to get your money back. The salesman tells you that he cannot make such an adjustment (procedural counterpersuasion) and that you will have to talk to the manager. You talk to the manager, and he offers to let you have another car, which you refuse. The manager tells you he cannot give you your money back. You persist (appeal), and he tells you that you will have to speak with the owner of the car lot (procedural persuasion).

You arrange an appointment. Again you ask for your money back. The owner tells you this is impossible because the car is already registered (procedural counterpersuasion). You stand firm and repeat that you want your money back (petition). The owner gets angrier and angrier, but you remain calm and continue to state that you want your money back. Finally, the owner of the car lot gives in and agrees to take the car back and gives you your money.

By resisting the temptation to become angry and counteract force with force, you were able to get your money back through a series of assertive behaviors. The individual employing this strategy calmly and coolly restates again and again, as many times as necessary, what he or she wants, regardless of how angry and unreasonable the representative of the institution becomes. The institutional representative does not know how to deal with this type of behavior and soon realizes that he or she will be dealing with you all day if he or she does not respond to your demands. This strategy is quite costly for the institution because it disrupts the normal functioning of the institution.

Other strategies that you might have employed would have been more costly to you because they would have taken more time and might not have been as effective. It would have been easy for the institution to ignore a written petition. You could have appealed to the Better Business Bureau or to a local consumer protection agency, but such agencies are usually unable to employ sanctions against a dealer in these cases. They must rely, instead, on voluntary compliance or on voluntary enforcement by the car dealers' trade association. Promulgation and organizing would have cost you a great deal of time and effort, regardless of whether you got your money back.

For the car dealer, the least costly strategies were used up early in the encounters. Because you were not going to go away, it was less costly for the dealer to refund your money than to continue to have you tie up the time of a number of people.

Whenever you are involved in a dispute with an institution, this type of analysis of the strategies available to you and the institution will be helpful to you in selecting the best tactic. Experience 6.9 will give you some practice in analyzing strategies.

EXPERIENCE   6.9   BATTLING AN INSTITUTION

DIRECTIONS   Assume the following set of facts:

1. You took your car for a grease job and an oil change.
2. On your way home from the service station, the oil pressure light comes on, but you are on a busy freeway and must drive several miles before you can get off.
3. You check the oil and discover that there is none in the engine.
4. You call a wrecker to have your car towed.
5. The driver of the wrecker notices that the oil drain plug is missing. You tell him where you just had the car serviced, and he suggests towing the car back to the station for repair.
6. You get back to the station, and the mechanic informs you that the engine is ruined and that it will cost you $500 for an overhaul.

   The following matrix shows what moves are available to you (the individual) and to the gas station (the institution). The dialogues demonstrate the use of these strategies. Identify the strategies used by each party in the dialogue by writing the appropriate letter and number (from the matrix) in the blank following each dialogue.

EXAMPLE   You: *I would like my car restored to the condition it was in when I brought it in here, and I don't expect to pay anything extra for it.*

Mechanic: *Well, I can't promise anything. The manager is out of town this week. I'll check with him when he gets back.*

Cell that represents strategies being employed: <u>A1</u>

Institution

	(1) Avoidance	(2) Procedural Persuasion	(3) Substantive Persuasion	(4) Adjustment	(5) Suppression
Petition (A)	A1	A2	A3	A4	A5
Appeal (B)	B1	B2	B3	B4	B5
Promulgation (C)	C1	C2	C3	C4	C5
Organizing (D)	D1	D2	D3	D4	D5
Resistance (E)	E1	E2	E3	E4	E5

Individual

DIALOGUE 1

Manager: *What can I do for you?*

You: *You can fix my car. I brought it in here, and someone didn't tighten the oil drain plug properly when I had the oil changed. It won't run now, and I want it repaired.*

Manager: *The oil was in the engine when it left our station, wasn't it? We can't be responsible for something that happened after you left our station.*

You: *I want my car repaired to the condition it was in when I brought it here. What are you going to do about it?*

Manager: *I'm sorry. There's nothing we can do unless you agree to pay for the repairs.*

Cell that represents strategies being employed: _____

DIALOGUE 2

You: *Two weeks ago I brought my car to your station at 45th and Cook Boulevard for an oil change and grease job. Someone failed to tighten the oil drain plug, and the oil drained from my engine. My engine is ruined, and I want it repaired to its original condition.*

District manager: *Let me check with the station, and I'll call you right back.*

You: *I'll be waiting for your call, but I want my car repaired.*

District manager: *I checked with the people at the station, and it appears that your facts are correct. We'll either have the car repaired for you or pay for reasonable repairs at a garage you choose. We apologize for your inconvenience and hope that you will continue to do business at some of our other stations.*

Cell which represents strategies being employed: _____

SUMMARY

The potential for conflict is always present in life. A predominant American value is that conflict is usually undesirable and should be avoided. But some conflicts are inevitable, necessary, and even desirable. Conflicts do not always result from poor communication, nor will they always be resolved by good communication.

Intrapersonal conflict often occurs because of the demands various roles and situations place upon the individual. Other intrapersonal conflict occurs when various values must complete for priority in a role or situation. People often experience intrapersonal conflict because they seek but cannot achieve perfection.

Interpersonal conflicts may be differentiated along several dimensions. One dimension is whether the conflict is over scare resources. Interpersonal conflicts are often seen by the participants as win-lose situations. A second dimension of conflict involves the goals of the parties. A problem-solving outcome of a conflict usually requires mutual understanding of both parties' goals. Conflicts may also be differentiated according to the relative power of the parties. An understanding of the power bases and vulnerability of the parties is essential in dealing with most conflicts.

Conflict-management strategies include the following:

1   *Problem solving.* Problem solving assumes that both parties can be winners. Issues are openly discussed, and the goals of the opponents are understood. Power differences are minimized.

2   *Forcing.* Forcing strategies create win-lose situations. Power differences are emphasized, as are differences in goals of the parties. In forcing strategies, the most powerful party wins.

3   *Compromise.* Compromise usually treats resources as scarce. In this strategy, neither party can win, but each can prevent the other from winning. Usually, neither party finds a satisfactory solution.

4   *Smoothing and Withdrawal.* Smoothing and withdrawal are used mainly to put off or avoid conflicts, not resolve them. They can be used positively to diffuse more serious forms of hostility, but they lead to trouble if they are the only strategies used to deal with conflict.

5   *Reframing.* Reframing is a nontraditional strategy for resolving conflict. It involves a change in the way the parties view the situation. This can be accomplished by getting the parties out of a more-of-the same situation.

Individuals dealing with large institutions frequently find themselves in conflict with the institution. In such a situation, several strategies are available to the individual: petition (the least cost and involvement), appeal, promulgation, organizing, and resistance (the most costly). The institution also has a series of strategies at its disposal: avoidance, procedural persuasion, substantive persuasion, adjustment, and suppression.

CHAPTER 7
CROSSING CULTURAL
DIFFERENCES

The following passage was written by a Peace Corps volunteer:

Life is very slow here and plenty real. It will be sporting for you at first—to be constantly adored as the strangest and most god-like individual ever to have turned his eye onto an isolated village, otherwise unknown. Very soon, I think, the game goes out of it. Then you must know what you're there for, what you are going to do, and why. I think you should have the answers ready because you're going to need them.

Let me describe a somewhat typical day in my life as a change agent. A chicken wakes me up, he is crowing about something indiscernible to me: Not even the chicken speaks English. Language is essential. . . . I brush my teeth for a while, not that they really need brushing, but this is a habit I've formed. The lady next door is watching from a screenless window. I feel a sense of pride that, having been awake for only ten minutes, I am already functioning as an agent of change. Trouble is, my neighbor's teeth are hopelessly blackened. She's about as likely to adopt my technique as I am to begin chewing betel nut.

Later, at a restaurant in the village marketplace, run by a retired prostitute, I order a bottle of orange soda. I've been ordering this every morning partly because I don't trust the water . . . and partly because it is the nearest equivalent to orange juice. She looks at me, in disgust, as if to say, "What the hell kind of man would drink orange soda pop for breakfast?"

A crowd begins to gather. Eating breakfast is my first big performance of the day. I sit as tall as I can and eat with vigor. I invite the nearest villagers to sit down with me—the ultimate of democratic gestures—but they refuse, as expected, because it's not their place to be seen eating with a superior. They're not sure whether I'm a superior or not, but they know I was placed there by some distant and very important machinery of government; they are, consequently playing it safe.

Small talk concerning hunger, food customs, and health soon leads to a question beyond my language capabilities. "Eh?" This is the word which I use most often during the day. The villager repeats his question, leaving me even more confused. One of the other peasants explains to the questioner that he must speak very slowly because the foreigner does not know "how to listen to our language." A couple of children giggle and repeat: "Foreigner." In their language the word also means the guava fruit, and, with a short modifier, bird manure.

The crowd thins. This curious new thing in town, a full-grown man who does not know how to speak, can sustain interest for only so long. I walk around the market, and stop to thump a few pineapples. I don't know how a good pineapple should thump, but this seems to be the proper thing to do, like kicking tires in a car lot.

Later, with a government change agent who is my counterpart, I visit the local barber shop. There are a half-dozen men seated in the barber shop and my colleague says a few brisk words to them in his language. The man in the barber's chair gets up and takes a place on a bench. I try to indicate that I want to wait my turn, but my language fails me. The barber, smiling, waits with cloth in hand. All eyes watch me. My counterpart says, "You sit down there." Everyone seems happy about it.

We retire to a tavern for rice whisky. There are five glasses on the table: one for me, one for my colleague, three for some soldiers. There are a dozen more persons around the table, but they are only peasants, watching the soldiers drink.

The sergeant at my right seems to be in charge; he is a counterinsurgency soldier. He explains that they have come to check over the village. He wears a pistol. He is drunk. He hates Communists.

By means of his G.I. English and my meager knowledge of his language, we reach a few understandings. He questions me about who I am and what I am doing. I have written my English name, to which I add "Peace Corps, U.S.A." He assumes that we are in the same line of work. He is anxious to prove to me his knowledge of propaganda and other counterinsurgency methods.

"Allies," he says in English.

"Allies," I agree.

"The American country and our countries—allies. You and me. We know how to kill the Communists together." He eyes the intent crowd keenly.

I hold up my hands. I announce, for the second time, as clearly and publicly as my vocabulary will allow, "I am not a soldier. I am a volunteer come from America to help the peasant, because you and the American are a pair of friends together."

The sergeant has another drink. "Allies," he says, and then: "Help the rotten villager. Look at this man." He orders him to stand up. "We help this man. This man is always lazy. This man is always dirty. Look."

The best way to handle those soldiers is to stay away from them. I decide to leave. I look over at the peasants who sit with their hands folded soberly. I had not even remembered to invite them to drink with us.

By way of a parting gesture, I order two bottles of whisky. The soldiers protest; this is their party, they pay. Then I order six glasses, which I pass out to the villagers. We drink, I shake hands with each person, including the soldiers and my counterpart. This is not the customary manner of taking leave, but they know that Americans always shake hands and say "okay," or "hello," or "goodby."

As I leave, the sergeant winks at me and says one English word: "Psychology." I wink back. "Psychology."

Now read this second story.

Rick and Pamela had been married for about a year. She suddenly began to pick fights with him over small matters, which seemed out of character for her. She sometimes nagged if he did not come home precisely when she expected. She commented that he did not care about her. The resulting fighting and unhappiness finally led the couple to seek marriage counseling.

The counselor quickly discovered that a major period of stress for the relationship occurred when the couple met at home after Rick had worked all day at his office. The following facts also emerged: When Pamela was a child, her father always came home at the same time each day. Before he left his job for the day, he would also call her mother to say that he was on his way. When he arrived home, he would hug and kiss his wife for about thirty seconds. When Rick was a child, his father might come home from work at widely varying times. He almost never called in advance. When he entered the house, his greeting to his wife was entirely verbal. He would stand across the room from his wife, and the two would exchange conversation about the day's events.

The counselor noted that both Rick and Pamela were behaving in ways that they thought were most appropriate to the situation but that the expectations of each were different. Pamela thought that Rick's practice of coming home at varying times and greeting her with words showed lack of attention and love because she was used to a man who came home at one time and who called first. Furthermore, she interpreted Rick's verbal greeting as rather standoffish. Rick, on the other hand, felt that Pamela was complaining unjustly and asking him to keep to an unreasonable schedule.

These two stories have something in common: Both describe difficulties that communicators face in their expectations about another's communication behavior. This is obvious in the first story because the communicators involved speak different native languages and were reared in cultural backgrounds widely different from each other. The expectation differences in the second example are of a different order. Rick and Pamela share a language and cultural background. But each has some routine expectations about behavior that the other does not share. The problems of the Peace Corps volunteer involve expectations tied in with language, race, and country of origin. Pamela and Rick's social expectations grew out of smaller social groups, their childhood families. When communication occurs between people from different nationalities, racial groups, or language communities, it is called *intercultural communication.*

Intercultural communication and the special problems it presents are the subjects of this chapter. We will not teach you a set of details to make you an expert on the subject of other cultures, but we will present a set of concepts and skills that you can use to figure out how to deal with intercultural communication.

Intercultural communication is a topic that suggests remote places, famous diplomats, and world travelers; as such, you may think that it is a remote subject. It may seem less remote when you realize that nearly all communications have an intercultural dimension, a sense in which *differences in cultural expectations lead to communication problems* (our definition of intercultural communication). Admittedly, communication between strangers from different nations is likely to be more complex than communication between members of different racial groups who live in the same city but who have different expectations. Nevertheless, each kind of interaction can be examined from an intercultural standpoint.

In Chapter 1, we discussed the importance of common fields of experience. That is, communicators who have had similar experiences will share a larger number of meanings with each other than those who have had different kinds of experiences will. Two communicators from similar cultural backgrounds who had lived through rather similar experiences might be pictured this way:

```
┌─────────────────────────────────┐
│ A's experience │  B's experience │
└─────────────────────────────────┘
```

But two communicators from diverse cultural settings, different levels of economic well-being, different educational levels, and so on might be pictured this way:

```
┌──────────────────┐──────────────────┐
│ A's experience  │  B's experience   │
└──────────────────┘──────────────────┘
```

Most of the overlapping information in common fields of experience can be called *social information.* Such information is less about a communicator as an individual than it is about the communicator as a member of some group. Your cultural background is a set of social information associated with residence in a location and membership in a group of communicators. For example, the answers to the following questions would be cultural information:

What is your nationality?
How wealthy are you?
What is your language?
What is your ethnicity?

Each question asks about cultural groups you belong to. There is a group of U.S. citizens of which you may be a member. There is a group of persons whose family income is between $5,000 and $10,000 per year. There are groups of people speaking your language. There are groups of people sharing any given racial characteristic. In contrast, the following questions index social information that is not cultural information:

Does your family demonstrate affection physically?
Do you belong to a college fraternity?
Do you participate in sports?

These questions also relate to groups to which you belong, but these groups are not strongly related to nation, race, or language. Rather, these social questions concern groups of associates with whom you identify (see Chapter 10). Differences in expectations that these groups give rise to may be more subtle than intercultural differences.

Finally, the following questions are not about social matters at all. Instead, they are about you as one person:

Are you ambitious?
Are you shy?
Do you like to quarrel?
What is your self-concept like?

Questions such as these call for *individual* information, unique to one person.

We do not mean to suggest that there are neat, hard-and-fast lines separating individual information, social information, and cultural information. In some cases, the distinctions are difficult to make. For example, if Jack wears a ring on his index finger today he is just wearing a ring. If you notice this about him every day for a month, you might classify him as "one of those people who wear rings on their index fingers." He is defined as a member of a group as well as an individual. When that step takes place, the thinking turns to social features. You might consider yourself to be one of those persons who wears rings on the index finger. If so, you may feel that wearing rings on index fingers is part of the common field of experience that you share with Jack.

If Jack wears a ring on his index finger but you never have considered such a thing, chances are you might communicate about that fact to someone. You might ask him about it, but you would probably find someone else who is not wearing an index finger ring and point out Jack's. You would have chosen to communicate with the person with whom you have a common field of experience (not wearing index finger rings). At this point, some problems of intercultural communication might arise:

Person 1: Do you notice that that guy is wearing a ring on his index finger?
Person 2: Oh, all Polacks do that.

Person 2 not only makes judgments about the existence of a group of people who wear index finger rings but also makes a (probably) disapproving cultural-group evaluation of the practice. This represents a sort of guilt by association. Everyone makes such cultural judgments many times every day. Most seem to work out fairly well. But every now and then—for example, when talking to a black person or a person who does not speak English—people make erroneous cultural judgments. Such occasions provide examples of problems in intercultural communication.

Some students have expressed the opinion that only career diplomats, social workers, and anthropologists need to study intercultural communication and that for everyone else intercultural communication might only come in handy on a trip to a foreign country. But we believe some awareness of intercultural communication is necessary every minute of the day.

Experience 7.1 will show you that you, too, make all kinds of cultural judgments in everyday life.

EXPERIENCE 7.1 CULTURAL JUDGMENTS

DIRECTIONS For each of the following situations, make a snap judgment about what you might infer or guess on the basis of the description. Then describe your probable response. Finally, add two descriptions of your own and respond to them.

EXAMPLE

Description	*My judgment*	*What I might do*
A male student from Iran displays strong body odor when you get close to him on the elevator.	This person does not bathe often. That might be OK in Iran, but I have a feeling of disgust.	I might turn away from him and avoid him. I certainly would not speak to him.

	Description	*My judgment*	*What I might do*
1	A woman acquaintance wears sheer blouses.		
2	A male from Panama appears to stand awfully close to you when you talk to him.		
3	A male acquaintance speaks in a high-pitched voice and wears bright purple shirts.		
4	Your best friend of the opposite sex expresses a dislike of french kissing.		
5	You are considering buying your friend's car. You offer him $100 less than his price. He looks offended and hurt.		
6			
7			

Review your reactions to each of the situations in Experience 7.1. Label each judgment you made as involving individual differences, social group differences, or cultural differences. Did you use different procedures for responding to different kinds of situations? Compare your responses with those of friends and classmates to see whether everyone agrees on which differences are cultural.

In order to understand the difficulties of crossing cultural differences, examine how the groups you belong to come to exert such strong influences over you. No one knows exactly how culture becomes part of communication behavior, but some theories have been offered. In any communication situation, communicators make predictions about appropriate behaviors. The more you function within any group, the more accurate you become at picking up what others expect you to do.

These expectations are based on what has happened before. The first time an event happens, you may not think about it too much. But if any behavior seems successful, you are likely to try the same behavior again later. By that next time, you will have begun to expect another favorable outcome. After dozens of repetitions, your expectation is so definite that to violate it seems almost impossible. Here are a few expectations Americans usually develop:

1   Public restrooms will be labeled by sex of users. Adults use only the same-sex restroom.
2   When walking around outdoors, grown-ups wear clothing that conceals their genitals and generally their chest (especially true for women).
3   When a stranger passes you on the sidewalk, you begin to look away from him or her when the two of you are about eight feet apart.
4   If all seats on a public vehicle (bus or subway) are taken, you stand.

Of course, these are only a few of the culturally normative expectations people assume and use all the time. Think about these examples as you read the following stories:

1   Bob visits his old college while on a vacation. He graduated ten years ago. He is on the fourth floor of a classroom building at eight o'clock on a Saturday morning. Nobody else is in the building. He is badly in need of a public restroom but can find only a women's room. He hesitates long at the door. Finally, he enters, his heart beating wildly, and hastily uses the facility. Then he bursts through the door, fully expecting someone, perhaps a crowd of people, to greet him with howls of derision. A wave of relief floods him as the door closes and he is alone in the hall.
2   The fireman reported that a woman was found burned to death in the front room of the house, right next to an open door. Apparently she did not run outside because she had no clothes on.

3   You decide to experiment with looking at strangers as they pass you on the sidewalk. Instead of breaking eye contact with them, you continue to look at them. Usually, they look away and hurry past. Sometimes they return your glance, smile, and say hello. Your heart beat speeds up; it is an intense experience. Sometimes they return your glance and do not smile. You feel your own face becoming hard, even hostile. You feel like a peeping tom who gets caught.

4   The teacher of the psychology seminar (Stanley Milgram) asked the students to perform the following experiment: On a full subway, approach a stranger of your own sex and ask, matter-of-factly, "Excuse me, may I have your seat?" Most students were unable to do this. Those who did reported that it was one of the most difficult experiences they could remember.

The point of these stories is that most humans conform quite rigidly to cultural norms. They behave in a way that is not usually expected, they become agitated, fearful of the consequences, even though they may have only a very vague idea of what those consequences would be. For example, is there any law against using an opposite-sex restroom? Would anyone have disapproved if the woman had run out of the burning building naked?

People feel constrained by social-cultural norms. They have internalized those norms and follow them more reliably than they follow orders. If they violate norms, or if others do, then reactions may be surprisingly extreme. People's reactions to young men with long hair, women who do not shave their legs, young adults who live communally tend to be visceral-emotive reactions.

Which items in Experience 7.1 did you react to emotionally? You may or may not have reacted predictably. You may have had a cross-cultural shock reaction to some items but not to others. The reason why not all students have the same reactions to Experience 7.1 is that there are cultural differences among people.

What are the things that really bother you, to which you react emotively in a way that seems to involve cultural norms? Experience 7.2 will help you to answer that question.

EXPERIENCE 7.2 NORMATIVE REACTIONS

DIRECTIONS   **Describe four events that would really surprise you and violate your cultural norms. Then describe how you would probably respond. The examples are not meant to prescribe what should offend you; they are merely examples of past responses to this experience.**

EXAMPLES   *Event description*   *My probable reaction*

I arrive at school and remove my   **I would put my coat on hurriedly**
winter coat only to discover that I   **and go home, even if it meant miss-**
forgot to put on a shirt.   **ing school and an important test.**

I see someone setting an   **I would scream at that person, try**
American flag on fire.   **to grab the flag, and fight if**
                                            necessary.

1 _____   _____
  _____   _____
2 _____   _____
  _____   _____
3 _____   _____
  _____   _____
4 _____   _____
  _____   _____

Now that you have completed Experience 7.2, it may be relevant
to ask yourself how the items that you cited there got to be so
troublesome. Can you remember any childhood experiences that
reinforce your feelings. Can you remember any sayings or childhood
rhymes you used to say that fit the pattern? Can you remember any
stories you knew or heard while young?

Stories, whether from books, TV, or people, seem to be a
prominent mode of learning about one's culture. Think, for instance, of
the norm, important to the authors' childhoods, that men should rarely
express their feelings, that men's faces should show control. The theme
dominated cowboy movies of that time. The strong, silent hero never
said anything about personal feelings; his feelings were observable only
through decisive actions he took, such as bringing bad guys to justice.
The most extreme example was the Lone Ranger, a mysterious man
dedicated to justice who always spoke in a quiet monotone and wore a
mask over his face.

Try to remember one story you knew as a child that illustrates
each of the four norms you chose. Write out the stories in detail if you
can. Compare stories with classmates or friends. See whether you all
heard similar stories. Differences between your stories and those of
others are likely to represent cultural differences between you. Such
differences can lead to cross-cultural communication problems. Such
differences also keep life fascinating.

In a sense it does not matter very much how common fields of experience get built. The point is that people use them. You try to communicate with others by seeing what you have in common with each other, making guesses about what groups the other person belongs to, and trying to put youself in the other person's shoes.

Generally, you are unaware that all this is taking place. It all seems to happen so smoothly when communicators have lived through similar backgrounds. Communicators can simply assume that others have the same beliefs and belong to many of the same groups they do. But when you talk to someone from a very different cultural background, that assumption is no longer valid.

A person who wishes to communicate across cultural differences is often given lots of advice about how to behave: "Be yourself." "Develop empathy with the other." "Communicate with others as you would have them communicate with you." The problem in trying to apply such advice is that when someone's field of experience is markedly different from your own, you often lack sufficient data about how the other person is responding to you to put yourself in his or her shoes. An example of this dilemma occurred when an organization that had been experiencing breakdowns in communication decided to schedule some interracial sensitivity sessions. The caucasian members of the organization were shocked to find that they as individuals were seen by black members of the group as problems. One white member expressed this shock in a parable form:

> It is as if a group of lions had walked into the sheep meadow and sat down with the sheep, saying, "I know what it's like to be a sheep and attacked by lions." The lions come in with warmth and friendship, sheathing their claws and their strength and smiling warmly. And then they're dismayed, shocked and hurt to discover that the sheep don't trust them! They say things like: "Some of my best friends are sheep. When I was a kid I palled around with sheep. I never ate any sheep. My family did and all the lions I grew up with did but I never did. Of course, when we grew up and started in with our jobs—you sheep doing your job of lying around and grazing and us lions getting to our work of chasing animals and killing them for food (after all, we are meat-eaters)—then my sheep friends and I tended to grow apart. But I still have the greatest respect for all the sheep that I see, and I tell my kids that they should always be nice to any sheep that they see and never kill any of them except if they have to feed their kids or protect property values or things like that."
>
> The lions are astonished when they find out that the friendly sheep have always been mad at being kept in the meadows and being chewed up on occasion. They always thought that the sheep liked the way it was, and that the sheep understood that all the lions were trying to do was to keep their children well-behaved and well-educated at school, that all they cared about was that their young cubs should grow up to be outstanding and upstanding Lion Club members.

And it is with real horror and anguish, soon turning to fear, that the lions discover that many of the sheep have actually turned into Panthers.*

Why is interpersonal communication with someone from a culture markedly different from your own so difficult? Why should it involve particular difficulties and pitfalls that are somewhat different from those encountered in other types of communication? To examine these questions, complete Experience 7.3.

* Ferdinand Jones and Myron W. Harris, ''The Development of Interracial Awareness in Small Groups,'' in *Confrontation: Encounters in Self and Interpersonal Awareness*, ed. Leonard Blank, Gloria B. Gottsegen, and Monroe G. Gottsegen (New York: Macmillan, 1971) pp. 417–418.

EXPERIENCE   7.3   AN INTERCULTURAL ENCOUNTER

DIRECTIONS   **Describe the essential details of a communication encounter you had with someone who is culturally different from you. The other person need not be a native of another nation; A young person (under five) or a person from a different ethnic background will do.**

1   **Who was the other person in the encounter?**

2   **How well did you know the person before the encounter?**

3   **Describe briefly what happened.**

4   **Which of your norms or values were important in the encounter?**

5   **What did you perceive some of the other persons's norms or values to be in the encounter?**

6   **On what basis did you predict what some of the other person's reactions to you and to the situation might be?**

7   **What difficulties occurred as a result of your not being able to understand the other person's language?**

8 On the basis of what you have read so far in this chapter, what would you do differently if confronted with a similar situation?

Experience 7.3 points to a number of the difficulties faced by communicators crossing cultural differences.

First, it is likely that you did not know the other person well. Our society, like most societies, structures interaction so that people talk mostly to others of similar cultural background. It is fairly unlikely that persons who are culturally different will become close associates. This is a vicious circle because only by communication (sharing) with different cultural groups can groups build up a common field of experience and successfully cross cultural differences.

In a sense, half the battle is over if you get to know a person better. When people get to know each other better, they interact mostly

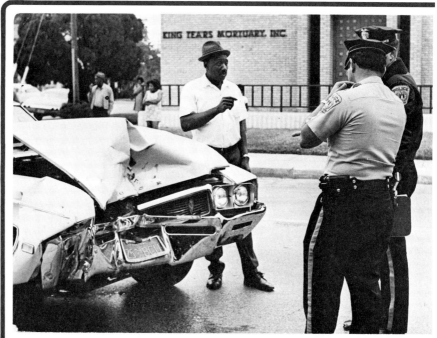

Sometimes the difficulties of an intercultural encounter are compounded by troubled circumstances or by rules about authority.

on the basis of what they know about each other as individuals, rather than on the basis of guesses about social or cultural information. Thus, you often hear close friends who are culturally different say things like, "I hardly think of Jon as a white person anymore. He's just an individual with virtues and faults like any other individual." Such an observation is accurate and helpful. It also represents an ideal: When you can use information about another person as an individual, communication is likely to be more efficient and accurate than communication structured mainly on the basis of cultural information.

But what do you do while you wait to get to know another person? What do you do when you are not really interested in a close relationship with the other but merely wish to share a table at a restaurant or buy a new pair of shoes? On such occasions, cultural information is the main determinant of how the other person is likely to react to your messages.

Second, you may have noted that different cultures seem to use different value systems and work toward different objectives in life. In Chapter 6, we discussed value conflicts faced by individuals. In this chapter, we concentrate on differences in values across cultures. Problems may emerge in communicating with people from other cultures because you assume that they value the same practices and things that you value. Cultural differences in *codes* (language and nonverbal codes) are related to cultural differences in value systems. Communicators must have common symbols in order to get messages across to each other. This is not always a problem, but accents, dialects, and idioms can get in the way of effective communication if these usages trigger negative stereotypes in receivers.

The rest of this chapter will examine the problems of differences in values and codes. We will not tell you particular tricks to use with members of different cultures. Nor will we suggest how to relate to Afro-Americans or Europeans or Mexicans or any cultural groups. Rather, we will emphasize the kinds of inferences and guesses you have to make in everyday interactions. Remember that all communication is to some extent intercultural.

VALUES IN INTERCULTURAL COMMUNICATION

How do you feel about the custom of brushing your teeth? Most North American adults feel clean after brushing their teeth and believe they are taking proper care of their teeth by brushing. The description written by the Peace Corps volunteer in Asia indicates that there are cultures in which brushing the teeth is of little value. The Peace Corps worker notes that it would be very difficult to persuade Asians to brush their teeth because they have no notion of why he finds the practice valuable. When persons from markedly different social groups communicate, a problem often emerges if the parties attempt to make clear what similarities and differences in values each brings to a communication situation.

Values can lead to communication difficulties even when communicators are culturally similar if communicators do not make clear to each other where value differences exist. In the case of Rick and Pamela, for instance, the communicators differed in norms but held similar values. Rick had customarily greeted Pamela only with talk to show affection. Pamela had expected physical contact to show affection. But both shared the value that husbands and wives should feel affection for each other and should demonstrate that feeling through affectionate behavior. Given these similarities, the simple act of pointing out that each valued certain forms of expression improved communication dramatically.

This example points up the differences between norms and values. Norms show themselves as everyday acts that we use to communicate values, but the acts are not the values. Rick and Pamela, for instance, shared the value that affection is central to a marriage. Only their norms for expressing this value differed. Problems of intercultural communication usually result from the *inference* that someone else's behavior violates your values.

Look back at the examples of intercultural problems that you listed in Experience 7.1. Did you infer a value difference from a norm violation. That error can be fairly easy to prevent if you become aware of your norms and values.

The problem is more difficult if parties differ in both values and norms. Suppose, for instance, Rick and Pamela did *not* both value affection in marriage? Would this not have made communication more difficult? Suppose the counselor said, "Rick, your wife is asking you for a display of your feelings of affection." Suppose that Rick responded, "Well, I don't think that a man should express such feelings. Besides, I'm not sure that man and wife should try to cultivate too much affection." Most of you would think that Rick is a cold fish. That is because most of you share the value that couples should feel and express affection for each other. But remember, not all cultural groups share this value. Imagine a culture in which all marriages are arranged by the parents of the bride and groom for political or economic reasons and in which any open expression of tender feelings could be construed as a sign of weakness. In such a culture, Rick's behavior might be normal and Pamela's would be abnormal. The point is that in intercultural communication, there is no such thing as abnormal values; there are only different values. If Pamela had come from an affectionate, demonstrative culture and Rick had come from a standoffish, undemonstrative culture, both could indulge in behavior that they think is clear and normal, and both parties could perceive the other as perverse.

To get a better understanding of how this valuing process works, complete Experience 7.4.

EXPERIENCE 7.4 AMERICAN VALUES

DIRECTIONS   Indicate your agreement or disagreement with the following statements by circling *SA* if you strongly agree with the statement, *A* if you agree, *N* if you hold no strong feelings either way, *D* if you disagree, and *SD* if you strongly disagree.

1   People are basically rational.
SA   A   N   D   SD

2   The best ideas and products usually win out in the free marketplace.
SA   A   N   D   SD

3   People are responsible for their own destinies.
SA   A   N   D   SD

4   The best ideas are often the simplest ones.
SA   A   N   D   SD

5   Individuals in our society can best be viewed as independent, unique, decision-making personalities.
SA   A   N   D   SD

6   If people fail to succeed in our society, it is because they are somehow personally inadequate.
SA   A   N   D   SD

7   Every individual, regardless of background, has the opportunity to rise in our economic and social system.
SA   A   N   D   SD

8   Changes in the way we do things are both necessary and beneficial.
SA   A   N   D   SD

9   The best ideas are often those that are most practical.
SA   A   N   D   SD

10   Good housing, nutrition, transportation, and medical care are essential for every individual in our society.
SA   A   N   D   SD

     The statements in Experience 7.4 reflect some values that run deep in American tradition and culture. You probably agreed with more of them than you disagreed with. Americans generally believe that people are rational, responsible for themselves, capable of making decisions for themselves, and have equality of opportunity. There is a pragmatic strain in most Americans that likes practical and efficient ideas. They also tend to value change, progress, and scientific ways of doing things, and they place high value on material comforts and obtaining the necessities of a comfortable life.

There is nothing wrong with the statements in Experience 7.4. In fact, we tend to agree with them ourselves. But to members of certain cultures, such pragmatic belief in progress, for example, seems absurd. Even in countries that are quite similar to the United States, widespread differences from some of these attitudes are quite common. In Britain, for instance, items 6 and 7 would probably provoke some disagreement. English society is more class-conscious than American society, and moving to a higher station in life is comparatively rare.

If someone disagrees with your values, that does not mean that the person is wrong, a fool, or crazy. Usually, it means that that person is somewhat culturally different from you. If you jump to conclusions about another person on the basis of information that that person's culture interprets differently, then you are acting ethnocentrically.

If you travel to Egypt, you may see adult males strolling in public hand in hand or arm in arm. If you are disgusted with this practice and think about homosexuality, you are responding in an ethnocentric manner. If your car breaks down while you are in Egypt and you find that it takes three weeks to get fixed and you become enraged after the

An activity that is highly valued in one cultural setting may be despised or ridiculed in another.

first four days of trying, your response may be ethnocentric. If you cannot bring yourself to eat raw fish or seaweed while traveling in Japan, you are responding ethnocentrically. All these examples concern a response that happens on a gut level. You have encountered something that is strange or even taboo in many sections of the United States but appropriate in the culture where you have observed it.

You may believe that you are a mature person who would not react in these ways. You may be correct; some travelers react quite well to foreign customs. Others find the experience of visiting a foreign culture quite upsetting. You have learned to respond quite automatically in your culture. When you travel to another culture, those responses are still automatic, but they become less appropriate. For example, on a first trip to Mexico, many North Americans are shocked by the condition of public restrooms. The facilities are not clean by U.S. standards, and toilet paper is rarely provided. Suppose that you are on your first visit to Mexico and that you need to use a public restroom. You are appalled at the squalor, but you decide to use the toilet anyway. You reach for the paper, only to find that there is none. You are in a vulnerable position. You are used to having toilet paper there when you need it. When you are at home, and the paper runs out, you can ask someone else to get some or get some from a cabinet. But if you are in a public place in Mexico, none of those options are available. At such trying moments, some tourists get angry. They enter the first phase of what is usually called *culture shock.*

Culture shock is what happens when your expectations of what is normal are routinely violated by others around you simply because they belong to different cultures that have different values and practices. You value toilet paper and the standard of cleanliness you feel it implies. Most North Americans share those values. But they do not apply in Mexico. Some U.S. tourists think Mexico is squalid and unhealthy. Can you see how that constitutes an ethnocentric response?

Suppose you show your outrage to a Mexican: "Hey, don't you people ever clean your restrooms?" The Mexican will quite justifiably treat you like a fool or worse. According to the Mexican's rules, you are behaving inappropriately. The Mexican probably regards you as a stereotypical Yankee who keeps getting upset over trivial things. If you cannot find anyone who understands your outrage, your anger may increase, and that makes you very vulnerable. You are likely to have a wretched vacation, become depressed, get distracted and have an accident, become ill, or have a host of other problems.

You can do much to ease such problems by accepting the fact that persons from many cultures simply do not share mainstream U.S. values. Experience 7.5 will show you the extent to which your values are not shared by the other peoples of the world.

EXPERIENCE   7.5   WORLDWIDE VALUES

DIRECTIONS   Here is a list of values that some people hold. For each value, indicate
whether it is of primary (*P*), secondary (*S*), or negligible (*N*) importance
to you by placing a check mark in the appropriate column. After you
have completed this task, compare your classifications with those of
your classmate, and discuss similarities and differences in values.

Value	*Primary importance*	*Secondary importance*	*Not important*
Individuality			
Motherhood			
Hierarchy			
Gratefulness			
Peace			
Money			
Modesty			
Punctuality			
Saviorism*			
Karma**			
Firstness			
Aggressiveness			
Collective responsibility			
Respect for elders			
Respect for youth			
Hospitality for guests			
Inherited property			
Conservation			
Color of skin			
Sacredness of farmland			
Equality of women			
Human dignity			
Efficiency			
Patriotism			
Religion			
Authoritarianism			
Education			
Frankness			
Masculinity			

* *Saviorism:* the notion that a person or idea can solve most problems.
** *Karma:* the belief that actions of past (even past lives) continue to affect us. That is,
suffering pays for past wrong.

The values listed in Experience 7.5 were used by Sitaram and Cogdell to determine what values are universal or held by many cultures. Sitaram and Cogdell classify the values listed as of "primary," "secondary," or "tertiary" importance, which is very similar to your rating of the values as of primary secondary, or negligible importance to you. Values that were rarely mentioned as important were assigned to a "negligible" category (of little or no importance). Sitaram and Cogdell classify cultures into five broad categories.

1   Western (W) cultures include caucasians who live in the Americas and Europe.
2   Eastern (E) cultures refers to cultures dominated by Hindu or Buddhist historical backgrounds.
3   Black (B) cultures refers to Afro-Americans.
4   African (A) cultures refers to common factors in continental Africa.
5   Muslim (M) cultures refers to those in which Islam has traditionally been the predominant system of belief.

Please note that these categories are not strictly geographic. Hindus and Muslims often live in the same country or the same town, as do Anglo-Americans and Afro-Americans. The classifications reflect the values of those involved, not their geography.

Table 7.1 (page 181) presents Sitaram and Cogdell's conclusions about which cultures share which values. It is interesting to note that nine of the values in Experience 7.5 are of primary or secondary importance to nearly all groups. Yet, there are surely political and cultural differences in how these values are expressed (norms), and members of each group may have some disagreements. Eight values are of at least some importance in all the cultural groups examined:

1   Hierarchy (the value of authority)
2   Masculinity
3   Respect for youth
4   Human dignity
5   Patriotism
6   Religion
7   Education
8   Frankness

The interesting thing about the Experience 7.5 list is that these are values about which you would probably expect members of other cultures to have some strong feelings. In contrast, six values held by Westerners are not considered of primary importance in any cultural settings.

1   Individuality
2   Punctuality
3   Saviorism
4   Firstness (as in being first on the moon)
5   Equality of women
6   Efficiency

TABLE 7.1   **Worldwide values**

W = Western   E = Eastern   B = Black (Afro-American)
A = African   M = Muslim

Value	Primary importance	Secondary importance	Not important
Individuality	W	B	EM
Motherhood	BE	MW	—
Hierarchy	WEMA	B	—
Gratefulness	EA	MB	W
Peace	E	B	WAM
Money	WAB	M	E
Modesty	E	BAM	W
Punctuality	W	B	MEA
Saviorism	W	M	EBM
Karma	E	—	MWBA
Firstness	W	B	EAM
Aggressiveness	WB	M	AE
Collective responsibility	EAM	B	W
Respect for elders	EAM	B	W
Respect for youth	W	MABE	—
Hospitality for guests	EA	B	MW
Inherited property	E	—	MWAB
Preservation of environment	E	BA	WM
Color of skin	EWB	M	A
Sacredness of farmland	E	A	BMW
Equality of women	W	EB	AM
Human dignity	WB	EAM	—
Efficiency	W	B	EM
Patriotism	BMAE	W	—
Religion	WBMAE	—	—
Authoritarianism	EMA	WB	—
Education	WB	EAM	—
Frankness	W	BEMA	—
Masculinity	BMEWA	—	—

If you express these values in a speech to a culturally different audience, you should be less than surprised if that audience is less than enthusiastic. They also may have ways of being impolite that you are not used to.

It is necessary, as we have noted, to be careful about what generalities we draw from Sitaram and Cogdell's chart in Table 7.1. It is easy to use the educated guesses in this table to form stereotypes of persons from other cultures. For instance, you could say that Easterners (E) place high value on motherhood, hierarchy, masculinity, gratefulness, peace, modesty, karma, collective responsibility, and so on but place little (negligible) value on aggressiveness, saviorism, and individuality.

To get an idea how dangerous such generalities can be, choose the column that most closely resembles you. If you are a Westerner (W), the table says that you are someone who primarily values individuality, hierarchy, masculinity, money, punctuality, saviorism, firstness, aggressiveness, respect for youth, color of skin, equality of women, human dignity, efficiency, patriotism, religion, education, and frankness. If you are like most of the students who have compared the table's list with their own classifications in Experience 7.5, you will probably say that you are not a typical member of the culture. You probably disagreed with some of the values Americans hold most dear (according to Sitaram and Cogdell). Your friends' values probably resemble yours more closely than they resemble those specified in Table 7.1. It is unlikely that that one person will be entirely typical of the culture. Obviously, some Americans are not patriotic or savioristic. The table is intended to refer to statistical norms for whole populations, not individuals.

In a sense then, Sitaram and Cogdell's findings represent cultural stereotypes. These stereotypes will have something in common with how many people from a given culture act, but they cannot be used to predict the behavior of each individual all the time. Stereotyping is a natural consequence of ways in which human perceptual systems work. Certain forms of stereotyping are closely allied to language and its use. Therefore, although we do not deal with stereotypes in general because the nature of stereotyping can be far removed from communication processes, we do discuss the process of linguistic stereotyping in intercultural communication.

LANGUAGE AND STEREOTYPING

Words do not have fixed meanings that belong to them, no matter what you may think when you use a dictionary. Rather, meanings are in people. Dictionaries try to describe the meanings that people hold in common for words. Dictionary definitions can be taken as clues to the meanings that humans assign to words, whether or not they are conscious of those meanings.

EXPERIENCE 7.6 DICTIONARY WORDS

DIRECTIONS **Look up the dictionary meanings of the following words. List briefly as many different meanings of each word as you can find.**

1 red _____

2 yellow _____

3   **white** ————————————————————

4   **black** ————————————————————

5   **mankind** ————————————————————

6   **dumb** ————————————————————

7   **blue** ————————————————————

**Racial
stereotypes**

    Dictionaries vary, but most of them note one major difference among the four color words listed in Experience 7.6: The word *white* has mostly fortunate and positive meanings; whereas the other three words, all of which are used to refer to ethnic minorities, have mostly unfortunate, negative meanings. The *Random House Unabridged Dictionary* includes the following definitions: *yellow*, "cowardly," "sensational [*yellow* journalism]," "envious," "jealous," and "sallow"; *red*, "radically left politically," "communist," "operating at a [financial] loss," and "angry"; *black*, "soiled," "gloomy," "pessimistic," "sullen," "deliberate," "harmful [a *black* lie]," and "evil [*black* magic]"; *white*, "free from spot or stain," "morally pure," "innocent [a *white* lie]," "harmless," "without malice [*white* magic]," "auspicious," "fortunate," "dependable," "honest," "silvery," and "radically conservative."

    Note that the word Caucasians use to describe their own race is assigned favorable interpretations; whereas the other race labels are assigned unfavorable ones. Do you think that is merely a coincidence? There is an interesting chicken-or-egg question here: Is it possible that the negative connotations are related to social realities? Is it possible that *white* means happy things because Caucasians are powerful in English-speaking countries? Members of certain cultures believe that there is a force (karma) which works in a small way through each small act to build the forces of evil in a person's life. The use of derogatory color words (or sex words) may work like that. That is, the user of the words intends no harm, but the harm exists in the usage nevertheless.

    Here is another interesting question: Are the colors of racial groups in the United States accurately represented by the color words commonly used? If you look carefully, you will see that Caucasians are not white at all; rather, they are a pink-beige color similar to peach ice cream. Native Americans are not actually red; they are a bronze-rust color. Orientals are not really yellow; they are slightly yellowish in relation to other skin tones. Blacks exhibit many shades of brown. Within each group, there is a wide variety of pigmentations. For example, there are many so-called Caucasians whose skin is darker than that of many so-called blacks.

    In fact, the designation of persons into racial categories is probably nonsense. It is likely that each reader of this book carries genetic input from members of two or three so-called racial groups.

The main point is that certain realities described by language are primarily sociocultural realities. For example, we could pick holes in the practice of using color words to refer to racial groups, as we have here, but the fact remains that the racial categories described are real to users of the English language. Just as you can tell a sentence from a nonsentence, you can tell a black from a Caucasian. In most cases, you can tell both by looks and by speech. Certain members of one group can pass for members of the other, but generally anyone can tell what racial group you belong to and can refer to it by using a color word. These words define cultural groups of speakers. People use these groupings in choosing neighborhoods, spouses, and most close friends, although in the U.S. government it is now illegal to use these categories to decide who gets a job, who may move into a neighborhood, or who may go to a particular school.

Boundaries between these cultural groups are often symbolized by language. After all, any language is spoken by people who form themselves into cultural groups. For example, consider the word *dumb*. Its original literal meaning referred to persons unable to speak. Many such persons also could not hear (*deaf and dumb*). Obviously, persons unable to speak become outsiders in most groups. Consequently, speakers are likely to think of them as stupid. Eventually, that connection led to the use of the word *dumb* to mean "unintelligent." Today, the "stupid" definition is the primary one given in some dictionaries.

Sexist language   A better example is the word *mankind*. It refers to all humanity, not just males. That is partly because the word came into use in a time when women were considered lesser beings than men. Today, language appears sexist because our culture is changing its values. Language will catch up eventually, but until it does, words such as *chairman, mailman, craftsman, linesman, draftsman, helmsman, spokesman, repairman*, and *headman* and phrases such as *all men are created equal* continue to reflect cultural realities that are out of date. Many English teachers still require that masculine pronouns be used whenever the antecedent is of indeterminate or mixed sex. Such linguistic wrinkles serve as constant reminders to women of inferior status, and that is why many communicators object to them, just as many object to referring to a black man as a *boy*. The use of masculine pronouns in indeterminate situations seems a strong blow to the self-respect of women because it implies the nonexistence of the female sex.

Just how pervasive are words that make men visible and women less so? Experience 7.7 presents a test case.

EXPERIENCE 7.7 SEXISM IN LANGUAGE

DIRECTIONS
(PART 1)

The following paragraph is taken from William Faulkner's Nobel Prize acceptance speech. Draw a line under all words that show some possible sex bias. Then rewrite the paragraph so that all sexist expressions are eliminated.

*I decline to accept the end of man. It is easy to say that man is immortal simply because he will endure—that when the last dingdong of doom has clanged . . . there will still be one more sound: that of his puny inexhaustible voice, still talking. I refuse to accept this. I believe that man will not merely endure: he will prevail.**

DIRECTIONS
(PART 2)

Many words assume the maleness of all people. Suggest substitutes for each of the following words and phrases. Indicate which words you think should be used as they are, in spite of possible problems?

1   manhunt
2   policeman
3   draftsman
4   man on the street
5   man-of-war
6   manpower
7   men's room
8   man-made
9   man of the house
10 freshman
11 woman
12 manhole
13 manual

* *Nobel Prize Library: Faulkner, O'Neill, Steinbeck,* New York: Helvetica Press, 1971, p. 8.

Experience 7.7 has pointed out a number of things to our students. The Faulkner quotation, for all its masculine emphasis, is a hauntingly beautiful and moving piece of prose. Faulkner's language in this passage displays language as well as some sexism. Changing *man* to *person*, *he* to *she/he*, and *his* to *his or her* would eliminate sex bias, but it would also destroy much of the rhythm and power of the passage. Whole sentences, perhaps the entire idea, must be recast to retain some of the style of the original. That is no small task; few of us can ever expect to write as well as William Faulkner.

It is important to realize that there is more to changing our speech and writing than just deleting sexist words. We must almost recast the whole style we have grown accustomed to using. To get some idea of the scope of this task rewrite the Faulkner paragraph without trying to repeat all the important phrases. Just try to capture the general idea in your own style and avoid using sexist expressions.

The individual words in Part 2 of Experience 7.7 present almost as many problems as the Faulkner passage. After you have made your decisions about each of these words, you may find it helpful to discuss your choices with other class members. Our students have disagreed violently on many of these items. Some prefer to change none of the usages because the newly coined words sound ludicrous. "How would you react," asked one student, "if someone told you to beware of an open *personhole?*" The word *person* has become a tiresome suffix in recent years, and alternatives should be sought wherever possible. For example, *drafting technician* is a more inventive term than *draftsperson.*

Many students have wanted to change all the words and phrases in Experience 7.7, even though that might result in a loss of precision. But some exceptions will be needed. For example, unless men and women wish to share public restrooms, sex-specific terms will still be needed. Other terms present a deeper challenge. A phrase such as *man of the house* is offensive, not because it refers to men, but because it puts men in the dominant role in family politics.

Some authors want to invent new pronouns to use in place of the male pronoun when the sex of the referent is nonspecific or mixed. The best example is the word *s/he.* That seems a clumsy alternative, but such clumsiness may be necessary. We favor such usages as *she/he,* or *he and she,* or even an occasional *they,* even though these might be jarring to a traditional ear. Also, it is often possible to phrase a sentence in ways that avoid pronouns altogether. Consider the following sentence:

Each student is responsible for care of his own textbooks.

It can be rewritten in two ways:

Students are responsible for care of their own textbooks.

and

Care of textbooks is each student's responsibility.

Dialects and standard english

Any time of social or language change is likely to involve some awkwardness, especially when the currents that are being changed run deep. Some of the deepest social currents in American society involve each person's attitudes toward the language itself. Language reflects social divisions, and when people violate certain rules of language, they are violating social taboos. The study of attitudes toward language and language varieties constitutes an important portion of sociolinguistics.

Take the word *dialect*, for example. Dialect influences are used by communicators to address certain groups of people. Certain features of your speech indicate something about where you grew up, how well-off you are, how much education you have, or what your ethnic background is. These are dialect markers. Everyone's speech displays such markers. Experience 7.8 examines some of your beliefs and feelings about dialects.

EXPERIENCE 7.8 DIALECT ATTITUDES

DIRECTIONS (PART 1)   **Rate your own speech on the following scales:**

My own speech is:

educated	___	___	___	___	___	___	___ uneducated
standard	___	___	___	___	___	___	___ nonstandard
intelligible	___	___	___	___	___	___	___ unintelligible
ethnic	___	___	___	___	___	___	___ mainstream
familiar	___	___	___	___	___	___	___ unfamiliar
city	___	___	___	___	___	___	___ country
Northern	___	___	___	___	___	___	___ Southern
dialect-marked	___	___	___	___	___	___	___ not dialect-marked
intelligible to others	___	___	___	___	___	___	___ not intelligible to others

DIRECTIONS (PART 2)   **Answer the following questions about dialect.**

1   **List here some identifying labels for some dialects you have heard spoken, and list one person you know who speaks each of those dialects.**

_____

2   **Can you list any dialect influences that exist in your speech?**

_____

3   **How do you feel about the way your speech sounds?**

_____

_____

We got some surprises when we started asking students about their attitudes toward dialect. To begin with, many students did not believe they spoke dialects; they maintained that they spoke good English. Those students who admitted to speaking dialects, which we all do, often felt some negative attitudes toward the sound of their own speech or feared that they would be unintelligible to others. Most students also felt that dialects were nonstandard, uneducated, and unfamiliar.

Somehow, the word *dialect* has acquired negative connotations. Perhaps because of stereotypes, perhaps because of dialect comedy, many people believe that only country bumpkins and members of minority groups speak dialects.

Since ancient times, many people have believed that their customary ways of talking are the right ways and that all others are a bit strange or undesirable. That is not necessarily bad. But what if some people in society gain the power to say that *their* way is the only correct way. In the United States, those who hold power and suppose there is one proper way to talk have invented the term *standard English* to describe that proper way. It is often supposed that those who do not speak this so-called standard are dialect speakers, but linguists have universally pointed out the nonsense of this view. Linguists define a dialect as *any variety of speaking that is tied to an identifiable group of people.* You speak a dialect each time you open your mouth.

In the United States, most differences between dialects are actually quite small and simple to understand. Most are differences in pronunciation of words. These sometimes create homophones and other sources of potential confusion, but only rarely do dialects actually get in the way of understanding. A fair number of middle-class Caucasians experience difficulty understanding some so-called nonstandard speakers, but those difficulties are not primarily linguistic. Rather, they are social. It is important to contrast these social difficulties with the difficulties that are actually traceable to language causes (such as gobbledygook). There are some undeniable linguistic differences between dialects. For example, most speakers of English can distinguish the speech of black people from that of Caucasians on tape recordings. Speakers (most often non-Caucasian ones) who speak in ways notably different from mid-western dialects spoken by radio newscasters are often said to speak nonstandard dialects of English. Some educators consider such nonstandard English to be a major handicap in school. But such opinions are primarily cultural, rather than linguistic. These language differences are comparatively small and only become important when social meanings or stereotypes are attached to them.

The very use of the term *nonstandard* implies that some spoken standard exists. But what is standard in Texas is different from what is standard in Massachusetts. Nevertheless, most Americans believe that such a standard does exist, although it seems almost impossible to define linguistically.

However, standards are easier to define culturally. They are what Caucasian speakers who are well off speak. The definition is as much a part of the status of the speaker as it is a set of speech characteristics. One study of attitudes toward black speech had teachers rate videotapes of white and black children. The tapes were edited so that some of the utterances of the Caucasian children seemed to come from the mouths of the black children. Teachers rated the same speech more nonstandard when spoken by black children than when spoken by Caucasian youngsters.

One source of the myth of standard English is language education in school. Grammar books have traditionally identified as correct some features of English spoken by middle-class Caucasians. As such, standard English is a high-prestige dialect, particularly in formal writing (such as English themes). In fact, although standard English is spoken by few people, much public writing uses a formalized style that approximates such a standard. The real importance of standard (written) English is that speakers of all dialects from Ireland to Australia can read the same written message without difficulty. There is no need to learn a new dialect in order to read. Speakers of different dialects do show some differing pronunciations when they read aloud. It is indeed unfortunate that some reading teachers label such pronunciations reading errors and correct them, thus helping to sour children on the process of learning to read.

Educated people are expected to speak standard English. But their speech actually contains many sentence fragments, frequent mispronunciations, and numerous informalisms such as *watcha doin'* and *howsit goin'*? Such aberrations rarely lead to serious difficulties unless speakers from a low-prestige social group consistently use some linguistic items that are unique to them. These differences then call attention to their status. That means that *listeners* call attention to their linguistic status labels. Listeners notice such a speaker. That is why comedians get a lot of mileage out of sounding like Italian gangsters or Jewish mothers. Such imitation involves cultural stereotyping processes.

How does such linguistic stereotyping work? Consider a Caucasian listener receiving a message from a black speaker. The listener is able to recognize black speech even over the telephone. Most Caucasians *expect* most blacks to sound nonstandard and will hear such speech even if the clues for it are extremely subtle or nonexistent. Thus, the linguistic and visual (in the case of face-to-face interaction) aspects of the situation trigger social, conformity-related decisions about the most appropriate way to behave toward black people. The judgment is social, although it may be partly triggered by details of language. To say that the details of the black speaker's dialect *are* the problem is like saying that the details of his or her pigmentation are the problem, which is to subscribe to nonsense and worse. The problem is the social judgments to which listeners leap on the basis of such cues. These judgments are learned attitudes based on stereotypes. The social biases that make black skins unwelcome in some quarters are the same ones that made Irish backgrounds and accents less than desirable to employers in 1900. Who knows what will be undesirable next?

Most people are capable of prejudiced against absolutely anything. Jane Elliot, a third grade teacher in Riceville, Iowa, conducted a two-day experiment in prejudice in her classroom. There were few non-Caucasians in Riceville, so Elliot divided her class into a brown-eyes group and a blue-eyes groups. On the first day, one group received extra praise and privileges and was thus made to feel superior. Members of the other group found themselves criticized for slowness and were allowed less access to recess, favored seats, and water fountains. On the second day, the roles were reversed. Elliot found that children who were accused of being stupid and clumsy really began to act that way. Even children with excellent academic records did poorly on tests during their membership in the dumb group. Self-fulfilling prophecy seems the flip side of stereotyping.

Without minimizing the diversity of American dialects, it can be fairly stated that speakers of these different dialects are usually able to make themselves intelligible to each other because they have much in common. If people changed their biases that certain dialect differences equal lack of intelligence, the effect could be relaxing. People could learn to enjoy the diversities that separate them instead of being frightened. After all, think how boring it would be if everyone sounded the same.

Listen to the voices around you. With a little practice, you will soon find that you can understand nonstandard speech.

To confirm our points about language and attitudes, tape-record several brief conversations you have with people over the next few days. Try to record yourself speaking with different individuals: males, females, members of different racial groups, and so on. When you listen to the tapes, ask yourself the following questions:

1   How do you feel when listening to your own voice?
2   How do you feel about the dialect(s) you spoke?
3   Does your dialect change when you speak to different people? In what ways?

SUMMARY

Communicators frequently attempt to send messages across cultural differences. These differences relate to different sets of expectations. Cross-cultural communication difficulties are easy to spot when you talk to someone raised in a different culture. But all communication has a cross-cultural component. If you understand how this aspect of communication works, you can avoid some of the difficulties it presents.

Cultural expectations are learned through socialization processes. Socialization is taught largely through experiences of conforming to norms and values of the social groups people grow up in. It makes little sense to label such sets of norms or values right or wrong. Rather, it is more effective to be aware of how they affect behavior, so that you can understand others' messages as clearly as possible. We believe that it is important to understand that each person and each culture possesses unique values and norms.

We encourage you to build usable stereotypes. Stereotypes are an inevitable part of the human perception process. A stereotype is a set of predictions based largely on inferences about the social groups to which a person belongs. As long as you realize the limits of stereotyping, you can use it effectively in many casual encounters with persons who are culturally different from you.

Not all stereotypes are simple; some are quite complex. That is the case with some interactions between stereotyping and language use. Some social stereotypes are so deeply buried in the language code that they may be triggered unintentionally dozens of times every day.

CHAPTER 8
DEVELOPING RELATIONSHIPS

Uh . . . I guess I'd better tell you that I don't like eggs fried in butter.

But . . . but . . .

I'm sorry, but it's true.

But . . . oh, why the hell didn't you tell me before? God, all this time, I've been frying your eggs in butter and . . .

I didn't want to hurt you.

—RAY SMITH

n this vignette, writer Ray Smith captures a piece of the absurdity of trying to function within a close relationship. Most Americans seek to live within such relationships, and relationships ordinarily present a multitude of communication difficulties. Who can think of their family or their first steady or their best friend without recalling occasional unhappy communicative experiences.

This chapter seeks to help you develop understanding and skills in forming and developing relationships with other persons. We begin by stressing the understanding of concepts about relationships. We examine the nature of relationship messages and distinguish them from content messages. We also examine the matter of accessibility to other persons. We then describe two predominant dimensions of relationship communication: dominance and friendliness. Finally, we stress the building of communication skills in developing relationships.

To get a better idea of your own thoughts about relationships, complete Experience 8.1.

EXPERIENCE 8.1 EGGS IN BUTTER

DIRECTIONS   **Imagine that your lover or spouse has been cooking your eggs for the past month and has always fried them in butter. You hate eggs fried in butter; you prefer them scrambled or poached. Write a conversation in which you tell your lover about the problem and she or he responds. Write actual dialogue, not a description of a conversation.**

_____
_____
_____
_____
_____
_____
_____
_____
_____
_____
_____

If you followed instructions, your conversation probably did not turn out to be much more pleasant than the one that opened this chapter. Many students in the past have refused to do so, saying, "I'd choose a better time to tell him." "I'd never have let it go for a month like that." But timing is vital to this example. The point is that it is *because* of the passage of time that there is a problem.

When would have been the best time to tell your lover that you do not like eggs fried in butter? What would be the worst way to say it? How would the other person probably respond? How would you feel if he or she continued to prepare eggs fried in butter afterward?

By now, you may believe that this example is overdone. Most Americans want to enter and maintain close relationships. What does a conversation about eggs have to do with such relationships? In fact, people rarely talk about relationships except when problems develop. Usually, they talk about eggs, TV, books, how the children are doing, passing the next test, whether the president is doing a good job, or whether premarital sex is right or wrong. Those all represent messages about *content*. Most people normally think of their communication as being about content, which it is. But nearly every message you send or receive can also be interpreted in terms of what it says about the relationships involved. Suppose a mother says to her son, "Straighten your tie." She may be demonstrating that she cares about how he looks, and she is certainly asserting her advice-giving position over him. These are messages *about the relationship*.

Suppose a college student says to someone of the opposite sex, "I'm thirsty. Let's go have a beer after class." There is obviously content to the statement; there are references to time, acts, and persons. But the predominant message is about the relationship. Although the exact content of such a message may be difficult to put into words, a feeling of attraction is certainly involved. Messages about relationships are most commonly discussed in terms of feelings, and part of the expression of these feelings is ordinarily nonverbal and hence still more difficult to translate into words. Nevertheless, describing feelings can add precision to messages about relationships. Here are some adjectives that people commonly use to describe feelings:

adequate	cheerful	doubtful	good	hostile
affectionate	childish	eager	gratified	hurt
angry	clever	empty	greedy	ignored
annoyed	confused	envious	goofy	immortal
anxious	cruel	excited	guilty	inspired
astounded	crushed	exhausted	gullible	intimidated
bad	deceitful	fascinated	happy	isolated
beautiful	defeated	fearful	hateful	jealous
betrayed	destructive	foolish	helpful	joyful
bitter	determined	frustrated	helpless	jumpy
bored	discontented	frightened	high	kind
brave	distracted	free	homesick	lazy
calm	disturbed	furious	honored	lonely
capable	dominated	glad	horrible	loving

low	obnoxious	pleased	restless	tense
lustful	odd	pressured	sad	tired
mad	opposed	pretty	satisfied	trapped
mean	painful	proud	scared	ugly
miserable	panicky	refreshed	sexy	violent
naughty	peaceful	rejected	shocked	vulnerable
nervous	persecuted	relaxed	stupid	worried
nice	pitiful	relieved	stunned	

Any message can be examined both from the viewpoint of content and from the viewpoint of the relationship. The content dimension involves the facts, subject matter, and explicit propositions that are presented. Consider this sentence: "I'm tired of Joe pushing people around." The content involves a person named Joe who has been literally or figuratively forcing people to do things against their will. The speaker describes this state of affairs and states disapproval.

The relationship dimension of an utterance involves people's feelings about each other and their maneuvers to get closer to or more distant from others. It may be more difficult to understand the relationship dimension of a single utterance than to decipher its content aspect because the past history of an utterance (part of its context) constitutes a large part of the relationship dimension. For instance, suppose a man calls a woman on the telephone and invites her to see a movie. The woman responds with a multiword obscenity and hangs up. The relationship dimension of the woman's utterance may be difficult to understand without some background information about the parties and their relationship. Suppose that a woman calls her husband "that old creep" while speaking to a group of woman friends. Such a term may serve as an expression of fondness in the context of her relationship with her husband, or it may be a strong insult.

In spite of such problems, you can learn to interpret the relationship dimension of utterances. Here are some questions that may tap relationship information: What feelings are being expressed? What does the speaker want this utterance to do in terms of his/her relationship with the listener? Is the sentence to be taken literally, metaphorically, or ironically?

Once again, consider this sentence: "I'm tired of Joe pushing people around." The speaker is complaining, expressing bitterness and hostility toward Joe. A more important clue is that the speaker is taking the listener into confidence with this complaint. Perhaps the speaker feels persecuted or scared or vulnerable. The action of telling the listener about this reveals both anxiety about the situation and dependence on the listener for support and acceptance of those feelings. The speaker is working to strengthen the relationship with the listener through expressing these emotions.

Sometimes both content and relationship dimensions are clearly specified in an utterance; sometimes either the content or the relationship aspect may be implied by nonverbal or contextual cues. You will be more effective in relationships if you are certain you can make this distinction. Practice making the content-relationship distinction by responding to Experience 8.2.

EXPERIENCE 8.2 CONTENT AND RELATIONSHIP

DIRECTIONS For each of the following picture-dialogue situations, write a description of the content message and a description of the relationship methods. Include as much information as you can about what cues you have discovered. In describing relationship states, use the list of feeling words on page 195.

SAMPLE

DIALOGUE:
Person A (not pictured): *I see you're frustrated.*
          Person B: *I can't get started.*

CONTENT:
A discussion of frustration. Person B is having trouble getting to work.

RELATIONSHIP:
Person A displays empathy, caring concern. The eyes seem important to this. Person B reveals frustration, fear, and perhaps guilt. The knit brows help communicate this. The relationship may grow closer through such an exchange of feelings.

1

DIALOGUE:
Teacher: *Can anyone tell me the relationship between frustration and aggression?*
Student: *No, mame.*
Teacher: *Did anyone read last night's assignment?*

CONTENT:

_____

_____

RELATIONSHIP:

_____

_____

_____

2

DIALOGUE:

He: _I'm interested in the play on campus this Saturday. Can you see it with me?_

She: _I'd love to, Jim, but I'm going out of town this weekend._

CONTENT:

_____

_____

RELATIONSHIP:

_____

_____

_____

_____

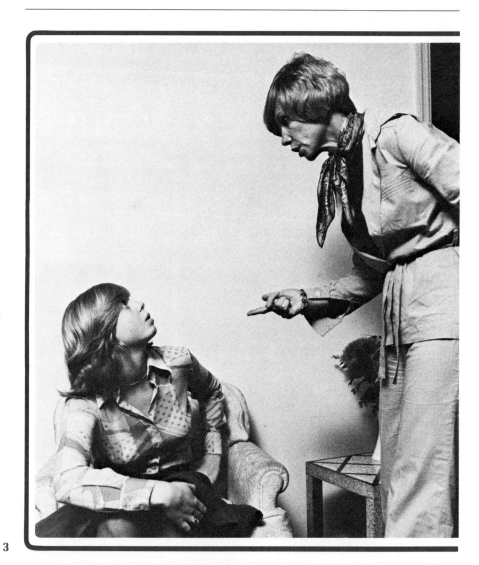

3

DIALOGUE:

   Mother: *Where were you last night?*
Daughter: *Oh, no place special.*
   Mother: *I want more detail than that. What time did you get in?*
Daughter: *A little past twelve.*

CONTENT:

_____
_____

RELATIONSHIP:

_____
_____
_____
_____

In working through Experience 8.2, you may have noted that messages of relationship are not always explicitly discussed. Relationship messages are often carried by nonverbal cues. Speakers tend to seek eye contact with persons or sit close to them. Thus, in exercise 2, the young man looks at the young woman and leans toward her. She, however, averts his gaze and turns away slightly, which may indicate avoidance of his advances.

A second reason why words rarely tell the whole story about a relationship is that *within certain contexts*, statements and actions take on implications that have little to do with the meanings of the same utterances under different circumstances. In Chapters 1 and 5, we discussed the importance of context in communication. Suppose, for example, that you pass a friend on the sidewalk this afternoon. You might say, "How are you?" But you are not interested in your friend's health. If he or she responded by describing a recent operation, you would probably be startled. You might say, "Nice day, isn't it?" You would probably be surprised if he or she responded, "I understand that there's a low-pressure system coming tonight, and it will get colder." Your original questions actually had nothing to do with your friend's health or with the weather. Rather, they served as signs of greeting within the contexts of this culture, a casual friendship, and a chance meeting on a sidewalk.

Messages about context may also be nonverbal. You pass your friend on the sidewalk and say, "Nice day isn't it?" But you keep on walking, without slowing your pace. Your behavior indicates that you have no desire to start a long conversation right now and helps place your utterance in context. Such messages are usually sent and received unconsciously and implicitly; they are understood by both parties in much the same way as individual items of code are understood (see Chapters 4 and 5).

One major relationship meaning carried by such contextual cues is attraction, that fuzzy, warm feeling that makes you want to spend more time with someone. Attraction is a sort of drive state that provides fuel for relationships. Under the magnetic pull of attraction, separate beings begin to move closer to each other, and the pull of attraction grows stronger as the parties grow closer.

ACCESSIBILITY
People who are attracted to each other also become accessible to each other. The term *accessibility* concerns the degree of attraction, closeness, trust, and interpersonal sharing that occur within a relationship. Two (or more) people who share an extremely close relationship are very accessible to each other. People who share less closeness can be described as less accessible. Your accessibility to another person is the degree to which that person knows you, can accurately read your messages, shares your secrets, predicts your behavior.

To get a firmer grasp on the concept of accessibility, complete Experience 8.3.

EXPERIENCE 8.3 ACCESSIBILITY

DIRECTIONS **To complete the chart on page 203, put a check mark in the column that best describes your willingness to talk about each topic. You may check more than one column per topic. Add some topics of your own to our list.**

The topics that you checked as things you could discuss with anyone are matters about which you are easily accessible. They are matters that everyone could know about you. The topics that you checked as discussible only with a few people, such as a lover or a member of your family, or with nobody are topics that you would not like to risk having most people know about. Those topics are highly personal information. When you talk about such personal information with someone, you give that person a certain power over you; you make yourself accessible to that person. It is like a boxer lowering his guard. He can see more clearly, but he is also more vulnerable to a punch in the nose.

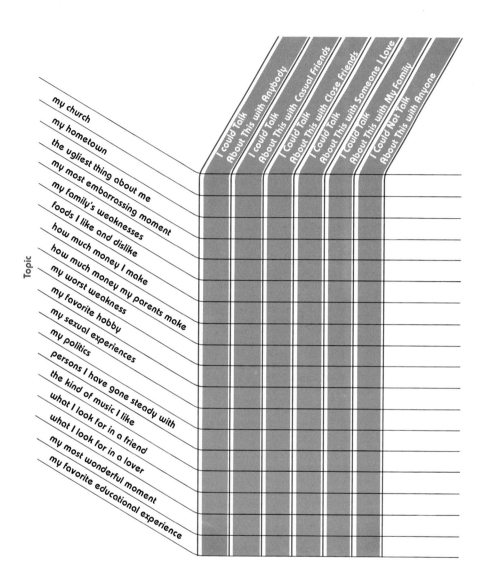

Different people will select different topics as the ones they are most unwilling to discuss. Some people do not wish to discuss religion; others avoid discussing sex or money or personal weaknesses. Many people are afraid to discuss anything they like but enjoy complaining about a wide variety of topics. Thus, the inventory of topics that you checked can be a valuable tool for self-analysis. For example, the topics you checked as things you could tell only to an intimate friend (or to nobody) are probably those topics about which you are most potentially vulnerable. Talking to somebody about these topics seems risky for you because it makes yourself accessible to the other. Are you curious about your accessibility to others? Experience 8.4 will tell you something about your accessibility to particular other persons.

EXPERIENCE 8.4 ACCESSIBILITY TO MY ASSOCIATES

DIRECTIONS This chart is similar to the one in Experience 8.3 except that the columns are blank. Fill in the heads of the columns with the names of five people you know who represent a wide spectrum of acquaintance

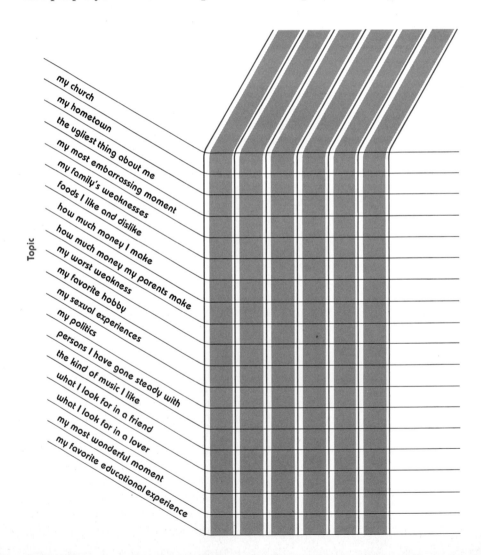

Topic

- my church
- my hometown
- the ugliest thing about me
- my most embarrassing moment
- my family's weaknesses
- foods I like and dislike
- how much money I make
- how much money my parents make
- my worst weakness
- my favorite hobby
- my sexual experiences
- my politics
- persons I have gone steady with
- the kind of music I like
- what I look for in a friend
- what I look for in a lover
- my most wonderful moment
- my favorite educational experience

and affection: a member of your family, your best friend of the opposite sex, somebody you barely know, your worst enemy, and so on. Then complete the chart by indicating which of these people you are willing to discuss each topic with.

You are highly accessible to those people you would tell rather personal information. Probably, such persons are also highly accessible to you. There may be only a few such people. Talking to others about such matters constitutes the process of *self-disclosure,* the willing giving of information about yourself to another person. Other people serve as mirrors in this process, and it is often only through the act of telling someone else that you become aware of something about yourself. (You may find it helpful to review our discussion of this issue in Chapter 3, "Communicating the Self-Concept.")

You may feel that self-disclosure is an exhibitionist tendency. But that impression is usually incorrect. Self-disclosure is ordinarily a by-product of straight talk between persons. Communicators rarely enter conversations with the intention of revealing large amounts of personal information. Rather, information comes to the foreground in the course of conversation and can be either withheld or shared. You can reveal as much of yourself talking about eggs fried in butter as you can talking about your most intimate feelings.

Self-disclosure can be rewarding, but it is also risky because it involves the unknown. Communicators build barriers around personal information as psychological fortifications that protect them from insult, oversight, or personal attack. You can get closer to another person only by letting the other through some of your protective walls. That can be a frightening experience. Eldridge Cleaver, in *Soul on Ice,* describes it this way:

> *Getting to know someone, entering that new world, is an ultimate, irretrievable leap into the unknown. The prospect is terrifying. The stakes are high. The emotions are overwhelming. The two people are reluctant really to strip themselves naked in front of each other, because in doing so they make themselves vulnerable and give enormous power over themselves one to the other. How often they inflict pain and torment upon each other. Better to maintain shallow, superficial affairs; that way the scars are not too deep. No blood is hacked from the soul.*

Although self-disclosure involves risks, they may not be so dramatic as Cleaver suggests. Nevertheless, it will not help to laugh those risks off or pretend that they are not real or rationalize that you are not afraid. Actually, close friends and lovers do not betray each other's confidences all that often, nor do they recite their intimates' secrets to enemies. Still, close relationships have their ups and downs, and somehow, the down parts seem inconsistent with the accessibility you have been building.

Everyone has had feelings hurt by a loved one or has taken a walk to let tempers cool. The risk in relationships is as much a risk of *involvement* as of betrayal. Once you are involved with and accessible to another person, you cannot easily pretend you do not care about his or her frustrations. You cannot easily refuse to listen to the other's gripes or refuse to help him or her out of troubles. Relationships may grow into invasions of privacy, and the selfish individualism that has been nurtured in most people sometimes finds that the demands of close relationships become uncomfortable and confining.

A PARABLE

There once was a happy couple who loved ice cream. They never really had discussed ice cream, but at dessert each night when the good wife placed the frosty bowl of ice cream before her husband the two grew closer spiritually.

One day in the grocery store, the good wife was trying to choose between vanilla and strawberry. "Which would *he* like best?" she asked. "I bet he'd like vanilla. He always eats that with such gusto!"

She placed the dish of ice cream before him. He raised one eyebrow and asked, "Vanilla again?"

She was crestfallen. "I thought that was what you'd like," she muttered. "I really would have preferred strawberry."

"Strawberry would have been better," he agreed. Next time, she chose strawberry because he preferred it. She really would have liked butter brickle, which was on sale that week. But she placed the dish of strawberry before him with the sure joy in her heart of one who has been considerate.

He raised both eyebrows and said gently, "I sure would like a sweet buttery flavor sometime instead of these old standards."

She went to the bedroom and slammed the door.

For months, she did all she could to please him. Their relationship deteriorated. They rarely spoke at supper. Both were tense.

One day at the grocery, deliberating over another impossible choice between flavors, she exclaimed in despair, "The devil take *his* preferences; I feel like spumoni."

And they lived happily ever after.

EXPERIENCE   8.5   A CONVERSATION

DIRECTIONS   **Before you respond to the questions in this experience, do the following: Find someone to talk to. It does not have to be someone you like. Buy him or her a soda or a pizza, or ask his or her advice; use any handy excuse. Probably the conversation will go better if you do not tell them you have to have this conversation or you cannot continue** reading. Spend at least 20 minutes talking; spend a whole evening if you like. Then, *immediately* after you end the conversation, return to this book, and complete this experience.

Stop reading.
Did you find someone to talk to? Do *not* proceed until you have had the conversation.

The following scales are designed to measure your attitudes toward the person you have just talked to. The adjectives at the ends of each scale describe possible extremes of relationship styles; the middle point represents a neutral judgment. Your task is to check the point on each scale that best describes your relationship.

1　In my conversation just now, the way I acted toward the other person tended to be:
dominant ____ ____ ____ ____ ____ ____ ____ submissive
List some actions (statements, nonverbal clues, and the like) that you observed during the conversation and that serve as evidence for this judgment.

_____
_____

2　In that same conversation, the way I acted toward the other person was:
friendly ____ ____ ____ ____ ____ ____ unfriendly
List evidence for this judgment.

_____
_____

3　In that same conversation, the way that the other person related to me was basically:
dominant ____ ____ ____ ____ ____ ____ ____ submissive
List evidence for this judgment.

_____
_____

4　In the conversation, the way that the other person related to me was:
friendly ____ ____ ____ ____ ____ ____ ____ unfriendly
List evidence for this judgment.

_____
_____

As you have probably guessed, most relationships can be evaluated fairly concisely by using two dimensions of judgment: dominance and friendliness. Most communication situations that you encounter can be described by examining the messages for evidence of dominance and friendliness (and their opposites) in the messages.

Kim Giffin and Bobby Patton discuss these dimensions of relationships in their book, *Interpersonal Communication*. They note that dominance-submission is the control dimension of a relationship because it relates to who gets their way, who wins arguments, and who backs down in a confrontation. Usually, dominant behavior on the part of one person leads to submissive behavior on the part of the other. For instance, if someone gives a direct order or bludgeons a listener with an opinion, the listener rarely responds with a counterorder or opinion. The listener may get angry, but chances are, he or she will defer. To answer dominant behavior with dominant behavior might cause open conflict. Similarly, when one communicator makes a submissive move, the other is likely to respond with dominant behavior. Otherwise, as the following exchange demonstrates, nothing happens:

"What do you want to do tonight, Sally?"
"I don't know, Fred. What do you want to do?"
"Whatever you want to do is fine."

Friendliness-unfriendliness is the affective dimension of a relationship because it deals with liking, interpersonal attraction, who compliments whom, who engages in self-disclosure or friendly humor. Unlike dominant behavior, friendly, affectionate, or caring behavior leads to response in kind. If you compliment a friend, the friend will be likely to return the favor. If you insult a friend, you can probably expect unfriendly behavior in return.

Some communicators develop a personal style—for example, dominant but friendly—which they use to respond to many different situations. Other communicators are more flexible, which is more likely to make them effective in wide varieties of situations. Similarly some relationships develop a rut, a pattern that the communicators use repeatedly to respond to each other. For example, a husband's paternalistic (dominant yet friendly) responses to his wife consistently produce submissive and affectionate (childlike) responses from her. These ruts limit the expression of a range of feelings. A strong, flexible relationship allows some spontaneity in the way the parties act toward each other. Either party may be dominant on a given occasion, and there is room for expression of hostility without destroying the relationship. Some psychologists call such a relationship *authentic* because both parties are able to act freely, without being constrained by ways they have acted in the past.

Once you have determined whether the way you relate to someone is primarily dominating or primarily friendly, you can plot the characteristic nature of your relationship on the following diagram:

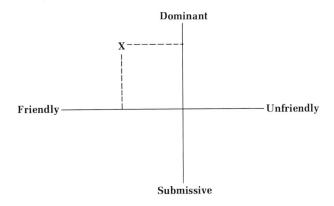

For example, the symbol X shows that you relate to this hypothetical other person in a way that is somewhat dominant and somewhat friendly. Note that X applies to one set of behaviors toward one person. It is not a statement about personality. Another dimension can be added, as the next diagram demonstrates, to show that the other person related to you in a complementary fashion (somewhat submissive and also friendly). The relationship between these two points signifies the state of your relationship at that moment.

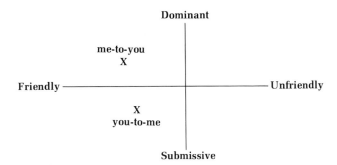

EXPERIENCE 8.6 DOMINANCE AND FRIENDLINESS

DIRECTIONS **Plot the relationships indicated by the following situations on the accompanying diagrams. Then write a sentence or two justifying your decisions.**

1 Situation: Man standing over desk of other man. Man standing looks dominant.

      Ted: *Harvey, do you think you could have a quotation on the Bales account by three o'clock?*

  Harvey: *I'm not sure, Ted, but I'll give it a whale of a try.*

      Ted: *I wouldn't push you, Harvey, but Bales has really been bugging me.*

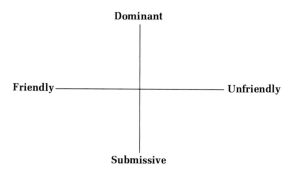

2 Situation: Two women seated in a messy apartment. They are looking at each other angrily.

Margie: *Sally, you never do the dishes or dusting. This place looks like a pigpen.*

  Sally: *It seems like you're always complaining.*

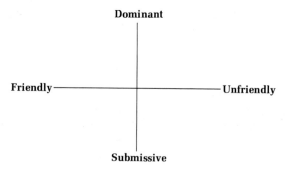

3 Write a brief dialogue you have recently had with another person. Then plot the relationship dimensions that it illustrates on the graph.

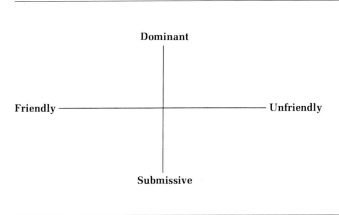

RELATIONSHIP SKILLS

Throughout this book, we have tried to discuss concepts and skills together as often as possible. The remainder of this chapter presents skills that build upon your understanding of relationship concepts. Four sets of skills seem particularly important to developing useful, productive, efficient, and meaningful relationships: empathy, feedback, expressing feelings, and making declarative statements. The use of each requires common sense and moderation. For example, it can be useful to give full and accurate expression to feelings, but if you attend to this ability only, you may become the kind of bore who talks about yourself all the time.

Empathy is the ability to put yourself in the other's shoes (see Chapter 2). An empathetic listener relates messages to his or her own experience in order to feel a feeling similar to that expressed by the speaker. Empathy is a skill that begins in early childhood when communicators learn that there are other points of view besides their own. A four-year-old child is considered egocentric because of an inability to distinguish his or her point of view from that of others. For example, suppose you sit across the table from such a child and hold up a picture that shows a ball on one side and a doll on the other side. You ask the child to hold up the picture so that you (the adult across the table) can see the drawing of the ball. The child will hold the picture so that *she* or *he* can see the ball; you will be looking at the doll on the reverse side. The child assumes that if he or she can see the ball, others can, too.*

Adults often fail to see the other's point of view when communicating about relationships. If a man is having an argument with his roommate about how dirty their apartment has become, he finds it easiest to see his own feelings. He may be so angry that stopping to see the other's point of view is the last thing on his mind. If a teenager complains because his brother uses the phone when he wants it, does he stop to examine the situation from the brother's point of view? If a communicator does this, she or he is practicing empathy.

Empathy is particularly important in listening. Suppose your roommate begins to complain about the mess in your apartment. Is your first thought that you have more important things to do now than cleaning? Or do you try to understand as completely as possible the viewpoint your roommate is expressing? Only after taking the role of the other are you likely to understand the message thoroughly.

If your friend complains to you about a problem with her parents, do you immediately begin to suggest ways they could improve the situation, or do you first make sure you have the whole story? Can you ask any clarifying questions about the facts of the case or about your friend's feelings on the matter? Obviously, an empathetic listener makes the process of self-disclosure most productive and efficient.

One key to developing and practicing empathy is being interested. If you care about another person in a way that cannot be faked, you are likely to listen to them. Probably the biggest block to empathetic listening is the feeling that you already know what the speaker is talking about. When people think they know all about what is happening, they tune out the speaker and miss critical points in the message. In fact, many people tend to interrupt others to complete sentences for them, a response that represents an almost total absence of empathy. A second block to empathetic listening is the tendency to evaluate what the speaker says. Consider a situation in which someone tells you about an act you disapprove of or about something that you would have done differently.

Husband: (answering phone) Hello.
　Wife: Henry, I'm afraid I've wrecked the car.
Husband: Oh, heavens, I hope you didn't admit it was your fault. Was the car badly damaged?
　Wife: It's totaled. They towed it away.
Husband: You let them do that? Did they tell you how much it cost?
　Wife: No, Henry, but—

* John Flavell, *Communication and the Development of Role-Taking Skills in Children,* New York: Wiley, 1968.

Husband: Honey, how many times have I told you—Well, you stay right where you are, and I'll come get you.

Wife: Don't bother. I'm in the hospital with four broken ribs.

How many times have you been so busy evaluating somebody's actions that you did not bother to get the straight story about what happened? If you want to be able to put yourself in the other's shoes, you have to listen to the whole story without evaluating what is being said. There will be plenty of time for evaluating after you get all the facts. To find out just how empathetic a listener you are right now, respond to Experience 8.7.

EXPERIENCE 8.7 EVALUATING AND JUMPING TO CONCLUSIONS

DIRECTIONS Read the following list of items, and perform the behaviors that are indicated. Be sure to read *all* items carefully before you write down anything.

1 Make a list of three people with whom you are usually dominant in a relationship.

2 Make a list of two of your friends whom you feel tend to evaluate what other speakers say rather than listening carefully.

3 Write the name of a person with whom you have been able to maintain a friendly relationship.

4 Give two examples of this person's behavior that contributed to the friendly relationship.

5 Write a short statement in which you define empathy in your own words.

6 In a short paragraph, describe your personal style of interaction in relationships.

_____

_____

7   Write two sentences that summarize the contents of this chapter so far.

_____

_____

8   Write your name at the top of this exercise.
9   Write your instructor's name at the top of this exercise.
10   Do only items 3, 8, and 9 of this list.

Did we catch you not following instructions? Most students responded to each item as they read it, in spite of the instruction at the beginning that they were not to do so. This experience serves as an example of being so set in your habits that you jump to conclusions about what to do before you have heard the whole story. If you react rashly in emotional crises, your actions can contribute to the problem rather than to the solution. Empathetic listening requires the ability to listen to an entire story and internalize what it means before evaluating it or taking action.

Feedback is one of the basic principles of effective communication (see Chapter 1). In interpersonal communication, obtaining feedback is the surest way to be certain that you are getting the whole story. The question is your most effective tool. Questions that flow from the topics discussed and are well focused can make communication much more accurate and efficient.

Husband: (answering phone) Hello.
Wife: Hello, Henry, I'm afraid I have some bad news. Are you sitting down?
Husband: Yes. What is it?
Wife: I've wrecked the car.
Husband: Oh, Lord, how did it happen?
Wife: I'm not sure; it all happened so fast. But I'm afraid it was my fault. Are you angry?
Husband: Are you all right?
Wife: Actually, I'm calling from the hospital.

If you doubt the efficiency of a few questions to help get the whole story across, remember Experience 1.4, in which you described shapes to another person without the other person being able to ask you questions. The degree to which the other person's drawing came close to your description was a measure of the accuracy of your communication. Experience 1.4 demonstrated that without feedback, it is extremely difficult to communicate accurately.

Another useful feedback tool is _reflective listening,_ or paraphrasing. Although this technique is sometimes overdone, it can be helpful in improving the accuracy of messages. To use this skill, you simply repeat in your own words what you think the speaker said. Your paraphrase serves as a reflection of the other person's words. The speaker can then agree that your reflection is what he/she meant or can make modifications in the message to clarify its meanings to you. Experience 8.8 gives you an opportunity to practice this skill.

EXPERIENCE 8.8 REFLECTIVE LISTENING

DIRECTIONS   Engage someone in a conversation on any topic that interests you. The discussion is to be unstructured except for a single ground rule: Before each participant speaks, he or she must first summarize in his or her own words and without notes what the other speaker has just said. The first speaker must agree that the summary encompasses what he or she intended to say before the second speaker can proceed. Continue the conversation for 7 to 10 minutes; then answer the following questions:

1 Did the process of reflective listening aid you in increasing the accuracy of your communication?

_____

2 What was your greatest problem in listening to the other person?

_____

3 What problems did the other person incur in paraphrasing your comments?

_____

4 How would the use of this skill in a less exaggerated fashion affect you in everyday conversations?

_____

_____

    Expressing feelings accurately can aid almost any relationship. It is important to remember that all feelings are OK, that there is no such thing as an undesirable feeling, although there surely are undesirable *behaviors*. Sometimes the accurate expression of feelings to yourself or to understanding others can prevent events from coming to a crisis in which unhappy or undesirable behaviors occur.

    In order to express your feelings, you must first become aware of them. (You may find it helpful to review the material aimed at this objective in Chapter 3.) Experience 8.9 is a warm-up exercise in expressing feelings.

EXPERIENCE **8.9 EXPRESSING FEELINGS**

DIRECTIONS   Complete the following statements:

1   If I had an extra fifty dollars, I would:

   _____

2   After doing this, I would feel:

   _____

   In expressing feelings, it pays to be vivid. Use names of colors when appropriate: "I feel an orange glow when I'm with you." "I feel pretty gray today." References to experiences you and the other person have shared can be effective: "I feel the same kind of exasperation today that I felt when those noisy kids camped near us last month." Be creative; use literary references and references to nature. Keep these points in mind as you respond to the following statements. Here are a few.

3a   In my relationship with my parents (or parent or guardian), the one thing that frustrates me most is:

b   Have you and your parents discussed this problem? If you have, how did the discussion make you feel? If you have not, how do you feel about that?

   _____

   _____

4a   Right now, I feel closer to _____ than any other person because:

   _____

b   When I'm around this person I feel:

   _____

5a   The most embarrassing moment I can remember was:

   _____

b   At that moment, I felt:

   _____

   The benefits of expressing feelings are undeniable, but expressing feelings can also be overdone. Most discussions of expressing feelings assume that you have absolutely no control over your feelings. The phrase "you *make* me angry" is quite typical in American society. It implies that you had no option but to become furious and that therefore you were not responsible. But in reality, you did have some options. As we noted in Chapter 1, you can stop fighting to answer the phone. Your feelings may seem powerful, but they are not powerful enough to absorb responsibility for your actions. People who claim that their feelings made them do something are often excusing childish tantrums or trying cheap tricks to get their way.

In this chapter, we have used the term *self-disclosure* to refer to expressions of feelings. It bears repeating that most self-disclosure occurs, not in the form of intimate revelations of experiences, but rather through sharing your reactions to events and experiences. Sometimes your reactions help the other person to feel good; sometimes they do not. Both kinds of information can be useful.

Self-disclosure involves your personal feelings. However, communicators tend to get lazy and use the same few terms over and over again. The words that we listed on page 195 may help you to increase your feelings vocabulary. It may be worth your while to put that list someplace where you can refer to it.

It is important to disclose about yourself, not just the other person. Statements that try to disclose to another person what they are like or how they feel are likely to be less than productive. "You never talk to me," "you are so bossy," "you are really sexy when you get mad" are not self-disclosures. They are *you-statements*, accusations. The you-statement is practically guaranteed to infuriate the other person. To disclose about yourself, use *I-statements*, descriptions of your own feelings.

Make your statements specific. "I feel elated today" is more specific and informative than "I am a happy person." Listeners can relate a statement about what is happening now to what they observe and feel, but a statement about generalities or personalities is less concrete. A good rule for making self-disclosure specific is to avoid the words *always* and *never*.

"I always end up taking out the trash."
"You never listen to me."

Always-never statements generally are weak messages. In the first place they are vague. In the second place, they are easy to deny with one counterexample.

"Wrong! I took out the trash twice last February."
"Not so. I'm listening to you now. You always exaggerate!"

A more useful beginning to these conversations might be:

"I resent having to take out the trash tonight."

or
"I think you're not listening to me now."

In summary, self-disclosure can be aided by making precise I-statements. Remember that you are the one person you have power to change.

Declaring statements

In their very informative short book *Declare Yourself,* John Narciso and David Burkett argue that if you express yourself in precise I-statements, you can achieve "first-person-singular freedom." That is, you can for the first time gain control over your own actions and the freedom to choose what you do next. Not only are you able to change your own behavior; you can also free yourself of the expectations of others. The secret weapon of the Narciso-Burkett approach is called the *declaring statement,* an I-statement that tells in very precise, or *operational,* terms what you would like to have happen.

You may notice that saying what you want to happen is not the same as expressing feelings. Narciso and Burkett argue that the expression of feelings is not very precise and therefore can be interpreted very differently by different listeners. In contrast, an operational statement is about something that can be observed. You cannot observe your friend's anger. You can observe your friend's wrinkled nose, hard stare, and compressed lips; from these clues, you may infer that anger is what your friend is feeling. Operational statements are concerned with facts. Feelings are not facts. They happen inside; they are not observable. (You may find it helpful to review the difference between facts and inferences, discussed in Chapter 4.)

If you are trying to figure out what making operational statements means, try what Robert Mager has called the "Hey-Dad Test."* The test uses this sentence:

Hey, Dad, let me show you how I can _____

Completing the sentence with the statement that you want to test. If the statement sounds OK, then probably the statement is probably operational; it describes something that can be observed. These statements are operational:

Hey, Dad, let me show you how I can go to the movies today.
shine my shoes.
tell Marge I don't like her.
get my homework finished.

In contrast, the following completions of the Hey-Dad Test sound exotic or at least imprecise. That is, Dad could not observe whether you were doing what you asked him to observe.

Hey, Dad, Let me show you how I can become aware of myself.
feel pitiful.
resent Marge.
love my husband.

* Robert F. Mager, *Goal Analysis,* Belmont, Calif.: Fearon Publishers, 1972, p. 29.

These sentences demonstrate why the declaring-statement approach avoids expressing feelings altogether. Although this may be an extreme position, we believe that the declaring statement is a skill you should master so that when extra precision is needed, or when you understand precisely what you wish to have happen, you can use this option. Being able to use declaring statements adds to your range of behaviors. It helps you cope with new situations.

In summary, declaring statements meet three criteria:

1 Declaring statements use *I*.
2 Declaring statements are operational, factual, and observable (Hey-Dad Test).
3 Declaring statements avoid expressing feelings and concentrate on issues instead.

To check your understanding of declaring statements, complete Experience 8.9.

EXPERIENCE 8.10 DECLARING STATEMENTS

DIRECTIONS Read the following imaginary conversation. Place a *D* in the blank to the left of each statement that satisfies all three criteria for a declaring statement. If a statement fails to qualify as declaring, write the numbers of the criteria it does not meet in the blank to the left of the statement.

_____ 1 **Agnes:** *George, would you like to go to a play on Thursday?*
_____ 2 **George (looks at newspaper):** *I'd rather talk about it later.*
_____ 3 **Agnes:** *Are you listening to me? What should we do Thursday night?*
_____ 4 **George:** *We have to go to Jonny's game. We can't miss that.*
_____ 5 **Agnes:** *I get bored at games. Do we always have to do what you want?*
_____ 6 **George:** *You know Jonny likes to see us at the games, and it helps him play better.*
_____ 7 **Agnes:** *Everyone is talking about the play. I'll kick myself if we have to miss it.*
_____ 8 **George:** *I am most interested in the game. I would prefer to have you come with me.*
_____ 9 **Agnes:** *Well, I prefer the play. I would like you to come, but I'm willing to go without you.*
         (A short time later.)
_____ 10 **Agnes:** *George, I'm going to the play. I'm going with Jim Walsh.*
_____ 11 **George:** *Agnes, you can't do that to me.*
_____ 12 **Agnes:** *Well, it's all arranged. He's got the tickets. He took time off this afternoon to drive over for them. I'd hurt his feelings if I back out.*

_____ 13 **George:** *Well, you're a free person. You can do what you want (picks up **newspaper, turns away**).*

_____ 14 **Agnes:** *I believe you're jealous.*

_____ 15 **George:** *I don't want you to go to the play with Jim.*

_____ 16 **Agnes:** *Well, maybe I would hurt your feelings.*

_____ 17 **George:** *Of course, I trust you. But others don't know you as well as I do.*

_____ 18 **Agnes:** *But how can I explain to Jim? And I'll be so disappointed if I miss the play.*

You probably did not identify every statement in Experience 8.10 correctly. That is to be expected. Declaring statements take some getting used to. The only declaring statements are numbers 2, 8, 9, 10, and 15. The others all fail to meet at least one of the criteria. Recheck your answers. Ask your teacher about any statements that puzzle you.

In Experience 8.11, we have rewritten the conversation between Agnes and George using all declaring statements. You will note that declaring statements do not solve basic conflicts. In fact, they sometimes make issues and differences clearer and that can lead to conflict.

Expect to have some problems in responding to Experience 8.10. You may discover that the declaring-statements approach fits extremely well with the problem-solving approach to conflict resolution. Declaring assumes that the conflicting parties are equal in power, and it makes goals and values as clear as possible.

EXPERIENCE 8.11 A DECLARING CONVERSATION

DIRECTIONS **Try your hand at writing an ending to the second part of the following conversation. Make sure that all the statements you write are declaring statements. Try to resolve the conflict according to problem-solving techniques as outlined in Chapter 6.**

> **Agnes:** *George, I want to go to a play on Thursday? Whirlwind is at the Bijou.*
>
> **George:** *I think Thursday is the night of the next game. I hate to miss any of Jonny's games.*
>
> **Agnes:** *I forgot the game, but frankly, I'd prefer the play. It has gotten good reviews. Bubbles Sorrell is the guest star. Could I talk you into it?*

George: *Sorry, I'd rather go to the game.*
  Agnes: *I don't see how we can settle this except by going to
          different places. It's more important to me to go to the play.*
George: *Is the play on any other night? I'd go if I didn't have to miss
          the game.*
  Agnes: *The play is Thursday only.*
George: *I guess you're right, then. I'll go to the game; you go to the
          play.*

  (A short time later.)

  Agnes: *George, I'm going to the play with Jim Walsh.*
George: *I don't want you to go.*
  Agnes: *I've decided already. We have the tickets. I don't want to
          back out.*

_____
_____
_____
_____
_____
_____

   After you have completed Experience 8.11, tape-record a conflict
discussion that you have with a friend or that two friends have with
each other. Rewrite their conversation using all declaring statements.
You will find that the conversation gets much briefer and is more
understandable and that conflict resolution is easier.

SUMMARY   Any message can be examined from two points of view: content
and relationship. Messages about relationships often represent feelings
and emphasize nonverbal cues over verbal cues. The degree of
closeness in a relationship is described by how accessible the people in
the relationship are to each other. You vary in accessibility with
different people and about different topics with the same people.

   Revealing personal information to others constitutes the process of
self-disclosure. By definition, self-disclosure is risky. That is, because
you usually cannot be certain of the consequences of disclosing
yourself to another, you venture into the unknown. You also risk
getting yourself involved with another person because high disclosure
on your part usually leads to reciprocal behavior on his or her part.

   Relationships may be described fairly concisely according to two
dimensions: friendliness and dominance. Almost any communication
situation that you encounter can be described by looking for evidence
of dominance and friendliness (and their opposites) in messages.

Four skills are helpful in developing meaningful relationships: empathy, feedback, expressing feelings, and declaring statements. If used with moderation, these skills will improve your listening, help you avoid evaluating what others say before you have all the facts, and help you to make clear to others where you stand, what you want, and even how you feel.

CHAPTER 9
INTERVIEWING

n Chapter 8, we examined the relationship level in interpersonal communication. In Chapter 9, we analyze the level of content in a structured situation, the interview.

The word *interview* puts a scare into many students. They think of interviews that can determine whether they get the job they want or of reporters putting a public figure on the spot with embarrassing questions. Those situations are interviews, of course, but there are also many commonplace situations that are so routine we often fail to realize that they are interviews or to plan them adequately. This chapter's goals are to help you to be a more effective interviewer and a more effective interviewee. We discuss the interview as a social situation, preparing for interviews, performing during interviews, and evaluating interviews. After reading this chapter, you can expect to be more productive when you ask for information in interviews, more precise when you interview someone to give them information, and more effective when you attempt to change another's behavior.

Interviews usually occur between two people, and at least one of the people generally has some purpose for the conversation beyond just talking to somebody. One person, designated as the interviewer, ordinarily begins the interview, sometimes by telephoning for an appointment, sometimes by suggesting that conversation cover a particular topic. The interviewer's purposes usually involve either sharing information or changing behavior.

Experience 9.1 shows you some examples of everyday situations that are really interviews.

EXPERIENCE 9.1 SOME INTERVIEWS I HAVE KNOWN

DIRECTIONS **Think of at least three interviews you have been involved in lately. In the first column, list the participants. In the second column, describe what you think the interviewer's purpose was (e.g., inform, gather information, change behavior). In the third column, describe how the interview began. As you can see from our examples, interviews can be extremely casual and brief. Chances are that you are involved in several such interviews each day, either as the interviewer or as the person being interviewed.**

EXAMPLE	*Participants*	*Purpose*	*Interviewer's opening tactic*
1	**Joe and Bill**	**Joe wishes to tell Bill to put gas in Joe's car when he borrows it.**	**"Bill, before you take the car tonight, there's something I want to talk about."**

	Participants	Purpose	Interviewer's opening tactic
2	Student and teacher	Student needs information to clarify what is expected on an assignment.	"Professor Jones, I have a couple of questions about today's assignment. May I come in?"
3	Two co-workers	One of them wants information from the other about a new reporting system.	First worker approaches second worker's desk: "Joan, do you know how to fill out these reports?"
1	_____	_____	_____
2	_____	_____	_____
3	_____	_____	_____
4	_____	_____	_____

CHARACTERISTICS OF INTERVIEWS

Did you find that you could think of several interviews almost immediately? If you could not, consider interviews that helped you to choose a college, interviews with advisers to set up your course schedule, interviews in which you asked someone for a date, interviews in which you asked your parents to increase your allowance. Try working on Experience 9.1 for two minutes more.

Because interviews are so pervasive in people's lives, there is a tendency to think of them as just talk. That misconception can lead to lack of preparation for an interview. It is important to realize that an interview requires skills and preparation just as much as any planned form of interaction does.

Doctor: How are you, Ted?
  Ted: Actually, I'm a bit ill. That's why I'm here.
Doctor: What seems to be the problem?
  Ted: I've had a sore throat for three days, and it's really been getting me down.

Doctor: Let's have a look. Hm—I can see some inflammation of the right side of your throat. Does the pain seem to come mainly from that side?

Ted: Well, mostly, but it's fairly hard to tell.

Doctor: Um-hum. (*Looks at record*) I see you have a slight fever this morning. Have you taken your temperature regularly since being ill?

Ted: No. Would that be a good idea?

Doctor: Well, it can be helpful because if the temperature shoots up suddenly, it's a good danger signal.

Ted: Oh.

Doctor: Let me swab this across your throat. I want to take a culture to be sure you don't have a strep infection. We'll analyze this and call you. Unless you hear otherwise, you can assume this is a throat virus. I recommend that you get lots of rest the next few days, drink plenty of liquids, and take one of these four times a day to relieve discomfort.

Ted: Thanks. I'll call this afternoon to check on the culture.

Doctor: That will be fine. See you later.

Ted: Good-bye.

In order to prepare effectively for interviews, you must first understand some of the basic dynamics of the interview situation. Consider the interview between Ted and the doctor. It is quite typical.

Obviously, most interviews occur on the level of the dyad, the two-person communication situation. It focuses on one person and allows for an efficiency that exists in few other situations. That efficiency can be effectively channeled toward a dominant *purpose* for the interview.

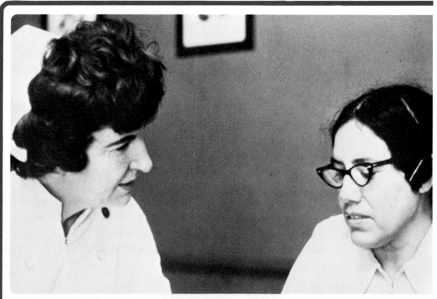

The interview allows a focus on one other person.

The purpose is the goal of the interviewer; it stresses the predominant reason for the interview. The main criterion for evaluating the success of an interview is whether the purpose was accomplished. There are four major purposes for which interviews are conducted:

1 to give information
2 to collect information
3 to change the other's attitudes or behavior
4 to reach a decision

Which of these purposes was predominant in the doctor's mind in our sample interview? Did you say to collect information? So did we.

Purpose
Obviously, it is vital to keep your purposes in mind during an interview. This is particularly important because participants in interviews frequently find themselves at cross-purposes. Consider, for example, TV interview shows that feature prominent personalities in the news. These shows were originally created because Sunday is a slow news day and reporters wished to create stories: "Senator Fogbound said on "Meet the Press" today that he would not run for president this year but might accept a draft at the convention." The reporters try to gather information from the public figures and also try to get them to say things that will create news. The public figure, on the other hand, may view the interview as a chance to become well known and make positions clear (transmit information, change voters' minds). Ordinarily, the public figure also wishes to say nothing that might prove embarrassing. This leads to a cat-and-mouse game in which reporters and the public figure spar for control of the interview. In these situations, the public figure's ability to think quickly, remain calm under pressure, and give informative answers becomes highly valuable because many voters seem to believe that such abilities make a person qualified for public office. Can you see how the interviewers and the public figure have somewhat different purposes for the interview?

The challenge in cross-purpose interviews is to see whether it is possible to gratify both sets of expectations. When a person interviews for a job, for instance, the employment interviewer's purpose is to find the best employee; whereas the interviewee's purpose is to be chosen and hired. A successful job interview will satisfy both purposes. Suppose, example, that you take your car to a repair shop. You are interviewed by someone who asks you what the problem is and has you sign a work order giving permission for the repairs to be made. Your purpose is to get your car running properly. The mechanic has a different purpose: to help the business to do well by persuading you to agree to the most costly repair that would be useful. Do not misunderstand. We are not accusing any mechanic of dishonesty; we are simply pointing out the different interests of the two parties. Under these conditions, arriving at solutions agreeable to both parties is a delicate process requiring some knowledge of automobiles and some communication skill.

EXPERIENCE   9.2   INTERVIEW PURPOSES

DIRECTIONS   List four or more interviews you have had recently. (You may use those you listed in Experience 9.1.) In the first column, list the participants. In the second and third columns, list the purposes of each participant. Try your best to figure out the other party's purpose. Finally, in the fourth column, describe the outcome of the interview. Be sure to state whether either or both parties achieved their purposes.

	Participants	Your purpose	Their purpose	Outcome
1				
2				
3				
4				
5				

Did you see any patterns emerging in your answers to this experience? Did you usually achieve your purpose? What do you think leads to one person's obtaining objectives in an interview? If one person achieves her or his goals, does that mean that the other person cannot? Which person controlled the interview?

Control   These questions bring us to the second major characteristic of interviews: *control of interaction*. In the interview between Ted and the doctor, the doctor exerted control by asking a series of diagnostic questions. Obviously, a person who exerts control of the interaction has a greater chance of reaching his or her goals. The word *control* sounds manipulative, but we do not mean that interviewers should bludgeon others into submission. We mean that an awareness of whether the parties to the conversation are satisfying their goals can help you see when interviews are taking unproductive paths.

Who controls interaction? Two factors are important determinants: relative status and interviewer planning.

Most interviews take place between individuals of unequal status: student and teacher, supervisor and worker, applicant and employment interviewer, doctor and patient. Sometimes status distinctions are not obvious to the parties, but an analysis of the interaction shows them to be operating. For example, suppose one student seeks the help of another about a study problem. The student sought may not be the boss of the one who needs help in any conventional sense, but he or she does have information the other needs and the power to give or withhold it. At another time, of course, the tables may be turned between these two students. In a discussion of social life, campus politics, or a different academic topic, the high-status student may have a lower status.

In summary, one factor that controls interaction is the status of the parties involved. The subordinate is more likely to listen carefully, less likely to jump to conclusions, less likely to offend the other. In such circumstances, it is likely that the high-status person will exert control over the flow of interaction.

The status factor can be offset somewhat through interviewer planning. If you plan to interview someone who is of superior status, careful planning is necessary if you are to accomplish your goals while allowing deference to the other's status.

Of course, the concept of control does not necessarily mean that one person has complete power over the other. In the most productive interviews, both parties generally contribute effective control strategies.

Degree of structure

Another factor that emerges as a major dimension of interviews is *degree of structure*. Some interviews are tightly structured around the interview's purpose; other interviews seem to ramble. Each of these courses can be productive in certain circumstances, and the choice among many possible degrees of tightness in structuring often results from how often an interviewer conducts a particular type of interview. When an interviewer conducts many interviews of the same type, such as employment interviews, it may be desirable to ask a standard set of questions in each interview. The less frequently a particular interview is conducted, the less structured it needs to be.

Some interviews also may take predictable courses of which neither party is aware. For example, a teacher may ask a student who often turns in late work whether an assignment is complete. The student interprets the question as nagging and makes a sullen excuse that leads to further disciplinary actions, all of which changes nothing about the continuing late work. There are dozens of familiar roads to failure in interviews. Experience 9.3 will help you to examine some.

EXPERIENCE 9.3 CHARACTERISTICS OF YOUR INTERVIEWS

DIRECTIONS **Choose two of the interviews you described earlier in this chapter or two new ones, one successful and one less than successful. Describe each interview according to the characteristics we have discussed in this section: purpose, control, and degree of structure. Describe both the parties and the occasions. Which party was the interviewer?**

Characteristics	*Interview 1*	*Interview 2*
1 **Purposes of *both* parties**	_____	_____
	_____	_____
2 **Did the interviewer or interviewee control the interaction? Was control exercised primarily by status or by interviewer planning? How was control exercised?**	_____	_____
	_____	_____
	_____	_____
3 **What was the degree of structure? Describe what sort of structural pattern emerged.**	_____	_____
	_____	_____
4 **What reactions have you to the interview now?**	_____	_____
	_____	_____

PREPARING FOR THE INTERVIEW

Preparing for an interview is more difficult than planning some other kinds of messages. If you prepare a public speech, you can be sure that you will have your say. Nobody is likely to interrupt your plans by interrupting you in the middle of a speech. But in an interview, you share control of the course of interaction with another person. That makes preparation more of a challenge. Planning your exact words may not be helpful if the interview should take an unexpected turn. You should be aware of this because by making proper use of the steps in preparation of an interview, you can anticipate these difficulties and cope with them more successfully.

The best way to teach interview preparation is to take you through the actual steps of preparing an interview and then to help you interpret what happens. The circumstances have been chosen to make the experience as easy as possible.

We suggest that you choose for your first planned interview a situation in which your purpose is to gather information; that is the easiest kind of interview to plan. Most students are interested in information about jobs that they may wish to hold at some time in the future. The rest of this chapter will help you plan, accomplish, and evaluate an interview with a person holding a job that interests you. Your purpose is to gain information about that job. Go ahead and dream. Pick something you would enjoy. You get no extra points for being realistic, so choose a job that would be fun to investigate.

Your next step is to gather some *background information* about that job. Such background information can often be found in the nearest library. The first book to look for in your library is the *Occupational Outlook Handbook,* which is published by the U.S. Department of Labor. It lists most of the job categories that are defined by the Department of Labor. Each listing includes a description of the work, average salaries, best areas of the country for employment, the requirements for the job, and opportunities for advancement.

If the job that interests you has a commonly used title, you may also be able to find information in the card catalogue or the *Reader's Guide to Periodical Literature.* Look under the job title in the subject section. If your job is known by several titles (such as clinician, therapist, or counselor), look under them all. Do not give up. You will be surprised at the information lurking there, waiting for you to find it.

In addition, ask librarians whether there are any trade or professional publications in the areas you are interested in. Of course, each of these encounters with librarians and other persons is itself an interview. Do not overlook such interviews as sources of information.

Using whatever sources you can find, begin to rough out a picture of what the occupation is like. Experience 9.4 will be helpful in this context. We raise some questions that you might be interested in answering, and we also provide spaces for you to note the sources of your information.

EXPERIENCE 9.4 BACKGROUND INFORMATION

DIRECTIONS **Indicate the job category you have selected, and answer the following questions about it. Note the sources of your information, including page numbers (if appropriate).**

EXAMPLE **JOB CATEGORY: Insurance Claims Representative**

Questions	*Information gained*	*Source*
1 **What is the nature of the work?**	**Investigate claims, negotiate settlements with policyholders, authorize payments.**	*Occupational Outlook Handbook,* **1976–1977 edition, U.S. Dept. of Labor Bulletin 1875, pages 117–120.**

2	Where are people employed in the job?	Insurance companies that sell property and liability insurance.
3	What type of training is needed?	Usually college degree plus specialized training by company.
4	What is the outlook for growth and advancement?	Industry will grow about same as the average for all occupations through the 1980s.
5	What earnings can I expect after I get the job?	In 1974, the average was $11,200 to $13,200.

JOB CATEGORY: _____

	Questions	Information gained	Source
1	What is the nature of the work?	_____ _____	_____ _____
2	Where are people employed in the job?	_____ _____	_____ _____
3	What type of training is needed?	_____ _____	
4	What is the outlook for growth and advancement?	_____ _____	
5	What earnings can I expect?	_____	

After you have gathered background information, your next step is to plan your interview's *purpose*. You can see that you have already begun to do this. In fact, it is usual for the purpose of an interview to be partly planned before you even realize that there is to be an interview. For instance, you may be working on a project and get stuck because you need a certain kind of information. After a while you think of somebody who might have access to that information. You decide to interview that person. By this point, you have already decided your purpose: to gain information, and you may have some rather specific thoughts about what kind of information you want to gather.

Nevertheless, it is important to be aware of your purposes and also of any purposes the other party might have. Many an interview has been undermined by lack of attention to this point. One student decided to interview an insurance salesperson. The salesperson's purpose for agreeing to the interview was to sell the student some insurance; the student's purpose was to find out about selling as a career. These cross-purposes created problems for the student, and the interview was a failure.

You've decided to interview for the purpose of gathering information, rather than to transmit information or to influence someone's behavior. You know some things about the persons you wish to interview, and some things about the job. Your next step is to seek more specific information about both. A good way to do that is to write down three questions you want the person you interview to answer for you. You can use questions such as those in Experience 9.4 or others. Do these questions represent any general theme or dominant purpose for the interview? Do they focus on some particular aspect of the job? The focus provided by these questions can be called the *specific purpose* for your interview.

EXPERIENCE 9.5 SPECIFIC PURPOSE FOR THE INTERVIEW

DIRECTIONS   Identify the job you wish to interview about. Then list three important questions that you selected. On the basis of those questions, formulate a statement describing the specific purpose of the interview.

EXAMPLE

1   **Job: Librarian**
2   **Three questions:**
   a. How did you get into library work?
   b. What is your greatest satisfaction in working as a librarian?
   c. Does the work get boring sometimes?
3   **Specific purpose: To gather information concerning a librarian's feelings about the job.**

1   **Job:** _____

2   **Three questions:**
   a. _____
   b. _____
   c. _____
3   **Specific purpose:**
_____

_____

You may have found that it was not easy to merge the purposes of your three questions into one statement of specific purpose. The purpose statement in our example incorporated only our second and third questions.

Look at the questions you listed. Could they be answered from a written source as well as through an interview? For example, we could have listed this question: How many different kinds of librarian jobs are there? It is, of course, an important question, but it could be answered just as easily by reading the college catalogue of a library school as by using valuable interview time. A serious problem with the information-gathering interview is that some beginning interviewers use it when more accurate and economical ways could be used to get the same information. It is more productive to find out background facts for yourself. Use the interview time to ask about the worker's perceptions, attitudes, satisfactions, feelings, or problems.

If two of your three questions in Experience 9.5 could just as well be answered from other sources, return to the preparation phase (Experience 9.4) until you answer these questions and formulate more suitable questions for the interview format.

Now that you have refined your specific purpose, contact a person holding the job you are investigating, and set up an appointment for a day or two from now (or longer if their schedule demands). The interview procedure will take about half an hour, and it would be courteous to inform the party of the amount of time you wish to spend. State the purpose for which you wish the interview clearly but briefly: "I'm gathering information about your line of work because such a job might interest me." Express your personality. If telephones scare you, it is doubly important for you to do this part of the exercise.

Your next major step is to formulate the key questions you want to ask. You have already had plenty of experience formulating questions in this chapter, and you know that some questions are more informative than others. Experience 9.6 gives you a chance to sharpen those skills. Try the "Meet the Press" game.

EXPERIENCE 9.6 "MEET THE PRESS"

DIRECTIONS   **You have been selected to appear as an interviewer on "Meet the Press." You are given three pieces of information: a brief biography of the interviewee prepared by the network staff and two news stories about her. The producer feels that the interviewee may be a dangerous demagogue in the making and wishes to use the interview to get a** complete picture of her motives. Your task is to prepare five questions you wish to ask the interviewee, Ms. Swaim.

BIOGRAPHY   Jane Wesley Swaim is thirty-four years old, a lawyer, mother of two children, and self-proclaimed protector of exploited housewives. Three years ago, Ms. Swaim was propelled into the spotlight by her best-selling book *Professional Homemaker,* which documented how many dollars a year the average housewife is worth to her family and demanded recognition of the status of "homemaker" as a profession parallel to doctor, lawyer, retail merchant, or craftsperson. Since that time, Ms. Swaim has attempted to influence credit managers and manufacturers of household products. She presently is leading a group of Newark housewives in boycotting all businesses that refuse credit to wives on the basis of their profession. Creditors complain that they cannot give charge accounts and loans to housewives because they have no income. Ms. Swaim maintains that the homemaker's economic value to the family is income and that this practice is simply old-fashioned sex discrimination.

MEET THE PRESS   NEWS ARTICLE 1
Newark Housewives Boycott 215 Businesses (Newark, NJ-AP)

A group of professional homemakers announced today a boycott of 215 local businesses on the grounds that these businesses denied credit to housewives. The group, calling itself "Homemakers for Independent Credit" (HIC) was originally concerned mainly with store charge accounts but has broadened its scope in recent weeks to lending institutions and other businesses as well.

Spokeswoman Jane Wesley Swaim, author of the best-selling book *Professional Housewife,* explained the campaign this way: "Businesses have always denied credit to homemakers on the grounds that they had no income. We've shown that this is not the case. The value of the homemaker's services to the household is rarely worth less than $8,000 per year. Technically, the homemaker is paid by other wage earners in the family, for whom these services are performed."

HIC has attracted about 2,000 sympathizers to date, almost all women. Newark businesses aren't screaming for help yet. "A bunch of radicals," snapped a drugstore chain executive who asked not be to identified. "This stuff will never amount to a hill of beans."

MEET THE PRESS   NEWS ARTICLE 2
Swaim Called Opportunist

(Washington-AP) An aide to Senator Bob Bailiwick (R-NJ) charged today that feminist Jane Wesley Swaim seems to be a dangerous opportunist. Characterizing Ms. Swaim's involvement in a host of feminist causes as a bid for political power, the aide predicted that she would "show her true colors in this Newark business." Those true colors involve building up distrust and hatred between men and women and trying to use a power base of women alienated from their families to run for public office.

The aide noted that this strategy was a grave threat to the family unit, which has already been much weakened in recent decades by geographic mobility, religious changes, and crumbling moral standards.

MEET THE PRESS

YOUR INSTRUCTIONS

Write five questions you wish to ask Ms. Swaim. Then describe the specific purpose you wish these questions to accomplish.

1 _____

2 _____

3 _____

4 _____

5 _____

6 **Specific purpose:** _____

The order in which you ask the questions in an interview is very important. Ordinarily, the initial questions set the tone for an entire interview. The first question should probably be a fairly easy one for the interviewee, one that will not threaten him or her too much. Similarly, the most controversial and difficult questions often seem more effective near the close of an interview.

Subsequent questions may build on each other. You can use follow-up sequences. Some questions are necessary only if the answers to the earlier questions are unsatisfactory. There is not always one right sequence for the questions in an interview, but some sequences may be more productive than others.

EXPERIENCE 9.7 INTERVIEW QUESTIONS

DIRECTIONS Rearrange the following list of questions so that the easier question has the lowest number and the most difficult question has the highest number.

_____ 1 What sorts of political problems with the city council do you encounter as a member of the planning staff?

_____ 2 What interested you in TV news in the first place?

_____ 3 How long have you worked as a stockbroker?

_____ 4 How did someone as young as you get to be general sales manager?

_____ 5 How would you characterize your relationship with your superiors?

Now that you have had some experience in deciding the most productive order in which to ask questions, return to the five questions you prepared for Ms. Swaim in Experience 9.6, and apply your new knowledge to them. In the blanks to the left of the question numbers, indicate the order of difficulty.

You are now ready to formulate a set of questions for your job-information interview. Experience 9.8 will guide your work.

EXPERIENCE 9.8 YOUR INTERVIEW QUESTIONS

DIRECTIONS (PART 1) Write five questions you now plan to ask in your information-gathering interview. Then arrange them in numerical order, the first question receiving the lowest number.

_____ 1 _____

_____ 2 _____

_____ 3 _____

_____ 4 _____

_____ 5 _____

DIRECTIONS (PART 2) On the basis of your interview questions, formulate a revised statement of your specific purpose.

Specific purpose:

_____

_____

It may be a good idea to tear out the sheet with the five questions on it or copy them, in their most effective order on another sheet of paper. You could easily carry a legal pad or clipboard into the interview and have these questions with you in case you should become tongue-tied. It is also useful to have your statement of purpose in front of you; it can come in handy when you have to make instant decisions.

Finally, take just a moment to think about time. How much time will you have? We suggested a half-hour interview. How busy is the person? Is he or she likely to be relaxed and cordial or anxious to get the thing over with. It is helpful for you to consider how they see the time you have. Will you have time to ask all your questions? If you have to leave one out, which one would it be best to skip?

Now you are ready for the interview itself.

CONDUCTING THE INTERVIEW

Most interviews are conducted between participants who do not know each other well; they are generally strangers. Because the interview is often short, you will have little time to build the interviewee's confidence in your skills and attitudes. Therefore, the first item on your agenda in most interviews is *establishing rapport.* You must build some common ground of acquaintance and trust between yourself and the other party. Beginning interviewers commonly make the mistake of devoting too little attention to this phase of the interview because they are impatient to get on with the task at hand. If the interviewer does not build trust, defensive behavior can occur throughout the interview. It does little good to ask questions of an interviewee who does not trust you.

In order to build rapport, you must understand the interviewee fairly well. Remember, you are the guiding force in the interview. Therefore, you cannot expect the interviewee to be as well prepared as you are. Do research about the person you are interviewing. For example, you can attempt to find out all you can about the interviewee's likes and dislikes. Do you have any friends who are well acquainted with the interviewee? What have you found out about this person's occupation? What have you found out about the organization for which the person works? All these sources of information are important to your understanding of the other person's point of view. In a sense, you need to build a minirelationship with the interviewee. (You may find it helpful to review the discussion of developing relationships in Chapter 8.)

Like everything else, of course, building rapport with the interviewee can be overdone. The interviewee could become uncooperative if you seem to be wasting his or her time. Remember, an interview is brief. If an interview is half an hour long, for example, you probably should not spend more than five minutes building rapport.

Building rapport in the interview: Well begun is half done.

How can you plan to do just the right amount of rapport building? Well, of course, you cannot plan it. It varies with each interview. The point is to let yourself be aware of how much is enough. If your senses are open, you will see the place. Nonverbal cues often help. If the interviewee fidgets in the seat and leans forward expectantly, it may be time to get to the heart of the interview.

Every interview is different. Greet the other person warmly; show the genuine interest you feel. Shaking hands is usually an asset for both men and women. Remember that you chose to interview this person out of dozens of possibilities. Probably you are delighted to be interviewing him or her.

The second thing you must do during the opening of the interview is to *build a common field of experience.* You and the interviewee need to have an understanding about the things you have in common and the purpose for which you are together. Often, an interviewee is not certain of the purpose of the interview. So even if you think *your* interviewee knows why you are here, it does no harm to review your purpose:

Mr. Walden, I'm here because I'm curious about how you see your day-to-day work as a lawyer. That means a lot to me because I'm seriously considering law as a career. So I'd like to get as far as a half hour can take us toward how your work strikes you.

Your opening gambit does not need to sound this involved, but note what the interviewer has accomplished in three sentences: She had stated the basic purpose of the interview, shown why she is interested in the information sought, and reminded the interviewee of the time limits they have previously agreed to.

The interviewee may question you about your opening statements, giving you opportunities to clarify them. If that happens, you will have worked out a number of expectations for the interview. You want to test to see whether the categories you have roughed out for the interview have any meaning for the person you are interviewing. For example, you might arrange to interview a lawyer with the idea that you will ask how it feels to argue a case in court. Yet many lawyers never do trial work. You could find that out in the opening phase of the interview and reorient subsequent questions to any change in perspective.

Perhaps the most straightforward way to gather contextual information is to volunteer some information and ask for confirmation or elaboration. For example:

The popular image of lawyers, Mr. Walden, is that they spend a lot of time in the courtroom. Is this true for you?

In summary, here is a checklist of things you might wish to think about in preparing to open an interview.

Checklist for interview opening:
Build rapport
_____Help the other to trust you.
_____Learn about the other person's job.
_____Watch what's happening to the relationship.
Build context
_____State your purpose clearly.
_____Note time limit early in interview.
_____Check your basic perceptions about the job and about the interview.

EXPERIENCE   9.9   WORK SHEET FOR INTERVIEW OPENING

DIRECTIONS   **The following items can be prepared before the interview to help make your opening be a success. Answer all items completely.**

1   Rewrite the specific purpose of the interview.

      _____

      _____

2   List the words you plan to use in actually stating your purpose to the interviewee. Use quotation marks.

      _____

      _____

3   List two statements you might make about yourself or your interests that might increase the other's trust in you.

      a. _____

      b. _____

4   List two questions that you might ask early in the interview to check your perceptions or your research about the job the interviewee holds.

      a. _____

      b. _____

5   List one question that is not necessary to your specific purpose but that you might ask to gain time if you get flustered or to flesh out information if you get through with other things too early.

      _____

You may feel that Experience 9.9 amounts to overpreparation. That can be true if you try to use exactly the same words in your interview. But if you speak conversationally, using the ideas you developed, the dialogue will flow naturally.

Once the interviewee seems comfortable and is responding well to your questions, you can move to the heart-of-the-interview questions, the questions designed to gather information related to your specific purpose. As this occurs, you will see the interview unfold as a growing interaction. The success of the interview depends upon continued interest in the topic and the skills of participants. You may observe this recurring sequence of events:

1   You ask question.
2   The interviewee responds.
3   You respond to the interviewee's response with a comment or a follow-up question.
4   You ask another question.

You will probably find that your responses (item 3) are as important to successful interviewing as the questions you originally planned. When the interviewee makes a statement, there are several classes of response you can use.

Sometimes, it seems you need to do little except nod in *agreement* because you are sure that the interviewee has some other things to say. Or you may wish to *summarize* a point that has just been completed in order to be certain that you understand it. A third alternative is to build and develop the response by *probing* for more information or asking for an example. Or you may wish to *change the topic* and move the interview in a direction related to your specific purpose. This is frequently necessary; after all, you cannot expect the interviewee to share or even understand all your purposes for the interview. It is your job to take charge of the interaction and gently nudge it in the direction useful to achieving your purpose.

The four kinds of responses to your interviewee's answers are illustrated in the following dialogue:

Interviewer: What is your greatest satisfaction in your work?
Professional: I would say that the greatest satisfaction I take in my work is the challenge of helping other people solve problems. I know also that I make more money when I tackle the most interesting and difficult problems.

Interviewer: (*Nods*) Um-hum.   Agreement

or

Interviewer: So the greatest satisfactions are the challenge of   Summary
solving problems and knowing that you are paid
what you are worth.

or

Interviewer: What sorts of problems do you often   Probe, follow-up
find yourself solving?   question

or

Interviewer: You mentioned making more money.   Topic shift to
How important to you was the level   related area
of pay when you chose this job.

or

Interviewer: What types of people do you find yourself working   Topic shift to
with on a day-to-day basis.   new area

Note that the same answer from your interviewee can take you in a number of different directions. As interviewer, it is your role to guide the interview in the direction you find most useful. Some beginning interviewers feel ill at ease changing the topic and fail to get to important areas of the interview because a good opportunity to ask their big questions never occurs. If you face this problem, you may wish to deal with it simply and bluntly: "I'd like to shift topics for a minute and ask you. . . ." Interviewees rarely object.

EXPERIENCE 9.10 LEVELS OF RESPONDING

DIRECTIONS Write five responses to each of the following statements using the format just outlined.

1 "When I was in college, I never dreamed that I'd be doing what I'm doing now. I guess there are some jobs you just can't train for."
a. Agreement: _____

b. Summary: _____

c. Probe: _____

d. Shift to related area: _____

e. Shift to new area: _____

2 "My experience in the service taught me that changes, if they come at all in this job, must be introduced at a slow, moderate pace."
a. Agreement: _____

b. Summary: _____

c. Probe: _____

d. Shift to related area: _____

e. Shift to new area: _____

The questions you prepared earlier can also be looked at from this perspective. Look back at the five polished questions you listed for this interview in Experience 9.8 and ranked in the order you wished to ask them. Label each of those questions as probe, shift to a related area, or shift to a new area. This experience will help you predict better the circumstances in which you will ask the question and may also help you to identify questions that will be difficult to ask at all.

If you have been successful to this point in the interview, you have observed the interviewee's nonverbal behavior, remained aware of how fast time is passing, and asked all your crucial questions. Only one more thing needs to be accomplished: the successful *closing of the interview*. Most Americans are not adept at finishings. They usually hate good-byes. Sometimes, an interviewee will begin to show signs of impatience (fiddling with objects, looking away, arranging arms so as to rise from the chair). In such circumstances, the interview is likely to end clumsily. It will be worth your while to think about how the interview may best be closed before you begin it. You may not use the tactics you have planned, but you can fall back on them if you have to. Thanking the interviewee for his or her time, asking for any final comments, standing, and offering your hand are all effective techniques.

In an information-gathering interview, closings are relatively simple once you have all the information you desire. But interviews that aim at changing behavior face a more significant problem: The interview closing can be critical to whether a behavior change does in fact take place as a result of the interview.

EVALUATING THE INTERVIEW

After each interview, it is useful to make a quick postmortem to evaluate your own performance and the overall success of the interview. It is wisest, especially for the first several interviews, to conduct this self-evaluation *immediately* after the interview has ended, while the facts are still fresh in your mind.

First, jot down some quick notes of things covered in the interview. You may not have had time to write in full during the interview. You need detailed information, especially in information-gathering interviews. If the place of the interview has a public waiting room, that can be an excellent location for the recall phase. Otherwise find a nearby place where you can collect your thoughts and write.

In recording your information, be certain to separate facts and inferences (see Chapter 4). Ask yourself whether the interviewee would agree with all the details of your account. One way to find out for sure is to prepare a written summary of the interview and mail a copy to the interviewee. If there is ever a question about what happened at the interview, you then have a written record that the other party has seen and that supports your recollection.

If the purpose of your interview was to change someone's attitudes or behavior, it would be useful to record the details of what was accomplished in the interview. If the two of you came to an agreement about a principle or course of action, or if the interviewee ordered some product or service from you, it can be vital to have accurate records of the transaction.

Once you have recorded the results of the interview, you can proceed to evaluate what happened in greater detail. Here are some questions to ask:

Did I ask all the questions I planned to?
If not, why did I leave some out?
Did my interview accomplish its specific purpose?
How can I tell whether it did?
Did I create a warm and friendly climate?
Did I create trust in me on the part of the interviewee?
Did I gain the interviewee's cooperation?
Did I maintain control of the direction and flow of the interview?

Experience 9.11 will give you practice in evaluating an interview. Respond to it after you have completed your job-information interview.

EXPERIENCE   9.11   INTERVIEW EVALUATION

DIRECTIONS   After you have completed your information-gathering interview, evaluate it according to the following scales. Circle the number that best describes your reaction.

  1   **How well prepared was I for this interview?**
       Not very well   1   2   3   4   5   6   7   Very well
  2   **What kind of climate did I create?**
       Cold and hostile   1   2   3   4   5   6   7   Warm and friendly
  3   **How interested was the interviewee in answering my questions?**
       Not very interested   1   2   3   4   5   6   7   Very interested
  4   **How cooperative was the interviewee?**
       Not very cooperative   1   2   3   4   5   6   7   Very cooperative
  5   **How much indication did I have that I was trusted by the interviewee?**
       Not very much   1   2   3   4   5   6   7   A great deal
  6   **How much control of the direction and flow of the interview did I exert?**
       Not very much   1   2   3   4   5   6   7   A great deal
  7   **How did the physical setting affect the interview?**
       Hindered   1   2   3   4   5   6   7   Facilitated
  8   **How much distraction was there by outside influences?**
       Very much   1   2   3   4   5   6   7   Very little
  9   **How efficiently was the time utilized?**
       Not very efficiently   1   2   3   4   5   6   7   Very efficiently
 10   **Now that the interview is over, how would the interviewee respond to a similar request from another person in my circumstances?**
       Not very favorably   1   2   3   4   5   6   7   Very favorably

EXPERIENCE 9.12 INTERVIEW PLANNING FORM

DIRECTIONS   **Use this form when planning your interview for this chapter. A duplicate of this form could be used for planning another interview.**

1   **Who is the interview with?** _____
2   **What do I know about this person?**

_____

_____

3   **How much time do I have with this person?** _____
4   **What is the general purpose of the interview?**

_____

_____

5   **What are some of the questions I need answered or things I need to get out of this interview?**

_____

_____

_____

6   **Which of the questions listed in item 5 can better be answered through other resources? (Try to answer them before the interview.)**

_____

7   **Place a number to the left of each remaining question in item 5 to indicate the order in which you plan to ask them.**
8   **State as concisely as you can the specific purpose of your interview**

_____

_____

BEING AN EFFECTIVE INTERVIEWEE

Everything we have said so far in this chapter has been designed to prepare you to be a more effective interviewer. But you will not always be the interviewer in your daily life. Most of you will be interviewees at least as often, unless you choose a career in sales or personnel interviewing.

An interview, like a relationship, requires the cooperative efforts of two persons in order to be effective. The interviewer is in the best position to set a course for the interview *if* the interviewee cooperates. But the interviewee can block any strategy tried by an interviewer. No matter how well thought out an interviewer's questions are, an interviewee can still obstruct, lie, or refuse to answer.

An interviewee can also try to set a different course for the interview. For example, when one of the authors worked as a salesman, he called on a potential client. The client seemed interested but kept referring to his own job, which was selling a different product. In the end, the encounter became a sort of double-edged selling interview, in which each was trying to get the other to buy his product.

As we pointed out earlier, parties usually have different purposes for an interview. For instance, the professional whom you interview has different motives from yours. Therefore, when preparing to be interviewed, you may find it helpful to go through many of the steps we have prescribed for interviewers. For example, it makes sense for an interviewee to understand his or her own purpose for granting the interview. Write this information down. Perhaps the interviewer wishes to gain information about your job. Why did you agree to the interview? Out of friendship? Because you could not say no? Because you are interested in encouraging intelligent young people to pursue your line of work? Because you want this person to work for your company some day?

Obviously, your reason for granting the interview will affect the way you act. If you granted the interview out of friendship or because you could not say no, you may be primarily interested in keeping things friendly but brief. If you want to encourage the person to join your occupational category, you may wish to make the occupation seem as attractive as possible.

Up to this point, we have also implied that if an interviewer asks his or her questions properly, the information asked for will be forthcoming. But suppose it is the primary interest of the interviewee to *hide* some information? As an interviewee, it is your right to give and withhold information as you please. If you wish to be interviewed but do not want to talk about a certain area, do not be afraid to say something like, "That's an area I don't feel free to talk about. Let's try a different subject." "I won't go into specifics about that case, but I can offer a general point of view." Do not lie, but be your own gatekeeper.

Similarly, in a sales interview, the interviewer's purpose is to sell a product or service; whereas the interviewee's purpose is to make a judgment. If the decision is not to buy, some sales resistance may have to be called into play as the salesperson asks for commitment to the sale.

These suggestions should make it clear that every interview is a two-party matter and that the most successful interviews are those which accomplish the goals of both parties. Most interviews are not situations in which one party wins and the other loses. Rather, they are likely to be situations in which both parties succeed or both fail. A sales interview is most successful if the customer buys the products

Both interviewer and interviewee may alter the tone of the interaction through nonverbal signals.

that will be useful to him or her and resists pressure to purchase others. The salesperson makes a living, and the customer is satisfied and likely to trust that salesperson with future business. An interview in which a salesperson manipulates a customer into buying more of a product than is needed does not serve the interests of either party. The interviewee will waste money, and the salesperson will probably lose business in the long run.

This is also true in most information-gathering interviews. If a person agrees to let you ask occupational questions, the two of you probably have some interests in common and both of you can be satisfied with the outcome. If the interview is unproductive, you are both likely to lose.

Job Interviews

There is one other situation that we have barely mentioned but in which your behavior as an interviewer may determine the course of your future life. This is, of course, the *job interview*. Most desirable professional positions pose the interview as a necessary hurdle to be cleared before obtaining employment. You will be interviewed by your potential boss or by a professional employment interviewer, perhaps by both. The success of your performance in this interview will be a major determinant of whether you get the job.

As a college graduate or a person with at least some college background, you will probably be interviewing for positions where the employer will be interested not only in the specific skills you now possess but also in your long-range potential as an employee who can grow with the organization and make positive future contributions. Thus, you should not be surprised if the interviewer asks many questions regarding your background and goals and attempts to get a feel for how ambitious you are and what sort of attitudes you are likely to have toward your job. You must prepare for such probing questions by taking a serious inventory of your characteristics, traits, goals, and preferences. Experience 9.13 is designed to help you do just that.

EXPERIENCE   9.13   MY BALANCE SHEET AS AN EMPLOYEE

DIRECTIONS   **The following pairs of adjectives describe qualities that many employers look for in potential employees. Take an honest look at yourself, and evaluate yourself on each of the adjective pairs by circling the number that best describes you in relation to the two ends of the scale.**

Dishonest	1	2	3	4	5	6	7	Honest
Unhealthy	1	2	3	4	5	6	7	Healthy
Do only what is asked	1	2	3	4	5	6	7	Eager for more things to do
Often absent	1	2	3	4	5	6	7	Seldom absent
Immature judgment	1	2	3	4	5	6	7	Mature judgment
Cannot be trusted	1	2	3	4	5	6	7	Trustworthy
Defensive	1	2	3	4	5	6	7	Open
Make decisions based primarily on hunch or intuition	1	2	3	4	5	6	7	Make decisions based on data
Disrespectful	1	2	3	4	5	6	7	Respectful
Uncooperative	1	2	3	4	5	6	7	Cooperative
Hard to work with	1	2	3	4	5	6	7	Easy to work with
Rude	1	2	3	4	5	6	7	Courteous
Unreliable	1	2	3	4	5	6	7	Dependable
Talk too much	1	2	3	4	5	6	7	Know when to be quiet

Both these favorable and the unfavorable characteristics in Experience 9.13 presume that you are skillful at whatever you are hired to do. Dissatisfaction with employees after they have been on the job often relates to interpersonal problems or a mismatching of people and jobs. Thus, it pays to become aware of the type of job you are interviewing for and consider it carefully. It makes sense to choose a job that you can perform well in and be happy with rather than just any good-paying job. You can get some of this information from interviews such as the one you prepared for this chapter. The career counseling center on your campus can help you get further information and prepare a resumé.

Resumé writing is essentially writing an advertisement for yourself. Again, that means taking inventory of yourself and then choosing those elements that best represent you to a potential employer. For example, what previous experiences or interests do you have that will make you attractive to an employer? Give a lot of thought to selecting the best ways to display the information on the actual resumé. It should be quite brief, probably a single page. There are no hard-and-fast rules, but most resumés will include the following categories or types of information:

1. *Heading.* The heading may include name, address, and phone number or name only (leaving address and phone number for the end). You can omit such data as age, marital status, weight, and height because the law does not consider these job-related qualities.

2. *Career goals.* This is a one-sentence statement of your career objectives. Serious job hunters often tailor this goal to a particular advertised position. In other words, they tailor a new résumé for each new job possibility. It also helps to indicate your ambition for increasing your knowledge and responsibilities. The following statement fulfills this requirement well: "An entry-level position as assistant buyer, leading later to merchandising management."

3. *Experience.* Whether you discuss education first or experience first will depend on which you feel is strongest in relation to the position you seek. Think about the paid jobs you have had and the positions of responsibility you have had in voluntary organizations. These activities will help create a positive impression. Use action words to describe your accomplishments under this section: for example, *developed, implemented, achieved,* and *performed.*

4. *Education.* List the institutions you have attended since high school. Give the names and dates of degrees conferred and any honors that you received, such as honors programs or dean's list. Be sure to list your major areas of concentration as well as any special projects you completed.

SUMMARY

The main purpose of this chapter has been to involve you in interview experiences.

There are many interview situations in everyday communication. An interview is a two-person conversation in which one of the parties has purposes or tasks to accomplish that predominate over the relationship dimensions of communication (see Chapter 8). The most common purpose for interviews is to gather information. Some interviews also transmit information or seek to effect behavior changes. To undertake persuasive interviews, combine the ideas of this chapter with those in Chapter 14, "Persuading Others." In most successful interviews, it is the interviewer who controls interaction. Consequently, the interviewer is usually more prepared than the interviewee. One exception is the job interview. Interviewer planning revolves around such issues as: status, control of interaction, and degree of structure.

In preparing for any interview, follow these steps: (1) pick an interview you will enjoy and profit from, (2) do background research, (3) state a specific purpose, (4) formulate questions, (5) arrange the questions in the most effective order, and (6) practice the opening and close of the interview.

In conducting an information-gathering interview, follow these steps: (1) establish rapport, (2) ask follow-up questions, and (3) probe, summarize, and change topics where needed. To evaluate the effectiveness of an interview, record information immediately and compare your accomplishment with your specific purpose.

A successful interview demands the cooperation of two effective communicators. Interviewee behavior can scuttle any interview or can help to salvage the efforts of an inept interviewer. The interviewee should examine his or her specific purposes for agreeing to the interview. Perhaps the participants of the interview will be found to operate at cross-purposes.

One important interview for all students is the job interview. Successful communication as an interviewee is crucial to getting the best possible job. Two major components of preparing for the job interview are analyzing your strengths as an employee and preparing an effective resumé.

CHAPTER 10
WORKING IN SMALL GROUPS

When a major long-term problem is recognized in the United States, the president appoints a group of distinguished citizens to discuss it, do research, and make recommendations. Such groups have studied pornography, riots, presidential assassinations, and many other topics.

When a piece of legislation is proposed in the U.S. Congress, it is referred to a committee, a small group of legislators who have some experience and expertise in the area being considered. Congress features committees that specialize in matters concerning the armed services, the judiciary, finance, foreign affairs, and so on.

When an executive wishes to revitalize the organizational structure of his or her department, a small group of individuals often considers the question. Such groups are able to question people within and outside the department. Similar processes are followed in schools, churches, and civic organizations.

A comedian once remarked that a committee is "a group of the unprepared appointed by the unwilling to do the unnecessary." That wisecrack derives its humor from our society's widespread reliance on task-related groups. The group has been important in every conceivable area of business and government. A group met to declare the United States' independence. Another group convened to write a constitution. In rejecting monarchy as a form of government, the Founding Fathers felt that rule by groups was more desirable than rule by individuals. The U.S. government has three branches. One branch is headed by an individual; the other two branches are headed by groups. That model has been followed in every state. Most cities are governed by city councils.

The existence of both executives and groups in government suggests that there are some kinds of jobs best done by individuals and other kinds best handled by groups. When speed of decision or specialized knowledge is needed, it would be foolish to ask groups to haggle. But if a decision has to be made that changes a law affecting many people, then a group may come up with a better decision.

Most groups that we have mentioned so far seem relatively *formal*. The groups have names, and some members are elected or appointed. The visibility of famous groups may obscure the fact that most groups that operate in and affect people's lives are relatively *informal*. People band together in groups for entertainment, study, promoting causes, worship, and so forth.

The purpose of this chapter is to help you examine how you operate in groups so that you can communicate more effectively in them. You already operate within many groups. Many students are surprised when we say this, but it is almost invariably true of even the most inveterate loner. To examine your behavior in groups, you must first find out the sorts of groups to which you belong. Remember, groups can be formal or informal. Start by thinking of any collection of people you commonly find yourself with. List some of these groups in Experience 10.1. Many students find this a bit difficult at first, so do not be discouraged if it takes a few minutes for you to think of group descriptions.

EXPERIENCE 10.1 THE GROUPS I FIND MYSELF IN

DIRECTIONS   **List all the groups you belong to, and state the number of members in each of them. A group may have a name, or you may just describe its purpose or the occasions when it finds itself together. Be sure to list at least six groups.**

EXAMPLE

Description of group	*Number of members*
First Street Church Softball Team	12
A communication class informal study group	3 to 5
Roommates	3

Description of group	*Number of members*
1 _____	_____
2 _____	_____
3 _____	_____
4 _____	_____
5 _____	_____
6 _____	_____

Students tell us that listing groups becomes easier once they get started. Their lists have usually contained about 8 to 14 group affiliations, including everything from work groups to social clubs to families. Some of the groups you listed may have 30 or more members (e.g., a class you attend). Others may have only 3 members. This chapter focuses on small groups in which almost everyone is likely to get a chance to talk. We guess that such groups usually have from 3 to 12 members. If there are only 2 members, the group can best be considered as a single relationship, or dyad (see Chapters 8 and 9). If there are more than 12 members, it is difficult for more than a few members to participate. Have you ever noticed how the same 3 or 4 people usually talk in a college class containing 30 or more members? The class is too large for everyone to participate. There were 12 apostles; there are usually 12 persons on a jury. Sometimes even 12 can be too many. Researchers have found that for most tasks in job settings, groups of 5 to 7 people are more effective.

If you look again at your list of groups, you will find that some groups are more *formal* than others. Some schedule meetings, set up agendas, try to finish things by deadlines, and so on. Other groups meet more by chance or on occasions when a meeting seems useful. Another dimension of formality is the group's role structure. Some groups have a leader who calls the group together and tells others what needs to be done. Some groups have secretaries or treasurers to keep important records. Some groups issue minutes or written reports. All these indicate formality in the group.

Closely related to formality is *task orientation*. Some groups, such as congressional committees, curriculum revision committees, and a gathering to study for the midterm exam, are created to perform tasks. Other groups, such as families, residential groups, and fraternities are primarily social. Some groups, such as charitable groups, garden clubs, and athletic teams, perform both functions. Indeed, as we will discuss later in this chapter, most groups come to perform both task and social functions.

How important to you is each of the groups you listed in Experience 10.1? Obviously, you are more committed to some groups than to others. Which groups do you care about most? Which groups would you most want to see accomplish something important? If all the groups you listed in Experience 10.1 were meeting at the same time, which meeting would you attend? Is *that* group most important to you? These questions are designed to determine your degree of commitment to, or involvement in, each group. We ask you to answer them formally in Experience 10.2.

EXPERIENCE 10.2 KINDS OF GROUPS I BELONG TO

DIRECTIONS   List five groups you belong to. You may list the same groups you cited in Experience 10.1 or others, but limit this list to groups containing from 3 to 12 members. Describe each group according to its formality, its task orientation, and your degree of commitment to it.

EXAMPLE

Description of group	Formal/ informal	Task or social orientation	Degree of my commitment
Study group	Informal	Task and social	Medium
My family	Sometimes either one	Social	High
Young Democrats	Formal	Task	Low

	Description of group	Formal/ informal	Task or social orientation	Degree of my commitment
1	_____	_____	_____	_____
2	_____	_____	_____	_____
3	_____	_____	_____	_____
4	_____	_____	_____	_____
5	_____	_____	_____	_____

In responding to Experience 10.2, you probably found that the categories formal-informal, task-social, and high-low commitment were not clear-cut. A given group, such as a family, can be formal on some occasions and informal on others. A task-oriented group may serve social functions. A group that requires high commitment at some times may be almost forgotten at other times. For example, a group affiliated with a national political party would require greatest commitment around the times of important elections.

And what of your own role in these groups? Does it change, too? Most people find that roles they take change over time. In family groups, for instance, young children play a subordinate role and depend on parents and other family members for support. As children get older, they join other groups, and the family may become less important to them. If the child goes to college, the family may fade into the background for several years. And by the time a child reaches college age, he or she begins to address parents as equals rather than as bosses.

The nature of the group may affect your tactical choices. A leader in one group may be a follower in another group. For example, a person confident of his or her religious views might be more of a leader in religious groups than in political or other groups. The important thing is to act in ways that feel most comfortable. Our objective is, not to change what you are, but to show you how you can use your strengths to become more effective.

PHASES OF GROUP BEHAVIOR

How does a typical small group function? It turns out that, at least in work settings in the United States, groups usually go through a predictable series of phases in almost any deliberation. It is possible to observe these phases and construct a sort of natural history of the group process. The purpose of this section is to relate such a phase-by-phase description to groups you are involved in. Perhaps the best way to do this is to generate a group experience and then discuss what happens. You may wish to participate in or observe an in-class discussion in conjunction with reading this section. Observation of how the group process unfolds will give added meaning to our description.

The most effective group discussions proceed through four predictable stages: the polite phase, the orientation phase, the role division phase, and the constructive phase. Groups that ignore one or more of these stages usually prove to be less productive.

Polite phase

The first phase in most group encounters is the *polite* phase. Group members are polite and restrained with each other because they do not know how else to be. If the group members are already well acquainted, this stage may be brief. During this stage, members get acquainted with each other, learn each other's names, share information, and in general feel each other out to see what modes of interaction seem most successful. The polite stage is a period of first impressions; little actual business is transacted. There is practically no conflict, self-disclosure, or task orientation.

In spite of how little seems to get done during this phase, there is some tension in the air. Group members are figuring out what roles are most appropriate for them. It is normal for some group members to grow impatient and want to get on with the business at hand.

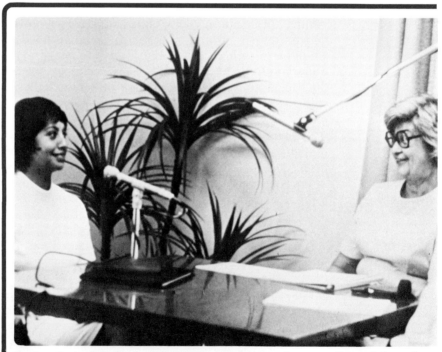

During the polite phase of group discussion, members are determining what roles seem most appropriate to the setting.

Ironically, the group *is* dealing with the business at hand by learning to deal with each other as people. If the polite phase is shortened and the meeting is prematurely called to order by an impatient chairperson, the personal issues are left unresolved, and they may rear their ugly heads at later points of deliberation. It may seem that the polite phase is only small talk, but research has shown its importance to effective group decisions. Knowing this often helps to quiet impatience when you are in groups that appear to spend too much time in the polite phase.

You will know that the polite phase is ending when several members begin to turn the discussion from personal matters to questions about the group's goals.

Orientation phase

The stage in which the group sets its purposes is called the *orientation phase*. It is during this phase that leaders begin to emerge in a group (assuming none were appointed at the start). Leaders appear when a critical question is asked—such as, "What exactly are our goals?" After the question is asked, watch people's eyes. They will often (but not always) look in the direction of someone whom they expect to speak. That someone may have seemed particularly confident or knowledgeable. That someone may be an authority figure. For example, when teachers work in small groups with students, the students usually look to the teacher.

It is during the orientation stage that alliances form. Persons who express similar views begin to look to each other for support and to agree with each other on other issues. Individuals feel that their influence is increased when others agree with them. The cliques formed in this way maintain influence throughout the life of the group. There is nothing inherently destructive about cliques, but they can become troublesome if they are competing with each other and cannot reach agreement with each other about the definition of the larger group's task.

During orientation, leadership may emerge somewhat passively, the followers push the leader to take over by looking at the leader, by reinforcing his or her comments, and by accepting the leader's definition of the task.

Role division phase

During the third phase, *role division*, the leader and other members of the group become more assertive in seeking out their roles and defining how they are to be acted out. This phase reveals bids for power on the part of potential leaders.

During the orientation phase, a potential leader might wait to be asked for an opinion. During role division, people may volunteer unsolicited comments about the group's purpose or about what should be discussed first. These are bids for group leadership. Rivals are likely to question such statements, and the nature of these interchanges provides another way to distinguish this phase. Arguments are a sign of jockeying for role positions. The cliques formed during the orientation phase also prove important during leadership struggles, and role positions within the cliques appears at this point. One member of a clique becomes its leader or spokesperson; others assume lieutenant roles. The supporters usually wait for the spokesperson to speak, then voice support.

Not all group members vie for task leadership. There are other important roles in group discussion. First, there is the role of the *easer of tensions*, the person who cracks a joke and puts others at ease. Then there is the *compromiser*, the person who seeks agreement and defines areas in which people can get together. The role of *questioner* is also often valuable. The questioner serves as a sort of outsider to the deliberations, asking pointed questions and indicating weakness in group positions. Finally, there is the *reinforcer*, the person who smiles, tells others when their contributions are worthwhile, and solicits contributions from those who have fallen silent.

There are of course many unworthwhile roles, including the sulk; the terminal cynic; the failed leader, who wants to sabotage the whole business; the practical joker, who wants center stage; the hard-nosed arguer, who wants to hold a position at all costs; and the blocker, who resists any novel position.

For some reason, people tend to assume roles rather inflexibly and having acted in a certain way are likely to continue to do more of the same. They expect it of themselves, and others expect it of them. Their roles assume some characteristics of self-fulfilling prophecy (see Chapter 3). When a group member is perceived as a leader, other members reinforce leadership attempts; when a member is defined by the group as a questioner, the group respects that person's questions and stops to ponder them. After several such reinforcement cycles, the characteristic behavior can become fixed. Unfortunately, many groups never pass through this stage and allow members role flexibility. Therefore, it is important to realize that a role need not be rigidly held by one person. Leadership is often shared. Any group member can ask a sharp question, any member can suggest a compromise, and so on.

Once roles have been divided and some flexibility established for operating within them, the group is finally ready to begin work on the task.

Constructive phase

The group now enters the *constructive* phase. Why does it take so long? Does the process seem dreadfully inefficient? Well, our language or our courtship customs often seem inefficient in the same sense. That is, a lot of things happen before what appear logically to be the critical acts. But the point is that if these introductory actions are skipped, the critical acts suffer. There can be no effective relationships without acquaintances, there can be no effective interviews without preliminaries, and there are few consistently effective groups that do not pass through the first three phases of the process.

During the constructive phase, group members share to some degree all roles defined during the third phase. They ask questions about the task and listen to responses. Personal roles, such as leader and the social facilitator, may still exist, but any group member can perform any of these functions when it is helpful to do so. Thus, different members take on varied tasks. Members lay out facts, alternative courses of action, and opinions to help the group reach the best-possible conclusions. Members may change their points of view on the issue in light of new information, which is quite rare in earlier phases.

The productive cooperation that emerges generates a group commitment, a spirit of identification among the members. Members feel attracted to the group and to its members. Although members may not always agree on particular subjects, they understand and respect alternative positions. They become satisfied with the group's output.

Incidentally, this group spirit generates a kind of conceit. The group becomes united against others who have not had the group experience and therefore understand the issues less clearly. If a new member joins a group that has already moved into the constructive phase, the new member may be treated as an outsider for some time and may even disrupt the group's productivity. This happens partly because the outsider is unaware of group norms in the same way that a tourist is unaware of the norms of the city or country he/she is visiting.

The phases of group development are not absolutely invariant. They do not always occur precisely as we have described them. For example, a group that has worked together many times may move quickly through the early stages. But researchers have observed the four phases in many successful groups that met in many times and places for many purposes. They have also found that groups which allow all these phases to unfold unhurriedly have the greatest chance of being efficient, successful, and satisfied with their accomplishments.

If you keep this natural history of a group in mind, you will be able to recognize where a group is at any given time. That recognition may prevent frustration or fears that a job will not get done. Effective groups start more slowly than inexperienced group members realize. If, for example, the group you are impatient with is still in the orientation phase, it is unrealistic for you to expect it to grapple seriously with problems at hand. Experience 10.3 gives you a chance to practice your skill in identifying the four phases of group activity.

EXPERIENCE   10.3   THE PHASES OF MY GROUP'S DISCUSSION

DIRECTIONS   Recall a recent group experience or observe one, and describe what
happens in each of the four phases. Be sure to include an explanation
of how you knew that each phase was in operation as part of your
answer in the What We Discussed column.

Phase	What we discussed	My contributions and feelings then
polite	_____	_____
	_____	_____
orientation	_____	_____
	_____	_____
role division	_____	_____
	_____	_____
constructive cooperation	_____	_____
	_____	_____

1   What is your overall evaluation of this group's effectiveness?
_____

2   What is your evaluation of your effectiveness in this group?
_____
_____

3   Did you assume predominantly one role?
_____
_____

Optional: Here is an extra form so that you can observe these phases
in another group discussion.

Phase	What we discussed	My contributions and feelings then
polite	_____	_____
	_____	_____
orientation	_____	_____
	_____	_____

role division   _____   _____

                        _____   _____

constructive   _____   _____

cooperation   _____   _____

1   What is your overall evaluation of this group's effectiveness?

    _____

2   What is your evaluation of your effectiveness in this group?

    _____

3   Did you assume predominantly one role? Describe your role tactics.

    _____

GROUP NORMS AND COHESIVENESS

Every group generates its own climate and expectations. You probably recognize the truth of this statement in general, but to see it more concretely and specifically, turn back to Experience 10.2. Choose two groups you mentioned there that are quite different from each other. The purpose of Experience 10.4 is to get you to think about differences in group norms and about differences among all groups to which you belong by taking another look at these two groups.

EXPERIENCE 10.4 COMPARATIVE GROUP NORMS

DIRECTIONS   The following forms list behavior descriptions that are appropriate in some groups but less appropriate in others. Write the name of one of the groups you have chosen from Experience 10.2 in the Group A blank; write the name of the other group in the Group B blank. For each behavior circle the number that best describes its degree of appropriateness or acceptability in each group. These ratings indicate the groups' norms. After you have completed the ratings for group A, rate group B without looking back at the group A ratings.

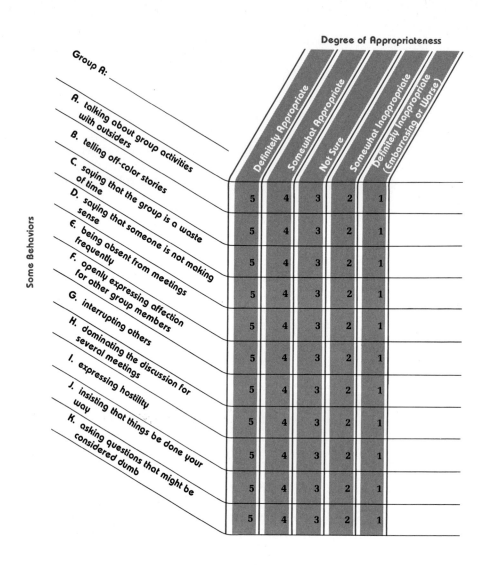

Degree of Appropriateness

Group A: _____

Some Behaviors

	Definitely Appropriate	Somewhat Appropriate	Not Sure	Somewhat Inappropriate	Definitely Inappropriate (Embarrasing or Worse)	
A. talking about group activities with outsiders	5	4	3	2	1	
B. telling off-color stories	5	4	3	2	1	
C. saying that the group is a waste of time	5	4	3	2	1	
D. saying that someone is not making sense	5	4	3	2	1	
E. being absent from meetings frequently	5	4	3	2	1	
F. openly expressing affection for other group members	5	4	3	2	1	
G. interrupting others	5	4	3	2	1	
H. dominating the discussion for several meetings	5	4	3	2	1	
I. expressing hostility	5	4	3	2	1	
J. insisting that things be done your way	5	4	3	2	1	
K. asking questions that might be considered dumb	5	4	3	2	1	

If you compare your ratings for groups A and B in Experience 10.4, you will probably find several differences between behaviors that are appropriate. Other group members in each group would probably agree with most of your ratings because every member of a group gains some knowledge about what communication strategies are most appropriate. This knowledge, like knowledge of codes (see Chapters 5 and 6), is often implicit. Appropriate behavior in groups is something people ordinarily do without even stopping to think about it.

An example of group norms is how much work the group considers it should do on any one occasion. Most groups evolve

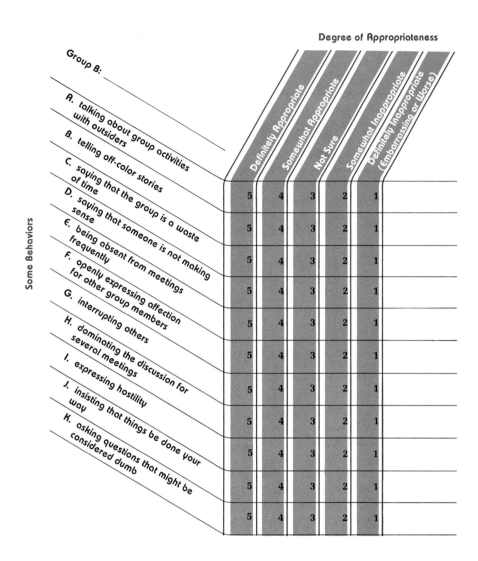

Degree of Appropriateness

Some Behaviors

Group B: _____

A. talking about group activities with outsiders
B. telling off-color stories
C. saying that the group is a waste of time
D. saying that someone is not making sense
E. being absent from meetings frequently
F. openly expressing affection for other group members
G. interrupting others
H. dominating the discussion for several meetings
I. expressing hostility
J. insisting that things be done your way
K. asking questions that might be considered dumb

	Definitely Appropriate	Somewhat Appropriate	Not Sure	Somewhat Inappropriate	Definitely Inappropriate (Embarrassing or Worse)
A	5	4	3	2	1
B	5	4	3	2	1
C	5	4	3	2	1
D	5	4	3	2	1
E	5	4	3	2	1
F	5	4	3	2	1
G	5	4	3	2	1
H	5	4	3	2	1
I	5	4	3	2	1
J	5	4	3	2	1
K	5	4	3	2	1

expectations in this area. This kind of norm is fairly difficult for a newcomer in the group to pick up, and a newcomer may be particularly anxious to please veteran group members by hard work. The newcomer may generate so much work that he or she becomes a rate-buster. That is because the newcomer did not understand the group norm against getting too much done at once.

The preceding example may give you the notion that group norms are all negative (against too much work, against outside authority, against telling off-color stories, and so on). Actually, group norms can just as easily favor high output and creative contributions from each member. In fact, certain norms cement a group together, generate warm feelings, and aid productivity. Such norms often allow members with differences of opinion to confront each other and talk them out. Then, when decisions are reached, group members are committed to them. (If these statements seem vague to you, it is because researchers do not yet fully understand group processes. Nevertheless, researchers agree that groups that have these characteristics are consistently more productive and satisfied than groups that lack them.)

More productive and satisfied groups are often called *cohesive* groups. That is, they stick together. Cohesiveness bonds members together into a larger unit that is more powerful and effective than individuals working alone. Cohesive groups are more than the sum of their parts. They tend to be friendly and cooperative, to encourage a lot of discussion and participation that includes all members. Less cohesive groups talk less, criticize each other and the group frequently, and frequently experience low productivity. A cohesive group, like a fulfilling personal relationship, is difficult to define. When a group has cohesiveness, things seem to get better and better. But when a group is struggling, things are as likely to go from bad to worse as they are to improve.

Probably the most important thing an individual can do to increase cohesiveness is to practice thinking of the self as part of something (the group) that is larger than individual members. Individuals can also encourage the group to set some concrete, obtainable goals. Just as cohesiveness leads to productivity, productivity leads to cohesiveness. If a group can accomplish some task, members are likely to feel good about the accomplishment and about their partners in it. Successful completion of a task provides the group with a piece of happy history and also builds norms that favor high productivity. Finally, individuals can give recognition for the accomplishments of other group members. When you recognize that the skills of another have been helpful, you make it more likely that the person will try similar productive strategies in the future. The rewarded member will feel increasing ties of sentiment to the group.

However, do not overestimate what an individual can do to foster cohesiveness. Some mixtures of people, like some mixtures of chemicals, cannot work effectively under any circumstances. Cohesiveness is a happy event that sometimes comes about, and if you are aware of what is happening, you can ride the crest of good fortune.

DECISION MAKING AND CONSENSUS

Most task-oriented groups face decisions. Successful decision making is the hallmark of effective groups. Not all good decisions are made in the same way. There is no one royal road to effective decisions. Here are some of the most common ways decisions get made:

1. *Dictator decisions.* A leader makes the decision for the group without checking with group members.

2. *Advice decisions.* A leader makes the decision for the group after checking with the group members for opinions. The president of the United States has traditionally run cabinet meetings this way.

3. *Expert decisions.* The group selects the person most qualified to decide and then allows that person the power of decision for the group. Groups of technical experts sometimes follow this method because one member usually has more knowledge on any given subject.

4. *Clique decisions.* Two or three influential members get together and make the decision, then persuade the group to go along with them. Sometimes the group agrees reluctantly.

5. *Compromise.* The group members state their opinions; then the group tries to arrive at an average position that will not dissatisfy anyone too much.

6. *Vote.* The members of the group vote, and the majority rules. This is the method used by most legislative and judicial bodies.

7. *Consensus.* The group discusses several alternatives and tries to hammer out a decision that everyone can be satisfied with. This is akin to problem-solving methods for resolving conflict (see Chapter 6).

Chances are that you have participated in groups that use all these methods. Check your understanding of the methods by completing Experience 10.5.

EXPERIENCE 10.5 METHODS FOR DECISION MAKING

DIRECTIONS   List the five groups you listed in Experience 10.2, and describe the method of decision making most commonly used in each group. Perhaps more than one method is used, or perhaps your group uses a method we have not listed. In either case, describe the method as clearly as you can.

	Group description	*Method of decision making*
1		
2		
3		
4		
5		

Each of the decision-making styles listed on page 267 has been used successfully by some small groups. Each method has some strengths and some weaknesses. For example, having a group leader make a final decision alone provides an efficient method for getting to decisions quickly. The disadvantage is that the resources of the group are not fully utilized; in fact, there might as well not be a group. In this situation, the leader may make a decision that the rest of the group disagrees with. Similarly, a vote to determine the majority opinion helps to resolve some quarrels fairly, but decisions made in this way may alienate many members and spawn a competitive, polarized atmosphere.

Most researchers consider consensus the most effective method of decision making for most kinds of problems encountered by small groups. Consensus occurs when members come to an agreement on the essential elements of a decision. Consensus is stronger than voting because it is more likely to take into consideration all issues involved and all important alternatives. It is also most effective in ensuring that everyone who will have to implement a decision is committed to its implementation. Finally, consensus puts the resources of the group to good use. Everyone with potential input has the opportunity to make his voice heard, and the group has the opportunity to take advantage of the experience of all group members. Although consensus usually takes more time than other methods, it is not necessarily inefficient. Rather, consensus shortens the time needed to secure commitment and therefore prevents problems at later stages of discussion and implementation.

Experience 10.6 will give you some concrete experience in working toward consensus.

EXPERIENCE 10.6   CHOOSING A CAREER

DIRECTIONS   **A good friend of yours is interested in several different professions and comes to you for advice. Use your best judgment in trying to rank the alternatives in terms of their outlook over the next ten years. Take into account the potential for growth in the number of jobs, starting salaries, salaries for established professionals, and entry prospects for qualified job seekers. Assign the number 1 to the most promising career, the number 2 to the second most promising, and so on through number 12, the least promising.**

After you rank the professions, your instructor will provide time for discussion of this topic. The class will be divided into small groups, each group will arrive at consensus rankings. The purpose of this discussion is to compare the accuracy of individual and group decisions. Later, your instructor will provide you with rankings of experts to compare with both individual and group choices.

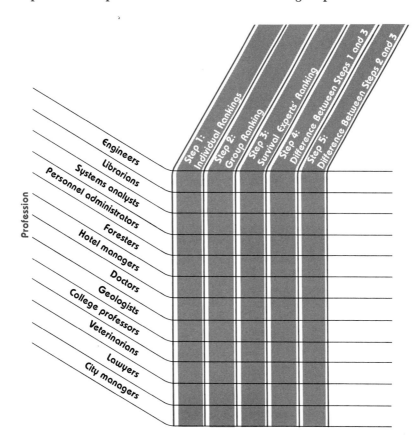

When our students have tried Experience 10.5, there has usually been a 10- to 15-point improvement of group scores over individual scores. If you really were choosing a career, that much difference in decision-making efficiency might mean the difference between happiness and its opposite.

Why does consensus lead to better decisions? Well, for one thing, having everyone publicly defend ideas acts as a sorting procedure. High-quality ideas get sorted out from those that are less worthwhile. This is, of course, a basic assumption of democracy: that good ideas will triumph over inadequate ideas in free argument. Of course, the process is far from infallible. Its strengths and weaknesses can be examined in terms of two characteristics of each group member's input into a decision: accuracy and influence.

Accuracy reflects the quality of your ideas. In Experience 10.5, each career could be quantitatively ranked by experts in terms of its outlook. In real-life groups, quantity and quality are not so highly related and easy to get at, but some ideas are more powerful, more productive, more useful—in short, more accurate than others. You can make an evaluative accuracy continuum that looks like this:

High accuracy

Low accuracy

A person's persuasive influence over others is somewhat independent of the accuracy of his or her ideas. Some people in your group for Experience 10.5 were probably confident that they knew what they were talking about and convinced others to take their advice; these people were high in influence. On the other hand, there may have been persons in your group who rarely uttered a constructive word that anybody listened to; these people were extremely low in influence. Everyone in the group can be placed somewhere on an influence continuum like this one:

Low ─────────────────**High**

　　　　Influence

When these two variables are put together, you can draw a diagram of any individual's contribution to the group. It looks like this:

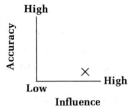

High

Accuracy

Low

　　　×　─ **High**

　　Influence

What use is this diagram? Any person's contributions to the group's discussion in Experience 10.6, for example, could be indicated by placing a mark somewhere between the axes of accuracy and influence.

For instance, a person who was highly influential but whose ideas turned out to be nearly worthless could be represented by the X in the preceding diagram.

Do you understand how it works? Use the same diagram, to rate your own performance in Experience 10.6.

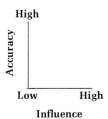

My Performance in Experience 10.6

Now rate the performances of two other members of your group. Write each person's name in the blank to the left of the diagram.

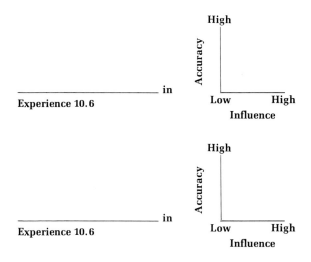

_____ in
Experience 10.6

_____ in
Experience 10.6

In completing this exercise, you have perhaps noticed that certain persons in your group seemed to have more fortunate combinations of accuracy and influence than others. For instance, a person with innaccurate ideas would be most helpful to the group if his or her influence were quite small. Conversely, a person with great influence is most helpful to the group if that person has top-quality or highly accurate ideas. In fact, it is possible to posit an ideal accuracy-influence line. It pictures the degree of influence in relation to the quality of ideas.

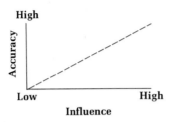

Ideal Influence-Accuracy Line

We return to the question: What makes consensus decision making effective? The answer is that something in the process of arriving at a consensus exposes ideas to the light of day and pushes the role of group participants closer to the ideal influence-accuracy line. The method is not infallible, of course. Nevertheless, consensus has proved to be the strongest method for group decision making in a wide variety of settings.

LEADERSHIP

You are now ready to act as a leader. Does that sentence sound strange to you? When informed that they were ready to exercise leadership, our students have reacted with statements such as: "Not me." "I can't do that."

If you think you are not ready, you have accepted a myth about what leadership is. Let us explore where that myth came from. During World War II, the U.S. Armed Services wanted leadership. Because armies work according to systems of rank, they wanted top-quality officers to "be" great leaders and make decisions. That is a valid model for a military organization because decisions must be made quickly and people down the chain of command must obey orders without question or exception. But a problem emerged because a number of leading social scientists worked in the effort to cultivate good officers in World War II and received important parts of their scientific training in this kind of job. Upon returning to civilian life, some of these psychologists were used to looking at leadership from a military perspective.

In everyday life—in schools, churches, factories, corporate conglomerates—there are many areas of decision making that are better faced from a group perspective than from an individual perspective. Groups, as we discussed earlier in this chapter, are usually most effective when *leadership is shared.* In the fourth phase of group development, constructive cooperation, leadership functions are to some degree shared by all group members. Can you see how that conflicts with the view that leadership belongs to single individuals?

Recent research does not support the great-leader myth. Rather, psychologists now feel that groups which share leadership often come up with the finest results. *Individual* credit or blame is very often beside the point.

Task and leadership functions are shared among group members.

When we say that you are ready for leadership, we mean that you are prepared to function effectively in group situations. You are ready to *exercise* leadership, not to assume the title of leader. If you show skills in working with others to achieve consensus, that is leadership. In Experience 10.5, you were able to look at your leadership skills in action in a particular setting. In the consensus groups, each person's influence attempts and accuracy of ideas interacted with the functions and natural history of the group to produce consensus. It was probably the case that one person did not perform all leadership tasks and that, instead, leadership functions were shared. Look back at your discussion of the career alternatives from this perspective. Perhaps there were two categories of leadership behaviors in your group.

Group leadership behaviors are directly related to completing the task. *Task leadership* behaviors include consolidating key points, clarifying, orienting, setting agendas, and making substantive contributions. These are all behaviors that propel the group directly toward its goals. Note how different individuals were best at various group functions in your group. One person may have been particularly skilled at looking at the overall picture; another may have excelled at summarizing key points. But neither was the group's leader. Rather, both shared leadership; both revealed task leadership skills.

Not all leadership is directly related to tasks. An equally important leadership skill involves maintaining good relations and open channels of   communication within the group. These *maintenance leadership* behaviors enhance friendly, constructive relationships among participants. They include settling disputes, releasing tension, and encouraging support from all group members. Maintenance leadership is not a frill; it is as necessary as task leadership. Task leadership is like gasoline; maintenance leadership is like grease and oil. Task leadership propels the group toward the goal, but the working parts of the group will burn out prematurely unless proper maintenance skills provide lubrication.

Can you see now that the notion that any group has a leader is an oversimplification? Both task and maintenance functions must be performed effectively in every group, and the most effective groups generally share these leadership functions among a large number of group members.

Can you also see that the notions of task and maintenance leadership have been implicit in most of this chapter? In Experience 10.2, for example, we asked you to note whether a particular group was primarily task or social (maintenance). Most groups appear to emphasize one of these functions. Nevertheless, probably all groups require both kinds of leadership behavior. Imagine a group formed for pleasure only, a completely hedonistic group of no social significance. Even such a group must face some task-oriented decisions. How can the group best achieve a good time? Should the group go to a football game, have a party, or go to a discotheque? Even purely social groups require task leadership. The reverse is also true. No matter how focused on a task group members are, friction is likely to subvert the task goal if maintenance functions are not performed.

The distinction between task and maintenance leadership behaviors and the fact that all functions of leadership are shared by group members are among the most important concepts in this book.

Teaching group skills is gratifying to us because of the behavior changes we see in students over the short term. You have probably changed some of your thinking about groups and group behavior. To look at these changes, respond to Experience 10.7.

EXPERIENCE 10.7 AGREE-DISAGREE STATEMENTS ABOUT GROUPS

DIRECTIONS **The following statements express some common attitudes about groups. Read each statement carefully. Then indicate in the Private**

Decisions column whether you agree or disagree with the statement. Write *A* if you agree; write *D* if you disagree. Take about five minutes to complete your private decision making.

Then your instructor will divide the class into small groups for further discussion of these statements. Each group is to employ the method of consensual decision making in reaching a Group Decision about each statement. The goal of this experience is to determine the effectiveness of each group in using the full range of available information as a basis for making a group decision.

	Statements	*Private decisions*	*Group decisions*
1	A concern for group functioning is more important than a concern for individual functioning.	_____	_____
2	The primary responsibility for the success of a group lies with the leader.	_____	_____
3	It is sometimes necessary to ignore the feelings of others in order to reach a decision.	_____	_____
4	Solutions to group problems should not be affected by personal feelings and wishes.	_____	_____
5	When the leader feels a group cannot decide an issue without a lot of hassle, he or she should go ahead and make the decision and inform the group later.	_____	_____
6	Although getting to know one another is important, a group should not spend much time early in its discussions on social things.	_____	_____
7	The best way to think about leadership is in concrete terms. That is, either you are a leader, or you are not.	_____	_____
8	Although there are several acceptable methods of decision making, the method of voting is preferable because it is closest to ideals of democratic action.	_____	_____
9	Even though cohesiveness is a desirable state for groups, there is little an individual member can do to promote it.	_____	_____
10	Although group norms may sometimes be unwritten, they are usually voted on and publicized by the group so that everyone knows them.	_____	_____

SUMMARY

Experience 10.7 is probably the best summary to this chapter. Your skills and your attitudes about what happens in groups are both important determiners of how effectively you function within task groups. Probably you will spend as much time in small groups as you will spend participating in any of the tasks described in this book. American society makes widespread use of decision-making groups. In fact, the notion of democracy rests largely on faith in group decision-making processes.

The groups you work in may vary widely in formality, in orientation to the task, and in the degree of commitment of their members. But within these limits, there are some common principles about how groups operate: Most effective group discussions proceed through four predictable phases. These are the polite phase, the orientation phase, the role division phase, and the constructive phase. Group norms, whether they favor effectiveness or not, exert strong influences on member behavior. Certain group norms are favorable to cohesiveness, a state of high commitment and high positive feelings for the group that often aids effectiveness.

Groups practice a number of decision-making styles. No one style is most appropriate for all situations. However, for most tasks, faced by small groups, working toward consensus has been found most productive. Consensus decision making uses tactics very similar to those used in problem-solving approaches to conflict.

Finally, there are two categories of leadership behavior: task leadership and maintenance leadership. These behaviors are exhibited by various group members under various circumstances.

CHAPTER 11
COMMUNICATING
IN ORGANIZATIONS

Human beings are organizers. They form and join organizations in vast numbers and develop communication strategies to define themselves within these organizations. In Chapter 3, we asked you to list answers to the question: Who am I? Your list may have included some organizations you belong to: an honorary organization, a special-interest organization, a service organization, a church, a commercial organization, a professional organization. People tend to identify themselves partly in terms of what organizations they belong to.

This chapter's goal is to help you communicate more effectively within the organizations of which you are a member. Of course, materials from all chapters of this book will prove helpful in organizational settings. The discussion of task groups in Chapter 10 is particularly relevant here because most formal organizations can be viewed as groups of groups. This chapter begins with a discussion of the nature of formal organizations, including superior-subordinate communication and the notion of informal communication channels. Then we ask you to consider in detail your own place as an individual within the organization. We ask you to analyze the various messages you receive within the organization in light of their influences on your behavior. Finally, we describe problems of coordination, task selection, and supervision that emerge in job settings.

What is the nature of organizational communication? Ordinarily, a distinguishing characteristic of organizations is that they pursue goals. Personal relationships are formed primarily because participants find them rewarding. In organizations, however, the motive is often more specific: A committee is appointed to study admissions policies in a university; a partnership is formed to run a store; a charitable organization is formed to aid hurricane victims. All these organized activities have in common the principle that participants join together to accomplish sets of tasks leading to long-range goals.

Organizations come in all sizes. Theoretically, if you joined with a friend to form a society for preserving plant lice in your apartment and the two of you meet weekly to consider projects you might undertake, an organization has been formed. If you take a job with a vast international conglomerate, you have joined an ongoing organization.

Can you describe your organizational memberships? Most students tell us that they live in an organized world. Many students have jobs or work during the summer. Many have joined service or social organizations. Unless you plan to become a hermit, you will probably become involved with an increasing number of organizations during your college career. Think about the organizations you are or have been involved with, and complete Experience 11.1.

EXPERIENCE   11.1   MY EXPERIENCES IN ORGANIZATIONS

DIRECTIONS   In the first column, list at least five organizations you belong to (you may include some that you listed in Experience 10.1. In the second column, list the goal of the organization. Try to do this in two or three words or phrases. In the third column, state whether all members perform the same tasks or different tasks.

EXAMPLES

Name of organization	*Goal of organization*	*Same or different tasks*
Newspaper	Make a profit by selling newspapers	Different
Food Coop	Provide food to members at reduced prices	Same
Prelaw Society	Provide social contact, share information about future profession	Different

Name of organization	*Goal of organization*	*Same or different tasks*
1 _____	_____ _____	_____
2 _____	_____ _____	_____
3 _____	_____ _____	_____
4 _____	_____ _____	_____
5 _____	_____ _____	_____
6 _____	_____ _____	_____
7 _____	_____ _____	_____

Most students had no difficulty listing ten or more organizations to which they belong. Experience 11.1 stimulates you to thinking about some attributes of organizations. For example, all organizations pursue

One of the major organizational blocks to effective communication is hierarchy.

goals. But in some organizations, goals dominate the members' thinking; whereas in other organizations, goals are rarely mentioned.

In most organizations (those that are quite small may be exceptions) tasks are distributed in ways that are supposed to increase the chances of their being accomplished effectively. In other words, labors are divided. Not everyone does all the jobs in the organization. This job specialization is one of the major features of organizations. Each member of the group performs only those tasks that he or she can do well, and if the organization's tasks are all well coordinated, an efficient group product emerges. Such coordination may not be easy. It requires effective communication because members of organizations commonly exchange messages to coordinate their work.

One of the major organizational blocks to effective coordination is *hierarchy*. As soon as different people in organizations perform different tasks, they also tend to assume different roles. One such role is that of superior, who keeps track of what everybody is doing and coordinates matters. If someone watches over your work in an organization and has the institutional power to tell you to do something different in order to fit in with organizational goals, then the relationship between you is hierarchical. A popular article by Jerry Farber explains student-teacher interaction in this way: "A student at Cal State is expected to know his place. He calls a faculty member "sir" or "Doctor" or "Professor" and he smiles and shuffles some as he stands outside the professor's office waiting for permission to enter."

Studies of communication in small groups have shown that when people find themselves structured into authority-centered hierarchies, free and efficient communication in both directions becomes less likely. H. H. Kelley conducted an experiment in which two sets of college students discussed problems supplied to them. In one experiment, the subgroups were labeled as a group of superiors and a group of subordinates. Kelley found that there was less communication between superior-subordinate groups than between equal groups. When applied to organizational settings, this finding implies that effective communication channels between superior and subordinate are difficult to establish and maintain.

Kelley's finding that superiors and subordinates talk to each other less than equals do is only part of the problem. Some subordinates talk to their bosses a great deal. They are the ambitious ones, the ones who hope to be bosses themselves someday. Such people tend to flatter their superiors, to tell them what they want to hear. Consequently, even bosses who want accurate information from subordinates often cannot get it. Teachers and corporation presidents often cannot find out what their subordinates really think. The most extreme example of this

Describe how these two persons are attempting effective communication across hierarchical boundaries. Are the parties likely to achieve their goals in this interview?

problem is that nobody seems to be able to tell the president of the United States that he is wrong. They are afraid they might offend him. Consequently, presidents often hear only good news about how their policies are doing.

Efficient communication is difficult in hierarchical situations because subordinates are likely to say what they think the boss wants to hear. But hierarchies seem essential to organizations. A nonhierarchical organization does not seem possible. For example, if you ever have worked in a large organization, you probably were given a set of instructions called a *job description* that summarized your responsibilities and told you who would be checking to see that you carried out your responsibilities. Unless you are the boss's child, chances are that you started out near the bottom of the organizational hierarchy. Lots of people could tell you what to do. One traditional way of describing this state of affairs is to say that you start out at the bottom of the organization chart. Figure 11.1 is an example of such a chart.

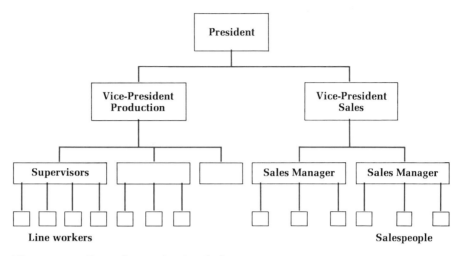

Figure 11.1   Formal organizational chart

The lines in the organization chart represent communication channels. In Figure 11.1, salespeople or line workers report to supervisors, who, in turn, communicate with or report to vice-presidents; the vice-presidents report to the president. It is through this formal structure that the organization divides up the work to be done.

Can you diagram the formal organization of an organization you belong to? Experience 11.2 gives you a chance to try.

EXPERIENCE   11.2   FORMAL ORGANIZATIONAL CHART

DIRECTIONS   **Select one organization you listed in Experience 11.1, and try to diagram its formal organizational chart. It can be much less complicated than Figure 11.1. Remember that formal organization is reflected in job titles and supervising responsibilities.**

You may have had some difficulty listing all the formal channels that operate in your organization. That is not surprising. Most people do not think about formal organization too much; they simply accept what is there.

Several aspects of formal organization are important in relation to your organization. First, the formal organizational structure depicted in an organizational chart is static; whereas the actual organization it represents is dynamic. This means that the chart can never fully describe who does what. The organizational chart becomes outdated almost as soon as it is completed. Second, the formal organizational chart does not take into account the interpersonal relationships that develop among members in various departments that interact with each other. They frequently bypass the formal channels of communication in order to accomplish their jobs efficiently. Third, many groups or committees are formed by organizations to respond to particular problems at given points in the organization's development. Such temporary groups are not reflected in the chart. These interpersonal relationships among individuals and within groups in the organization constitute the *informal organization*.

Even though there is a division of labor in an organization, people frequently need to coordinate their activities in order to do their jobs. For example, in a retail organization buyers need to stay in frequent contact with salespeople in order to know what is selling. Every organization recognizes the need for such contact, but these contacts are rarely institutionalized. Therefore, they are rarely reflected on the organization chart.

Experience 11.3 gives you a chance to try to visualize the informal organization operating within a group to which you belong.

EXPERIENCE 11.3 INFORMAL ORGANIZATION

DIRECTIONS **Sketch the informal contacts between members of the organization that you described formally in Experience 11.2. Include most of the people you placed on the organization chart, but put the names of these people in little boxes around a circle, as in the example shown here.**

Draw lines between pairs of the people to show who talks to whom fairly frequently. Do not connect people who rarely talk to each other. If the connections are slight, use only a dotted line. Feel free to leave many people unconnected with each other. You may also find that you have to include new people you did not show in your formal diagram, such as staff advisers, secretaries, or technicians.

Along the lines you have drawn, write descriptions of the kinds of information that are exchanged between the individuals.

Finally, darken five of the lines you have drawn to indicate that these seem the strongest and most frequently used informal channels of communication connecting individuals in the organization.

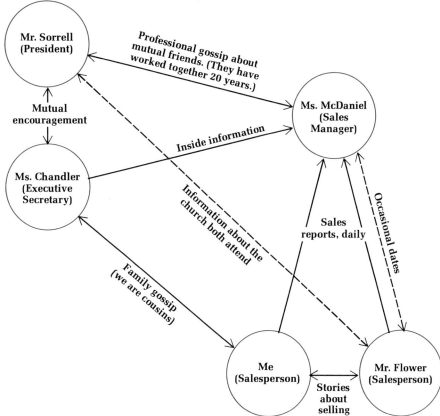

EXAMPLE

The first thing you probably noticed in trying to detail the informal organization is its complexity. Many relationships exist for each person, and many different kinds of information are exchanged. Some information is work-related; some information is gossip about work; some information concerns outside interests or relates primarily to peoples' feelings about each other. Friendships may be based on cooperation at work, living in the same neighborhood, or an after-hours romance. Clearly, the informal organization is much less cut-and-dried than the formal organization.

The informal organization also changes more rapidly than the formal organization. If the sales manager falls in love with one of the salespeople, the informal organization may change immediately, even though the formal organization remains unchanged. If a colleague you do not know very well engages you in conversation one day, you may be left with positive feelings toward that person and be willing to communicate with him or her in the future. This newly developing relationship can be vital to getting work done, but it will not be reflected in the formal organization chart.

Another difference between formal and informal organizations is that the formal organization deals fairly well with routine situations (i.e., situations for which there are rules or well-defined procedures). But when a unique situation or special crisis comes up, the formal organization may not be able to function as well. These are the situations in which most people want to be able to turn to friends for help or in which people want to make an exception to a rule. In such cases, the informal organization can be useful.

For example, suppose a friend calls you and says he has two tickets to the home team's opening game, which takes place next Tuesday afternoon during work hours. You have used up all your time off, but you are caught up with your work and would hate to miss the game. You know that to go to the president and ask this favor would be putting him on the spot. On the other hand, you and the president's secretary are close friends, so you confide in her. She informs you that the president will be out of town on Tuesday; if you clear the absence with your own supervisor, the president would never know about it. Many such decisions are made in the informal organization. We do not argue that *all* such decisions are fortunate. In the example used here, you are taking advantage of the system, and that tactic could affect productivity or make others jealous. Those are the things that the formal organization is set up to prevent.

In summary, you need to use both the formal and the informal communication systems in organizations, just as you need two hands to applaud or two scissor blades to cut. And an organization needs both systems if it is to remain effective.

THE INDIVIDUAL IN THE ORGANIZATION

What is the place of each individual *me* in an organization? The individual *me* gets buffeted about by a large number of influences. Sometimes, the individual may feel like the rope in a tug-of-war. Various forces push and pull in different ways. Some of these forces (influences) have already been detailed in our discussion of formal and informal aspects of organization. For example, both formal and informal organizations make demands on the individual much of the time. You can tell what kind of demand is occurring largely by the channels through which it arrives. Messages from people in formal power positions arrive through formal channels of communication, which are the legitimate paths for messages about work. Formal channels follow the organization chart. Most formal messages are about things which must get done; most are also written or given verbally by bosses to their subordinates. If you send a message directly to the president, bypassing your boss, you may be accused of failure to work through proper channels (That phrase gets used by politicians when their constitutents, instead of writing letters and politely requesting appointments, stage boycotts or sit-ins.)

Sales summaries, progress reports, annual employee evaluations are all critical documents and all written. Some officials are sticklers for form and insist that everything be put in writing, but that is usually a mistaken overdependence on formal channels. Such officials may be less comfortable than most people are about using informal channels of communication.

Informal channels carry both business and social messages. Informal channels also include many statements made off the record, meaning that participants may speak freely (informally), without worrying that their messages will become permanent or that their frankness will be used against them.

The persons who wield the greatest influence in the informal network may not be the persons who hold the highest positions in the formal organization. For example, when the president has to make an important decision, chances are he or she asks somebody's advice first. According to the formal organizational chart, that person is less important than the president. But the formal chart does not tell the whole story.

What factors within your organization influence your everyday behavior? Think about what happens when you are functioning primarily as a member of the organization. What is influencing your behavior? Focus on yourself as an individual, rather than on people in general in the organization. What factors help you to decide how you behave on any occasion? Experience 11.4 is designed to help you to place yourself as an individual within the organization.

EXPERIENCE 11.4 ORGANIZATIONAL INFLUENCES ON ME

DIRECTIONS   **Write the name of the organization you used in Experiences 11.2 and 11.3 in the Organization blank. Now, around the circle marked *me*, try to diagram all the influences (the things that cause you to perform and react the way you do) operating in the organization. (Use any type of diagram you wish to represent these influences.) Try to include everything that influences the way you think, work, and interact with others in the organization.**

EXAMPLE   **ORGANIZATION: Campaign to Elect City Council Member**

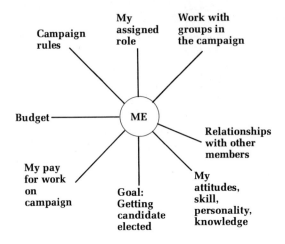

Campaign rules · My assigned role · Work with groups in the campaign · Budget · ME · Relationships with other members · My pay for work on campaign · Goal: Getting candidate elected · My attitudes, skill, personality, knowledge

ORGANIZATION: _____

ME

Most students have reported that filling in the diagram of Experience 11.4 was not too difficult, even though they usually had not thought about all the factors before. Most people realize that there are many events and relationships which influence us to communicate as we do. This is not to suggest that humans are programmed machines with no options. Rather, it means that the actions of others and the conditions in an organization make some actions more desirable than others. In most organizations, these actions and conditions include:

1   relationships with individuals and memberships in groups (the informal system)
2   organizational structures such as formal rules, resources of the organization, and stated goals of the organization (the formal system)

An organization is a complex system of factors. The organization affects the individual. Both the organization and the individual are affected by larger systems of events. Communication processes are the carriers of such influences. In other words, communication is what keeps organizations organized.

Figure 11.2 is a formal model of the influence structures in organizational communication.

Most of the terms in this model of the individual within the organization should be fairly familiar to you by now. Most of our

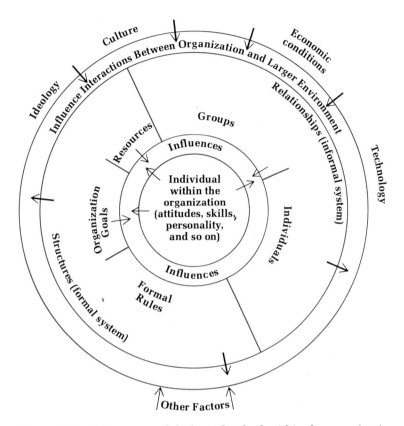

Figure 11.2   Influence model: the individual within the organization

students have noted that the model is quite similar to the diagram they created in Experience 11.4. Did you find that similarity? If you did not, what were the differences? Why do you suppose students' diagrams often turned out a lot like ours?

One major reason is that we have been discussing many of these variables for much of this chapter. The organizational structures include many items discussed as part of formal organization. Interactions with individuals and groups were discussed both in earlier chapters and as aspects of informal organization. The variables in this model have also been discussed in a number of places in this book. Formal and informal communication in large organizations functions in much the same way as the task and relationship dimensions of small groups. Large organizations such as industrial companies are groups of groups working toward common goals. The goals, the formal rules, and the constraints of resources are guidelines that organizations use to assist these individuals and groups in their tasks. Relationships between individuals and groups constitute the organization's informal communication system.

A note on the process of influence seems necessary. Figure 11.2 shows a donut-shaped space between the individual and the larger organization and another space between the organization and larger social structures. This space, which we call the *influence donut,* is where communication influence happens. Certain persons are often described as "having a lot of influence," but such influence is not really a personal possession. Rather, it is something that happens as people communicate with each other and with organizations.

Just as individual and organization influence each other, the entire organization is influenced by the larger environment in which it exists. It also influences that larger environment. Influence is always a two-way process. If the organization is to grow and survive, it must constantly interact with its environment. For example, retail stores must maintain contact with the customers they serve. No doubt, there were once stores in your community which sold dressy clothing to college students. Many such stores faced a crisis when students opted for a more casual, comfortable, natural look of blue jeans. Stores that adjusted to these changes in the environment began carrying more casual clothes; stores that did not respond to the changing tastes and life-styles of college students found themselves short of customers.

Numerous examples of organizations that did not adequately respond to the demands imposed on them by their environments could be cited. To avoid this state of affairs, businesses spend millions of dollars to research markets and respond to changes in tastes, economic conditions, and life-styles. To do this, the organization must be flexible and open to change.

Some interactions between organizations and society are more global in scope. The factors listed around the edge of Figure 11.2 represent some areas of such interaction: technology, politics, cultural forces, and social change.

Consider technology. In many cases, a person's job requires interaction with machines as well as with other persons. Keypunch operators, computer programmers, auto mechanics, and stereo repairpersons all work with machines. A worker who cannot adapt to changes in the technology of his or her field has little chance of either enjoying a job or performing it effectively.

Technology seems to stimulate change. The more technology unfolds, the more it leads to further technological development. Rates of change escalate toward limits that Alvin Toffler has dubbed *future shock.* The term was borrowed from studies of culture and communication. We noted in Chapter 7 that travelers to foreign countries frequently experience culture shock, a paralyzed reaction to differences between cultures. Many travelers report stress associated with not being able to communicate with anyone because of language barriers and seeing events that would be bizarre in their own familiar culture. One reaction is to go into shock, that is, to lose appetite, to become ill, to become apathetic and unable to function. Toffler argues that technological change disorients people just as readily as cultural differences do. Technological changes makes tomorrow as different from today as Egypt is different from the United States. The environment can become unfamiliar and strange to someone whose job is taken over by machines, his or her entire way of life changes in a few days. Under such conditions, the everyday predictions that individuals made and that always seemed to work are no longer effective. Future shock may emerge as technological changes influence individuals within organizations.

In summary, the model of the individual within the organization demonstrates how people function within job settings. It provides a way to conceptualize the factors that influence behavior in such settings. It also seems similar to the way most people picture their place in such organizations.

Now, it is time to tell you something rather startling. We are now going to turn the framework of this chapter upside down. Up to this point, we have been discussing communication in organizations as something that happens in well-defined organizations such as companies. That is the easiest way to talk about organizational communication. Corporations have offices and prestigious titles. Everyone knows what a company is and what a boss is. But we believe that the most important focus for communication study is the individual within the organization. Each such individual receives messages from many sources. Those messages *are* that person's organization.

In a sense, any organization is less the building and furniture and organizational chart and informal channels than *a set of meanings inside the head of the individual within the organization.* That is, each person uses messages and the meanings he or she gives to those messages to organize reality and give it structure. In this sense, communication *is* the organizing strategy for human life. Formal organizations are simply documented, stable sets of messages. Thus, although it is possible to describe communication as one thing that happens in organizations, it is equally possible to claim that communication is the source of organization itself. This perspective makes it possible to apply the ideas in this chapter to all forms of communication, not just those that happen on the job.

COMMUNICATION PROBLEMS IN ORGANIZING: CHANNELS, GATEKEEPING, AND SUPERVISION

In our discussion of the informal organization, we mentioned that it performed important functions by getting information to people who needed it. You may wonder why organizations do not just do away with formal structures and make the informal ones into official channels. One answer is that this kind of move would make the informal channels formal and that would defeat their informality. Probably a whole new set of informal channels would emerge.

A more thoughtful answer is that an organization has uses for both kinds of communication channels. There is plenty of vital information which travels through each. If an organization had only one kind of communication channel, it might often become "overloaded" with unsorted information. This development could lead to several consequences. First, if a channel is overloaded, messages take longer to get to their destination. If you want to send packages to relatives at Christmas time, for instance, you must send them early because the mail channels are clogged with a lot of traveling information at that time of year. Similarly, if you want to make a long distance phone call on Christmas Eve, you often have to try several times before you can get through. All available lines are in use. The channel is clogged with information.

Another likely outcome of an information overload in single channels is that certain key individuals in overloaded communication systems have too much information for them to handle. An example is the executive who can't catch up with his or her mail. Sorting through a large volume of mail and responding to it is a time-consuming task. Many people simplify this task by throwing out some information. For example, when mail gets too heavy (which may be hard for most college students to imagine!), some receivers respond by simply throwing away all third-class mail.

Information overload happens to everyone at some time or other. You probably feel its effects when you have to study for an important exam. The most common way to deal with overload is to make priority decisions. Throwing out junk mail is a priority decision; deciding which facts to memorize for a test is another.

Complex organizations often hire persons whose major job responsibility is making priority decisions. Communication theorists have labeled such responsibilities *gatekeeper functions*. The simplest example is the person who selects what information goes into a daily newspaper. There is only a certain amount of space in any newspaper, but there are many messages that might appear in it. Millions of events happen in the world every day, and thousands of these reported to the offices of a typical daily newspaper. Some come through the wire services, organizations that mass-distribute stories about topics of national and international importance. Many potential news items are composed as news releases by public relations specialists or other interested parties. At the office of the newspaper, a gatekeeper function must be performed to reduce this mountain of data and choose which stories should appear in the newspaper.

Gatekeeping is performed in many places. Even your perception system (see Chapter 2) seems to simplify the basic data that it takes in, using some process of throwing away extra material. Then there is the executive secretary or administrative assistant, a person whose job consists largely of keeping track of information that an executive needs to know and deciding which information reaches the executive. The assistant may summarize some lengthy reports for the executive, forward other documents with portions marked for the executive's attention, or decide that some document does not need attention. The assistant may also decide who gets to see the executive for a personal meeting because the executive does not have time to see everyone without risking overload.

It should be obvious from these descriptions that gatekeeping functions are extremely influential in determining how an organization works. Perhaps no other single activity makes more difference to a newspaper than the selection of newsworthy items. Perhaps nothing is more important to how an executive functions than what information he or she receives and who is granted personal contact. If most of an organization's gatekeeping functions are performed by one person, that person is obviously important and influential.

To get a better idea of how gatekeeping works, respond to Experience 11.5.

EXPERIENCE 11.5 GATEKEEPING

DIRECTIONS **You are a gatekeeper at a radio station. There is to be a two-minute newscast, which allows selection of only four items. The news director tells you that the most important item should be listed first, the second most important item second, and so on. The stories from which you choose are described here. Place the appropriate number (1 for most important, 4 for least important) in front of the news stories that you would choose for the broadcast. Then write a sentence or two explaining the reasons for each of your choices.**

_____ 1 **City council votes yes on a tough new leash law requiring all owners** of dogs and cats to keep their animals on a leash or fenced at all times. Vote by council was unanimous.

_____ 2 State agency directors and heads have been ordered by the governor to prepare budgets for the next two years that reflect a 10 percent cut in expenditures.

_____ 3 Ethics committee in House of Representatives convenes in Washington to consider disciplining a member who was charged with a conflict of interest.

_____ 4 Two persons were killed 15 miles east of town in a head-on crash on a rain-slicked highway.

_____ 5 Talks continued today aimed at bringing about a settlement between warring factions in a small African nation. Diplomatic sources reported that some progress in the talks had been noted in recent days.

_____ 6 New community theater opens with a performance of *Hamlet.* The theatre was built by volunteer laborers with materials donated by community groups.

Our students have gotten into some dandy discussions about which of these news stories are most important. Importance turns out to be highly subjective. To some people, a fatal automobile accident is the most important form of news because it involves tragedy and human lives. To others, national and international affairs take precedence. To still others, news of local politics or cultural events deserves the spotlight. Deciding among all these conflicting pulls is an example of the gatekeeping function in its purest form.

Everyday life shows many forms of gatekeeping that are less strictly involved with the message and more involved with the persons to whom the messages get sent. For example, if an administrative assistant knows that the executive does not like to hear news about a given topic, then such news may get omitted on many occasions. Similarly, some items are not put in a newspaper or on TV news because they are tasteless or illegal and because some audience members could become irate.

Perhaps most important, all of us *systematically delete information from messages we pass on to others.* Experience 11.6 will illustrate this.

EXPERIENCE   11.6   WRITING HOME

DIRECTIONS   Imagine that you wish to write to your parents or other closest relatives about your recent college experiences. Your experiences include the following:

a. You just ran into a very good friend of theirs whom they had not seen in years.
b. You just flunked an exam.
c. You have just written a check that will bounce unless they put some money in the account.
d. You have just fallen in love.
e. You forgot to lock your bicycle, and it was stolen.

Now write your parents a letter about these recent experiences.

_____
_____
_____
_____
_____
_____

Nearly all our students told their parents about the mutual friend, and most informed them of the rubber check. Very few mentioned the flunked exam or the stolen bicycle. Those who did mention the bicycle deleted certain information. That is, they noted that the bicycle was stolen but omitted mention of having left it unlocked. Some students said they had fallen in love; others would not mention such an item to their parents.

This exercise is informative because parents are in a sense organizational superiors. When children are very young, parents are the big bosses. Even college students are obliged to take into account their parents' opinions, especially if parents provide financial assistance so they can attend college. It is essentially this authority dimension of parents that leads to omissions and distortions in writing letters home.

As we have noted, hierarchies distort communication. Hierarchies are the essence of formal organization. Whenever you send information to another person higher up in the organization, you tend to imagine his or her reaction to the information and to present it in a way that will please the higher-up. No one likes to send bad news or news that will reflect badly on the sender. Consequently, people who are high in the organizational chart sometimes do not receive the kind and quality of information they need to guide the organization. For example, salespersons who lose an important account to a competitor may withhold this information from higher-ups because they feel it may reflect badly on their work, even though the reason for the lost sale is that the other company is able to provide faster delivery. If persons up the line are given that information before several accounts are lost, they can make some modifications in shipping procedures to get deliveries back on schedule. Without this information, other accounts may be lost before the problem is identified.

A related problem occurs when subordinates do not feel free to discuss things openly with their superiors. This is often a problem when the supervisor employs an authoritarian style of supervision. To find out how this works, complete Experience 11.7.

EXPERIENCE 11.7 STYLES OF SUPERVISION

DIRECTIONS **You will need a partner for this exercise. You are going to rank a series of organizational characteristics according to their importance in contributing to the effectiveness of the organization. Flip a coin to determine which of you will be the supervisor for Part I.**

DIRECTIONS **INSTRUCTIONS AND INFORMATION FOR THE SUPERVISOR:**
(PART 1) **1 You are clearly in charge of this task.**
2 The supervisee may have some good ideas, but you have no good reason to believe that he or she does.
3 Your goal is to represent your own ideas and move toward a ranking as soon and as directly as possible.

INSTRUCTIONS AND INFORMATION FOR THE SUPERVISEE:
1 You are a follower in such situations.
2 You are to go along with the supervisor's sense of the situation.
3 Work on this task with the preceding ideas in mind.

TASK
Rank the following characteristics of organization X in terms of their importance in creating a climate for flexibility and responsiveness to change:

_____ a. Organization is highly centralized, with decisions made at the top.
_____ b. Members have many contacts with other professionals outside the organization.
_____ c. Jobs in the organization are highly structured and governed by rules.
_____ d. Members have strong informal communication network.
_____ e. Organization has many uncommitted resources that can be used to develop new ideas.

DIRECTIONS (PART 2)   Switch supevisor and supervisee roles.

INSTRUCTIONS AND INFORMATION FOR SUPERVISOR:
1. You want to use your own ideas, but you also want to get the perspective of the person working with you. You seek joint agreement on the ranking task.
2. Move toward completion of the ranking as soon as possible.

INSTRUCTIONS AND INFORMATION FOR SUPERVISEE:
1. You are to go along with the supervisor's sense of the situation.
2. Move toward completion of the ranking as soon as possible.

TASK
Rank the following characteristics of organization Y in terms of their importance in creating a climate for flexibility and responsiveness to change:

_____ a. Budget is very tight, and few resources can be committed for innovations.
_____ b. People are encouraged and rewarded for transmitting negative information up the chain of command.
_____ c. Organization is highly decentralized, with decisions made at lower levels of the organization.
_____ d. Members tend to have few contacts outside the organization.
_____ e. Jobs within the organization are highly formalized and governed by rules.

DIRECTIONS (PART 3)   Answer the following questions about the two supervisor-supervisee interactions.

FOR PART 1: LEADER   FOLLOWER (CIRCLE ONE)

1. How satisfied did you feel with the amount and quality of *your* part in reaching a joint decision?

completely   not at all
satisfied   1 2 3 4 5 6 7   satisfied

2. How much responsibility did you feel for the work?

completely   not at all
responsible   1 2 3 4 5 6 7   responsible

3. How committed do you feel to the list you and your partner made as a pair?

completely   not at all
committed   1 2 3 4 5 6 7   committed

4. How much frustration did you feel during the work on the decision?

completely   not at all
frustrated   1 2 3 4 5 6 7   frustrated

5. How good was the ranking you made as a pair?

excellent   1 2 3 4 5 6 7   poor

FOR PART 2: LEADER   FOLLOWER (CIRCLE ONE)

1. How satisfied did you feel with the amount and quality of *your* part in reaching a joint decision?

completely   not at all
satisfied   1 2 3 4 5 6 7   satisfied

2. How much responsibility did you feel for the work?

completely   not at all
responsible   1 2 3 4 5 6 7   responsible

3. How committed do you feel to the list you and your partner made as a pair?

completely   not at all
committed   1 2 3 4 5 6 7   committed

4. How much frustration did you feel during the work on the decision?

completely   not at all
frustrated   1 2 3 4 5 6 7   frustrated

5. How good was the ranking you made as a pair?

excellent   1 2 3 4 5 6 7   poor

The instructions for the two situations in Experience 11.7 were the same instructions with one exception: In the second interaction, both the leader and the follower were to expect a cooperative relationship between them; whereas in the first interation, both parties expected the leader to get his/her way. You probably recognized the difference between these two styles of leader-follower relationship as being similar to the difference between forcing and problem-solving tactics in conflict resolution (see Chapter 7).

Most students reported the following results in Experience 11.7: The second interaction was perceived as more satisfying to both parties. Both parties in the second interaction felt a greater sense of participation (more responsibility for outcomes) than those who participated in the more authority-centered interaction. Both parties in the second interaction also felt greater commitment to the decisions they made. Parties to the cooperative (second) interaction were more satisfied with what happened and liked the other party better as a person.

Of course, few real-life situations are as clearly cooperative or authority-centered as those presented in Experience 11.7. But to the extent that superiors and subordinates alike incorporate the meanings of cooperative problem solving, in their interactions, more effective outcomes to interaction will result.

SUMMARY

Groups of communicators who share a common purpose or set of purposes often form organizations. Organizations come in all sizes, and some are more permanent than others. Most organizations differentiate the roles of participants in terms of what work each member is to do. This differentiation of tasks leads to hierarchy in the formal system of the organization, as reflected in the organization chart of a company. Although hierarchy is necessary to efficient operation, it creates communication difficulties because information is passed up and down hierarchies quite selectively.

Alongside the formal organization and its communication channels operates the informal system, which consists of the relationships between the people in the organization. The informal system carries both work-related and social information. It plays an essential role in avoiding inflexibilities and unfairness created through the rules and customs of the formal organization. Both formal and informal messages act upon the individual within the organization at all times and influence the individual's behavior. If you look at organizational communication using these terms, as we do in our influence-donut model, almost any social system—families, cultures, classes—can be considered a communicating organization.

Communication problems beset any organization. One of the most common is information overload at key points in the communication system. The gatekeeping functions performed at such critical points have important effects on how effectively the organization operates. All people perform some gatekeeping functions with the information they process whether they are aware of it or not. Even the human perceptual system is based on gatekeeping to avoid information overload. One of the most consistent sets of problems of gatekeeping relates to hierarchies. In reporting to superiors, gatekeepers often destroy information essential to proper functioning of the organization. Some of this difficulty can be handled through use of participative styles of decision making between superiors and subordinates that allow both informal and formal information to come into play and also equalize the parties' perceptions of their power over each other. This sort of climate makes problem-solving communication increasingly likely and increases both efficiency and job satisfaction.

CHAPTER 12
PUBLIC SPEAKING:
SITUATION AND PURPOSE

So far, we have focused primarily on communication in informal settings. Interaction flows freely in ways that often seem unstructured in such settings. But some settings are more structured, more carefully planned, more formal. For example, the setting in which a senator gives a patriotic speech on the Fourth of July may be planned in detail. An agenda of events is usually followed. Such planned events are often public in the sense that the audiences are made up of people from diverse backgrounds. Another characteristic implied by public settings is that there is one message sender and a number of message receivers (the audience).

In this chapter, we begin our discussion of public communication events. We focus on one particular event: the public speech. The term *public speech* refers to an event in which there is one speaker who delivers a planned and prepared message to a number of listeners. We guide you through the first steps in preparing a public speech: analyzing the speech situation and determining the purpose of the speech.

There are a number of reasons for studying the public speech as a communication form. First, there is a long tradition of such study, dating back to ancient Greece. It has been formalized as training in rhetoric throughout Western civilization. Second, there are a number of occasions in the life of any American when he or she has the opportunity to affect important decisions or advance a career through the use of public presentations. But many people shy away from public speaking opportunities. Given the importance of public presentations, that is astounding. This leads us to a third reason for studying public speaking: Most Americans are terrified of speaking in public. We are not quite sure how this stage fright syndrome got started, but we know that it is epidemic at the beginning of public speaking classes. "I can't speak in front of groups!" many people claim. "My legs turn to jelly!" We deal specifically with this problem in Chapter 13. At this point, the important thing for you to remember is that one cure for stage fright is giving speeches. Even if you never make another public presentation, being cured of stage fright is reason enough to study speechmaking.

Fourth, the skills that you learn through the speech experience can be useful in other aspects of your communication life. Practice in speech composition and delivery can help you to be a better interpersonal communicator in everyday life. For example, speech composition is excellent practice in logical thinking; if you can think better, that will help you with other aspects of communication. Improvement in public speaking skills is also likely to mean improvement in writing. These skills can have a significant affect on how successful you will be in the world of work.

**SPEECH
SITUATIONS**

Public speeches happen at a particular time and place. This differentiates them from written communications. You can pick up a book anytime during your life or read a weekly newsmagazine at any hour of the day, but speeches happen all at once. If you write someone a letter, they may read it several days later; but if you give a speech, it is usually received by audience members as you deliver it. Therefore, the situation in which a speech occurs is part of the speech itself. The first step in speech preparation is analysis of the situation.

There are several interacting aspects of a speech situation. The first is the *audience*. A speech without an audience is absurd. For example, on one occasion, only one student out of thirty showed up for a class. At the appointed hour, the professor entered the room, looked around briefly, and began lecturing in his usual style. He gave a speech to one person. That was an absurd feeling for the audience member. Different audiences respond to different speeches, and effective speakers plan their presentations with the nature of their audiences in mind.

The *occasion* is another aspect of the speech situation. Sometimes, a gathering is called together only to hear a speech; sometimes, a group meets for other reasons and listens to speeches, too. Often, there is an uneasy compromise. At church or at a banquet, there are other activities besides public speaking, but it is easy for the speech that is delivered on such occasions to be either the high point of the occasion or quite the opposite. A speaker needs to plan the speech in terms of the occasion. How much time will there be? What is the setting like? How well will people be able to hear?

Finally, there is the *topic*, the subject matter and treatment of the speech itself. The situation often dictates the topic. A professor gets a call asking her to speak at a lunch seminar on the topic of grade inflation. In that case, the invitation sets the topic. If Senator Fogbound is asked to speak at a Fourth of July rally, the precise topic is not set, but the senator's remarks must be suitable for a patriotic occasion. In other cases, the topic choice is more open. For example, when you give in-class speeches, you are likely to have free choice of topic. In many churches, the preachers have a fairly free rein in choosing topics to speak about.

In summary, any speech situation is a dynamic mix of the speaker, the occasion, the audience, and the topic. With all these factors operating, you cannot always predict what will happen. There is a strange chemistry involved that makes effective speechmaking a challenge.

In this chapter, we will ask you to think and write about both speech situations in general and speaking situations you will soon face.

We will use the four elements of the situation (speaker, occasion, audience, and topic) as the basis for these exercises.

It is not necessary to talk about the speaker in great detail. In your case, the speaker is you. Sometimes, the identity of the speaker is one of the most important aspects of the speech occasion. In fact, some people make a fair amount of money going around giving speeches. People will not pay to listen to you yet. First, you must develop speaking skills. Then, who knows what will happen in the future?

You and I are only us. Someday, we may become famous, but probably we will not. What is important, regardless of circumstances, is to know your strengths and weaknesses as a communicator. That is what this book is about. By now, there is only one more precaution you need to take to be sure you are ready to speak: Prepare. Do your homework. Get ready.

One way to get ready is to start thinking about the speech occasion. That is what Experience 12.1 is designed to help you do.

EXPERIENCE   12.1   DESCRIBING SOME OCCASIONS

DIRECTIONS   The following list presents several descriptions of a speaker and a purpose or topic for a speech. Describe one occasion on which each speech might be extremely effective and one occasion on which the speech might be ineffective. Your description should include the reason for the audience's getting together (i.e., are they there to hear the speaker or for another reason), the place in which the speech occurs, and the probable length of the speech.

A   A noted researcher in population control is giving a speech advocating the use of abortion as a means of birth control.
1. Occasion on which this speech would be effective:
   a. reason for gathering

   _____

   b. room or place

   _____

   c. length of speech

   _____

2. Occasion on which this speech would be ineffective:
   a. reason for gathering

   _____

   b. room or place

   _____

     c. length of speech

    _____

B   A candidate running for president of the United States on the Communist Party ticket is giving a speech entitled "Principles of Communism at Work in a Democracy."
1. Occasion on which this speech would be effective:
   a. reason for gathering

    _____

   b. room or place

    _____

   c. length of speech

    _____

2. Occasion on which this speech would be ineffective:
   a. reason for gathering

    _____

   b. room or place

    _____

   c. length of speech

    _____

C   An employee of IBM is giving a talk to inform an audience of businessmen about practical uses of computers for small businesses.
1. Occasion on which this speech would be effective:
   a. reason for gathering

    _____

   b. room or place

    _____

   c. length of speech

    _____

2. Occasion on which this speech would be ineffective:
   a. reason for gathering

    _____

   b. room or place

    _____

   c. length of speech

    _____

     Most students have little trouble figuring out speech situations for Experience 12.1. They usually choose as effective examples occasions on which the audience already feels friendly to the speaker or the topic. For instance, the Communist candidate was often pictured as effective when speaking to other Communists. That is right to a point, but it depends on how you define effectiveness. A candidate for president in the United States will not be effective in the long run unless he can be effective with some non-Communists, too.

Many students noted that other things besides the occasion contribute to the effectiveness or ineffectiveness of a speech. For instance, what is the nature of the audience? But the question Experience 12.1 explored was: What kinds of differences can the occasion by itself make?

Is the purpose of the gathering primarily to hear this speech, or is there some other reason? Did the audience gather to hear a large number of speeches, as is the case in most public speaking classes? For example, if a speaker thinks that the speech is the featured event at a banquet and, just before the speech, finds that he or she is only one of fifteen speakers, he or she will probably have to make a quick change of plans. Was the meeting called for some purpose having little to do with the speeches, such as a club meeting? Is it a meeting that people attend for economic reason, such as a stockholders' meeting? Is it a meeting that people are required to come to, such as many college classes? Analyzing the purpose of the meeting at which the speech is to be given can yield many insights that will make your effort more successful.

The actual setting (room or outdoor place) in which the speech is to be given is also an important part of the speech occasion. The kind of setting you are in places some limits on what you can do. For example, you cannot show slides at an outdoor rally held at noon

Settings can be important influences upon message effectiveness. How might you adjust a message to this setting?

because there is too much light and no projection facility. If you had planned a talk accompanied by slides, you would have to make some adjustments.

Where do you stand or sit when you make your presentation? Is there a lectern? Is its height good for you? How far away from the audience will you be? How far away is the farthest person? Can that farthest person see you clearly and hear you satisfactorily? If not, is there anything you can do about it?

Sometimes, a few changes in the situation can make the difference between a success and a failure. If the audience is scattered all over a large room, it may be worth your while to request those in the rear to move forward. If the microphone is at the wrong height, take as long as you need to adjust it. If there is too little light, raise a shade. After all, you are giving a performance. Actors and directors spend weeks or even months perfecting scenery, relationship of scenery to curtains, relationship to audience—all aspects for the setting of the drama. If you make favorable changes in your setting, you give yourself a little advantage. You also gain added respect in the eyes of the audience because your actions demonstrate that you care about the kind of impression you make.

If you give in-class speeches, the setting is fairly constant and familiar. But you should realize that a constant setting (or one you thought was constant) can still be changed to your advantage. Is there something about it that you would like to change? Do you feel uncomfortable using a lectern? Do you feel uncomfortable without one? Do you feel most comfortable if you move the lectern a few feet closer to your listeners? How is the light? Can everyone see any charts you plan to show? Could you improve your presentation by adding slides or sound recordings? Ask your teacher whether these can be provided.

If your are going to speak in a new setting, it is wise to visit the scene before the event so that you will have time to plan. Stand at about the place where you will be when you speak. Look around; see how it feels. Check for sources of distraction. Will the sun be in someone's eyes? Is there any source of noise, such as loud passing traffic? How are the acoustics? Are there easy-to-use facilities for slides, overhead projectors, tape recorders, and other aids.

How much time will you have? Perhaps the biggest bore is the speaker who exceeds the time limit, droning on after the audience expected to be listening to something else. If you have more to say than the time allows, which things will you leave out?

In summary, put some thought into the purpose for the meeting and the physical setting. These frequently neglected aspects of the speech situation can pay juicy dividends to the prepared speaker. Practice your occasion-preparation skills by completing Experience 12.2.

EXPERIENCE 12.2 ASPECTS OF SPEECH OCCASIONS

DIRECTIONS
(PART 1)

Design a speech topic or purpose statement suitable for each of the following speech occasions.

1 a Fourth of July speech

_____

2 a banquet speech at a lawyer's lawyers' convention

_____

3 a meeting of students interested in working for Democratic candidates

_____

4 a meeting of the local Kiwanis Club

_____

5 a sales meeting of a manufacturing company

_____

DIRECTIONS
(PART 2)

Match each of these five speech topics with its most appropriate time limit. Write the letter in the blank to the left of each topic.

_____ 1 a morning sales meeting at a retail store before the store opens

a. two minutes

_____ 2 acceptance speech for most valuable player on volleyball team at awards banquet

b. five minutes

_____ 3 a speech before the school board as they deliberate about raising taxes

c. twenty minutes

_____ 4 introduction of a guest lecturer

d. one hour

_____ 5 dimensions of american foreign policy

DIRECTIONS
(PART 3)

Answer the following questions designed to analyze your classroom as a speech setting.

1 List a speech topic you would like to use.

_____

2 List two disadvantages of your classroom for that kind of speech.
   a. _____
   b. _____

3 List two advantages of using the classroom for this speech.
   a. _____
   b. _____

4 List two alterations you wish to make in the environment when you speak (changes in seating or lighting, addition of slide projector, and so on).

a. _____

b. _____

5 How much time do you expect to have for your speech? Do you think there will be any trouble covering it in the time allowed?

_____

6 Draw a diagram of this room. Include places for a slide projector, charts, or other aids.

Audience characteristics

The successful public speaker thinks of an audience as a collection of individuals. There will be as many messages received as there are persons in the audience, even though only one message is sent. Thus, the more the speaker can find out about the people in a given audience, the better he or she can make strategy decisions.

There are a number of things about audience members that a speaker will want to know before preparing a message. First, is the audience *homogeneous*? That is, are the audience members like each other or different from each other? Sometimes, it is difficult to stereotype an audience in any specific way; there seem to be people of all ages, races, educational levels, interests, and political views. It is easier to speak to a homogeneous audience. You can make some educated guesses about how they will react to your messages.

If an audience is heterogeneous (each member having little in common with the others), what pleases one person may well offend others. That is the problem of most television shows, which aim for a huge heterogeneous audience. Almost any message could cause offense to someone in such an audience. Consequently, most TV programs suffer from blandness springing from the effort to offend as few people as possible.

There is no single solution to this problem. You should keep looking for some things that the audience might have in common with each other and with you as a speaker.

Demographics are social characteristics that are used by census takers as key facts about people. Age is a demographic characteristic. So are sex, race, and the number of years a person goes to school. Demographics can be used as a guide to what might be acceptable and interesting to audiences. For example, if you spoke to a group of middle-aged women who were members of a fundamentalist church, you would be careful not to tell off-color jokes or stories about getting drunk because your audience might be bothered by such topics.

Educational level is a crucial demographic variable. Knowing the approximate educational level of most audience members can give a speaker an idea at what level to aim the message. For example, some terms commonly used among people who have a college education are either unknown to less educated audiences or considered pretentious and arrogant. Such words as *dependency, demographic variable, ego involvement, deficit spending,* and *dysfunctional* fall into this category. If you were addressing a less educated audience, you might consider deleting such words and if the words are essential to your message, you would want to give brief, nonpatronizing definitions.

The *group memberships* of audience members are closely related to demographic characteristics. The groups people belong to can influence the way they react to a speaker. For example, what could you infer if you found out that most of your audience members were members of the Sierra Club or members of the Young Republicans Club?

Group memberships can serve as clues to the *opinions and attitudes* of audience members. Members of political parties may share beliefs about welfare, military spending, foreign affairs, taxes, and government social programs.

As you look at the characteristics of the audience, try to make *speaker-audience comparisons.* For example, certain generalizations may be possible about elderly audiences, middle-aged audiences, and young audiences. The principal generalization is that most age-groups prefer to listen to speakers of similar age. If your audience is considerably older than you are, you may need to find ways to tell listeners about your qualifications to speak on this topic or to refer to testimony of persons the older audience respects. Your audience's age might also influence your choice of clothes. For example, if your audience is much older, you might decide to de-emphasize the age difference by dressing up.

Most demographics and most opinions become important largely in relation to similarities between speaker and audience. Audiences generally prefer to take advice from others who are like themselves. If you have ethnicity or age or some other variable in common with your audience, shape your presentation in ways that take advantage of the similarities.

Experience 12.3 will give you important practice in analyzing your audience.

EXPERIENCE 12.3 THE AUDIENCE

DIRECTIONS
(PART 1)

Select a speech you have attended in the past year. Then analyze the audience according to its stable characteristics and its relationship with the speaker.

Speech occasion and location _____
Topic _____

1   Answer the following questions about audience characteristics:
   a. Was the audience homogeneous? (check one)
      _____ extremely
      _____ somewhat
      _____ not at all
   b. What were the ages of audience members?
      _____
   c. What ethnic groups were represented?
      _____
   d. What groups did members belong to?
      _____
   e. What were the political and religious attitudes of audience?
      _____

2   Describe the similarities and differences between speaker and
   audience for the variables discussed in items 1b to 1e.
   _____
   _____
   _____
   _____

DIRECTIONS   Analyze the class for which you are reading this book as an audience.
(PART 2)

1   Answer the following questions about audience characteristics:
   a. Is the audience homogeneous? (check one)
      _____ extremely
      _____ somewhat
      _____ not at all
   b. What are the ages of audience members?
      _____
   c. What ethnic groups were represented?
      _____
   d. What groups do members belong to?
      _____
   e. What are the political and religious attitudes of audience?
      _____

2   Describe the similarities and differences between speakers and
   audience for the variables discussed in items 1b to 1e.
   _____
   _____
   _____
   _____
   _____

Topic

Now we come to a vital decision: the topic of your speech. Giving a speech in a class in which your classmates also take turns giving speeches is a very different experience from giving a speech in other situations. One of the most important differences is in the area of choosing a topic.

In outside-the-classroom speaking situations, the choice of a topic is rarely a problem. Often, the topic is set by the situation. In other cases, there is a burning issue that you want to be talking about, otherwise you would not have accepted the invitation to speak. In nearly all cases, you care deeply about your topic. Strong caring about the topic is a necessary ingredient of speech success. But in class, things are different. You may not care whether you deliver your speech, but you know it has to be done.

This can be a problem because the same rule applies for class speeches as for any other speeches: If you get involved in a topic, you are well on your way to an effective speech. If you do not care, you are

The speaker's strong interest in a speech topic can help hold the attention of audience members.

well on your way to a bland message; your speech may have everything that is required (good organization, good evidence, good reasoning, good delivery), but you will be a bore to yourself and others. The thing to do, then, against all the odds, is to choose a fascinating speech topic.

Some students do not want to talk to their teachers about the topics they care about. But remember, your teacher is in the other half of the same box you are in. There is nothing your teacher wants more than for you to find a speech topic important to you.

How do you choose a speech topic you care about? There is no sure way, but we can give you a couple of hints:

1   If you decide on a speech topic because you browsed through a magazine until you came to an article that sounded like a good topic, throw that topic away.
2   If you choose a topic because you have already thought a lot about it and/or talked to your friends about it before you ever thought it was time to find a speech topic, then you are in good shape.

Here is the point: Most students choose speech topics by looking *around*. If you want to succeed, try looking *in* instead. The stuff you care about is already *in* your head. Write down some of your thoughts; keep a journal. Some of the things you know and care about might make good speech material; some might not. How can you tell the difference? The key to this sorting process is to mirror your own criterion. That is, ask yourself *what your audience will be likely to care about.*

List four or five things that you care about; then ask yourself some questions about each topic: Is there anything that an audience can learn from this topic? How does the topic fit with their other attitudes? Is this a topic they have probably thought of before? If so, would they wish to hear more about it? Is there a viewpoint they have not heard before? Do not be overly pessimistic. If you care about the topic, chances are that you can make it vital for others, too.

We have given quite a few general ideas about choosing a topic. What do you do right now, *specifically*? Try to turn an area you already care about into a public message topic. If your major is accounting, for example, you might choose topics such as how an audit is conducted, how to read a financial statement, or ethical standards of CPAs. Other academic majors offer many possibilities, too. For example:

Prelaw
How lawyers select juries
Types of law practice
How lawyers become members of the bar association

Education
Behavior modification techniques used in elementary school
    classrooms

Changing patterns of teacher education
Counseling practices in high school

Sociology
Jobs sociologists perform
Demographic trends in the United States
Training and certification of social workers

Engineering
How building materials are evaluated
New trends in the construction of mass transit vehicles
Energy resource depletion

Management
Current theories of management
Types of management
How management performance is evaluated in organizations

Nursing
New trends in the use of paraprofessionals in health care
Changes in nursing emphasis to care of the total person
Employment trends in nursing

Architecture
How to select an architect
How architects make use of research in nonverbal communication
How architects design a custom-built home

Government or political science
How a bill is passed in the state legislature
Types of local government
Current trends in the reform of campaign financing

Journalism
The urban magazine as a new journalistic form
How editorial policy is established at a particular newspaper
Public access and press freedom

Other good sources for ideas are your hobbies, interests, and
sports. You can find great ideas in your own backyard if you will just
take an inventory of the things that interest you. For example:
Photography
How to select a camera
How a photographer uses light to create special effects
How to judge a photograph

Music
History of jazz in big cities
Rock music of the fifties
How records are produced

Sports
How to select a canoe
How football players are recruited by colleges
Current trends in women's sports

These ideas are, of course, intended only as starters. We want you to select your own ideas for a speech topic. Experience 12.4 will help to do that.

EXPERIENCE   12.4   SELECTING A TOPIC

DIRECTIONS   Using the guidelines we have just presented, select two speech topics. Write them down in the appropriate spaces below; then answer the following questions about each topic.

Topic A: _____
1   How is this topic related to something you are currently interested in?
_____

2   How much thinking have you done about this topic before reading this chapter?
_____

3   What will be the audience response to this topic?
_____

4   What will be your instructor's response to this topic?
_____

Topic B: _____
1   How is this topic related to something you are currently interested in?
_____

2   How much thinking have you done about this topic before reading this chapter?
_____

3   What will be the audience response to this topic?
_____

4   What will be your instructor's response to this topic?
_____

We have discussed three components of the speech situation: the occasion, the audience, and the topic. Successful public speaking requires that you look at each of these factors of the situation and decide how to act on the basis of them. Experience 12.5 is designed to help you practice looking at the big picture.

EXPERIENCE   **12.5   A WHOLE SPEECH SITUATION**

DIRECTIONS   You have probably been assigned to give a speech for this class. Describe the basis dimensions of the situation you will speak in as you see them.

1   *Occasion:* Describe the most relevant properties of the purpose for the meeting at which you will speak and the setting (room). How will you take these variables into account in your speech?

_____

_____

2   *Audience:* Describe the demographic and attitudinal characteristic of your audience. Is the audience homogeneous? How are you similar to most members of your audience?

_____

_____

3   *Topic:* List three topics you are eager to talk to someone about. Which seems most appropriate to the audience and occasion? Why?

_____

_____

_____

_____

As we noted earlier, most of what we say here about speeches can be applied to written communications. A letter or essay also exists within a communication situation, with an occasion in which it functions, with an intended audience, and with the topic choice being critical to success. Remember that practice in speech preparation can improve many aspects of communicating.

General purpose   Many communication events are regarded as having purposes. If someone acts strangely toward you, you may ask yourself, "Why did he or she do that?" That question concerns the purpose of the act. Most conscious communication serves some purpose.

In interpersonal communication, it is not always easy to state the purpose or purposes of a message. If you have a close relationship with someone, any message you send to them may serve a variety of purposes; it may be unnecessary to have one well-defined purpose for any message. However, in formal public messages, formulating a statement of a clearly defined purpose is one of the most important steps in preparing the message. Public formal messages are sent to large groups of people. Each audience member has a different field of experience. Therefore, to be understandable, the purpose of a public message must be more explicit than those of most interpersonal messages.

Purpose statements describe the desired effects of the message on the audience. A public speech, a poem, or a news article aims to make contact with audience members and change them in some way. The change need not be huge. Maybe it gets across a new piece of information; maybe it tries to get audience members to change an attitude or to try something new.

Experience 12.6 asks yout to describe the purposes of several messages you have been exposed to recently. Any kind of message is OK, from a presidential speech to TV commercials to skywriting.

EXPERIENCE 12.6 SOME MESSAGE PURPOSES

DIRECTIONS **Describe some messages you have received recently. Then state some purpose that the message sender(s) seemed to be trying to accomplish.**

EXAMPLE

Describe speech situation	*Describe purpose*
A congressional candidate gave a speech to a college Young Republican club.	**To persuade audience members to vote for the candidate**
One of Nader's Raiders addressed a group of apartment residents who were worried about demands from their landlord	**To let audience know about their rights and about some procedures they could use to protect their interests**
A TV situation comedy	**To help the audience have fun**

Describe speech situation	*Describe purpose*
1 _____ _____	_____ _____

2 _____   _____
   _____   _____
                                            _____
3 _____   _____
   _____   _____
                                            _____
4 _____   _____
   _____   _____
                                            _____
   _____   _____
   _____   _____

STATING THE PURPOSE OF A MESSAGE

Did each of your purposes make a statement in terms of the audience? The number-one rule of a message purpose is: State purposes in terms of what will happen to the audience members. If any of your purpose statements do not refer to the audience, revise them.

The purposes that most students list can be divided into three categories: to inform the audience, to persuade the audience, or to entertain the audience. Of course, you may not have used those exact words. Instead of *to inform*, for example, you may have written *to tell about* or *to describe*. Nevertheless, the basic purpose—to get some facts or information across—is the same. Three infinitives—*to inform, to entertain,* and *to persuade*—are often called the three *general purposes* of public speeches. Most speeches serve mainly one of these general purposes. Thus, by using one of these in your statement, you can focus on what you want to do to audience members during the speech.

Deciding on a general purpose is one of the first steps in composing any speech. Here is a brief look at the three general purposes:

Messages whose purpose is *to inform* audience members are the easiest to understand. Their purpose is to get some facts from point A (your brain) to point B (the brains of the audience members). The usual assumption is that audience members can make use of this information.

Informative messages focus on various kinds of information. The *how-to-do-it message* explains or demonstrates how to achieve some practical end (how to refinish furniture, plant a garden, iron a shirt, play second base). There is also the *how-it-works message* (how a ten-speed bicycle works, how the bicameral legislative process works, how the digestive system of a frog works). Finally, there is the *idea message*, which informs the audience about some development in philosophy, medicine, space travel, or a thousand other topics. These kinds of messages are not pure types. Rather they are meant to show (to inform) you some potential directions that an informative message can take. Any message that passes data to the audience but does not try to manipulate their behavior in a particular direction can be classified as informative.

Any message that tries to change somebody's mind or to get them to behave differently can be classed as *persuasive*. Persuasive messages assume that the things people communicate to each other influence what we do or say later. What kinds of influence? Well, some messages try to get you to perform an act (buy a product, vote, give blood, fasten your seat belt). A salesperson's messages to you when you shop for clothes fall into this category. Some messages try to get you to avoid doing something (do not drink while driving, do not vote for candidate X). Finally, many persuasive messages try to get you to change an opinion or an attitude (to feel differently about the status of women, to begin to believe in God, to feel confident that you will be able to get a good job after college). These last examples do not ask you to do anything different, although different behavior might be implied. Rather, they aim at the attitudes and opinions in your head.

Most speeches contain information. Obviously, you are unlikely to change your mind on an issue unless you are provided with some information you have not heard before. But if a speech's overall purpose is persuasion, it is classed as a speech to persuade. The distinction can sometimes be tricky. A salesperson may come to your house pretending to be doing a survey and only begin the sales pitch after thirty minutes of giving you information. That entire event, once you see it clearly, is persuasive in nature.

Some speeches are purely for fun. These are the speeches you hear at dinners and banquets. As people enjoy dessert and coffee, a speaker tells a few stories, introduces a few people, thanks the audience for coming, and tells a few more stories. Being entertained does not always mean being made to laugh. A ghost story, a horror movie, or a murder mystery may scare the wits out of you and still be entertaining.

Can you tell the difference between the various kinds of messages? Find out by responding to Experience 12.7.

EXPERIENCE   12.7   GENERAL PURPOSES OF MESSAGES

DIRECTIONS   **To the left of each of the following descriptions of a message's objectives, write the general purpose phrase (to inform, to persuade, to entertain) that best describes the message.**

1 _____ After hearing this speech, audience members will be able to adjust the idle speed on most cars' carburetors.

2 _____ After hearing this speech, half the members of the audience will sign a petition to the city council protesting a change in the zoning ordinance.

3 _____ After hearing my speech, audience members will be able to describe the organizational chart representing my college's administration.

4 _____ After receiving this message, audience members will be able to list three causes of hypertension.

5 _____ After hearing this radio commercial, many audience members will purchase FrostiCola.

6 _____ After receiving this message, audience members will feel more cheerful than they did before.

7 _____ After receiving this message, audience members will be able to use a light meter for photography.

8 _____ After receiving my letter, mother will send me fifteen dollars before next weekend.

9 _____ After hearing my speech, audience members will feel proud of our country.

10 _____ After receiving this message, audience members will say they enjoyed themselves.

11 _____ After hearing this speech, my teacher will give me a grade of B plus or better.

12 _____ After hearing this speech, audience members will be able to describe some things God has done for them in the last week.

Specific purpose

Students quickly note several points about Experience 12.7. First, all messages, even interpersonal messages can be analyzed for general purpose, and an infinitive phrase can be applied to them. This is not to say that every message has only one purpose. Most interpersonal messages have multiple purposes. For example, you may ask your mother for money and have other purposes in mind besides persuasion. The most effective public messages, on the other hand, usually have one clear, planned purpose. If the purpose of a message is not too clear, that is usually an indication of poor planning. Items 9 to 12 in Experience 12.7 are examples of such poor planning.

Item 9 is stated as an entertaining purpose; some feeling is to be aroused, but no particular act is to be accomplished by audience members. Such speeches are often given on the Fourth of July and other patriotic occasions. From this purpose statement, you might guess that the speech would be one of that type. But the speech may in fact be primarily persuasive in nature; it may try to get people to change their attitudes and behavior in the direction of something that the speaker defines as more patriotic. Item 10 presents almost the same problem. That message almost certainly has informative purpose, but it is stated in a way that suggests a persuasive speech on the topic "you are having the time of your life right now." Item 11 shows a different kind of problem. If you are giving an in-class speech, chances are that your primary purpose is to earn a high grade. If the teacher assigns your grade, then the teacher may be your most important audience. *But* you cannot state your purpose in those terms because your teacher may downgrade you for not expressing your purpose in terms of the *classmate* audience. This paradox springs from the fact that you are speaking to two audiences. You must speak to your classmates almost as if the teacher were not there in order to make a favorable impression on the teacher. That is no different in principle from going to the malt shop with the guys when your real purpose is to impress Amy, who is there with a girl friend, and you pretend you do not notice her. Politicians have similar problems. If a U.S. president gives a televised address to the American people, he or she may have one planned purpose in terms of his or her political rivals and another purpose for the heads of foreign governments. For example, the president gives a speech on cuts proposed for the Defense Department's budget. The purposes may be stated as follows:

1   After hearing this speech, the majority of this country's voters will support cuts in the defense budget.
2   After hearing this speech, my political opponents will be convinced that it would be politically unwise to take a stand against my proposals.
3   After hearing my speech, the leaders of foreign governments, allies and others, will be convinced that U.S. military strength will not be diminished by these budget cuts.

Note that although this speech has three stated purposes, it does not violate the rule that a speech should have one purpose. We amend that rule slightly: A speech should have one clearly stated purpose for *each* audience. The presidential speech has three distinct and identifiable audiences in mind and only one purpose to be accomplished with each.

Suppose, once again, that your primary objective is to impress your teacher and receive a high grade. Mentioning this may actually lower your grade. The solution is not difficult. When writing early drafts of your purpose statement, you can make a distinction between your two audiences:

1   After hearing this speech, the teacher will give me a B plus or better.
2   After hearing my speech, my classmates will be able to make piecrust.

The final item in Experience 12.7 states that audience members should be able to describe some things God has done for them during the last week. This is stated (in form) as an informative purpose; the word *describe* is the key. However, many audience members might feel that this represents a persuasive topic because the existence of God and God's intervention in daily affairs is a controversial topic. The person giving the speech may have strong faith in the daily presence of God, and to that speaker, such a description may seem as matter-of-fact as listing what was bought at the grocery last evening. How is one to decide whether such a speech is informative or persuasive?

This is one of the most difficult problems that you can run into in trying to state a speech's purpose. It is often hard to separate informative speech topics from persuasive ones. There are, of course, certain clear cases of each. A speech on how to make pudding is certainly informative. A speech in defense of gay rights is clearly persuasive. But in between, it is often hard to tell. Furthermore, speech that is persuasive for one audience might be informative for another.

Many speech topics could be either informative or persuasive. The difference may be largely a matter of emphasis. Are you stressing how something is done (informative) or how wonderful that something is to do (persuasive)? Are you trying to get some information across or to get someone to change his or her mind? Are you describing some behavior or trying to change someone's behavior?

It has been argued (by Aristotle, for instance) that all speeches are persuasive. If you want nothing more from your speech than to get information across, you still must (in a sense) persuade the audience that what you offer *is* information, not fantasy or half-baked opinion. If you want to entertain your audience, you must persuade the audience that what you say is entertaining, not boring or merely ludicrous. If you want nothing more from your speech than that the audience stay awake, there is even a persuasion interpretation for that: to persuade the audience that they should stay awake during my speech.

In summary, it is worthwhile to plan a speech by stating its general purpose and then amplifying that general purpose with a statement of specific purpose. Of course, a speech's purpose is sometimes difficult to state. Usually, the best way to clarify the problem is to look at the nature and attitudes of the audience. Try to leave your own beliefs out of it. A purpose statement is a statement only of what happens to the audience. Furthermore, there is no need in most real-life situations to assume that you can have only one audience.

In the preceding paragraph, we used the term *specific purpose.*

You probably noticed that that was a new term. The general purpose of a message, you recall, is to inform, to entertain, or to persuade. The specific purpose is a more particular statement of what you want to happen to audience members as a result of your speech. Items 1 to 8 in Experience 12.7 were statements of specific purpose written in the form we want you to use. Turn back to Experience 12.7 and look at those statements.

The first thing you probably noticed was the repetition of something like "after hearing this message, the audience will. . . ." These *words* remind the speaker that purposes are stated in terms of what is going to happen to the audience. They also make it clear that what the audience is going to do is in some way related to receiving your message. The statement of purpose is not simply a description of something the audience members were going to do in any case; rather, it is a prediction about some way in which you plan to have your speech make a difference. We recommend that you state your specific purpose more or less this way:

> After hearing my speech, audience members will. . . .

A second thing you probably noticed was that most of the specific purpose statements are stated *in a way that can be measured.* This means that the specific purpose is to be stated in a way that sets of a goal for the speech; then, after the speech, you will be able to check to see whether the goal was accomplished. This can be very difficult to do. The closer you can get to being able to do it, the stronger and more useful your statement of specific purpose has been.

Here is an example of a statement of a specific purpose:

> After hearing my speech, audience members will know something about cameras.

The statement uses the words *After hearing* . . . , and it is clearly informative. But there are problems with it. Can you identify those problems?

> What is wrong is _____
> _____

> A better way to state it would be: After hearing _____
> _____
> _____

You were correct if you said that the purpose as stated was not measurable. A measurable specific purpose might be: "After hearing my speech, the audience will be able to operate the light meter on a 35-millimeter camera."

Here is another example: "After hearing my speech, the audience will be able to do a tune-up on an outboard motor." Can you explain what is wrong with this purpose statement for a five-minute speech to a college class?

_____

_____

The major problem in this case is that the statement of purpose is too much to expect from a five-minute presentation. Several hours of instruction as well as actual experience may be required before the audience could realistically be expected to accomplish this stated purpose. Depending upon the type of audience in the class as determined by the audience analysis, the topic (outboard motor repair) may or may not be appropriate. A better specific purpose might be: "After hearing my speech, the audience will know two things to try if a motor breaks down."

Here is one more example: "After hearing my speech, the audience will do something to support the causes of the Travis County Blood Bank." Explain what you think is wrong with that purpose statement?

_____

_____

If you said that this statement of purpose does not call for a specific behavior, you are on the right track. It is not clear what the audience is to do in order to support and otherwise further the cause of the blood bank. Revise this purpose statement.

_____

_____

In summary, an effective statement of purpose must meet three criteria:
1 It must be stated in terms of audience behavior.
2 It must state specific measurable behavior on the part of the audience.
3 It must be achievable within the limits of time and the speaking situation.

To see how well you understand these criteria and the concept of specific purpose, try your hand at Experience 12.8.

EXPERIENCE 12.8 SPECIFIC PURPOSE

DIRECTIONS
(PART 1)

Evaluate each of the following specific purpose statements according to these three criteria: (1) stated in terms of audience behavior, (2) states a measurable effect, and (3) is achievable in time and situation.

If a statement does not meet one or more of these criteria, put the number of that criterion in the blank at the left. If the purpose statement can be improved, rewrite it.

_____ 1 After hearing my speech, audience members will be able to write down four steps in cooking Chinese vegetables.

_____

_____

_____ 2 After hearing this message, the audience will support mental health programs.

_____

_____

_____ 3 The purpose of this speech is to inform about side effects of birth control pills.

_____

_____

_____ 4 After hearing my speech, audience members will be able to state the meaning of the term *qualified audit report* and tell why this concept is important to any business.

_____

_____

_____ 5 To inform about tuning guitars.

_____

_____

_____ 6 After hearing my speech, audience members will know three *good* things that England's King George III did during his reign.

_____

_____

DIRECTIONS
(PART 2)

For each of the following topics, below, construct a statement of specific purpose that satisfies all three of our criteria. Assume that each purpose statement is for a five-minute speech delivered to the class for which you are reading this book.

1 Planting a garden

_____

_____

2 Igneous rocks

_____

_____

3 Richard M. Nixon

_____

_____

4 The Oedipus complex

5   Unicorns, dragons and other mythical beasts

More messages fail because of a clearly defined purpose statement and the failure to analyze the situation than from all other causes combined. Practice may seem tiresome, but it is essential. Experience 12.9 consists of a work sheet that can help get you started toward preparing a successful public message. The work sheet outlines the topics discussed in this chapter and invites you to appraise the speech situation and generate a specific purpose.

EXPERIENCE 12.9 SPEECH ANALYSIS WORK SHEET

DIRECTIONS   Use the worksheet in this experience as a guide when working on an assigned speech.

1   Describe the reasons for the gathering to which your message will be addressed.

2   Describe the room or place.

3   How much time do you have?

4   Is the audience homogeneous?

   a. Describe audience demographics (age, sex, education, ethnicity).

   b. Is the audience similar to you? Explain the similarities and/or differences.

5   List three possible topics for your speech. (Do not worry if they seem too general).

a. _____

b. _____

c. _____

6 **Rank these three topics in terms of which interests you most.**

_____

7 **What is your general purpose (to inform, to entertain, to persuade)?**

_____

8 **Using your top-ranked topic from item 6, compose a statement of specific purpose (that fulfills the three criteria (stated in terms of audience, measurable, appropriate to situation).**

_____

_____

_____

SUMMARY

This chapter presents the preliminaries to the preparation of any public message: analysis of the situation and the purpose of communication. The chapter focused upon public speaking situations, but the experiences and concepts presented could apply to written or mass-media communication events as well.

The speech situation consists of a dynamic interplay of many forces, including 1) *the audience,* the analysis of which includes such considerations as demographic information, homogeniety, and similarity to speaker; 2) *the topic,* which is best analyzed in terms of areas interesting to both speaker and audience and suitable to the occasion; 3) *the occasion* itself, consisting of such factors as time limit, formality, setting and facilities; and finally, 4) *the speaker.*

After analyzing the speech situation, the speaker next states the purpose of the message. Public messages, unlike some interpersonal messages, are generally more effective if a concise purpose is stated. There are three general purposes: to inform, to entertain, and to persuade. A speaker may hone any of these general purposes into a specific purpose which describes the desired effect upon the audience. The more concise a specific purpose, the better. It is best to state your purposes in terms of measurable effects so there will be some realistic way of evaluating the speech.

The materials in Chapter 12 are the background for preparing an effective speech. They involve preparation for the speech that may not be obvious to a casual observer. You may be tempted to short-cut the process at first, but we encourage you to go through all of these steps.

CHAPTER 13
PREPARING THE PUBLIC SPEECH

In Chapter 12, we talked about analyzing the speech situation and composing the purpose of your message. In this chapter, we describe how to construct and put together the message itself. Again, although we emphasize the public speech, most of the discussion also applies to written messages, documentary films, news stories, and many other kinds of messages.

There are four basic steps to message preparation: gathering the information, outlining, polishing the style, and delivering the message. Speechmaking has been taught through these four steps at least since the time of the Roman Empire. It is a method that works. It produces messages with content, structure, style, and dynamism.

This is a nuts-and-bolts chapter; it takes you through a series of steps. We recommend that you follow this procedure: Study the chapter until you understand the flow of the speechmaking process; then use chapter materials as a handy guide and reference in preparing a few messages. When you get stuck, refer back to the chapter for advice on getting unstuck.

GATHERING INFORMATION

Taking notes

Ordinarily, you will need to gather information for your speech; only rarely will you already know all about everything you wish to say.

It will be helpful for you to take notes on what you learn. Nearly everyone takes some notes as they do research, but the way in which you take notes can save a lot of work and trouble if you give it some thought.

First, get a stack of paper so that you only write down *one idea on a sheet*. (Some people prefer note cards, which are easy to work with.) This method helps keep your ideas straight. The reason for writing only one idea to a page or card is that when you prepare the message, you can organize your notes for presentation by simply arranging (and rearranging) them in a stack.

Second, *note whether you are quoting exact words or paraphrasing general ideas*. Some research handbooks recommend always writing down an author's exact words; others recommend usually paraphrasing notes in your own words. There is really no right or wrong way. Just be sure to indicate whether you are using an author's exact words and to put quotation marks around them. That way you can give proper credit. Teachers get very angry if you quote someone without giving full credit. It is a form of plagiarism, the worst crime an academic researcher can commit.

One advantage of including quoted material in your notes is that if you paraphrase materials when you compile your notes and then paraphrase again in composing your final message, you may inadvertantly paraphrase back into the author's original words. Obviously, if you have the author's actual words in front of you, you will avoid this problem.

The following note makes creative use of quotation marks:

The FCC fairness doctrine requires broadcasters to devote part of their air time to discussions of important public issues. "Licensees have an obligation to see that the presentation of such issues is balanced and that opposing views are aired. They have an obligation to seek out opposing views from partisans who earnestly espouse them, and they may not exclude proponents of such views who are unable to pay the cost of airing their opinions." (From Anne W. Branscomb, "Citizen Access to the Media." In *Aspen Notebook on Government and the Media,* edited by W. L. Rivers and Michael J. Nyhan. New York: Praeger, 1973, p. 122.)

Third, *use topic headings* for each note. Put a key word or phrase in the upper-right-hand corner of the note; that will tell you at a glance what the note is about. These topic headings will be useful later when you begin to sort your notes to arrange the message. Headings are also helpful when you leaf quickly through your notes to ask yourself whether you have enough information to start active preparation and polishing.

Fourth, *record source data* for the information. If the source is a book, periodical, or other published material, record the necessary information for a footnote or bibliography listing: author, title, publisher, date, and page numbers. If the source of information is a personal interview, a letter, or some other kind of personal experience, note everything about that source that seems helpful.

Putting down this much information may seem extreme if you are preparing only a five-minute speech, but we have often found the practice useful. It takes little time to record this information while you have the source right in front of you; whereas later it might require a special trip to the library to get it. Also, listing your sources is a good, low-keyed way to demonstrate to the teacher that you looked in lots of places and took your research seriously. List your sources fully. Most teachers are unimpressed by a general entry such as the name of a magazine or book title.

Here are some examples of documentation we recommend:

Article: Mullay, Donald, "The Fairness Doctrine: Benefits and Costs." *Public Opinion Quarterly* (Winter 1969–70): 577–582.

Book: Rivers, William J. and Nyhan, Michael J., eds. *Aspen Notebook on Government and the Media.* New York: Praeger Publishers, 1973.

Interview: Martha Smith, interview conducted in Austin, Texas, on March 11, 1977.

People as resources

Information does not chase after you; you have to hustle it. That is not always simple. Some information is contained in easy-to-read magazine articles. Other information may not be in print at all. You may have to do some of your information gathering through interviews. You may decide to do a small questionnaire survey or write a letter or make a few phone calls. If you are willing to chase information, there is a lot you can learn.

Most students head straight for the library after choosing a speech topic. When they have found all they can there, they consider the job done. The most frequently overlooked resource for speech materials is *people.* People, after all, write everything you can read in the library. Sometimes, you can get the information from the people firsthand.

Is there anyone you know who can provide you with information about your topic? At most colleges and universities, there are experts in a large number of subjects right on campus. These people are usually happy to talk to any student interested in their subject matter. It is as easy as picking up the telephone to ask them.

If you do not know of any experts, try to guess what department such an expert might teach in. Call that department and see if someone can help. If no one there can help, they can usually refer you to someone else. Make phone calls during the early exploratory part of your search for people; you can make twenty calls in the time it takes to make one or two personal visits.

Sometimes, you will not find the people you want on campus. What about in the rest of the town? Do not worry about blind alleys. You will not get information or help from every phone call or visit you make. But eventually, you will contact somebody who can give you more useful information than ten magazine articles. Remember, you cannot ask questions of a magazine article.

People are a frequently overlooked source of materials for public messages.

You have a big head start in this kind of situation because you have learned a set of interview skills. (You may find it helpful to review the material in Chapter 9 on interviews to gather information before you go to see the person you have contacted.)

Here are two more tips. First, start early. Sometimes it takes a little time to track down the right person. Sometimes, for example, the best person can be reached only by mail; that could take a week. Go ahead and write to the person; you have nothing to lose. If you are in a time pinch, you can use other sources. Then, if you do not get an answering letter, you will not be stranded. You might also consider paying for a long-distance phone call.

Second, try the ten-referrals technique. Go to any person you know well enough so that you know he or she will be receptive regardless of what you ask. Ask if he or she knows anything about your topic. If your topic is as limited as it should be—say, the effects of radioactive fallout—your friend will probably know very little. But here is the important part of the technique: *Ask your friend for the name of somebody who might know something about radioactive fallout.* Do not accept no for an answer. Make sure the person is someone you can get in touch with. Next, go to the person recommended. Explain that your friend (use his or her name) recommended him or her as someone who might be able to give some information. The person will probably be a little flattered to have been recommended. Still, however, he or she probably will not have much knowledge about your topic. Get as much information as you can; then ask this person for a recommendation of someone who might help. Go to that person. Ask some questions. By this stage, you may be talking to someone who has really useful information. In any case, you are sharpening your questions. When you find the person with the information you need, you will have lots of good questions on the tip of your tongue. Ask the third person for his or her recommendation of someone he or she knows personally who could give you more information.

You will be astounded at how quickly you will find someone who is an expert on your topic. Five or six interviews should be sufficient. Researchers have found that even if you start with just anyone on the street, you will arrive at internationally recognized experts in about ten sets of interviews.

In summary, people are often the best resources for speech information. People can point you toward things to read faster than any index can. They can put things in perspective for you. They can also answer questions.

Experience 13.1 will help you to get started using people as resources.

EXPERIENCE 13.1 PEOPLE AS RESOURCES

DIRECTIONS
(PART 1)

For each of the following topics, list one person you know who could be helpful. If you do not know anyone, list a place you might call as a first try or a person you might ask as a first referral.

1 International trade _____
2 Women's college athletics _____
3 Growing vegetables _____
4 Modern art _____
5 Courtroom procedure _____
6 Etiquette _____

DIRECTIONS
(PART 2)

Using the topic you chose in Chapter 12 or some other topic, list at least three people or offices, bureaus, and the like that you might contact. List phone numbers and addresses to facilitate the contact.
Topic _____

1 _____
2 _____
3 _____
4 _____

DIRECTIONS
(PART 3)

Using the same topic, complete five rounds of the referral technique. Record each person's name; opposite the name, make a quick note of the information you obtained from him or her.

Names	*Information*
1 _____	_____
2 _____	_____
3 _____	_____
4 _____	_____
5 _____	_____

Libraries as resources

Facts, data, quotations, background, opinions, and many other printed items of helpful information live in libraries. You know this, so you go to the library and spend an evening looking for information for your speech. You come away muttering about libraries in general and that library in particular. You could not find what you wanted at the library—again. Perhaps you spent the last half hour of the evening sitting with a couple of friends who were also frustrated in their library search, griping about how poorly the library is run and so on.

We have talked to a number of students with such complaints to to find out what goes wrong. Here are some of the most common problems:

1. *The One-Library Problem*
   "I went to the library and couldn't find anything."
   What library did you go to?
   "The public library branch near my house. They didn't have anything on radioactive fallout."

There are many different libraries in most cities. Every library is strong in certain areas and less strong in others. If you try one library and have little luck, try another.

2. *The Card Catalog Problem*
   "I looked in the card catalog, but I couldn't find anything there."

Often students know how to look in the card catalog but do not know what to try next. In the Appendix, we show you how to use the card catalog more productively and where to look next if the card of the card catalog proves unhelpful.

3. *The How-to-Look Problem*. This problem is one of not knowing how to go about searching for information on a topic. Actually, the first two problems are specific examples of this one. This problem can occur at any stage of research. Your creative response to it determines how much you can get out of the library. Remember this ultimate strategy: Ask a librarian.

Do you need a new *library search strategy?* Experience 13.2 will help you to find out.

EXPERIENCE   13.2 WHAT IS YOUR LIBRARY SEARCH STRATEGY?

DIRECTIONS   **Rearrange the following steps in the process of researching a topic in the way that seems most efficient. Write the step numbers in the blanks to the left of the items. For the purposes of this experience, your topic is the uses of television in college teaching.**

_____   A   **look in the card catalog.**
_____   B   **search the *New York Times Index* for newspaper articles.**
_____   C   **ask a librarian for suggestions.**
_____   D   **look for a bibliography on the topic.**
_____   E   **look in specialized reference works for entries on instructional television.**

_____ F   browse through a shelf where there are many books about television.
_____ G   search the *Reader's Guide* to find magazine articles.
_____ H   look in encyclopedias or dictionaries.

Experience 13.2 demonstrates the problem of developing an effective library search strategy. Where can you look next to find the most material that you can understand and that will be helpful? If you were to give a report on instructional TV, chances are you would not use all the choices given in Experience 13.2. So if you left out one or two choices, your strategy was probably realistic. It would also be understandable if you did not know how to find four or five of the items referred to.

We suggest the following order of the steps in Experience 13.2. Try this order as a research strategy for the message you are now preparing. Our students tell us that it seems to work well for most topics. You need not use every item in every topic search, but we have found it generally helpful to follow this order for whatever items you do use. Try it without question for two or three projects. After that, you will be able to develop the order that works best for you.

1. dictionary
2. encyclopedia
3. card catalog
4. creative browsing
5. *Reader's Guide to Periodical Literature*
6. newspaper indexes (*New York Times Index*)
7. bibliographic index or statistical summaries
8. librarian

If you put five of the items in Experience 13.2 in this order and did not miss any item by more than two positions, you are ready to go on with this chapter. If you missed four items or feel that you need more experience with library materials, read the Appendix, "Doing Library Research." Then respond to Experience 13.3, using the speech topic you are preparing. The experience is intended to guide your library preparation for the speech.

EXPERIENCE   13.3 SEARCH STRATEGY GUIDE

DIRECTIONS   Use the following list of sources to guide your search for information. Consult the resources in the order listed. Be sure you write down the following information for each relevant source you find: author's name, title of article and magazine or book, volume number, page numbers, date, and call number. Use this list as your guide, but use other paper or note cards for taking the actual notes.

ENCYCLOPEDIAS

1   Subject headings used:

_____

_____

2   Relevant articles:

_____

_____

_____

BOOKS

3   Card catalog: subject headings used:

_____

_____

4   Relevant books:

_____

_____

_____

MAGAZINE ARTICLES

5   Title of index used:

_____

6   Subject headings used:

_____

_____

7   Relevant articles:

_____

_____

_____

OTHER SOURCES

8   Describe any sources that you have used that we have not included in this list.

_____

_____

_____

_____

Formulating a central idea

One place where students go wrong is in worrying whether they have enough information. Some students go on seeking new sources and taking new notes until the day before the assignment is due. That is usually a mistake. Remember, the later stages of speech preparation require some time, too. At some point, you have to break off the gathering of materials and get on with formulating the message. Knowing when is a subjective matter that improves as you gain experience.

The first step is to ask yourself this question on the basis of the purpose you formulated earlier and the information gathered: What is the central idea I am trying to get across in this message?

A message's *central idea* is a one-sentence summary of the entire message. It is a clear, condensed version of the point that it is most critical to emphasize in the speech. A central idea differs from a statement of purpose. A purpose is stated in terms of what you want to accomplish with the audience; the central idea is *what you want to say in terms of the subject matter.*

If you are able to formulate your central idea clearly, you are nearly ready to stop the research phase. If you formulate your central idea and have enough materials collected to support that idea effectively, you need not do more research. (In fact, doing more research might waste time.)

Experience 13.4 lets you sharpen your skills in differentiating between central ideas and statements of purpose.

EXPERIENCE 13.4 CENTRAL IDEAS AND STATEMENTS OF PURPOSE

DIRECTIONS   Read each of the following statements, and decide whether the statement is a central idea or a specific purpose statement. Write *CI* in the blank if the statement is a central idea; write *P* in the blank if it is a statement of purpose.

_____ 1   After hearing my speech, the audience will be able to load film into a 35-millimeter camera.

_____ 2   After hearing my speech, the audience will be able to state two major principles of the FCC fairness doctrine.

_____ 3   The fairness doctrine requires broadcasters to provide reasonable opportunities for broadcasting conflicting points of view on matters of public interest.

_____ 4   After hearing my speech, the audience will be able to state the three major sources of influence operating in organizations.

_____ 5 Loading a 35-millimeter camera properly will help assure good, clear, unfogged pictures.

_____ 6 The major sources of influence operating in organizations are interpersonal, structural, and technological.

_____ 7 After hearing my speech, the audience members will write to their representatives in Washington requesting that more federal money be channeled into research on solar energy.

_____ 8 Solar energy represents the nation's only hope for safe, efficient energy, without destroying our environment.

The central idea is a summary of the main idea or content of the message you want to get across. The purpose statement, although closely related to the central idea, is always stated in terms of audience behavior.

Now that you know the difference between central ideas and purpose statements, practice formulating some central ideas by responding to Experience 13.5.

EXPERIENCE 13.5 FORMULATING CENTRAL IDEAS AND PURPOSE STATEMENTS

DIRECTIONS Formulate a specific purpose and a central idea for two speech topics. One topic should concern something about your academic major or a job you hope someday to hold. The second topic should deal with some aspect of your favorite hobby or special interest. Be sure that the purpose is stated in terms of the audience. The central idea should contain only one major idea.

Topic 1: _____
Statement of purpose:

_____

_____

Central idea:

_____

_____

Topic 2: _____
Statement of purpose:

_____

_____

Central idea:

_____

_____

OUTLINING

Now you are ready to organize your materials. Clear organization is the hallmark of a clear message. If a message is well organized, the receivers can tell what is being said without having to rearrange the ideas.

The method most recommended for arranging messages is outlining. Outlining skills are essential to constructing effective messages. An outline is the skeleton of the message, the bones to which flesh gets attached. Without a skeleton, the flesh would collapse into a heap. Without a skillfully executed outline, the information you have gathered for your message will also collapse.

Outlining is not just arrangement. It is also a process of deciding which pieces of information are the most critical to what you have to say and deserve emphasis. Outlining is a continuation of the process that you employed when you composed the central ideal for your message.

Order

To begin with, you need to determine what kind of order you will use for your outline. Order may be determined by the nature of the materials you have gathered for the message. For instance, if your message tells a story, the best order will probably be to run through the story in *chronological order*, that is, in the same time sequence in which the events occurred. Here is a sample outline using chronological order:

  I. Topic: The arrest of a citizen. What happens?
 II. General Purpose: To inform
III. Specific Purpose: After hearing this speech, the audience will be able to list each major step in the process of confinement in a county jail.
 IV. Central Idea: If a citizen knows the process usually followed when someone is taken to jail, that citizen can make the most of his or her rights.
  V. Chronological Ordering of Materials
   A. arrest
   B. transport to jail
   C. booking
   D. search of files for previous record
   E. interview
   F. fingerprinting
   G. mug shot
   H. telephone call
   I. assignment to cell

Another way to outline a message is to follow the topic's *spatial order*. How would you describe the living room of a house or apartment in which you grew up? You would probably start at one place in the room and describe each object as you swept your imaginary gaze across the room. This form of organizing is useful in many messages that acquaint an audience with the workings of an object (such as an internal combustion engine) or a geographic area (such as the Sahara). Here is a sample outline that uses spatial order:

  I. Topic: Geography of the state of Texas.
 II. General Purpose: To inform

III. Specific Purpose: After hearing this message, audience members will be able to list and describe seven geographic areas of Texas.
IV. Central Idea: Texas is a state containing many climates and terrains.
 V. Spatial Ordering of Materials:
   A. the piney woods of east Texas
   B. the hill country in central Texas
   C. the desert area of west Texas
   D. the mountainous area: Big Bend and Davis Mountains
   E. the Rio Grande valley
   F. the coastal region on the Gulf of Mexico
   G. the Panhandle plains

You may have noted that spatial order does not seem so cut-and-dried as chronological order. Usually, there is only one time order in which events unfold. But with spatial order, you can start almost anywhere, so long as you follow a consistent framework. In the sample outline, material was organized from east to west across the center of the state, with a discussion of several areas near the edge of the state. The particular order you choose can create some problems. We will discuss them in the section "Main Points."

Topical order often provides even greater flexibility. Topical order divides the subject to be considered into a number of subsubjects, on the assumption that the discussions of those subtopics will add up to a discussion of the whole. For example, we have followed topical order in this section, describing each method of ordering (chronological, spatial, topical) as a separate subtopic on the assumption that mastery of each will constitute knowledge of the general topic of organizational arrangement of messages. In fact, topical order is the method of arrangement used most frequently throughout this book. Each chapter is a subtopic in our informative message about communication skills. (We have used other methods of ordering in some places. For example, the entire discussion of how to prepare a message has been based mainly on chronological order.) Here is an example of an outline using topical order:

  I. Topic: A balanced diet.
  II. General Purpose: To inform
 III. Specific Purpose: After receiving this message, audience members will be able to evaluate their own daily diet in terms of nutritional values.
 IV. Central Idea: A balanced diet is made up of foods from each of four major food families.
  V. Topical Ordering of Materials:
   A. cereals
   B. dairy products
   C. meats
   D. fruits and vegetables

Finally, a message can be arranged in *cause-effect order.* This method is used to show how particular events lead to other events. The cause-effect sequence is commonly used in persuasive speaking (see

Chapter 14), but it is also well suited to other purposes. Some topics could be arranged about equally effectively in cause-effect or chronological order. The occurrence of one event before another event is often used to argue that one caused the other. But this sort of argument is often false. For example, day comes before night but does not cause it.

Sometimes an entire message revolves around a single cause-effect sequence. In such a case, the major arguments for the causal connection become main points. On the other hand, a message may present several cause-effect sequences that are related to each other. For example:

   I. Topic: Causes of heart disease
  II. General Purpose: To inform
 III. Specific Purpose: After this speech, audience members will be able to summarize six conditions that often lead to heart disease.
 IV. Central Idea: There are a number of rather diverse problems that increase risks of heart disease.
  V. Causal Ordering of Materials (Each topic suggests a cause-effect ordering.)
    A. saturated fats
    B. calories
    C. high blood pressure
    D. lack of exercise
    E. smoking
    F. too much sugar

Other ways of structuring information can, of course, be used. The point is, not that any one order is better than another, but that some system of order, applied appropriately, will improve a message's coherence.

It is also possible to combine various sequences of ordering. The cause-effect sequence in the preceding example could have been combined with a spatial sequence noting which parts of the heart and circulatory system are affected by each abuse, or it could have been combined with a chronological sequence illustrating how repetition of one abuse (such as smoking) creates different kinds of effects over long periods of time.

To practice your skills in using the four orders of message organization, respond to Experience 13.6.

EXPERIENCE   13.6   MESSAGE ORDERS

DIRECTIONS
(PART 1)

Indicate which of the four methods of organizing messages (chronological, spatial, topical, cause-effect) would be most effective for each of the following topics:

1 Making adjustments on the gear mechanism of
   a bicycle   _____
2 Explaining what materials and services are
   available in each part of the library   _____
3 Describing the organizational chart of your
   college or university   _____
4 Explaining discipline problems in elementary
   school classrooms   _____

DIRECTIONS   Use a series of 3-by-5 cards or pieces of paper for this exercise. Return
(PART 2)   to the informative message that you began constructing in Experience
              13.5. You uncovered a large number of items of information for this
              speech. (Our students usually came up with six to fourteen items
              worth writing down.) Write each separate piece of evidence or
              information on one piece of paper or card. (Do *not* write more than
              one piece of information on one card. If you are in doubt, use more
              than one card.)
                   Look through your stack of pieces of information, and see if you
              can decide which of the four orders for presentation would be most
              appropriate. Make a note of the topic and the kind of order. Then
              arrange your cards or slips of paper in the desired order. When you
              are satisfied with the arrangement and feel that it makes sense, copy
              the items of information next to the numbers provided here.
              Topic _____
              Kind of order used _____

1 _____
2 _____
3 _____
4 _____
5 _____
6 _____
7 _____
8 _____
9 _____
10 _____
11 _____
12 _____
13 _____
14 _____

Main points   The major bones of the message skeleton (outline) are the *main
                   points*, the major propositions of the message. Added together, the
                   main points equal the central idea of the message.

After you have arranged your information, the next step is to pick out and/or compose the main points. For some messages, the main points jump out at you. But usually, the main points are less obvious.

The beginning student often feels that it is easy to figure out main points; after all, a bunch of ordered points have just been offered. Why not list those as main points? The answer is that the main points are the *major* bones of the skeleton, not the whole thing. Main points are simplifications of the list of topics you developed in the last section. Here are three criteria that main points must meet:

1. For a short speech, there should never be more than four main points or less than two. It is difficult to explain this rule of effective composition, but it seems related to how many things people can remember at once.

Considerable refurbishing of an idea is sometimes required to reduce the number of main points. The student who constructed the speech about the geography of Texas (page 341) originally wanted to give a detailed geographic tour of her native state. She noted seven regions in the state and wished to have a speech with seven main points. When told the speech must be reduced to no more than four points, she was puzzled. Eventually, she realized that her topic was too large for a five-minute message. She might have given a geographic tour of half of Texas, but that seemed less unified than talking about the whole state. Her solution was to give up the original objective and substitute the objective of informing the audience that Texas is a land of geographic contrasts. With this changed emphasis, she no longer had to talk about everything; she could concentrate on particular contrasts that would support this central idea. Compare her final outline with that on page 341.

I. Central Idea: Texas is not a unified geographic area, as some people believe, but a region containing diverse climates and terrains.
II. Main Points (topical order)
   A. The Great Plains, miles and miles of miles and miles
   B. The mountains, stark leftovers from Creation
   C. The thickets, flat and piney east Texas
   D. The beaches, seashore on a Texas scale

Notice that this is practically a whole new topic; none of the headings look precisely as they did before. Nevertheless, most of the same materials can be used. This kind of rearranging and changing is common in the preparation of effective messages. One of the worst pitfalls for the mediocre is unwillingness to rearrange a message.

2. Main points should be parallel to each other. That is, your expression of main points should have the same basic language form. This points out both to speaker and to audience the clear structure

provided by the main points. For example: which of these sets of main points do you prefer?

Topic: Houseplants

I. Cactus and succulents
II. Ferns add a touch of green
III. The durable, undelicate
    African violet

or

I. You cannot kill a cactus.
II. Your thumb will go green with ferns
III. You need not be afraid of
    African violets

The second set of main points is preferable because they are phrased in parallel fashion. Each is a full sentence focusing on what the gardener can or cannot do.

3. Each main point should contain only one idea. It does not help to combine ideas with each other in a list. Sometimes, in order to get a small number of main points each of which expresses only one idea, you must reorganize your material somewhat. For example, on page 343, we listed six items for a speech about heart disease.

    saturated fats
    calories
    high blood pressure
    lack of exercise
    smoking
    too much sugar

The objective is to combine these into between two and four main points, each containing one idea. We would probably do it this way:

I. Dietary causes of heart disease
    A. fats
    B. calories
    C. sugar
II. Circulatory system causes of heart disease
    A. blood pressure
    B. arterial problems, lack of exercise
III. Smoking as cause of heart disease

There is no one way to rough out main points. You may well think of a better scheme for this speech than the one we suggest. Note that our reorganization followed a cause-effect order combined with a topical order.

Notice, also, that our tactic for combining a large number of points to achieve a smaller number was to organize several together under a common theme. You may find this method useful.

In summary, the main points should add up to the central idea. The message should be structured so that the main bones of the skeleton are strong enough to hold all the flesh and mold the whole into the proper shape. Try your hand at Experience 13.7.

EXPERIENCE 13.7 MAIN POINTS

DIRECTIONS
(PART 1)

Using the materials from the research about arrest procedures (page 341), construct the main points for a speech. Write these main points below.

_____
_____
_____
_____
_____

DIRECTIONS
(PART 2)

Did your main points conform to our three criteria (no more than four points, parallel form, only one idea per point)? If not, please revise.

_____
_____
_____
_____
_____

Subpoints

You probably noticed that some of the arranging of main points described in the last section was accomplished by rearranging materials as subpoints under (and supporting) each of the main points. If subpoints do not emerge during the outlining of the main points, then they are the next thing you must work out.

Subpoints support the main point they appear under in the same ways that main points support the central idea of the message. The discussion of each of the subpoints should establish the main point as firmly as possible. Like main points, subpoints should be presented in parallel form. However, subpoints need not be parallel to the main point or to subpoints under *other* points. For example:

I. Putting film in a camera
   A. be sure it is right side up
   B. be sure it is really winding
II. Using the light meter
   A. the tolerance
   B. the needle
   C. the f-stop

In this example, the main points parallel each other and the subpoints parallel other subpoints under that same main point. Further parallelism is usually unrealistic.

Subpoints must really be subordinate to, or part of, the main points they are placed under. If they are better discussed as part of something else, do more rearranging.

Subpoints can be arranged under the main point using any of the orders we discussed earlier (chronological, topical, spatial, or cause-effect). However, it is not necessary to use the same order throughout the message, so long as subpoints under a main point fit together.

Subpoints can be supported by sub-subpoints. (Theoretically, the practice could go on forever; but in practice, the sub-subpoint is rarely further subdivided.) For example:

I. First main point
  A. subpoint
    1. evidence
    2. further support
  B. second subpoint
    1. sub-subpoint (support)
    2. further support
    3. evidence, testimony, analogies, and so on
II. Second main point
  A. subpoint
  B. subpoint
    1. evidence
    2. evidence
  C. subpoint

Generally, the symbols used in the preceding outline are preferred for message outlines: roman numerals (I, II, III, IV) for main points; capital letters (A, B, C) for subpoints; arabic numbers (1, 2, 3) for sub-subpoints; lowercase letters (a, b, c) if further subdivisions are needed.

The process of arranging main points and subpoints into outline form seems awkward the first few times you do it, but it becomes quite natural with practice. You can get some outlining practice by responding to Experience 13.8.

EXPERIENCE   13.8   OUTLINING WORK SHEET

DIRECTIONS   **Using your speech topic and your materials, complete this outline work sheet.**
Topic: _____
General purpose: _____
Specific purpose: _____
_____
Central idea:_____
_____

Outline (main points, with subpoints)

_____
_____
_____
_____
_____

What material will you use to introduce and conclude the message?

_____
_____
_____

**POLISHING THE
MESSAGE: STYLE**

Your message is now substantially complete, but it is not yet ready for delivery. It is still in rough form and needs polishing.

Polishing involves words and phrases. The use of the right word at the right time has saved many a message. In our speechmaking culture, listeners have often responded to eloquent phrases:

We have nothing to fear but fear itself.

Ask not what your country can do for you, but what you can do for your country.

Give me liberty or give me death.

. . . . and that government of the people, by the people, and for the people, shall not perish from the earth.

I have a dream. . . .

Such phrases get remembered. That is why speakers usually strive to say things that will be quotable or memorable. When you polish your message by adding a quotable quote or otherwise making it as suitable as possible to the audience and occasion, you are working on the style of the message.

Your first task in working out the style of your message is to decide what kind of _tone_ you want to achieve. Do you wish to sound formal or informal, dignified or folksy, ironic or straightforward? As far as general tone is concerned, the question of formality is the most important. Most communication events in American society could be rated on a scale of formal to informal. Church gatherings, weddings, government meetings, and other semiceremonial occasions tend to be extremely formal. Speakers speak more in dignified tones, use sentences that are more grammatically correct, and underplay humor. This paragraph, for example, uses a rather formal tone.

In contrast, an informal tone is likely to be more colloquial, to use more slang, to use more humor, to overstate a point for effect. Informal gatherings are likely to attract people who have fairly similar tastes or who know each other quite well. Most classroom public speeches may be more informal than formal. (Remember, however, that the formality judgment is a matter of degree.) Even in informal gatherings, there are rules of taste. Foul language, off-color jokes, outright slapstick, or strong insults are almost always out of place in public messages, even if you commonly use them in everyday conversation.

It has often been said that public speaking is a lot like conversation. Most public speakers today use a relatively *conversational* tone for speaking. Conversational tone connotes informality but not totally informal talk—and certainly not lack of preparation. Public speaking is, after all, *enlarged* conversation.

Style is a difficult thing to talk about. You can point to examples and say that one is stylistically interesting and effective and another is not. But determining just why each had the effect it did, can be difficult. Aside from telling you to gear your level of formality to the audience and the occasion and to strive for a conversational style, we can advocate only three stylistic goals for you to strive for: clarity, vividness, and emphasis.

Clarity

One thing matters above all: to be clear. To get the message across without being misunderstood is the most important goal of most public messages. Say what you mean in the simplest possible terms. Speakers often feel that they will be more impressive if they use big words. One result is the euphemism. (We talked about this in Chapter 4.) To sound impressive, some people say "chief executive" instead of "president," "the National Anthem" instead of the "Star-Spangled Banner." Such substitutions are harmless enough. But if used in large numbers, they can help a speaker to sound pretentious and arrogant. Words used to impress others can backfire. Experience 13.9 will give you a fuller idea of what we mean.

EXPERIENCE 13.9 CLARITY

DIRECTIONS   After each of the following words, list a word that has a very similar meaning but sounds less pretentious or pompous.

1   difficult _____
2   to purchase _____
3   eventuality _____
4   ascertain _____
5   inquiry _____
6   to rectify _____

7 **to terminate** _____

8 **to procure** _____

9 **to commence** _____

10 **to assist** _____

11 **at the present time** _____

12 **at that point in time** _____

13 **in the near future** _____

14 **in order to** _____

15 **in order that** _____

16 **endeavor** _____

Even in formal situations, a simple word or phrase can communicate best and fastest to a wide range of receivers. If you watched the Watergate hearings on TV a few years ago, you probably remember the phrase *at that point in time.* It was used repeatedly by witnesses to indicate when they knew or did something in connection with the Watergate cover-up. The phrase caught on and was soon being used in conversations instead of *then.* This phrase is a good example of pseudoclarity. That is, in an attempt to be very precise, speakers and writers select words and phrases that they feel will help differentiate their meaning; instead, they often produce confusion.

Legalese is also a good example of pseudoclarity. The lawyers who write and interpret our laws maintain that legalese is necessary for precision and clarity. In some cases, that may be true; but in most cases, obscure legalese just helps most people to remain ignorant about insurance, real estate, and other contracts that they sign, so that they have to hire lawyers.

Vividness

Effective styles of speaking and writing are sometimes described as having vividness. A vivid style shows life. A vivid style is an active style. Something seems to be happening. A key to vivid style is the use of verbs. If active verbs, rather than passive verbs, are used by speakers, they can add to vividness.

The preceding paragraph serves as an excellent example of writing that is short on vividness. The following paragraph makes the same points more vividly:

> Vividness lives in most effective messages. We cannot define vividness precisely, but active messages display vividness. You cannot miss it. A vivid style breathes movement, a sense of something happening. A vivid style creates listener interest. To make your style more vivid, use robust, thrilling, squirming, active verbs. Avoid puny 97-pound passive verbs.

After you write down a message or practice talking through it, note the verbs you have used. If they seem drab, bring in some less tired substitutes. Look at the following list of verbs. They are tired.

(They are also rather general.) Can you think of more vivid alternatives for each of them? The more vivid alternative need not be a complete synonym. Chances are it will be more specific than the word we list. For example, instead of *walk*, why not choose *stroll, amble, saunter, plod,* or *trudge.*

tell _____

hit _____

get _____

write _____

More descriptive substitutes for the word *tell* might include *disclose, advise, hint, inform, enlighten, recite, express, announce, specify,* and *describe.* You probably thought of others, too. For the word *hit,* you may have thought of *strike, jab, smack, slap, swipe, rap,* or *flog.* The meaning of the verb *get* might be expressed more vividly by *gain, acquire, obtain, purchase, retrieve, salvage,* or *find.* Similarly, the verb *write* could be expressed as *record, compose, abstract, summarize, condense, copy, draft, pen, scribble, scrawl,* or *transcribe.*

You may note, as some students have, that we seem to violate our suggestion that you stick to simple words to get your meaning across. The point we want to make is this: Select the word that is most descriptive of the meaning you have in mind and want your receivers to have. If it communicates more information, is more descriptive and vivid, and is likely to be understood by your listeners or readers, use it.

Emphasis   Not everything in a message is of equal weight or importance. Therefore, another aspect of style is the emphasis you give to the ideas or concepts. There are several ways of indicating relative importance within messages. The most direct is to use transitions that show relative importance. Statements such as "the most important step in the process is," or "if you remember only one idea from what I have to say, I'd like for it to be this one," indicate to a listener or reader what you consider to be most important.

Proportion can also be used to indicate importance. If in a 20-minute presentation on management, you spend 15 minutes on goal setting, the receiver will understand that goal setting is most important. Repetition can effectively indicate importance. Stating the same concept in slightly different ways will indicate to the receiver that it is important and should be remembered. You can use a visual aid to reinforce an idea and provide repetition.

Finally, you can reinforce an idea and indicate importance by using vocal cues. Varying volume or pitch will emphasize an idea for the receiver. In written communication, you can emphasize an idea by setting it off from the other prose, by underlining it, or by other visual devices.

DELIVERY   Now the message is virtually complete. All you need to do is deliver it. This is the part of the process that is easiest for some but most difficult for others. Speech teachers are amazed at how many capable students shake with fright at the prospect of delivering a speech, even a short speech to a group of friends. If you are a victim of such stage fright, we have some concrete suggestions about how you can overcome your problem. Take comfort in the fact you are not alone; more than half of your classmates have stage fright, too. Here are some things to keep in mind:

1. Most audience members cannot tell the difference between frightened speakers and confident ones. For example, students in speech classes are usually surprised when a fellow student they believed to be totally successful and confident suddenly faints from fright in the middle of a speech.

2. You do not need to apologize for your fear. Remember, most members of your audience share it. But if you feel you must apologize, use the following to your advantage: "I am afflicted by terrible stage fright. I probably will faint before finishing this speech."

3. Stage fright is a wholly natural physical response to stress. That inner churning you feel is your body getting ready for a time of trial. The same thing happens before many kinds of public events. Athletes feel it; actors feel it. And they put it to use. The good actors and athletes translate this energy into effective performances.

4. Stage fright diminishes with practice. This is not to say you will necessarily get less scared. Some people do; others do not. But however scared you get, you will become increasingly confident that you can handle it.

Stage fright, also known as communication apprehension, is experienced by most people, but each individual feels it in a unique way. To get an idea of how you feel it, respond to Experience 13.10.

EXPERIENCE 13.10 SPEECH ANXIETY*

DIRECTIONS **The following statements refer to the experiences and feelings that have been reported by students immediately before and while speaking to an audience. For each statement, circle the number to the right of the statement that indicates how you *generally* feel.**

* D. H. Lamb, "Speech Anxiety: Towards a Theoretical Conceptualization and Preliminary Scale Development, *Speech Monographs,* 39(1972), 62–67.

		Almost never	*Sometimes*	*Often*	*Almost always*
1	I feel calm as I rise to speak.	1	2	3	4
2	It is easier to prepare a speech than it is to give it.	1	2	3	4
3	Fear of forgetting my speech causes me to jumble my words.	1	2	3	4
4	I feel in a daze while speaking.	1	2	3	4
5	My ideas and words flow smoothly while I am speaking.	1	2	3	4
6	I feel awkward while speaking.	1	2	3	4
7	I am terrified at the thought of speaking before a group.	1	2	3	4
8	I am so frightened at times that I lose my train of thought.	1	2	3	4
9	At the conclusion of my speech, I feel that I would like to continue talking.	1	2	3	4
10	The audience seems with me while I am speaking.	1	2	3	4
11	I feel poised when I face an audience.	1	2	3	4
12	Although I am nervous just before getting up, I soon forget my fears and enjoy the experience.	1	2	3	4

We asked you to respond to the statements in Experience 13.10, not to test you or to label you as a person who is chronically anxious about speaking in public, but to encourage you to examine some of your feelings about the speaking situation and honestly confront those that may be giving you some trouble before you begin to speak. For most people, some form of speech anxiety is normal and predictable.

To make the most out of normal anxiety, we recommend the following procedures:

1   When you get up to speak, take a moment to breathe deeply and collect your thoughts.

2   Plan your introduction carefully so that you know exactly what you are going to say in the early part of your speech.

3   Be sure that you have the audience's attention before you begin. Do this by remaining silent until everyone looks up at you. A second or two will usually be sufficient.

4   When you are making self-statements about speaking, think about the positive aspects of what you will be doing. We all talk to ourselves. When we make statements to ourselves that are

negative, we develop self-fulfilling prophecies about our own behavior. If we can begin to make positive self-statements about speaking situations, we can develop positive self-fulfilling prophecies.

Types of delivery

There are several appropriate ways of delivering a message: manuscript, memorization, extemporaneous, and impromptu. Which one you use depends upon the situation and circumstances of the speaker. In *manuscript delivery*, the speaker reads from a prepared text. In *memorization delivery*, the speaker writes out the speech in advance and memorizes it for later presentation to the audience. In *extemporaneous delivery*, the speaker thoroughly prepares and outlines a speech but does not memorize the exact words he or she will use in delivering the speech. The speaker may refer to notes and respond to nonverbal feedback from the audience. In *impromptu delivery*, a speaker is given only a few minutes to prepare a short message. This often occurs at a meeting in which a speaker is asked to give a report or respond to a question.

Anxiety is a normal response to a public speaking situation. It can be controlled and directed toward dynamic effectiveness.

Manuscript delivery is used when speakers want to determine in advance exactly what will be said in a speech and how it will be said. It is used by public figures making important policy announcements because every word will be sifted, measured, and analyzed. However, it is not a method that we generally recommend for in-class speeches. The manuscript method often makes the material sound as though it was meant to be a printed essay, not a speech. A speech must be more than an oral essay. A badly delivered manuscript speech may lead listeners to wonder why the speaker does not just give everyone a written copy and be done with it. (Most people can read faster than they can listen.) The many speaking occasions on which manuscript speeches are given are largely ceremonial and symbolic or too critical to chance tongue slips (e.g., speeches made by U.S. presidents).

Speakers using the manuscript method are advised to make the speech sound as conversational as possible, using as many terms that include or make reference to the audience as possible. The speaker must also rehearse the speech thoroughly so that his or her nose is not buried in the manuscript. Also, words selected should be those that are usual and comfortable for the speaker and understandable to the audience.

The memorization form of delivery, although generally superior to the manuscript style in maintaining audience contact, has a number of shortcomings. First, memorizing a speech takes a tremendous amount of time. A speaker may not always have the time necessary to do a good job of memorizing. Second, this form of delivery does not allow the speaker to respond to feedback from his audience. Third, it is difficult to sound natural and spontaneous when delivering a speech from memory. Fourth, the speaker may forget what he is going to say next, resulting in an embarrassing silence in the message. However, in past generations, the memorized speech was a rather popular form. When done well, it is as much a work of art as a play, a poem, or a song. If you wish to try a memorized speech and are willing to prepare it thoroughly, you might have some fun.

The extemporaneous method of delivery allows the speaker the greatest degree of flexibility. After thorough advance preparation, the speaker makes a brief set of notes. These notes are used by the speaker to remind himself or herself of the main points to be made. However, the actual wording of the speech takes place at the time of delivery. You may think that this technique sounds conversational, and in fact, extemporaneous delivery often adds to the spontaneous feeling of a speech. It allows the speaker to adapt to the changing moods and responses of the audience. For example, the speaker can include or discard some materials, depending upon his or her assessment of probable audience response. The extemporaneous method is generally recommended for beginning speakers and for more experienced speakers who wish to sound natural, spontaneous, and conversational.

Impromptu speeches are given when a speaker is called on to answer a question or give a report on some event or activity without advance notice. The speaker should keep impromptu remarks brief and focused on the topic or question. Audiences generally like this method of delivery because they feel that the real person is being revealed in the speech. If the speaker is asked to comment on some topic he or she is unfamiliar with or to answer a question that is still unclear, he or she usually has the right politely but firmly to decline to speak. Many a political candidate has lived to regret off-the-cuff remarks made in response to a question that he or she was hearing for the first time and for which he or she therefore had no clear response formulated. "Better to remain silent and be thought a fool than to speak and remove all doubt."

Appearance

The audience reaction to your delivery begins with your visual appearance. The audience sees you and makes some perceptual judgments (see Chapters 2, 5, and 7) before you utter a word or even lift an eyebrow. Audience members seem to have certain expectations of appropriate appearance. Deciding what these are and to what extent you can or will conform to them can be a difficult task. Twenty years ago, it was simple. If you were going to make a speech, you put on a suit or a businesslike dress. You got a haircut if you needed one; you were well scrubbed. These were well-understood code items.

Today, the situation is more complicated. You can wear a short dress, a long dress, or blue jeans; you can wear a sweat shirt, a tie, or a tank top. Few would want to go back to the custom of dressing up for everything. But there are problems, too. Because there is fairly wide latitude in many cases, it can be difficult to decide what attire and grooming will be most effective with your particular audience. To explore this problem, respond to Experience 13.11.

EXPERIENCE 13.11 APPEARANCE EXPECTATIONS

DIRECTIONS   **Imagine that you have been invited to speak before each of the following groups. Describe the clothing and grooming you think would be most appropriate on each occasion.**

1   **Interviewing for a summer job**   _____

_____

2 **Speech to a civic club of businesspeople in your hometown.** _____

_____

3 **Oral report at a regular meeting of a campus organization to which you belong** _____

_____

4 **Oral report for your communication class.** _____

_____

5 **Oral report in some other class** _____

_____

In determining what was appropriate dress for each of the occasions, listed in Experience 13.11, you probably took a number of factors into account. One of these was probably what you knew or assumed your listener or listeners would be wearing. Perhaps another was your estimation of the formality or informality of the occasion. Finally, you might have considered the demographic characteristics of the audience.

Whatever your choices, you can be sure that appearance is an important variable in determining the audience's response to you. Good appearance alone will not make your speech a success, but it can go a long way toward making the audience more receptive. Certainly, an inappropriate appearance can place an unnecessary barrier between you and the purpose you want to achieve with your audience.

Vocal aspects of delivery

The voice is a tool that the speaker can use to enhance the message. Researchers have concluded that a large part of the communication of emotional meaning is accomplished through the voice. To get a better idea of how much you rely on vocal variables to communicate feeling, read the following passage in three ways. If you have a tape recorder, record your readings and play them back, listening for differences in rate, volume, pauses, vocal quality, inflection, and variety of the pitch of the voice. First, read the passage as if you really believe it and want your listeners to believe it, too. Second, read it as if you are bored by its content. Third, read it as if you are suspicious of its contents and do not endorse it.

> One of the errors of the early feminist movement in this country was that it assumed that men had all the goodies and that women could attain self-fulfillment merely by being like men. But that is hardly the utopia that today's college students envision. Rather, the logical extension of their value of self-fulfillment would require that society raise its children so that some men might emerge with the motivation, the ability, and the opportunity to stay home and raise children without bearing the

stigma of being peculiar. If homemaking is as glamorous as the women's magazines portray it, then men too should have the option of becoming homemakers. Even if homemaking isn't all that glamorous, it would probably still be more fulfilling for some men than the jobs in which they now find themselves. *

In what ways did you cue your listeners about your feelings? What would be the probable impact on listeners of each of the three modes of reading?

Beyond just making sure that you pronounce words properly and articulate clearly enough so that your listeners can understand you, there are numerous vocal characteristics that are under your control and that you can use to communicate to your listeners. Of course, it is important that you speak loudly enough for your listeners to hear you without straining, but volume can also be used for emphasis or to get the audience's attention. You may change your rate of speaking to indicate how you feel about the message and your audience. If you are bored, the rate is generally slower than if you are interested and enthusiastic. Pitch can be used to gain attention, communicate interest, and add variety to your presentation.

Eye contact

The criterion of appropriateness is applicable here, as it is in so many other areas of communication. Your entire presentation will be more effective if the vocal aspects of your delivery are appropriate to the audience, to the setting of your speech, to the content you are delivering, and to yourself as a speaker. The audience will be able to detect an unnaturalness in your delivery, and that will affect response to the total message you communicate. Maybe it is best to relax and not worry about it.

For more than fifty years, speech teachers have emphasized looking audience members in the eye. Most Americans seem to trust people who make eye contact, and research has shown eye contact to be an important variable in interpersonal communication. It is equally important in one-to-many communication. What would you think of a speaker who rarely looks at the audience and who never looks at the eyes of the audience members on those rare occasions when he or she does look at the audience? List several words or phrases you would use to describe a person who does not maintain good eye contact.

Now imagine a speaker who looks the members of the audience in the eye. This speaker attempts to look at each listener in turn. All other things being equal, how would you describe this speaker?

* Sandra L. Bem and Daryl J. Bem, "Case Study of a Nonconscious Ideology: Training the Woman to Know Her Place," in *Beliefs, Attitudes, and Human Affairs,* ed. Daryl J. Bem (Belmont, Ca.: Brooks/Cole, 1970), p. 95.

You probably described the person who does not maintain good eye contact as anxious, reticent, nervous, dull, closed, unanimated, not spontaneous, and not very self-confident. In contrast, the person who maintains good eye contact is usually considered calm, eager, open, spontaneous, animated, and self-confident. Audience members typically make such judgments regardless of whether they are warranted by any internal state of the speaker.

A speaker who wishes to create positive impressions will pay particular attention to eye contact, attempting to look each person in the audience in the eye at least once. Eye contact is used for *inclusion;* thus, it is important to include every member of the audience, if possible, without favoring any particular area of the room. Eye contact alone cannot make a speech successful. But a lack of good eye contact can create a barrier not easily overcome even if all other elements of the speech are excellent.

A word of caution is necessary here: Some researchers are now suggesting that not all members of American society value eye contact equally. Specifically, they maintain that Mexican-Americans and black Americans do not always place the same value on eye contact that Caucasians do. However, the evidence on this point is not clear. If a speaker who is a member of a social or ethnic minority group does not seem to look at the audience as often as most speakers, it may be because of cultural differences, or simply because of lack of trust and identification with audience members.

What would you do if you were giving a speech and members of your audience did not look at you? That happened to a friend of ours. His class read ahead in a text about nonverbal communication and made a plot to not look at their teacher at all one day. They attended class, paid attention, took notes, laughed at jokes, but did not ever look at their unsuspecting instructor. After about twenty minutes, the speaker was reduced to a stuttering blob.

Like most forms of nonverbal communication, eye contact is a set of code items. Code items differ according to language and culture. For example, there are cultures in which speakers can stare at each other for minutes at a time without blinking. In such a setting, the average American would appear evasive. Codes are not absolutes.

Our point is this: Speech teachers have tended to treat eye contact as an absolute for effective speaking, and it probably is for many audience members. As a general rule, learn how to look at audience members while talking. Do not worry about losing your place, a brief pause while you glance at your notes almost always adds dignity to a speech. *But* if you are making eye contact and it does not seem to be having the desired effect of increasing rapport with the audience, do not panic. You may be speaking to an audience to whom eye contact is unimportant or even offensive. When you listen to others speak, do not be too quick to judge them harshly if they fail to make eye contact.

SUMMARY

There are four basic building blocks to effective speaking: gathering materials, outlining, polishing the style, and completing the delivery. Each aspect of message effectiveness requires attention by the beginner or expert.

In gathering information, you should use both personal (human) resources and library resources. Take notes as you go, and put only one idea per note, so that the simple arrangement of these notes into a stack can do most of your difficult organizing work. If you have trouble using people as resources, we advocate that you try the ten-referrals technique. If you have difficulties getting needed information from libraries, study the Appendix, "Doing Library Research."

As you gather materials, formulate the central idea for your message. The central idea is best stated as a one-sentence summary of what you want the speech to say in terms of the subject matter. Central ideas differ from purpose statements in that purpose statements specify what your speech would accomplish in terms of audience members.

When your research is complete, arrange your materials into some sensible order, such as topical cause-effect, chronological, problem-solution, or spatial order. Then rough out between two and four main points. They should be written in parallel form and express the sense of the central idea. Complete your presentation of each main point by dividing it into subpoints. Use the same methods you used for structuring the main points.

Now you are ready to begin polishing the style of the speech. Be sure that the tone you choose expresses the appropriate degree of formality. Scan your wording for evidence of clarity, vividness, and emphasis. Then select a mode of delivery most appropriate for the occasion. Manuscript delivery (for very formal speeches) and extemporaneous delivery (for more conversational settings) are the most common methods. Do not worry if you experience considerable stage fright when you give your first few speeches. This is normal, and all speakers go through it. Speakers differ only in how much they show it. Dress appropriately for the image you want to create. Attend to eye contact and your vocal dynamism as you deliver the speech.

CHAPTER 14
PERSUADING OTHERS

We have discussed the presentation of public messages in general, but one very important kind of public message deserves special treatment: the persuasive message.

The purpose of this chapter is to describe the persuasion process and provide you with skills both as a message sender and as a message receiver. Persuasion can be defined as *the process through which messages change attitudes.* To clarify what that definition implies, we begin with a definition of attitude; then we discuss how attitudes are measured by researchers and pollsters. We examine persuasion (changing attitudes) from the view of both message senders and receivers. Knowing about persuasion is equally important whether you wish to sell a product (persuade others) or whether you wish to buy a product (evaluate persuasion by others). Finally, we discusses credibility, the believability or persuasiveness of individual speakers. We conclude by telling how you can improve your credibility when delivering a public message.

Persuasive messages are very much a part of modern living. The average United States citizen receives dozens of persuasive messages every day. Many are advertisements paid for by makers of products or deliverers of services to persuade you to change your mind in directions they favor.

Because persuasion is so familiar, most people have some definite opinions about it. To measure your opinions, complete Experience 14.1.

EXPERIENCE 14.1   AGREE-DISAGREE STATEMENTS ABOUT PERSUASION

DIRECTIONS   **Indicate whether you agree or disagree with each of the following statements write *D* if you disagree with it. In Group Decisions column, record the consensus if these topics are used for in-class discussions.**

	Statements	*Private*	*Group*
		Decisions	
1	**People generally agree about the most important issues in life.**	_____	_____
2	**One way to persuade others is to talk the way they do.**	_____	_____
3	**The people who have the most power to change things actually do not receive as many persuasive messages as the rest of us do.**	_____	_____

362

4   An outsider is generally more persuasive to
    an audience than a member of the group is.   _____   _____
5   Brute force is the best persuader.   _____   _____
6   When trying to get a new program adopted,
    one should concentrate on explaining details
    of how it will work because it is probably
    obvious what the benefits of the program are.   _____   _____
7   Most newspaper articles are not persuasive
    messages.   _____   _____

   Most of the statements in Experience 14.1 do not have simple
right or wrong responses. Statement 2 (about talking the way the
people you wish to persuade talk) is generally true, but there may be
some exceptions. For example, some people have rather negative
attitudes toward their own speech (see Chapter 4) and therefore might
be impressed by someone who talked differently. Statement 6 (about
explaining the details of a program) is usually false. Generally, the
benefits of what you advocate need to be spelled out in great detail.
Generally, persuaders underestimate the degree to which it would be
productive for them to explain the benefits of their positions.
   Statement 4 (about an outsider being more persuasive) is also
more often false than true. Generally, audiences are persuaded by
people who seem similar to themselves. An exception might be some
topics that group members do not know much about. Under
such circumstances, an outsider might find it easier to establish himself
or herself as an expert. Statement 7 (about newspaper articles) indicates
how very common persuasive messages are in our society. Many times,
people do not realize that the messages they receive are persuasive in
nature; newspaper articles are an excellent example. Many of the
items in the average daily newspaper are public relations releases, that
is, items that someone with a point of view to push has written and
sent to the newspaper as newsworthy. Newspapers generally run such
items as submitted by the original source. For the best example, look in
the real estate section of a Sunday newspaper. Generally, stories are
about the first family in an exciting new subdivision or about how
pleasant life is in some resort community. Frequently, these are straight
news pieces written by reporters. Often, real estate firms commission
public relations writers to supply text of stories to the newspaper.
   Sometimes, it is very difficult to tell the difference between a
message purpose that is persuasive and one that is informative. A
speaker can give only facts and still be most persuasive if most of the
facts presented favor one position. The item in Experience 14.1 that
refers to the persuasiveness of brute force brings up a similar question

of definition. Generally, pure force is not classed as a form of persuasion. In persuasive situations, the receiver has some freedom of choice: to do as the speaker is advocating or to remain unconvinced. If you hold a gun to someone's head and ask them to declare allegiance to the Republican party, you are not engaging in persuasion or, for that matter, in any desirable behavior. An offer that cannot be refused is not persuasion because the receiver has no options.

The ultimate aim of most persuasive messages is to change people's behavior. The persuader may argue that the listeners should vote for a candidate, buy a product, or be active in support of a particular cause. Messages that aim directly to change behavior make measurement of effects possible. If, for instance, you design a series of television commercials for Sudso Laundry Detergent, you can check the sales figures for Sudso in the markets where the messages are shown. If you design a publicity campaign for a candidate for public office, you can tell whether your campaign strategy succeeded by counting up votes.

For most persuasive messages, however, such behavioral measures are not available. In the first place, human behavior is quite complex, and it is difficult to say whether a particular behavior was a result of a particular message. In the second place, some issues do not lend themselves to behavioral tallies. Suppose you wish to deliver a persuasive message advocating strict controls for handguns. It would be unrealistic to expect one message to effect enduring change on this subject, and it would also be impossible for you to follow individual audience members to find out whether they register their guns or argue that others should do so. In such a situation, communicators generally aim to change attitudes, rather than behavior.

Attitudes are imaginary constructs, made-up items of theory that try to account for the fact that although a message makes a difference to you, that difference may not be immediately apparent in your behavior. For example, suppose you hear a speech urging you to drive defensively. The speech may have a great impact on you, but it would be difficult for the speaker to know that. After all, the speaker would not be likely to observe your driving. Even if your driving were observed, an outsider might not be able to notice that you were driving more defensively. Perhaps the changes are as much in the way you *feel* as in the way you drive. For example, you may become more patient with fellow motorists. All these changes, theorists claim, involve your attitudes toward defensive driving; they may have effects on what you do, or they may not.

An attitude is a liking or disliking for some concept or object. More than that, it is a predisposition to behave positively or negatively toward a concept or object of the attitude. Because it is very difficult to observe people's behavior after they receive a persuasive message,

The ultimate aim of most persuasive messages is to change a person's behavior or attitude.

MEASURING ATTITUDES

researchers studying the effects of various persuasive messages have opted for measuring attitudes through responses to paper-and-pencil questionnaires or pollsters' questions.

Most public opinion polls simply pose a question to an interviewee and ask for a yes or no answer.

> Should companies that strip-mine coal be required to reclaim the mined land?
>
> _____ yes
> _____ no

A variant of this approach asks the respondent to agree or disagree with a statement.

> Companies that strip-mine coal should be required to reclaim the mined land.
>
> _____ agree
> _____ disagree

Such measures are commonly used by political pollsters. We have used such statements in this book. But the information they provide is not so precise as it could be.

When more precision is desired and more of the dimensions of an attitude need to be tapped, a measurement technique known as the *Likert scale* may be used. A number of statements concerning a particular attitude object are presented, and the respondent is asked to indicate how strongly he or she agrees or disagrees with them. Sometimes, the option of a neutral response is also allowed. The responses are then added up to indicate a total attitude score.

Another more precise technique is the *semantic differential*. This is a series of adjectives and their opposites; the respondent is asked to indicate which adjective comes closest to expressing their feeling about a concept listed at the top of the adjective scales.

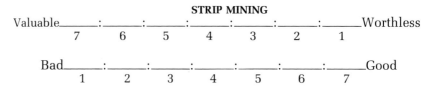

STRIP MINING

Valuable___:___:___:___:___:___:___Worthless
       7   6   5   4   3   2   1

Bad___:___:___:___:___:___:___Good
    1   2   3   4   5   6   7

The respondent checks the position on the scale that indicates which adjective comes closest to describing how they feel. These responses are averaged to give a total score for a person's attitudes. Both semantic differential and Likert scores can be used to measure the impact of persuasive messages, to compare two or more messages' impacts, or to chart the course of attitude changes over a period of time.

An example of a Likert scale is the Attitudes Toward Women Scale (Experience 14.2). After completing the experience, you may wish to compare your attitudes with those of your classmates.

EXPERIENCE 14.2 ATTITUDES TOWARD WOMEN

DIRECTIONS **The following statements describe attitudes that different people have toward the role of women in society. There are no right or wrong answers. You are asked to express your feeling about each statement by indicating whether you (A) strongly agree, (B) agree mildly, (C) disagree mildly, (D) disagree strongly. Please indicate your attitude by circling *A, B, C,* or *D* to the left of each item. After you have responded to the scales, cover your responses with a piece of paper and have one of your parents respond to the scale, using the column to the right of each item. If a parent is not available, respond to each item as you think your parents would.**

_____A B C D 1. Swearing and obscenities are more repulsive in the speech of a woman than of a man.

1. A B C D_____

_____A B C D 2. Women should take increasing responsibility for leadership in solving the intellectual and social problems of the day.

2. A B C D_____

_____A B C D 3. Both husband and wife should be allowed the same grounds for divorce.

3. A B C D_____

_____A B C D 4. Telling dirty jokes should be mostly a masculine prerogative.

4. A B C D_____

_____A B C D 5. It is insulting to women to have the "obey" clause remaining in the marriage service.

5. A B C D_____

_____A B C D 6. Women earning as much as their dates should bear equally the expense when they go out together.

6. A B C D_____

_____A B C D 7. A woman should not expect to go exactly the same places or to have quite the same freedom of action as a man.

7. A B C D_____

_____A B C D 8. It is ridiculous for a woman to run a locomotive or a man to darn socks.

8. A B C D_____

_____A B C D 9. In general, the father should have greater authority than the mother in bringing up the children.

9. A B C D_____

_____A B C D 10. Women should be concerned with their duties of childbearing and house tending, rather than with desires for professional and business careers.

10. A B C D_____

_____Total

Total_____

To score the scale, use the following key.
For items 1, 4, 7, 8, 9, 10:

A = 0　　B = 1　　C = 2　　D = 3

For items 2, 3, 5, 6:

A = 3　　B = 2　　C = 1　　D = 0

Write the value of each circled letter in the blank next to the item.
Then add up these values to get a total score for yourself and one for

your parents. **The lower the score, the more traditional the person's attitudes toward women. Higher scores indicate more flexible attitudes.**

Janet Spence and her associates administered a similar scale to students at the University of Texas and their parents. The average score for female students was about 20, for male students about 17, for parents about 15. These averages may have risen somewhat since that time. How did your attitudes compare with those of the University of Texas students? How different were your attitudes from those of your parents? How do you account for these differences?

A researcher could present you with a set of Likert or semantic differential scales and obtain measures of several of your attitudes on a subject (just as we did in Experience 14.2). Such measurement is a routine form of communication research. This kind of research makes some assumptions about attitudes that may or may not be true. For instance, it does not measure the *importance* of an attitude to a person. You may feel that women and men should have equal rights in the spheres of both dirty jokes (item 4) and social leadership (item 2), but chances are that these two issues are not of equal importance to you. However, your response to the Likert scale would show only the similarity between the two attitudes. You might favor a particular candidate for senator but not care enough to go vote on election day. Someone else might check the same item on a Likert or semantic differential scale and might care enough to devote hundreds of hours as a campaign volunteer. Your attitude is quite different from the attitude of the dedicated campaign worker, but the measurement would not show that.

CHANGING ATTITUDES

Attitudes are formed over a rather long period of time and circumstances. They represent habit patterns that are quite difficult to change. Your attitudes toward such issues as the role of women in society, the languages spoken by ethnic groups other than your own, or a political party are learned through interaction with others. Children usually grow up sharing social and racial stereotypes with their closest associates. Over time, a growing person finds himself or herself rewarded for making certain kinds of statements and ignored or punished for others. Similarly, some actions closely associated with attitudes seem to work well; others fail. If a child is rewarded for mocking cripples, that behavior and attitudes connected with it are likely to be strengthened. If a child learns that table manners are important, his or her attitudes toward people with uncouth table manners are affected.

If you learn attitudes, can you not just relearn a new set of attitudes when a change seems called for? For instance, now that increasing numbers of people are concerned about equal rights for women, can people learn new, more realistic attitudes on such issues? To a limited extent, they can. But such changes are often slow and difficult.

Attitudes are difficult to change partly because a human mind holds many attitudes simultaneously. You hold attitudes toward individuals, ideologies, money, power, God, and other matters.

Now suppose that you want to change your attitude toward equal opportunities for women. You might be able to do so easily if that attitude existed in a vacuum. But it does not. For instance, are there ways of speaking with women that you learned as a child which are different from ways for speaking to men? Is your own sexual identity tied up in such definitions? Can you change just one attitude? Or would you have to change a whole cluster of attitudes, some of which relate rather closely to what you think of yourself as a person?

Suppose you convince your friend George that his attitudes toward women in the world of work should be changed but such a change is not consistent with his other attitudes about behaving in a courtly manner toward women. That inconsistency might make him uncomfortable. It is usually easier to keep old attitudes than to change them, and people use processes of selective attention, selective interpretation, and selective recall to keep their attitudes consistent with each other.

For example, suppose that your friend George seems to exhibit a condescending, sexist attitude toward women, and you try to persuade him to change his attitude. George may agree that his attitude is troublesome in today's society, but then he remembers that his own girl friend prefers to be treated as a mindless sex object. (At least that is what he thinks she tells him.) George thinks, suppose I change this attitude, as my friend suggests. It might ruin my relationship with my girl. Furthermore, George's mother likes to be treated deferentially because she believes that it indicates respect for her sex. If George changes his attitude, what will her reaction be? Therefore, you can predict that attempts to persuade George to change his attitudes will meet with difficulties.

Still, you call George and announce that you want to change his mind. You propose that the two of you have a talk about women. George tells you he has a date tonight and that, now that he thinks it over, he is going to be very busy for the rest of the month. George is evading you. He is avoiding the messages you might send him because he knows that those messages could make him uncomfortable. This is *selective exposure*, a tactic many people employ to keep from receiving messages that would be inconsistent with present attitudes. If you are a

Republican, for instance, and you hear that the Democrats have scheduled a campaign show on TV, chances are that you will not watch it. If somebody visits you frequently and attempts to sell you a product you do not want, you will probably manage to be "busy" when this person calls.

Your sexist friend George is avoiding you, but you outwit him. You know his habits. He always goes to Ed's Bar on Thursdays after work. You are waiting there when he arrives. You buy him a beer and begin to talk about women's rights. After a minute, you notice George does not seem to be listening to you. He is providing an example of *selective attention* by tuning out a message that he would have trouble with. Has anyone ever failed to listen to you in situations that could be explained by reference to their attitudes?

"George," you persist, "think how you'd feel if you couldn't get a job because you were a woman, and interviewers, instead of hiring you, kept asking you for a date."

"Wouldn't that be super," he responds, "I could catch me a fat cat for a sugar daddy, and I wouldn't need to work at all. I could sit around all day, watch soap operas, and eat candy."

That statement indicates George's *selective interpretation* of your argument. He misunderstands the argument so that he will not have to face the discomfort it might bring to his consistent clusters of attitudes. George is not listening effectively. You could criticize him for that, but you would be missing the point. The point is that George is listening ineffectively *for a reason:* to keep his attitudes as they are.

You are not quite ready to give up on George. After buying him several beers (George has a favorable attitude toward beer), you finally hear him admit that his attitudes toward women have been unfair and that he will mend his ways. You go home satisfied. The next morning, you remind George of his new attitude, but he does not remember making any such statement. Yes, you discussed the subject when he was drunk, but his basic stance remains unchanged. George's behavior in this instance demonstrates *selective recall.* George remembers best those parts of the conversation that favor his former attitude. So what seemed to be persuasion yesterday was only a short-term change.

People's attitudes provide them with consistent pictures (sets of knowledge) about the world and how it operates. Thus, any major attitude change represents a big switch in the ways people view themselves and their place in the world. Major current theories about attitudes and attitude change stress this *consistency* among attitudes.

Consistency does not mean that all attitudes are alike and similar to all behaviors. Rather, it means that there is just enough similarity-consistency to hold the system together and keep it stable while allowing some change. What happens to attitudes at times of behavior change? If you take some new action, you may try to justify it on the basis of your previous attitudes or acts. You will also use selective exposure, attention, and recall, but in reverse ways (to get added information to support your new decision against your old attitudes).

For example, if you buy a new car, you probably see a lot of ads for that kind of car soon after you buy it. You had not noticed these ads before, but now you read them with great attention. If someone tells you something good about your new car, you are likely to remember it and even repeat it. If someone tells you your new car is a clunker, you may not even hear them.

Pregnant women describe a similar experience. A woman's first pregnancy is usually a striking event that introduces attitude difficulties. The woman finds herself feeling unwell and sometimes even unable to perform activities she is used to. More important, she usually faces several years of reduced freedom while she cares for her very young child. Justification of the changes takes many forms. A pregnant woman may talk about how exciting it is to have life growing inside her. She selectively notices pregnant women. As soon as a woman becomes pregnant, she notices other pregnant women wherever she goes (selective attention). She also talks to many of these women about their experiences and theories of pregnancy and motherhood. She is likely to choose to spend a lot of time with other pregnant women or mothers of small children (selective exposure). She is likely to accent the positive aspects of motherhood and minimize the negative (selective recall).

The principle: A decision leads to justification of that decision. The more important the decision, the more strong and lasting the justification will be.

The accuracy of this principle has been demonstrated by experiments.* As an example, suppose that someone asked you to rate the desirability of small appliances (toasters, blenders, etc.). Then according to how much you like a particular one, allowed you to choose an appliance to keep. Later, if you rate the appliances again, you may rate the chosen appliance higher than before, and those not chosen lower than before. In order to justify the choice they had made, you maximize information that would help you feel best about the choice. Another example: If you have trouble deciding between two kinds of car, but eventually choose one, you may begin to like the chosen car more and more, and the rejected one less.

If you were to cheat on a test in spite of moral misgivings about

* For a review, see Robert A. Wicklund and Jack W. Brehm, *Perspectives on Cognitive Dissonance*, Hillsdale, N.J.: Lawrence Erlbaum Associates, 1976, pp. 83–85.

such behavior, you would be likely to work hard to convince yourself that the cheating was justified. For example, you might claim that the test was too hard. On the other hand, if you were tempted to cheat but resisted temptation, you would probably justify your behavior by strengthening your attitudes against cheating. Keep this justification principle in mind as you respond to Experience 14.3.

EXPERIENCE   14.3   JUSTIFYING

DIRECTIONS   **Describe at least three recent changes in your own behavior or major purchases you made (stereo, bicycle, backpack, rental of an apartment). Then describe how you justified your behavior to yourself. Compare your ways of justifying your behavior with those of others in your class.**

EXAMPLE   *Behavior*

Purchase of a used Volkswagen

Justification

Reading classified ads to make sure the price was as low as possible. Noticing how many other wise people also own Volkswagens. Reading magazine advertisements for Volkswagens.

Behavior

1 _____

2 _____

3 _____

4 _____

Justification

_____
_____
_____
_____
_____
_____

Many students have expressed amazement about the amount of self-justification that surrounds important decisions. Actually, what is amazing is that, given the constraints of attitudes, people have the ability to act in new ways at all. Perhaps they are able to do new things primarily because of new influences that impinge on them. For example, communicators are often impressed by a new acquaintance and try to act like that acquaintance as often as possible or to express opinions that person might approve of.

Some researchers have even suggested that attitudes are more a matter of what people *say* than of what they do. That is, you might express different sets of attitudes, depending on who you are talking to. This fits with the concept that there are several selves in each individual (see Chapter 3). According to this view, the things we say are often aimed at aligning us with others we admire, wish to imitate, or wish to impress. For instance, you might emphasize different aspects of your attitudes toward religious groups when you talk to a minister than when you talk with peers. The difference does not reflect hypocrisy; rather, it demonstrates the fact that one social situation or the other may make different feelings appropriate. You probably will not directly contradict on one occasion what you say on the other, but different items surely will receive emphasis.

Talking to others is, after all, a kind of doing. Just as a decision to choose an appliance or to cheat on a test involves some change in attitudes, so do most opinionated statements you are likely to make in a day. The more you express an opinion to others, the more strongly you may feel it.

This tendency to justify actions with changes in attitude can be used quite effectively by people trying to sell things. One common technique is for the salesperson to get a foot in the door by getting a small commitment from a customer. An experiment conducted by Jonathan Freedman and Scott Fraser demonstrates how small commitments lead to larger ones.* Homeowners in a residential area were asked to sign petitions favoring safe driving. Very few refused to do this harmless act. Several weeks later, a man asked residents to allow a large, ugly Drive Carefully sign in their yards. Of the homeowners who had signed the petition, 55 percent allowed him to place the sign in their yards. Of those who had not been asked to sign the petition, only 17 percent allowed the sign to be placed in their yards. The small commitment to sign a petition actually led to some justification-related attitude change. This change made it easier to allow the large ugly sign to be placed in the yard.

One real estate salesman we know used this technique to purchase a piece of property that was "not for sale at any price." Other salesmen had not even been allowed to talk to the elderly woman who owned this choice piece of property in a downtown area. Our friend drove to the city where the woman lived, called on her, introduced himself, and announced that he was there to buy the property.

"It's not for sale," was her reply.

"Well, I've been driving for two hours, and I'm really thirsty. Would you give me a glass of cool water?"

* Jonathan Freedman and Scott Fraser, "Compliance Without Pressure: The Foot-in-the-Door Technique," *Journal of Personality and Social Psychology* 4(1966), 195−202.

"Certainly. Come on in."

After the salesman was in the kitchen, he saw a large bowl of apples on the table. "Would you mind if I had one of these apples?"

"Of course not! Go right ahead," said the woman.

Then they went into the living room, where the salesman saw a large sofa. He asked if he could "rest for just a minute before he drove back home."

"Sure! Have a seat," was the woman's reply.

They began exchanging pleasantries. They talked for two hours without ever mentioning the property the salesman was there to buy. Finally, the owner brought up the topic of the property. She explained her reasons for not wanting to sell the property: Her father had deeded her the property in his will.

The salesman, who had known of her father and of his penchant for cleanliness, finally had a lever to pry the property loose. He gave the woman a chance to admit that the tenants on the property were not taking good care of it. He told her what he would do with the property and helped her visualize how neat and clean it would be if he purchased it. She agreed on the spot to sell the property to him.

A series of small commitments by the owner made it easier for the salesman to talk to her. During the talk, the salesman built her confidence in him and led her to reveal her reasons for hanging onto the property. By bringing into her consciousness the inconsistency between what her father would have done with the property and what she was doing with it, the salesman gained his objective.

Companies often use this principle to increase sales of their products by sponsoring contests in which contestants write a 25-words-or-less essay about why they liked brand A. In addition to getting testimonials to use in ad campaigns, the companies invite thousands of people to persuade themselves to use of the products by writing testimonials. The people who enter the contests justify their actions by convincing themselves that the product really is good.

One inventive use of this principle was demonstrated by a shirt company at a recent trade show. The company wanted not only to sell shirts to retailers but also to have those retailers become long-term customers. They rented several booths at the show and set up a television studio, complete with lights, cameras, videotape equipment, and engineers. They played on the retailers' vanity by inviting them to make a TV commercial for the shirts in front of the cameras. These commercials were later sent to the retailers. Having made a public commitment about the shirts, the retailers were likely to justify their actions, probably by ordering more of the shirts than they planned to. Certainly, having made the commercial for the shirts, they were more likely to buy those shirts than a competitor's.

Such tactics may seem cute and effective when someone else is involved or when you are the persuader. But how do you feel when other people use such techniques on you? The result can be that you buy something that you have no use for. If you do not want to be manipulated by such techniques, you need to be aware of the way small commitments can be used to justify larger ones and the psychological pressure that this creates.

You see, these techniques of selling use your guilt against you. Most people want to be pleasant to others, not to refuse things without reason. Salespeople take advantage of this by asking for commitments that any reasonable person would give. If you say no, you feel guilty. Manuel J. Smith discusses this problem in *When I Say No, I Feel Guilty*. If you have problems with salespeople, we particularly recommend that book to you.

Smith points out that salespeople take advantage of questions which would be pleasant if they occurred in ordinary conversation and use these questions to gain the small commitments that lead to larger ones. If you deny the commitments by acting surly, the salesperson can deny that he or she was leading up to a sale and help you to feel guilty about your unpleasant behavior. If you give the seemingly harmless commitment asked for, you make it more likely that you will buy the product. Although there is no easy way to prevent this from happening, Smith does recommend a number of gimmicks. The simplest and probably most effective is called the *broken record*. Most people have a habit pattern that makes what they say depend upon what someone else says first. But they do not have to respond in this way if they do not want to. You do not have to answer a salesperson's questions or let him or her have a drink of water. Smith recommends that if you want to avoid the salesperson's persuasion, you simply reply, "I understand, but I'm not interested," regardless of what he or she says. Do this without raising your voice or showing any sign of anger. Experience 14.4 gives you a chance to practice this technique.

EXPERIENCE 14.4 BROKEN RECORD

DIRECTIONS **You will need a partner for this experience. Have the other person assume the role of a salesperson trying to come into your house to sell you an encyclopedia, a burglar alarm, or a vacuum cleaner. The salesperson should try to ask you questions or use any other technique he or she can think of to get inside your door and give you a**

demonstration of the product. **Regardless of what the salesperson says, you are to reply simply, "I understand, but I'm not interested." Do this as many times as is necessary to let the salesperson know that he or she has come up against a brick wall. Be a broken record. Then switch roles, and be the salesperson.**
After completing this experience, note your reactions and observations.

_____

_____

_____

_____

Experience 14.4 has produced some bizarre situations in our classes. Most students are amazed at how difficult it is to use the broken record technique. The first few responses are fairly easy, but soon students want to justify why they are doing the broken record. Here is a typical dialogue:

Salesperson: Hello, I'm doing some opinion work here in the neighborhood.
Broken Record: I understand, but I'm not interested.
  SP: I'm talking to as many of the residents as I can, and I'd like to take just a few minutes of your time. Would that be all right?
  BR: I understand, but I'm not interested.
  SP: I will just ask a few questions. You don't have to do anything. May I step in?
  BR: I really don't have the time—and I'm not interested.
  SP: (_Seeing an opening_) It won't take a minute. The first question is: Do you have an encyclopedia in your home at the present time.
  BR: I really don't like answering this question, and I don't want to buy an encyclopedia.
  SP: (_Smiling_) As I mentioned, I'm not a salesperson. I just asked a simple question about whether you have an encyclopedia in your home.
  BR: Uh—no, but—
  SP: Good, now would you tell me whether. . . .

This is what usually happens to the beginner when he or she tries the broken record technique. After a few repetitions of "I understand, but I'm not interested," the person begins to feel uncomfortable about using the same phrase in response to any come-on. The person feels that such a stereotyped set of responses would be hard to justify, so he or she tries to vary the responses just a little but still show lack of interest. As you can see, the salesperson is able to use these variations to continue with the pitch. In the example, the salesperson was able to move into the pitch in spite of the customer's active resistance. In real-life, this customer might have ended up buying an unneeded encyclopedia or at least wasted an hour talking to a salesperson. Contrast the earlier dialogue with this one, in which the broken record sticks to the line:

Salesperson: Hello, I'm doing some opinion work here in the neighborhood.
Broken Record: I understand, but I'm not interested.
SP: I'm talking to as many of the residents as I can. Can I take just a minute of your time?
BR: I understand, but I'm not interested.
SP: I will just ask a few questions. You don't have to do anything. May I step in?
BR: I understand, but I'm not interested.
SP: It won't take a minute. The first question is: Do you have an encyclopedia in your home.
BR: I understand, but I'm not interested.
SP: Do you mean you don't even have two minutes to answer questions?
BR: I understand, but I'm not interested.
SP: Is that the only thing you ever say.
BR: I understand, but I'm not interested.
SP: Listen, I'm not out to twist your leg off. I just need two minutes of your attention.
BR: I understand, but I'm not interested.
SP: Can you tell me the names of any of your neighbors who might have small children?
BR: I understand, but I'm not interested.
SP: I can't get to first base with you!
BR: I understand, but I'm not interested.

Successful broken record dialogues such as this were greeted by howls of laughter from our students. Why is that conversation so funny? It is unusual. The broken record *never tries to justify* what is being said. The broken record leaves himself or herself open to being called stupid, but he or she frustrates the salesperson's every move.

In summary, the broken record technique is effective because the speaker gives up the responsibility of justifying every utterance. Listen to yourself on the average afternoon. How many words do you spend justifying the rest of what you say. Much of this justification can be useful, but when you are tangling with an effective salesperson, it can be your undoing. Practice not justifying until you can take apologies on and off like a sweater. You will find this skill useful on a large number of occasions.

SOURCE CREDIBILITY

Our examination of the conditions under which attitudes are likely to change suggests that the most effective kind of persuasion is self-persuasion. That is, successful persuasion is most likely to occur if the person to be persuaded performs some behavior that later can be justified psychologically by attitude change. The rationalization processes help people convince themselves that they have good reasons for what they did. These good reasons become formulated as shifts in attitude. It is important to be aware that such processes work both for the persuader and for the one being persuaded.

The nature of the examples we have used, including some

experiments and the tricks of clever salespeople, may make it seem that such manipulations are usually available to everyone. But that is probably not the case. Usually, all you can do to persuade someone of your case is to assemble arguments and evidence favoring what you advocate and hope that the message produces attitude change.

When such persuasive messages are delivered to audiences, under what circumstances do they produce the greatest attitude change? You may be surprised to learn that the greatest changes in attitude seem related less to any details of the message than to the general believability of the source of the message. If a message comes to you from someone you trust and believe about that subject, you tend to believe the message and change your attitude. If a message is delivered by a less credible source, less attitude change results.

If two people try to convince you to buy an Acme Frypan, one of them a salesperson for Acme Frypan and the other a professor of engineering, which would you believe? Chances are, you would feel that the salesman is biased and that the professor of engineering knows enough to form an objective opinion.

As you can see, the fact that you believe some people more than others is a complicated business. There does not seem to be a simple

The degree to which you consider a person credible will influence the effect the message has upon you.

ranking scheme in each individual's head that ranks all the people in the world in terms of how well they can be believed. You may find that a friend who is highly credible on the subject of fashions gives terrible advice on social behavior, that the person who gives good advice on politics may have atrocious taste in clothes, and so on. How credible or believeable someone is on a particular topic is a blend of several variables: his or her general trustworthiness, how much he or she knows about the subject, and whether he or she is objective.

To examine the workings of some of your credibility attitudes toward important issues, respond to Experience 14.5.

EXPERIENCE   14.5   SOME CREDIBLE SOURCES

DIRECTIONS (PART 1)   **For each of the following topics, list at least one person you could be persuaded by on that topic. Then describe what makes that person a credible source. If you cannot think of a person for a particular topic, list those characteristics that establish source credibility for it.**

EXAMPLE

Topic	*Persons who are credible*	*Characteristics*
Renting an apartment	**My friend Sam**	**Sam used to be an apartment manager. He knows what to look out for. He has no ax to grind in renting me an apartment.**

	Topic	*Persons who are credible*	*Characteristics*
1	**birth control**	_____	_____
2	**selecting a major**	_____	_____
3	**getting your car repaired**	_____	_____
4	**repairing your tape recorder**	_____	_____

5 selecting a movie _____   _____
                                              _____
                                              _____

6 drugs   _____   _____
                                              _____
                                              _____

7 buying clothes   _____   _____
                                              _____
                                              _____

8 studying for a test _____   _____
                                              _____
                                              _____

9 selecting a novel to _____   _____
   read during   _____
   vacation
10 choosing a career _____   _____
                                              _____
                                              _____

DIRECTIONS
(PART 2)

Name one source that you believe on the *widest* variety of topics. List several of the topics, and describe what makes that person's messages so highly credible.

_____

_____

_____

Most students who complete Experience 14.5 have found the Part 2 quite difficult. If you were having some difficulty and left your answer unfinished, return to the experience and continue working on it for about two more minutes before reading on.

Part 2 of Experience 14.5 was difficult because there are very few people who seem credible on a large number of topics and when these people exist, you are not sure why you believe them. The most common reason seems to be a trust of this person's advice built up over experiences in which he or she gave good advice or made an accurate prediction.

The person who is credible is likely to vary with each topic, but the reasons for believing them usually have some things in common. Throughout Experience 14.5 you probably listed these characteristics quite often as contributing to the credibility of a source. Look over your own responses to see what characteristics occur most often. The following characteristics were cited most frequently by our students:

1   *Honesty.* People believe those whom they think are telling the truth and have strong principles about lying.
2   *Expertise.* People believe those who are in some position to know about the topic, whether through job, education, or other experience.
3   *Objectivity.* People believe those who seem unbiased more than those who seem to have an ax to grind or a product to sell.
4   *Similarity to selves.* All else being equal, people believe sources more if they are similar to themselves in some important way, such as beliefs, background, or similar past experiences.

The most credible sources listed by students commonly exhibited some form of all four characteristics. If a source has some of these qualities but not others, he or she is likely to seem less credible. The key point is that these characteristics are not really properties of the message senders. Rather, they are *your own attitudes* toward those senders. Thus, *source credibility involves a set of attitudes toward the source of the message.* These attitudes are quite similar to your attitudes on other subjects. That is, consistency among attitudes is the reason source credibility is so effective. If you have a favorable attitude toward a source's credibility, it is rational and reasonable for you to believe what that source tells you.

To get a better idea of how credibility works as a set of attitudes, complete Experience 14.6.

EXPERIENCE   14.6   RATING THE CREDIBILITY OF SOURCES

DIRECTIONS   **Watch five TV commercials in which persuasive messages are delivered by on-screen spokespeople, such as a famous athlete, an actor, or someone who is supposed to be a doctor. Pay particular attention to this spokesperson. Complete one of the following sets of scales for each spokesperson by circling the appropriate responses. Use this key in determining your answers:**

SA = strongly agree
 A = agree
 U = undecided
 D = disagree
SD = strongly disagree

Source 1: _____

a   **Speaker seems to know a lot about the subject.**   SA A U D SD
b   **Speaker seems to be a person I can trust.**   SA A U D SD

c	Speaker seems objective.	SA A U D SD
d	Speaker seems like me in many ways.	SA A U D SD
e	Other comments: include perceptions of sincerity, whether you would like to know this person better, or whether he or she talks down to the audience.	

_____

_____

f	Summary rating: This person is highly credible.	SA A U D SD

Source 2: _____

a	Speaker seems to know a lot about the subject.	SA A U D SD
b	Speaker seems to be a person I can trust.	SA A U D SD
c	Speaker seems objective.	SA A U D SD
d	Speaker seems like me in many ways.	SA A U D SD
e	Other comments: include perceptions of sincerity, whether you would like to know this person better, or whether he or she talks down to the audience.	

_____

_____

f	Summary rating: This person is highly credible.	SA A U D SD

Source 3: _____

a	Speaker seems to know a lot about the subject.	SA A U D SD
b	Speaker seems to be a person I can trust.	SA A U D SD
c	Speaker seems objective.	SA A U D SD
d	Speaker seems like me in many ways.	SA A U D SD
e	Other comments: include perceptions of sincerity, whether you would like to know this person better, or whether he or she talks down to the audience.	

_____

_____

f	Summary rating: This person is highly credible.	SA A U D SD

Source 4: _____

a	Speaker seems to know a lot about the subject.	SA A U D SD
b	Speaker seems to be a person I can trust.	SA A U D SD
c	Speaker seems objective.	SA A U D SD
d	Speaker seems like me in many ways.	SA A U D SD
e	Other comments: include perceptions of	

sincerity, whether you would like to know this
person better, or whether he or she talks down to
the audience.

_____
_____
_____

f   **Summary rating: This person is highly credible.**   SA   A   U   D   SD

Source 5: _____

a   Speaker seems to know a lot about the subject.   SA   A   U   D   SD
b   Speaker seems to be a person I can trust.   SA   A   U   D   SD
c   Speaker seems objective.   SA   A   U   D   SD
d   Speaker seems like me in many ways.   SA   A   U   D   SD
e   Other comments: include perceptions of
sincerity, whether you would like to know this
person better, or whether he or she talks down to
the audience.

_____
_____
_____

f   **Summary rating: This person is highly credible.**   SA   A   U   D   SD

Did you get a clear picture of some similarities between source
credibility and other kinds of message receiver attitudes? No one
communicator actually has credibility, and no two receivers apply
exactly the same standards of credibility.

As you worked on Experiences 14.5 and 14.6, you may have had a
gnawing feeling that if you are not a credible source, there is nothing
you can do about it. That is not true. In the first place, a speaker who
does well on one occasion may fail miserably on the next occasion, even if
the second audience seems quite similar to the first. For example, we
have had the experience of speaking one day to a class and having all
the pieces fall into place. At the end of a class hour, we felt that our
credibility was high. But the next day's class was a disaster.

Like most aspects of communication, a speaker's credibility
changes on the basis of messages that the speaker sends and the
changing climate of audience opinion. For example, if your argument is
obviously to your self-interest, your credibility may be diminished. If a
member of Congress advocates the adoption of a new military weapons
system that just happens to be made in his or her district, the credibility
of that argument suffers. Conversely, credibility can be improved by
somehow demonstrating that you have nothing to gain from the
acceptance of your argument. For example, if your child argued with

you, maintaining that his or her allowance should be made smaller, nearly any parent would be impressed because this measure would seem not to be in the child's self-interest.

Another example of the way self-interest limits credibility is the salesperson's commission. One reason why it is difficult to believe salespeople when they tell you how good a product is is that the salespeople generally make more money if you buy than if you say no. Under these circumstances, the salesperson is in a bind. He or she must attempt persuasion against resistance that exists because the audience knows that self-interest is involved.

Self-interest is related to the so-called credibility gap encountered by many politicians. When politicians are attacked, they generally respond by defending themselves and arguing for their positions. But everything they say must be taken with a grain of salt because these people make a living by getting elected to office, and it would be highly unusual to hear any politician say anything negative about himself or herself.

The major tactic used by American public speakers to combat self-interest problems is to try to establish their own objectivity as a source. An air of objectivity is often attempted by using a lot of *factual evidence* and testimony from experts in the field about which the speech is being given. A speaker may have self-interest in the outcome of a persuasive dispute, but he or she may be able to use testimony of a secondary source in a speech. Some expert or consumer advocate will not have the potential conflict of interest that the speaker has.

Another way to build source credibility is to *avoid lying* or even coloring speech materials in a way that overstates your case. It is amazing how fast the news of a little overstatement can travel and become distorted. Your credibility is your best persuasive weapon. Keep it clean by sticking to the truth. That sounds like Mr. Clean, but it is really Mr. or Ms. Practical. There is probably no particular end you want to achieve over a short run that is worth your risking the loss of your reputation for telling the truth. A large number of public speakers learn every day, to their regret, that the short run can become the short ruin. Once tarnished, credibility takes a long time to rebuild.

Closely related to telling the truth is *self-deprecation*. Without flogging yourself as an unimportant person, you can de-emphasize your importance to a speech or to a cause. For example, politicians often tell jokes that poke fun at themselves.

Dynamism can also build credibility. Audiences stay more interested in a speaker who seems alive, alert, and interested in the topic. Dynamism is very hard to fake and harder still to teach. Successful public speakers seem dynamic. A high activity level shows dynamism. Animated gestures, smiles, some movement all seem to increase the dynamism of the image you present. There is no point in trying to be charisma personified if you do not have the desire to ham it up a little. But even drab, matter-of-fact speakers can use gestures, movement, humor, and lively language to pep up the image they project.

Working on your stage fright (see Chapter 13) can also improve the dynamism of your effort. Sometimes, the most frightened speakers appear frozen or otherwise drab. It is partly for this reason that a little movement is often an excellent tonic for stage fright. Dynamism and confidence go hand in hand.

EXPERIENCE 14.7 CONSTRUCTING A PERSUASIVE MESSAGE

DIRECTIONS   Construct a persuasive message according to the following steps. You may wish to supplement some steps with material from Chapters 12 and 13.

1   Select a central idea that you would like to communicate to a specific audience.

_____

_____

2   How does your central idea differ from the audience's present behavior or attitude?

_____

3   What are the relevant characteristics of the audience that you need to consider in formulating your message and selecting a channel? How are they ranked in terms of importance?

_____

_____

4   Which audience characteristics tend to be favorable to the idea you advocate?

_____

5   Which audience characteristics tend to work against your proposal?

_____

6   What are the main points of the message you will present? (Use the outline form.)

_____

_____

_____

_____

7   How will you attempt to build your credibility?

_____

_____

8   Will you ask for small commitments first? List the commitments you
    will ask for ranked from small to large.

    _____

    _____

    _____

9   What indications will you have that your message is getting across?
    What feedback will you have?

    _____

    _____

SUMMARY

Persuasive messages are designed to change the attitudes and behaviors of receivers. Attitudes are theoretical constructs designed to make measurable the effects of persuasive messages upon others. Such attitudes are ordinarily measured through the use of pencil-and-paper questionnaires.

Attitudes are learned, and to change them one must deal with the likelihood that a receiver has interests in keeping his or her attitudes unchanged. One way of talking about such interests is by conceptualizing all of one's attitudes as a consistent system. If a given message is inconsistent with a number of such attitudes, there may be consistency related forces that will lead to the rejection of the message. Common vehicles for these drives toward consistency are selective exposure, selective attention, selective interpretation, and selective recall. These same consistency related forces also lead communicators to engage in justifications of past actions.

There are ways to change people's attitudes by using consistency. One such technique is to ask for a small commitment first, and larger ones later. This allows the subject to build attitudes consistent with the change during the process of change. Just as important as knowing how to persuade others is knowing how to resist change if you wish to, using techniques like the "broken record" to resist persuasive attempts such as the foot-in-the-door technique.

However one gets into the persuasive process—whether as sender or receiver—the notion of credibility is likely to emerge as important to the outcome. In most persuasive situations, the receivers' attitudes about the competence and trustworthiness of the source are major predictors of the effectiveness of a message. There are ways for speakers to build credibility as they deliver their messages; by showing that your interests do not bias you, by showing yourself to be objective, by citing other credible sources, and by simply telling the truth. The sad lessons of politicians of the last decade whose lies came home to haunt them highlight the importance of truth as a measure of long-term communicative effectiveness.

APPENDIX
DOING LIBRARY RESEARCH

n this appendix we examine some details of library research strategy, including dictionaries, encyclopedias, the card catalog, creative browsing, the *Reader's Guide to Periodical Literature*, newspapers, bibliographies, and librarians.

Looking up a few key words in a dictionary often helps clarify your beginning thinking about a topic. It allows you to define words thoroughly, to find synonyms for those words, and to see some areas of the topic that may have escaped you before. If you look at a dictionary that provides derivations of words from other languages, you may also run into some new ideas. If you are at the library, use one of the large unabridged dictionaries because these will contain the most thorough lists of information. For the synonyms and antonyms of your topic words, use Roget's *Thesaurus*.

DICTIONARIES

In addition to general dictionaries, there are subject dictionaries in several specialized fields. If your topic or words related to it fall within one of these fields, such dictionaries may be helpful. Here are just a few:

1   *Language of the Specialist.* This dictionary covers words used by specialists in 20 different fields. It is not comprehensive within a particular field, but it usually includes most of the words that are encountered by people outside the field.
2   *Webster's Graphical Dictionary.* This dictionary lists information on countries, cities, towns, and geographic features.
3   *Dictionary of Politics.* This reference gives information on a variety of political parties, leaders, movements, elections, and other events for the years 1933 to 1971.
4   *Chamber's Dictionary of Science and Technology.* This dictionary lists definitions used by scientists in many fields.

Once you begin to look around, you will be amazed how many kinds of reference dictionaries exist. If you wonder whether one exists in your area, ask the person who sits at the desk labeled *reference librarian*. Many larger libraries have an entire room (called the *reference room*) in which general reference works are collected. Generally, you use these books only in the library.

ENCYCLOPEDIAS

You will find encyclopedias on the shelves of reference rooms. Most of you have used encyclopedias before. In some circles, encyclopedias have a bad reputation because students sometimes use the rather general information in these collections and then stop. If you use *only* encyclopedia information in preparing your message, you will probably run into this reaction. But if you use encyclopedias as a natural focusing step that follows the dictionary and precedes other references, you may find them helpful.

Encyclopedias are particularly useful for historical events, geographic subdivisions, and popularized scientific information. Obviously, very recent events will not be dealt with in encyclopedias.

Whatever encyclopedia you choose, begin by looking in the index because even encyclopedias that have everything in alphabetical order may have information about your topic that is not in an article especially about that topic.

There are specialized encyclopedias, just as there are specialized dictionaries. Here are a few:

1 *Encyclopedia of Psychology.* This three-volume work defines and discusses many terms and concepts. There are extensive bibliographies to guide further reading and brief life stories of important psychologists.

2 *International Encyclopedia of the Social Sciences.* This work covers a broader range of topics than the psychology encyclopedia, including anthropology, history, law, political science, economics, sociology, and statistics. The articles are generally not too difficult to read.

3 *McGraw-Hill Encyclopedia of Science and Technology.* This encyclopedia provides information in the physical and natural sciences, technology, and engineering.

4 *World Mark Encyclopedia of the Nations.* Prepared for the United Nations, this work contains factual material on almost 150 countries. It includes data (as of 1971) on population, transportation, politics, agriculture, and education.

As you use encyclopedias, remember that they are only beginning sources. They give you a general orientation and point you to other places in the library where you can follow up.

CARD CATALOG   You have some general information, and you know some key words. You probably also know the names of two or three important writers in the area. Now you are ready to work with the card catalog. We say work with because the card catalog, like any other source of information, will give you helpful information only if you ask it useful questions.

There are two sections of the card catalog: an author-title section and a subject section. If your reading so far has suggested authors' names or book titles, look for them in the author-title section. If not, look up key terms used in the area in the subject section.

The card catalog is used primarily for finding where in the library the book is located. But it also contains other helpful information. Some of that information may help you to decide whether the book will be useful to you. Take a look at the cards on the following pages.

Note that the cards are identical except for the heading on the first line. These cards were filed in four different places in the card catalog so that each place you looked (authors, title, or the subject "children—language"), you would find this book listed.

That heading "children—language" deserves some discussion. It is often difficult to tell where a book will be listed in the subject

Call number identifies the subject of the book and tells you where to locate it.

Author

Title

Second or joint author

Place and date of publication gives you an idea of how up to date the book will be.

Information for librarian's use.

AUTHOR CARD

```
P
136
H6
COMMUN
```
Hopper, Robert.
   Children's speech: a practical
introduction to communication
development [by] Robert Hopper [and]
Rita C. Naremore.   New York, Harper &
Row [1973]
   x, 140 p. 21 cm.
   Bibliography: p. 135-138.

   1. Children--Language. I. Naremore,
Rita C., joint author. II. Title

TxU   JAN 20, '75   684065   IXJdc   72-86372

Roman numerals describe other places in card catalog where this card is located.

Height of book in centimeters. Useful because very large books are sometimes located separately in the library.

If the book had any illustrations, the abbreviation illus. would appear here.

The card notes whether there is a bibliography and lists the pages on which it can be found.

number of text pages

number of introductory pages

The arabic numbers tell you the subject headings used to describe the book. This book was described under only one heading. Looking under this subject heading will lead you to other books on the subject.

CHILDREN--LANGUAGE.
P
136   Hopper, Robert.
H6   Children's speech: a practical
COMMUN introduction to communication
        development [by] Robert Hopper [and]
        Rita C. Naremore. New York, Harper &
        Row [1973]
            x, 140 p. 21 cm.
            Bibliography: p. 135-138.

            1. Children--Language. I. Naremore,
        Rita C., joint author. II. Title

TxU   Jan 20,'75   584055 IXJdc   72-86372

Naremore, Rita C., joint author.
P
136   Hopper, Robert.
H6   Children's speech: a practical
COMMUN introduction to communication
        development [by] Robert Hopper [and]
        Rita C. Naremore. New York, Harper &
        Row [1973]
            x, 140 p. 21 cm.
            Bibliography: p. 135-138.

            1. Children--Language. I. Naremore,
        Rita C., joint author. II. Title

TxU   JAN 20,'75   584055 IXJdc   72-86372

Children's speech
P
136   Hopper, Robert.
H6   Children's speech: a practical
COMMUN introduction to communication
        development [by] Robert Hopper [and]
        Rita C. Naremore. New York, Harper &
        Row [1973]
            x, 140 p. 21 cm.
            Bibliography: p. 135-138.

            1. Children--Language. I. Naremore,
        Rita C., joint author. II. Title

TxU   JAN 20,'75   584055 IXJdc   72 86372

391

catalog. That is one reason why you collected several sets of key terms when looking through dictionaries and encyclopedias. Subject catalog headings are often two-word items, such as *children—language, political parties—Republicans,* or *ethnic groups—Italian-Americans.* Try phrasing something from your subject area by using a general term followed by a more specific term.

Do not be discouraged if the first six places that you look in the card catalog turn up nothing. That is quite common. Those who succeed in using the catalog are not necessarily more skillful than you, only more persistent.

Keep looking until you have written down the titles of at least five books that might help you. You need this many titles because you may not be able to obtain all of them. Make notes of the book titles, authors' names, and the call numbers (the numbers at left-hand side of the card). You will need call numbers to locate the books.

CREATIVE BROWSING

Now that you are armed with descriptions of where to find five books, you are ready for one of the most interesting challenges in scholarship: the process leading to that golden moment when you slip your fingers gently around the binding of a book that really might assist your search.

First, let us hope that the library you are dealing with lets you browse among the shelves. Many large college libraries have put into use a system called *closed stacks,* which means you have to give a clerk a slip of paper with the name of the book you want and the call number. The clerk looks for the book and returns to tell you whether it is there. This system seems necessary in certain crowded libraries, but alas, it is a horrible mess. In the first place, it deprives you of the right to dig into the shelves yourself; and in the second place, you are more likely to find the book you want than the clerk is because you want it more. If your library has closed stacks, find out if there is a loophole. Most closed-stack libraries allow graduate students or students with special permits to go into the stacks. Ask your teacher to write a short letter saying your research necessitates access to the stacks. Take the letter to the library staff and get a pass. Then you can browse creatively.

The purpose of creative browsing is that you will rarely find all the books that might be interesting on your topic in the card catalog. What you do get are the call numbers of some books. Books are shelved by subject categories. Consequently, there is a very good chance that other books of interest will be close by on the shelf to the book you are looking for. That is the secret to creative browsing.

Here is the procedure: Go to the shelf where the book you want is located. You will find that shelf by looking at the top line of the call number. Look at the tops of shelves for signs with that same top line.

In big libraries, you will want to consult a directory, which will be hanging on the wall in a central location. Now that you have found the right shelf, look down to the next row of numbers or letters in the call number. Match these numbers or letters to those of books on the shelves, until you come to the book you want. If your library is like ours, the book probably will not be there. Do not despair. Look at what *is* there. Is it on your topic? Browse six books to the right and six books to the left, looking for titles that grab you. If a book looks promising, study its table of contents. Then look at the index. Is your specific subject area mentioned? No? Go on to the next book.

A funny thing often happens during browsing. You find the book you were looking for; it was shelved six books to the right of where it should have been. Or maybe you will find a book that is even better than the one you were looking for.

Do not overlook creative browsing as a method. It is fun because it allows the unexpected element to creep in. It is a lot like operating a slot machine. If you understand that analogy, you have the makings of a true bookworm.

Suppose you do not have any specific book titles. Can you still browse creatively? Yes, but it is a little harder. First, find out what kind of classification system your library uses. There is probably a chart on the wall telling you this. Or you can ask a librarian. There are two main kinds of classification systems: Dewey decimal and Library of Congress. They are similar in principle, but whereas the Dewey system uses numbers from 0 to 999 to sort topics, the Library of Congress system uses letters of the alphabet. The Library of Congress System, invented for that biggest of all U.S. libraries, seems to be gaining in popularity. Here is a list of its major topic headings. If your topic does not seem to be under one of these, ask a librarian. It is in there someplace; *everything* is.

LIBRARY OF CONGRESS CLASSIFICATION

A	General Works		F	U.S. History (Local)
B	Philosophy		G	Geography
BF	Psychology		GF	Human Ecology
BL	Religion		GN	Anthropology
C	History		H	Social Sciences (General)
CS	History		HB	Economics
CT	Genealogy		HM	Sociology (General)
D	History		J	Political Science
E	U.S. History (General)		K	Law

L	Education	QD	Physics
M	Music	QL	Zoology
N	Fine Arts	R	Medicine
		RT	Nursing
P	Philology and Linguistics		
PH	Literature	S	Agriculture
PQ	Romance Literature		
PR	English Literature	T	Technology
PS	American Literature	TT	Handicrafts
PT	Germanic Literature		
		U	Military Science
Q	Science (General)		
QA	Mathematics	V	Naval Science
		Z	Bibliography and Library Science

READER'S GUIDE

Your next step is to look for periodicals on your topic. A number of indexes are available to help you in your search, depending on the topic you have selected and the depth of coverage you are seeking. If your topic is one that might be covered in popular magazines, you can begin with the *Reader's Guide to Periodical Literature*. This work indexes about 160 American periodicals of general interest. The author and subject entries are together in this index. Each entry gives you all the information necessary to locate the articles: author, title, name of periodical (this is abbreviated; look in the front of the volume for the complete name of the periodical), volume number, page numbers, and date. If the article contains maps, portraits, illustrations, or bibliographies, these are noted in the entry. Here is an example of the material found in *Reader's Guide* under the heading of solar energy:

SOLAR energy
  Fuel formation from aqueous ferric bromide by photolysis in the visible. S. N. Chen and others. bibl il Science 190:879–80 N 28 '75
  How to live on sun power. W. Thoms. il Mech Illus 71:37–9 N '75
  Solar energy reconsidered: ERDA sees bright future. A. L. Hammond. il Science 189:538–9 Ag 15 '75; Same with title Prospects for solar energy. Current 177:55–9 N '75
  Solar technologies. F. Von Hippel and R. H. Williams. bibl. il Bull Atom Sci 31:25–31 N. '75.
  Space colonies and energy supply to the earth. G. K. O'Neill. bibl il Science 190:943–7 D 5 '75

The title of the first article by S. N. Chen and others is "Fuel formation from aqueous ferric bromide by photolysis in the visible." It can be found in *Science* magazine, volume 190, on pages 879 and 880, in the November 28, 1975, issue. The article is illustrated and includes a bibliography.

If your topic is somewhat specialized and academic, you may not get help from the *Reader's Guide.* You will probably need to consult a specialized index. Most of these use entry formats similar to that used by the *Reader's Guide.*

1   *Humanities Index.* This index covers articles in about 300 scholarly journals concerned with archaeology, classics, folklore, literature, history, philosophy, religion, and so forth. This index has changed names several times. From 1965 to 1974, it was called the *Social Sciences and Humanities Index.* Before that, it was called *International Index.*

2   *Social Sciences Index.* This split off from the *Humanities Index* in June 1974. It covers academic journals in anthropology, psychology, government, sociology, and related fields. Both *Humanities Index* and *Social Sciences Index* also contain sections of book reviews.

3   *Public Affairs Information Service Bulletin.* This index has been published since 1915. It lists books, pamphlets, government publications, and periodical articles dealing with economic and social conditions, public administration, politics, human relations, and international affairs.

Those three may be the ones most often helpful in preparing speeches, but there are many other specialized indexes to periodicals, including *Art Index, Business Periodicals Index, Education Index, Current Index to Journals in Education, Psychological Abstracts, Environmental Periodicals Index,* and *Sociological Abstracts.* There are many others. Ask a librarian.

NEWSPAPERS

Newspapers often contain materials that can be helpful in message preparation. This is especially true with current events, such as election news and analyses or current court cases. But it is even more difficult to find information in newspapers by a look-till-you-find method than to use this method in magazines. Again, you need to use an index. Many libraries have a system for indexing local newspapers; ask a librarian.

For national issues, the best single source for information is the *New York Times Index.* It covers only one newspaper, of course, but that newspaper is very large and covers many topics thoroughly. The index also is useful because it summarizes the articles; many times you do not actually need to look up the article to see whether it will be useful to you. It is much faster to read summaries than to get access to the actual articles.

Each entry in the *New York Times Index* also provides the date, page, and column of the newspaper where the article can be found. The index can also be used in conjunction with other newspapers to isolate the dates when particular events were occurring. Once you know the approximate date of an event, you can browse through other newspapers published around that date to get additional information. Here is an example of the entry in the *New York Times Index* on solar energy:

Cross-references

Subject heading in boldface type

SOLAR Energy. See also Astronautics, D 29. Elec Light—US, Ap 10, Je 25, D 29. Energy and Power, Ja 31, Ap 22, O 28, N 7, 13, 16, 25, 29, D 5, 9, 12, 13, 19. Heating, N25, D 5, 9. Jewels, Jl 31. Space—Sun (for gen material on nature of solar energy). Watches and Clocks, Jl 31. Water Pollution—Sewage etc, D 23

Article in NY Times series on energy crisis discusses possibility of harnessing solar energy to solve current problems; current research and proposal of

Several articles are summarized in chronological order; date, page, and column are given for each.

Dr. Glaser to tap space solar power with photovoltaic batteries described; Glaser pro; solar power station illus. Ap 18, 21:2; 1r of J Marshall, of Wilderness Soc and Natural Resources Defense Council, urging US look to solar energy instead of nuclear energy as alternative for oil; citing problem of nuclear wastes from projected 1,200 power plants in US by yr 2000, urges fostering research and development of solar energy as safe substitute for oil. Je 25, 32:3; hundreds of scientists from 3 dozen nations are gathered in Paris on July 1 for 4-day conf sponsored by UNESCO to discuss ways in which solar energy can be more effectively harnessed to. . . .

The first article summary refers to an article that can be found in the April 18 issue on page 21, column 2. Notice that the year is not given. You have to write down the year of the index you are using. This entry comes from the 1973 index.

The final advantage of the *New York Times* is that nearly every college library carries it. If they do not have actual copies of the paper, they probably have microfilm copies. Ask a librarian to explain how to use a microfilm reader. It is like a projector, and what you read looks like a full-size newspaper page; and although it is hard on the eyes to browse through a whole day's paper this way, you can easily find and read the article you want.

Another useful index to newspapers is *Newsbank*, which indexes selected articles in over 100 U.S. newspapers. The articles are reproduced on microfiche. Less information is provided by the index, so you may need to consult the actual document to determine its usefulness. The entries in the index refer to microfiche cards and to grid locations on the cards. Information is provided in each book on how to use the index and then how to locate the information on a microfiche card. The index is useful if you want to get a range of viewpoints from across the country.

Other useful indexes of current news include the *Wall Street Journal Index*, *Editorial Research Reports*, *Facts on File*, and *News Dictionary*. These should enable you to locate all the relevant information on your topic that is available in newspapers.

BIBLIOGRAPHIES   Probably, by the time you have exhausted all of the preceding sources, you will have all the material you need. But if the search strategy outlined so far has not given you everything you need, you may wish to use other library resources to fill in gaps in your research. Bibliographies are available on a wide variety of topics. A bibliography can be a big time-saver. If you can locate a bibliography that lists references on your topic up until 1974, you need only to look for materials published since 1974 to fill in your research.

A valuable tool for finding bibliographies on your topic is the *Bibliographic Index*, a subject index that will lead you to articles, books, pamphlets, and bibliographies of books devoted to bibliographies. It also tells you whether the bibliographies are annotated.

You will also find that you need to support a statement, show some trends, or provide some comparative data in the form of statistics. Perhaps you have not yet found the exact statistics you were looking for. You may wish to consult *Statistics Sources*, a subject index that lists sources of statistical information on industrial business, social, educational, financial, and other topics for the United States and some foreign countries. Other specialized sources of statistical information include the following:

American Statistics Index
Handbook of Basic Economic Statistics
Agricultural Statistics
Statistical Abstract of the United States
County and City Data Book
UN Demographic Yearbook
UNESCO Statistical Yearbook
UN Statistical Yearbook
Harris Survey Yearbook of Public Opinion
Historical Statistics of the United States

LIBRARIANS

When all else fails, use librarians. They are professionally trained people who can tell you how to find the information you seek. You are an amateur detective; they are experts. Yet, most students confess to us that they do not use librarians effectively as resources.

Part of the problem seems to be the popular stereotype of librarians. It is something many children learned during their first visits to public libraries. Children find libraries fascinating, and the child's response to fascination is talk. The librarian is the person who tells you to be quiet. As children grow older and begin to use libraries to find materials for fun or school, the librarian appears in two more undesirable and stereotyped roles. First, a librarian is the protector of materials. The librarian is who tells you that volumes of the encyclopedia cannot leave the room and that copies of the *Readers' Guide* cannot be taken home. Also, the librarian is the one who levies library fines. All these things contribute to the problem some college students have with librarians.

The truth is that librarians can be especially helpful in looking for information. We previously mentioned that most college libraries have a particular person designated as reference librarian. This person often has a desk in a room in which many dictionaries, encyclopedias, special reference volumes, indexes, and so on are stored. The reference librarian is often the most knowledgeable person in town when it comes down to trying to trace a particular fact. Get to know the reference librarian. Here are a few things the reference librarian may be able to get you access to:

Addresses of almost anyone you wish to write to for information
Any dictionaries, bibliographies, or indexes, including many that we do not know about
Information on almost any imaginable person
Information on almost any geographic location
Census data for any year
Information on historical eras of the United States
Information on local political figures

The list is almost endless. You will be amazed at the magical powers of the reference librarian. Once you get hooked on using the reference librarian as a resource, the number of searches that end happily will increase dramatically.

Here are a few final words on using the library: You can now see that there is much more to using the library than making one or two attempts to find information. We find that nine of ten students who tell us that they could not find information in the library did not follow more than two of the procedures outlined in this appendix. Try them all, and we guarantee you will find significant information and gain confidence in your own skills as a researcher.

Keep records of your search as you go. Experience 13.3 provides a search strategy guide for you to use to keep track of which sources you have consulted and which you have not. As you use a given source, take notes on what you find, using whatever system you find convenient. You have probably learned a system in an English or history class.

Finally, remember the first law of research. We guarantee it to be true: When you do research, if there is any way for something to go wrong, it will. Every researcher makes mistakes, traces down sources of information that prove worthless, looks up and searches for the same source twice, spends several hours on a wild goose chase, finds only the same limited information in two or three sources. All these disasters and many more will befall you during your first five thorough message preparations using the method we have outlined. The only way to avoid these disasters is to avoid doing the job right. Then your final product will be the disaster.

But remember that this happens to every researcher, even the most experienced. Do not be too discouraged. It surely is not your fault; it surely is no reason to give up. The depression you feel is only temporary. It will be replaced by elation when you find the juicy fact you have been looking for. Keep at it.

REFERENCES

Allport, Gordon W. and Postman, Leo J. *The Psychology of Rumor.* New York: Holt, 1947.

Ardrey, Robert. *The Territorial Imperative.* New York: Atheneum, 1966.

Basso, K. H. "To Give Up on Words: Silence in Western Apache Culture," in Pier Giglioli (ed.) *Language and Social Context.* London: Penguin, 1972, pp. 67–87.

Bem, Daryl J. *Beliefs, Attitudes and Human Affairs.* Monterey, Calif.: Brooks/Cole, 1970.

Bowers, John Waite. "Communication Strategies in Conflicts Between Institutions and their Clients." In *Perspectives on Communication in Social Conflict,* edited by Gerald R. Miller and Herbert W. Simons. Englewood Cliffs, N.J.: Prentice-Hall, 1974, pp. 124–152.

Berger, E. M. "The Relation Between Expressed Acceptance of Self and Expressed Acceptance of Others." *Journal of Abnormal and Social Psychology* 47(1952): 778–782.

Bills, R. E.; Vance, E. L.; and McLean, O. S. "An Index of Adjustment and Values." *Journal of Consulting Psychology* 15(1951): 257–261.

Birdwhistell, Ray. *Kinesics and Context.* Philadelphia: University of Pennsylvania Press, 1970.

Browning, Larry D.; Hopper, Robert; and Whitehead, Jack L. "Influence: The Organizer in Communication Systems." *Group and Organizational Studies* 1(1976): 355–369.

Chomsky, Noam. *Language and Mind.* New York: Harcourt Brace Jovanovich, 1968.

Cleaver, Eldridge. *Soul on Ice.* New York: Dell, 1968.

Cook, Mark. *Interpersonal Perception.* Baltimore: Penguin Books, 1971.

Dillard, Annie. *Pilgrim at Tinker Creek.* New York: Harper's Magazine Press, 1974.

Doyle, Sir Arthur C. *A Scandal in Bohemia and Other Stories.* New York: Happy Hour Library, 1941.

Flavell, John, *Communication and the Development of Role Taking Skills in Children.* New York: Wiley, 1968.

Freedman, Jonathan, and Fraser, Scott. "Compliance Without Pressure: The Foot-in-the-Door Technique." *Journal of Personality and Social Psychology* 4(1966): 195–202.

Gergen, Kenneth J. *The Concept of Self.* New York: Holt, Rinehart and Winston, 1971.

——, **and Morse, S. J.** "Self-Consistency: Measurement and Validation." *Proceedings of the American Psychological Association* (1967): 207–208.

Giffin, Kim, and Patton, Bobby R. *Interpersonal Communication.* New York: Harper & Row, 1974.

Hall, Edward T. *The Silent Language.* New York: Doubleday, 1959.

Hopper, Robert, and Naremore, Rita C. *Children's Speech.* 2d ed. New York: Harper & Row, 1978.

Jones, Ferdinand, and Harris, Myron W. "The Development of Interracial Awareness in Small Groups." In *Confrontation: Encounters in Self and Interpersonal Awareness,* edited by Leonard Blank, Gloria B. Gottsegen, and Monroe G. Gottsegen. New York: Macmillan, 1971, pp. 417–418.

402

Kelley, H. H., and Thibaut, John W. "Group Problem Solving." In *The Handbook of Social Psychology,* 2d ed., vol 4., edited by Gardiner Lindzey and Eliot Aronson. Reading, Mass: Addison-Wesley, 1969, pp. 1–601.

Korzybski, Alfred. *Science and Sanity.* Lancaster, Pa.: The International Non-Aristotelian Library, 1933.

Laing, R. D. *The Politics of Experience.* New York: Ballantine Books, 1967.

Lamb, D. H. "Speech Anxiety: Towards a Theoretical Conceptualization and Preliminary Scale Development." *Speech Monographs* 39(1972), 62–67.

Mager, Robert. *Goal Analysis.* Belmont, Calif.: Fearon Publishers, 1972.

Mehrabian, Albert. *Silent Messages.* Belmont, Calif.: Wadsworth, 1971.

Milgram, Stanley, "Frozen World of the Familiar Stranger: Interview." Edited by C. Tarvis. *Psychology Today* 8 (June 1974): 70–73.

Narciso, John, and Burkett, David. *Declare Yourself.* Englewood Cliffs, N.J.: Prentice-Hall, 1975.

Occupational Outlook Handbook. U.S. Bureau of Labor Statistics, Washington, D.C., 1974.

Pirsig, Robert. *Zen and the Art of Motorcycle Maintenance.* New York: Morrow, 1974.

Rogers, Carl R. *On Becoming a Person.* Boston: Houghton Mifflin, 1961.

Rogers, Everett M., and Shoemaker, F. Floyd. *Communication of Innovations: A Cross-Cultural Approach.* 2d ed. New York: Free Press, 1971.

Schramm, Wilbur. *The Processes and Effects of Mass Communication.* Urbana: University of Illinois Press, 1954.

Sitaram, K. S., and Cogdell, Roy T. *Foundations of Intercultural Communication.* Columbus, Ohio: Merrill, 1976.

Smith, Manuel J. *When I Say No, I Feel Gulity.* New York: Bantam Books, 1975.

Spence, Janet, and Helmreich, Robert. *Masculinity and Femininity.* Austin: University of Texas Press, 1978.

Vonnegut, Kurt. *Wampeters, Foma, and Granfalloons.* New York: Delacorte Press/Seymour Lawrence, 1974.

Watzlawick, Paul; Beaven, Janet; and Jackson, Don D. *The Pragmatics of Human Communication.* New York: Norton, 1967.

Watzlawick, Paul; Weakland, John H.; and Fisch, Richard. *Change.* New York: Norton, 1974.

Wicklund, Robert A., and Brehm, Jack W. *Perspectives on Cognitive Dissonance.* Hillsdale, N.J.: Lawrence Erlbaum Associates, 1976.

Wiener, Norbert. *Cybernetics.* New York: Wiley, 1948.

Williams, Frederick, and associates. *Explorations of the Language Attitudes of Teachers.* Rowley, Mass.: Newbury House, 1976.